GHETTO BASTARD

a memoir

Russell Vann

Ghetto Bastard

Published by Russell Dynasty, LLC

ISBN-13: 978-0-9991540-0-7

Twitter: @Ghetto_Bastard

Facebook: www.facebook.com/profile.php?id=100018804571379

Website: ghettobastard.com

Editing and Book Design: www.529Books.com

Editor: Lisa Cerasoli
Interior Design: Danielle Canfield
Cover: Claire Moore

To God—without Him I am nothing and with Him there's nothing I can't do. Also, to my wife, a gift from God.

Note to the Readers

I was born in the South Bronx in the late sixties to a drug-addicted mother, who didn't know who my father was, and into a world that didn't want me. Growing up, I faced life or death situations every step of the way, it seemed. Not only have I struggled to overcome my own specters, but also those of my environment. I started to write these books as a form of therapy. In doing so, I realized that all the people around me, throughout my life, had been dealing with their own misfortunes. That's when it hit me that I was writing my memoirs to convey that "current situation" neither determines nor defines "final destination."

I've had to overcome many obstacles affiliated with living in the ghetto. Did I escape unscathed? No, but I'm stronger. And matters of the heart—that I've experienced because of the ghetto—have shaped me into the man I've become.

I'm no longer in the ghetto, and while those experiences haven't defined me, they haven't left me, either. I am truly blessed to have my loving family's support on this journey to become an author.

Regardless of where you come from or what you do, I hope my life story touches you. The threads of commonality that run through my memoir show that we all face similar struggles in life and must overcome much of the same troubles. Life and death battles don't lurk around every corner, but fears and worries haunt us all; love and heartbreak can change our lives in a moment. Because of that, *Ghetto Bastard* tells everyone's story.

GHETTO BASTARD

Born next to a Bronx city housing project.
I didn't know my father.
My mother didn't want me.

BOOK I
The Beginning

To
Rami
Enjoy !!!

Russell
Mann 333

chapter **ONE**

"**G**uy, go get me a switch. This muthafucker done pissed the bed again," Emma yelled to her eleven-year-old son. Guy did as his mother ordered. He went outside to retrieve the thickest switch he could find from the tree in the front yard. He had brought it back to his mother with such enthusiasm, anxious to see the beating she was going to inflict on the helpless two-and-a-half-year-old. Emma raised her arm, switch in hand, and struck the young boy with all her might. Once, twice, three times. She beat the young boy with so many strikes, even she lost count. In fact, she didn't even count; she just beat the young boy until she was out of breath.

Guy watched, laughing and yelling, "Get him, Mama!" The helpless toddler ran as the strikes of the switch hit his naked body on his back, legs, butt, and arms. The blows were random, with no special target, the only purpose to inflict the most pain possible. The toddler finally ran under the bed for safety. This was his safe haven. The beatings would usually stop once he was under the bed. Emma would beat him until all flesh was hidden.

This was my daily wake-up.

From my earliest memories, this is what always comes back. My mother was pregnant at age seventeen. She didn't want the responsibility of taking care of a baby, and neither did her thirty-six-year-old mother. So, she boarded me out to some people that she knew growing up. She had to pay them, and sometimes, I guess, she was late or didn't pay. When she didn't pay, she wouldn't call or show up. So, the repercussions of her actions were often taken out on me. The lady that my mother boarded me out to was named Nana. At least, that's what everyone I saw would call her—except for Emma, who would call her Mama. Nana was a very old, very light-skinned black woman. So light, she almost looked white. I knew—or thought—she was black because her daughter, Emma, was a heavyset, dark-skinned woman. Guy, her grandson, was just as dark as his mother, and he called the light-skinned woman Nana. I didn't know who this woman was, but I knew she was in charge. Every morning, when Emma arrived, she would complain about how I urinated in the bed. I could see the joy in her eyes as she beat me mercilessly with that switch.

When Emma left to go home, the torment was from the two or three other children Nana took care of. Some seemed a little older than me, maybe four or five. On many occasions, Emma would have them jump on me—for what reason, I couldn't say. Often, I found myself fighting back like a wild animal, swinging my fists, kicking, and even biting. I can remember seeing her out the corner of my eye, telling them, "Get him, get him!" Once, I was fighting back and bit one of the kids so hard on the thumb that it drew blood. Everyone stopped as the boy started crying, showing Nana his thumb. Nana was filled with rage and yelled to the boy and others, "Get that son of a bitch!"

The beating became more severe than when it started, and the young boy bit me on the top of my right eye, tearing away about a three-quarter-inch piece of flesh. When the beating stopped, I remember feeling dizzy. I looked into a long mirror hanging on a nearby closet door to see blood running down the right side of my face. There was no one to hug me, no one to comfort me. I just remember an older girl, about ten, taking me to the bathroom to wash my face.

These beatings were a common sight in the house. On one occasion, Nana was setting up her minions for another jumping. It usually started with a condescending remark about me, and the other kids would just follow her lead. I knew a beating was coming, so I hid behind the bed. They were yelling at me, and in defense of myself, unable to form full sentences yet, I yelled, "Stupid!".

That was their excuse to start. "You called Nana stupid!" one of them said. Just as the children were about to charge at me, a door to one of the bedrooms opened, and this slender, young black man, about twenty-three, named Norman, stepped out. I had seen Norman, but never knew who he was. He rented a room from Nana.

Norman yelled, "What the fuck is going on here?"

As if ignorant of the situation, Nana said, "What?"

"What the fuck you doing to that boy?"

Nana said, "He called me stupid!"

"Fuck that shit! Every time I turn around, you muthafuckers is kicking his ass."

"I don't treat him any different than anybody else," Nana said.

"Bullshit!" Norman yelled. "I see you muthafuckers all the time and don't say nothing. I'm tired of this shit! The next time I see this muthafucker getting his ass kicked, I'm gonna start kicking somebody's ass."

Then Norman went back in his room. I lay on the floor by Norman's door for the rest of the day. At last—someplace safe.

The morning beatings continued as usual. I guess Norman was at work by the time Emma arrived. But every night, I would lie on the floor by Norman's room, even if he wasn't home. It was my safe place.

Nana would say, "You think Norman's going to protect you all the time? He's not going be here forever." I would just look at her, knowing she meant every word. Norman did move out; however, Nana had died by that time.

At that point, a young, light-skinned black lady picked me up. She was about 5'6", with a big afro, and smoking Kool cigarettes. I got in a black car with her and a male driver. They drove me to this other lady's apartment, and the woman I was with called her Auntie.

I heard her tell the lady that Nana had died, and she asked if Auntie could watch me for a little while. The woman left, and the lady sat me at the kitchen table and gave me something to eat. She was dark-skinned, in her late fifties, and wore a black wig. She gave me a bath and put me in a twin bed in the room where her elderly mother slept in another twin bed. No one said much to me. In the morning, I got up, and of course, wet the bed. The lady wasn't upset. She just washed me up, sat me at the kitchen table, and gave me something to eat. This went on for a few days, until she said, "Your mother is coming to get you today."

I thought, *Who's my mother?* I didn't even know who my mother was. *Great! Now I have a mother. I don't have to go back to that house.*

The doorbell rang, and I was anxious to see my mother. When the door opened, it was the light-skinned lady with the afro who had dropped me off. I was surprised at this. When she picked me up at Nana's house, I had no idea who she was.

I yelled, "Mommy!" not from any joy or bond that we had developed, but just because I saw other kids do it when they saw their mothers. My mother took me back to Nana's house, but instead of Nana, Emma was there with her son, Guy.

Emma and Guy now lived in this house. My mother dropped me off, had a conversation with Emma, and left. No kiss, no hug—she just left. Here I was, back in the house of horrors, and the morning ritual continued. It got to the point that I just got used to the beatings. How I wished I could go back to that other lady's apartment. But who was she? I thought this lady, Emma, must be my family because I lived here. I was with Emma and Guy all the time. When they went to the store, I was with them. Any outing whatsoever, I was with her, Guy, and whoever else may have come along. They were my family—at least, the only family I knew.

One night, when Emma, Guy, two other children, and I were out riding in the car, there was a full moon. It was enormous, and a conversation started up between Guy and Emma. They were talking about the man in the moon, and how when it's big like that, he comes out and kidnaps little kids. This was one of the joys they had—frightening this three-year-old boy. I remember looking in the night sky, at the enormous moon, from the car window, full of fear.

When we got back to the house, I had to go to the bathroom. When I went in, the window was open and I saw the enormous moon. I was scared to death. I ran out of the bathroom, but I still needed to go. I didn't want to pee in my pants, because I knew a beating would follow. So, I saw the dog's bowl and urinated in that instead. While I was urinating, Guy walked in and saw me.

He yelled out, "Ma, Malik's pissing in the dog bowl!"

I could hear her say, "That little muthafucker! Get him!"

I quickly ran under Emma's queen-size bed to escape their retribution. Emma was on one side, Guy on the other, both reaching for me. At one point, they both had me. I thought they were going to tear me apart. Finally, Emma pulled me from her side and knocked me down to the floor. Guy got on top of me and put his legs on my arms. Emma poured the bowl of urine down into my mouth, all the while saying, "How you like drinking piss you little muthafucker?" I could not yell. I was choking as Emma and Guy were laughing. Even if I could yell, who would come? Norman didn't live there anymore. There was no place to run. No place to hide. No one to run to. No one to protect me. No one to love me.

To the world, I was just Rosemary's bastard son, and Emma and Guy knew it. They could do whatever they wanted to me, and no one would even care. I guess they figured no one in my family wanted me, not even my own mother, or else I wouldn't be there. The physical, emotional, and verbal abuse went on until I was four years old, and then there was a godsend.

chapter TWO

O ne day, no special day in particular, my mother came to pick
me up. She took me back to the other lady's apartment—the
one she called Auntie—and left. I didn't mind this lady because when I wet the bed, she didn't beat me. She let me take a bath,
and she had little boats in the tub for me to play with. Before I went
to sleep, she asked me if I wanted a bedtime snack. She gave me
some cookies and warm milk, and then put me to sleep. The next
day, my mother came by with another lady she called Mommy. At
four, I didn't know who anybody was. I heard them talking as I
stood invisible to all in the living room. They were talking about me.
By accident, I spilled a glass of liquid that was on the table. My
mother jumped up in anger, and from the way she jumped, I knew
her plan was to inflict punishment. I quickly ran to the bedroom
and hid under the bed.

I heard the lady she called Auntie say, "Oh, it's alright. It was
just an accident." She came in the bedroom, stuck her hand under
the bed to try to retrieve me, and I bit her thumb as hard as I could.
She pulled her hand back in pain and, somewhat surprised, she said,
"Look at that. He bit me."

My mother, more than ever, was determined to inflict punishment upon me. She came toward the bed and said, "I'll get his little
ass!"

But the lady called Auntie said, "No! Leave him. I like that. I see
he's a fighter."

I stayed under the bed until everyone left. The lady my mother called Auntie asked me, while I was still hiding, if I wanted to eat. I came out from under the bed. She sat me at the table and fed me some food. I could barely speak, but I was able to ask her who she was.

She said, "You call me Nana." She told me from now on, I was going to live with her. I was happy to hear that. This Nana treated me nicely. She didn't beat me.

So now, I lived with Nana, her mother, and Nana's husband, but they slept in separate bedrooms. I slept in the room with Nana's mother on a twin bed. I called her mother Granny. She was very old and quiet, and stayed in the bed a lot. The apartment was very large, with three bedrooms and two bathrooms. Nana stayed in one room, Granny and I stayed in the second, and Nana's husband in the third. I called Nana's husband Granddaddy. He was not related by blood. Nana was a waitress at a restaurant downtown on 37th Street, and Granddaddy was a chef at a different restaurant. Granddaddy didn't talk to me much, but when he did, he was always kind.

The first thing my Nana did was enroll me in Labor Sherman Daycare Center. She would drop me off every morning before she went to work. I was around other kids, but these kids weren't beating me up. I had three teachers who helped improve my speech by leaps and bounds. I was soon able to form full sentences and express myself.

I started asking Nana questions about my mother and the lady my mother called Mommy. She told me that the lady my mother called Mommy was my grandmother, and to call her Grammy. I asked Nana who was she to me, and she said, "I'm your great-grandmother." I asked if she was Grammy's mother, and she said, "No, I'm your grandfather's mother."

"My grandfather," I said. "Who is he?"

She told me I would meet him one day, that he lived in New Jersey.

Nana and I had a routine. Every day, she would wake me up in the morning, and I would eat something like oatmeal or cream of wheat. Then, she would walk me over to Labor Sherman to drop me off. Later, she would pick me up after work. We would go home, and she would feed me dinner. I would take a bath, have a bedtime snack, and be off to bed. She even came up with a solution for my bed-wetting: I would wear diapers to bed. No more beatings, no more cursing at me, no more hiding under the bed. At last, at four-and-a-half years old, I had someone that loved me.

On the weekends, Grammy would come to pick me up for a day. She had a boyfriend. He was a bald-headed man named Pete. They would take me to their apartment, a three-story walk-up. I would hang out for the day, but a lot of times, Pete was out, so Grammy and I would go to the movies, the park, or one of her friend's houses. At night, I would return to Nana's. I didn't see my mother at all.

One day, Grammy picked me up from the daycare center with this tall, slim gentleman. He was very light-skinned, like my mother. It was strange, because only Nana picked me up. Grammy introduced him as Uncle Maurice. They both took me home to Nana's house, where there were a lot of people sitting around the kitchen table. Nana met us at the door and thanked them for picking me up. She sat me in a rocking chair in the living room and told me to watch TV, and not to go in my room. As I sat watching, I saw, out the corner of my eye, Nana run into my room with her hands covering her face as she cried, saying, "Oh, Mama!" Granny had died. This would be one of the two only times I ever saw Nana cry in my life.

After the funeral, there were a lot of people at Nana's apartment. I saw my mother, but she didn't really show me any kind of special attention. I just knew it was my mother. I saw Nana's son, my grandfather. He didn't pay any special attention to me, either. I just noticed that he had the same complexion as my mother and her brother. Grammy was a bit darker. Grammy was my grandfather's ex-wife. After everything was over, Nana and I went on with our regular routine.

It was time for me to go to school. Nana enrolled me in a Catholic school called Saint Angeles, right around the corner from the daycare center. After school, the same teacher I knew would pick up a group of us and take us back to Labor Sherman. Nana would then pick me up as usual.

All of a sudden, Nana started to wake me up early on Sunday mornings to take me to church. This was new. I didn't know what church was. I knew they talked a lot about this person called Jesus in school, but what was this?

The church was in my school. I remember walking up the stairs to see this enormous statue of a cross with a white man on it. His hands and feet were nailed to the cross, and he had a crown of spikes. There was blood dripping from his head and hands. It looked scary.

I asked Nana who that was and she said, "That's Jesus."

I asked her who Jesus was. She told me he was God's son. I asked her, "Who is God?"

"He's our Father up in Heaven."

I asked what Heaven was. She said, "Be quiet. Church is getting ready to start." The ceremony started and ended. I still didn't know what Heaven was. I was six years old, and had never heard of God, Jesus, or Heaven.

Every Sunday, we went to church. And then, one day, Nana said, "You're going to get baptized." I didn't even know what that was, but if Nana wanted me to do it, I knew it couldn't be bad.

The day of the baptism came. It was 8:00 p.m. at the Saint Angeles Church. Grammy and Pete were there, for some reason, along with Nana. There was a tall white man in a black suit, with a white collar around his neck. It was just the five of us in the church.

The man in the white collar put his thumb in some oil, made the sign of the cross on my forehead, and said, "I baptize you in the name of the Father, the Son, and the Holy Spirit."

That was it, I was baptized. No fanfare, no music, no cheers. I still didn't know what it meant, but Nana was happy, and if Nana was happy, I was happy.

chapter **THREE**

C hristmastime was coming. I didn't even know what that was. I was six years old, and had never had a Christmas. I don't re-member anything about a Christmas when I was with Emma and the other Nana. This Nana decorated the apartment with Santa Clause pictures, and this was all new to me. I asked her who Santa Clause was, and she had me watch the *Santa Clause Is Coming to Town* and *Rudolph the Red-Nosed Reindeer* animated features on television. I was excited for my first Christmas.

Nana had a silver Christmas tree, and she and I decorated it. The day before Christmas, there were no presents under the tree. I asked Nana about this, and she said Santa would bring them when I was sleeping. *Oh, that's right*, I thought. I remembered from the show on television about Santa. I went to bed early that night. I looked out of the window to see that the moon was big and shining bright. For a moment, I remembered what Guy and Emma had told me about the man in the moon, but I wasn't scared. I was with Nana. She loved me. She would protect me, so I fell asleep.

When I woke up, the first thing I noticed was my diaper was dry. I went out to the living room, and I couldn't believe what I saw. It looked like a toy store. Nana stood by the tree and said Santa had come. I could see the joy in her eyes from the joy in mine.

She said, "Are you happy?"

I shouted, "Yes!"

I couldn't wait to tear into my gifts. I had everything! To this day, I couldn't tell you what toys they were. I have had many other

Christmases in my life since then, but that is the one I will always remember.

I had been living with Nana for about a year and a half by now. I loved her. This home was stable. I felt safe. I was going to school, and my life had structure. I hadn't seen my mother since Granny died. In fact, I never really even thought about her until the day Nana said, "Your mother is coming to see you."

When my mother came by the apartment, she was with this tall, dark-skinned gentleman. He had a beard, and she said his name was Jack. This wasn't the same guy from when she picked me up from Emma's house. My mother decided she would start picking me up on weekends. I would stay at her house with Jack, and come back on Sunday. It would start next week. I was fine with that, as long as I could come back to Nana's.

The first time my mother and Jack picked me up, we went to their place in Queens. Queens was also where Emma lived. When we arrived, to my surprise, there were three kids also living there. There was Jack Jr., who was also six; Curtis, who was five; and a baby girl whose name I forgot, still in the crib. I wondered what was going on here. My mother was living with a man with three kids and taking care of them? They seemed like such a family. I have to admit that I was rather jealous. They seemed so happy together, and I was the visitor.

My mother would pick me up on the weekends, as planned. I would come on Friday and leave on Sunday. It seemed like a big, happy family. However, I still felt like an outsider. Sometimes, I didn't want to leave. I wanted a daddy. I wanted brothers and a sister, and every time I left to go back to Nana's, I felt like the stepchild.

I did notice something, even at six. Whenever my mother would discipline any of us, she seemed to be just a little sterner toward me, as if to show Jack and the other kids that I held no favoritism in her eyes. This went on for several months. I remember when I turned seven, all of a sudden, the visits stopped. I asked Nana what happened, and she told me that Jack and my mother broke up. I didn't see my mother for a couple of months. Then she showed up, and Nana said that I was going to be spending the summer with her in Queens.

When my mother picked me up, we took the train back. Two trains, in fact. Usually, someone drove us. When we got off, we walked about ten blocks to a small basement apartment in a two-family house. When you walked in, there was a little living room, and then you would walk right into another small living room, with the bathroom right there. The kitchen was right next to this room and the bathroom. In Nana's house, I had my own room, and it was bigger than both of these living spaces. My mother said I would sleep in the room by the bathroom. This wasn't a room—you had to walk through it to go to the bathroom and the kitchen. It was just a space, and there was a small bed for me in the corner. I figured this was just for the summer, so I guess I could handle it.

My mother would have her friends over a lot, and they would smoke marijuana, drink, and play Monopoly. My mother had a new boyfriend named Lamar. She also had another guy she was seeing named Rodney. He raced cars. I don't know what Lamar did. Rodney never came over to my mother's house. We would go over to his place and just hang out—or, they would hang out, smoke marijuana, and drink, while I watched television in the other room. Spending that summer with my mother made me realize one thing: I didn't want to live with her. Sometimes, she was alright (usually when she was high). The other times, she was mean. She wasn't the loving and nurturing mother she had been with Jack's kids.

I couldn't wait for this summer to be over. My mother would make plans and not tell me anything. We would just get in a car and go. Most of the time, she was dropping me off at a friend's house so that they could babysit while she went out partying or roller-skating. She would always pick me up at 3:00 or 4:00 in the morning.

chapter FOUR

One day that summer, we got in the car with a friend of my mother's and started to drive. I heard them talking about a trip. As we drove, the area started to look a little familiar. It wasn't a long drive, and as we approached a house, my heart started to beat faster. The closer we got, the faster my heart was beating. I could feel the fear rising deep inside me. I thought, *This can't be!* I hadn't seen this place in years—three, to be exact.

It was Emma's house!

I thought, *What's going on here?* My mother was going away for two weeks, and she was going to leave me there. As we got out of the car, all of the horrors of the past came pouring back into my young mind. The daily beatings with a switch. The bowl of urine that was poured down my throat. The scar over my right eye.

When we entered the house, Emma greeted my mother with a warm welcome. She commented to my mother about how big I had gotten. Then, there he was—Guy, Emma's minion. He looked older now. He was about fifteen, and a lot thinner. I heard my mother say she would be back in a couple of weeks. There were two other kids in the house, too. There was a Spanish kid, about my age, but smaller, and a black kid, about six. The black kid was Emma's grandson, from an older son she had had. They called him Pop. I don't remember the Spanish kid's name, but we seemed to hit it off pretty well. My mother said she would be back in a couple of weeks, and then she left me with my tormenters. The only difference was I could talk now.

I slept in the same room as before, and all I could think about was not wetting the bed. My bed-wetting was on and off at my mother's, and let's just say, it wasn't well-received. Emma was a cab driver and worked the night shift, so during the day, I played with the other kids. When we went to bed, she went to work, leaving Guy to babysit. The first couple of days were uneventful, and thank God, I didn't wet the bed. I think pure fear allowed me to refrain from any accidents.

All three kids, along with Guy, slept in the same room, which was very small. I awoke one night to see Guy having sex with his girlfriend right next to me. I went right back to sleep as if I hadn't seen anything. The next morning, Pop, Emma's grandson, told me all about it, how he was wide awake and saw everything.

Besides that incident, the days and evenings seemed uneventful. I thought that perhaps they were treating me better because I could talk better, and they didn't want anyone to know if they did something to me. I was mistaken. One day, Emma worked the day shift and left us in Guy's care. The other boys and I were play wrestling in the back of the house. Guy and another boy about the same age as him came to the back. They said, "What you muthafuckers doing?" I knew by the tone in their voices, and the fact that they called us muthafuckers, something bad was coming.

The Spanish boy and I said, "We're playing." Pop remained silent. Guy and the other teen told us to keep fighting.

We continued to play, and then Guy said, "Fight for real."

"For real?" we asked.

"Yeah, for real, muthafuckers," he said while looking at the other teen and giggling. The Spanish boy and I continued as we were—still playing. Then Guy said, "If you muthafuckers don't fight for real, I'm gonna fuck ya'll up."

I knew he was serious. I didn't want to be at the end of another beating, so I struck the boy in the face with my fist. I felt bad, because he was my friend. The boy looked at me with such shock, and he began to swing his fist. There we were, like gladiators fighting for

15

the amusement of the Roman emperor. I was bigger than the other boy, and got the best of him. His nose was bleeding and he was crying. Guy and his buddy were laughing. Then the two older boys threatened us that if we told Emma, he was going to get us at night. The other boy and I never said a word, but after that, he and I were enemies.

The couple of weeks went by kind of fast before my mother picked me up. When she did, Lamar was with her. We went back to that small basement apartment, and I couldn't wait to get back to Nana's, where I felt safe. My mother was the type of person you had to walk on eggshells around, and I don't think she liked children. I was supposed to be spending the summer with her, but every time I turned around, she was dropping me off at someone's house. My mother would leave me with anybody. If her friend couldn't watch me, she would ask if they knew somebody. Many of my sitters were one-night stands, because most of them didn't like when she would come and pick me up in the wee hours of the morning, sometimes on weeknights.

Why did she even have me? I wondered. I could have just stayed with Nana and gone to Labor Sherman. I hadn't seen Nana for at least two months. I really missed her. I couldn't wait to get home.

My mother was always home during the day, and didn't go anywhere at night except to party. I often wondered how she paid the rent for this rat hole we lived in. It was late August, almost the end of summer. I knew I would be out of the rat hole soon. The anticipation was enormous. I would be back with Nana, back in my own room, back to someone who loved and nurtured me. Then, in an instant, it all came crashing down.

One day when my mother and I were sitting at the kitchen table, she said, "I been thinking, and I talked with Nana, and I decided to keep you." My heart sank. I wanted to cry, but didn't. She said, "You can visit Nana on the weekends."

At last, the plan was revealed. It was her intention to keep me the entire time. I was her meal ticket. With me, she was able to get welfare and food stamps, and the welfare paid her rent as long as she was registered in some kind of school. So, she enrolled in Hostos Community College in the Bronx, which was down the block from Nana. We lived in Queens. She went to school on Fridays when she dropped me off at Nana's, so she could go to one or two classes and the records would show she was in school. It didn't matter if she passed the classes; she just wanted the money. I went with her a couple of times, and all she did was play cards in the recreation area with other people that were running the same scam.

My mother registered me in the public school, which was right across the street. I was in the second grade. The bed-wetting became more frequent, and when my mother would wake me up in the morning, she would always vent her anger by saying, "Clean those pissy sheets and wash your ass." One time, in the middle of the night, she pulled the covers off me, woke me up, and accused me of wetting the bed on purpose. After school, she would just let me run around outside with no one watching me, which was fine with me as long as I didn't have to be in the house with her and Lamar. Lamar lived in Brooklyn, but he was there a lot.

In school, I was acting out. I was a disruption to the class, and one day, the teacher wrote something in my notebook regarding my behavior. She wanted my mother to sign it. I was afraid to show my mother, so I signed it. Of course, you could tell a kid signed it and not a parent. However, before I went back to school, I came out of the bathroom one morning to find my mother sitting at the kitchen table, looking at my notebook. She asked me what it was she was looking at, and I told her. She asked why I signed it, and I told her I was afraid. I didn't notice that she had a belt by her side. She began to beat me. I didn't have any clothes on, since I was just coming out of the bathroom to get ready for school.

When she beat me that morning, it was for more than just misbehaving in school and signing her name. There are two types of beatings; believe me, I know the difference. There's the one when a parent spanks to discipline the child, and there's the one when the child is beaten with anger. This was the second kind of beating. Each blow from the belt said something. It said I hate you. I hate that you pissed the bed. I hate that I got pregnant at seventeen. I hate that I have to take care of you. I hate that I have to live in this shithole. And who knows, maybe a dozen other resentments were taken out on my half-naked body that day.

Even though I was only seven years old, I realized that my mother didn't love me. Starting then, I did everything to avoid any more beatings, because I knew they would all be the same. In my heart, I hated her. I hated her not because of that beating, but because I knew she didn't love me. I knew she didn't care about me like Nana did. The only good thing in my life was that I got to see Nana on the weekends. I hated Sundays, when my mother and Lamar picked me up to take me back to Queens.

Now it was December, and my mother's idea of a Christmas tree was a single string of lights on the wall in the shape of a tree. That was it. No decorations, no presents under the tree. Comparing Nana's Christmas tree to hers, I really didn't expect much of a Christmas.

One night, the phone rang, and my mother answered it. It was Lamar. She was arguing with him, and all I could hear was something about "VD." When she hung up the phone, she called a friend and asked her to give her a ride.

During the car ride, I overheard her and her friend talking. She said, "That muthafucker said I gave him a venereal disease."

My mother and her friend were looking for a doctor so that she could be tested. However, it was late at night, and all the private doctors' offices were closed. My mother's friend took us back to the house.

Later that night, there was a bang on the door. It was Lamar. I could see the rage in his eyes, and I could hear it in his voice. He asked her about the test results. She explained that the doctors' offices were closed, and that she couldn't get tested. He demanded that she go to the emergency room at the local hospital with him to get it done. We all got in a cab and went to the nearest hospital.

The cab ride was dead silent. Lamar was fuming with anger with every passing second. When we arrived, we walked into the emergency room and waited in line. When we got up to the counter, my mother stated that she would like to see a doctor and, instead of saying VD, she described the symptoms of VD so as not to be embarrassed. Lamar was livid. He grabbed her by the arm and pulled her to the outside of the emergency room. I followed them.

What I saw next, I will never forget for the rest of my life. Lamar was yelling at the top of his lungs, right up in my mother's face, maybe half an inch away.

"Why didn't you tell the nurse what you were here for, bitch?"

My mother told him she was describing the symptoms, but Lamar yelled over her, saying, "You fucking cunt! You gave me this shit, bitch, didn't you?" He kept repeating the statement.

I was standing there just watching. All of a sudden, he took his left elbow and pinned my mother by her neck up against the barred metal gate behind her, and then punched her in the face. She fell to the ground. He picked her up by the collar of her shirt, pinned her by the neck again, and repeatedly punched her in the face.

I was in shock. I couldn't believe what I was seeing. I was yelling for him to stop.

I heard a woman say, "Look how that man is beating that woman."

I was yelling and crying out, with tears in my eyes, to anyone who would listen, "Somebody please help my mother!"

My cries fell on deaf ears. People were looking, but no one would help. Lamar continued his assault, mercilessly beating her. My mother was bleeding out of her mouth, and her face was swelling. I thought he was going to kill her, and there I stood, helpless, just like when Emma would beat me in the morning when I woke up from a wet bed.

I ran back into the emergency room, crying, yelling, and screaming, "Somebody please help my mother. He is going to kill her!" I saw a security guard. I grabbed his arm and begged him, "Mister, please help me! He's going to kill my mother! Please, please, please!"

The security guard followed me outside and walked up to Lamar while he was still assaulting my mother. The guard called out to Lamar. Lamar stopped punching my mother and released her from his elbow choke hold. When he did, she fell at his feet.

Lamar turned around and yelled to the security guard, "What the fuck do you want, muthafucker?" Lamar wasn't that big of a man, but he was bigger than the guard. "This is my muthafucking woman!"

My mother started to get up. I ran to help her to her feet while the security guard had Lamar's attention. I heard the guard tell him that he understood it was his woman, but he had to take his business off the hospital property. Lamar turned around, walked toward my mother, and said, "Come on, let's go."

She refused.

Lamar picked my mother up and slammed her body to the ground. He then grabbed her by her afro and started to drag her by her hair off of hospital property. He was yelling at her, "Get up and walk, bitch!"

She refused, knowing the brutal beating would resume. He continued to drag her by her hair when three more security guards came out and got his attention again. Lamar let my mother go and spoke to them. This time, he wasn't yelling; he was outnumbered, and a couple of the guards were much bigger than he was.

I helped my mother to her feet, and while the hospital guards blocked Lamar, we ran to a cab and got in. Lamar ran past the guards and started to bang on the cab window. My mother locked the doors.

The cab driver said, "Miss, you're going to have to get out my cab. I don't want any trouble."

My mother refused.

Lamar was now standing right in front of the cab, yelling to my mother. "Get the fuck out!"

He came around the side of the cab and banged on the window, and then tried to kick out the glass. At this point, the driver floored the gas pedal and took off. Lamar jumped on top of the cab and held on. The driver stopped the cab, and when Lamar got off, he floored it again. Lamar chased, but was unable to catch up.

I remember looking out the back window of the cab, watching Lamar chase it. He was running top-speed, and I could see the distance between him and the cab increase. I looked at my mother's face. Her eyes were almost swollen shut. She was bleeding from her nose and mouth.

We took the cab to the house of one of her friends. It was about 1:00 a.m. When the woman opened the door, she was shocked at what she saw.

"Girl, what happen to you?" she asked. My mother told her, and her friend said, "He did this to you in front of Malik?"

The woman was shocked at the brutality and the heartlessness of the man to beat a woman like that in front of her child. She gave my mother some cloths to clean her face off, and as my mother sat down in front of the mirror, she began to cry. This was the first time she had seen what Lamar had done to her face.

There was a knock at the door. Both my mother and I feared it was Lamar. We hid in the bedroom as the lady answered the door. I was terrified. The lady locked her bedroom door before going to answer the front door of her apartment. When she came back, she told us it was just a friend of hers. We were relieved, and for the first time that night, felt safe.

We left the friend's house about 3:00 a.m. and took a cab home. I went to sleep in my bed, and at about 5:00 a.m., I was awakened by a male voice. It was Lamar. He and my mother were talking at the front door. I walked out toward the light so he could see me.

He said to my mother, "If I beat your muthafucking ass again, I'd be wrong, right?"

I thought another beating was about to begin.

My mother said, "Just leave, please." She handed him a bag of things, and he left without further incident.

I lay down in my mother's bed that night, and she held me and started to cry. She was crying hard. She didn't cry during the beating. Even though I hated my mother and I knew she didn't love me, that night, I loved her. That night, I had compassion for my mother. I thought for that night, she loved me.

I went to Nana's that weekend, and on Sunday, when it was time for my mother to come, Grammy and Pete came instead. They were going to drop me off at my mother's. When we got to their car, Pete's large German shepherd was in there also. When we got to my mother's place, the dog stayed with us. I asked if we were keeping him. Pete told me that Lamar was scared of dogs, so he was going to stay with my mother and me for a few days.

The next few weeks went by, and life went on as usual. My mother was just as mean as before, and I visited Nana on the weekends. Sometimes when I went to Nana's, Granddaddy's grandson, Mitchell, was there. He was a year younger than I was. When I lived with Nana before, he would come by sometimes, and we played together. From what I could overhear when grownups were talking, Mitchell's mother and father were heroin addicts. Mitchell's father was Granddaddy's son, and his name was Mitchell as well. Mitchell's skin tone was very light. He had light brown eyes and reddish hair. People in the family always commented on how cute he was. Mitchell's mother was named Jewel, and he got his features from her. He looked just like her, in male form. We weren't related by blood, but we were cousins.

After a couple weeks, the dog returned to Grammy and Pete's. Soon, my mother was seeing this other guy named Rodney. This wasn't the Rodney who drove a racecar; this was another guy. He was skinny and had a beard. He was light-skinned, like my mother, and had a dog, a Great Dane. He didn't live with us; he lived in the Bronx, near Nana's house, with his mother. Sometimes, we would hang out there after my mother picked me up from Nana's. He lived in a housing complex near Ogden Avenue. My mother's friend from Hostos College, Sandy, lived in the same complex, in a different building. She had a son named Carrie, who was about six years older than I was. I met him once or twice. He was tall and skinny, and acted very feminine. He had a lot of comic books. Sometimes, when my mother would go to see Sandy, she would let me read his comic books in his room although he wasn't home. They would smoke marijuana in the other room.

One weekend when my mother picked me up, she was with some heavyset lady. We left my Nana's apartment and got into the car the heavyset lady was driving. We drove to my mother's place, and then they went upstairs to talk with the landlord. The landlord and his family lived above us. He was married, and they had two boys aged about eight and ten years old. I played with them outside sometimes.

My mother told me to go downstairs, and that she would be down shortly. When I went downstairs, our door was open. I opened it slowly, and the lights were out. I could see the shadow of a man standing by the lamp, and suddenly the lights came on. It was Lamar. I didn't know whether to scream or run. I stood in shock. He just stood there and smiled at me, as if savoring my reaction, my fear.

The night at the hospital came back to me as if it were only five minutes in the past. Every blow he gave my mother appeared in my mind. What was he doing here? About ten seconds later, my mother and the heavyset lady came in the door behind me. My mother walked up to Lamar and kissed him on the lips passionately. That's what he's doing here—they were back together! The heavyset woman was his sister. My mother had stayed in Brooklyn with Lamar that weekend. Lamar's sister left, and he stayed for a couple of days. What was she thinking? How could she take him back after what happened, especially in front of me? Didn't she know that if a man beats you, he has no respect for you?

I hated him, and now he was around even more than before. He was nice as pie to my mother for the next few weeks, but as the story goes, once a man beats you, he will always beat you. He wasn't doing it in front of me, but it was still happening.

A couple of times when my mother would pick me up from Nana's with Lamar, her face would be a little swollen. There were times I would hear them arguing, so I would say something to him like, "Don't hit my mother." He would be upset that I said anything, and then he started to hate me for it. Once, when the three of us were in a park, he and my mother were play fighting, but I thought it was for real. I hit him with an umbrella. He was furious. Later that day, my mother cursed me out because he was mad at her over what I did. Lamar told her he wasn't coming around for a while, and I was the reason. I couldn't believe it—my mother was cursing me out for trying to protect her against the animal that beat her like a dog in the street. He dragged her by her hair in front of her child! After that, I knew he hated me for sure. The way he would look at me, I knew he didn't want me around, and the feeling was mutual.

One day, my mother wanted to go someplace, but without Lamar. She told him we were going somewhere, and we left the house. When we got to the bus stop, she told me to go back to the house, but she had me wait until the bus came.

When I got back home, Lamar asked me where my mother was. I told him what had happened. He wanted to know where she went. I told him that I didn't know. He was really upset. I went back in my space and watched television. My mother was gone for several hours. During that time, I went to sit at the kitchen table to eat something. Lamar came into the kitchen and sat across from me.

He said, "Let me ask you something. Why you always in me and your mother's business?"

"I'm not in your business," I said.

"Yes, you are." Then he asked me, "Why'd you hit me with the umbrella? Why you got to say something when I'm talking to your mother?"

I said, "Because that's my mother" to both questions.

"You're just a kid, and you need to mind your muthafucking business," Lamar said. "I better not have to tell you again, you understand?"

I nodded yes, too scared to answer because of the tone of his voice, and because whenever people in my past addressed me as "muthafucker," it was never a good thing. I didn't say anything to my mother when she came back that night. I figured she would just take his side anyway.

On one of my weekend visits to Grammy's, I told her what happened. She asked if he hit me, and I replied that he didn't, but that his tone of voice scared me. Grammy and Pete were upset and spoke to my mother about it. Pete was a street hustler. You name it—if it was illegal, he did it. That's why he was often gone at night when I would stay at Grammy's. He told my mother that he was going to talk to Lamar to set him straight about abusing her and scaring me.

The next day, my mother, Grammy, Pete, and I got in the car and drove to some building. I think it was Lamar's school. Pete parked the car across the street from it. My mother, Grammy, and I stayed in the car while Pete went into the building.

My mother looked very nervous and was saying to Grammy, "I don't think this is going to work. He doesn't scare very easy."

Grammy rubbed her hand and said, "Everything is going to be alright, don't worry."

Pete came out of the building and started to cross the street toward us. Lamar stood out front and watched Pete. He saw us in the car, which made my mother start to panic.

She said to Grammy, "I know that look. He's mad." Then, she started to cry.

Pete got in the car, and then Grammy asked Pete what he had said to Lamar.

Pete responded, "I let him know that the next time I have to come and see him, only one of us is walking away. The other one is going to be carried away, and by other, I mean you." He then turned to my mother and me in the backseat. "You shouldn't have any more problems out of him."

Pete then drove off. All the while, Lamar stared at the car.

Pete was wrong. Later that night, Lamar called my mother, and I heard them arguing on the phone. The next day, my mother's friend was at the house—the woman whose house we went to the night Lamar beat my mother up. They were smoking marijuana together when there was a knock on the door. My mother opened it.

It was Lamar. He said, "I wanna talk to you." Then he looked at me, pointed, and started to yell, "You lying muthafucker! I never threatened you!"

My mother said, "He never said you threatened him. He said the tone of voice you used scared him."

Lamar said, "Fuck that little nigger! Why you have that bald-headed muthafucker come talk shit to me?"

My mother told him that Pete was just concerned about her.

Again, Lamar said to my mother, "Fuck that little nigger!"

My mother asked her friend to take me for a walk so she could talk to Lamar. As we were leaving, Lamar looked at me and said, "Yeah, get that lying muthafucker out of here."

My mother's friend and I walked around the block and came right back. The door was unlocked, and we could hear Lamar yelling. My mother's friend opened the door, and we saw my mother flying across the room as if she were pushed, and her face was red like she had been slapped.

My mother said, "I'm alright. Get him out of here."

My mother's friend and I left again, this time for a little longer. Her friend was worried, so we started to walk back toward the house again. When we came to the block where the apartment was, I saw Lamar on the other end, at the corner. I also saw a police car across the street. We walked to the middle of the block and looked up to see my mother in the window of the landlord's apartment. She was waving for us to come upstairs. When we got there, she told us that

Lamar was beating her, but she was able to get away and ran upstairs. She said Lamar was banging on the landlord's door, so the landlord called the cops.

The cops told her that they wouldn't come in; someone had to go out to them. My mother went out to talk to the cops while I stayed in the landlord's house. Lamar disappeared from the corner. She told the police all that happened, but she didn't want to file a complaint. The cops left, and Lamar reappeared on the corner. My mother was scared to go back to her apartment, so the landlord called the cops again. Lamar disappeared from the corner a second time, so the cops took a statement and left. Lamar did not reappear.

My mother called that guy Rodney, from the Bronx. She told him what happened and asked him to pick her up. Rodney was skinny. Although Lamar was bigger, Rodney had a black belt in karate. My mother and I waited upstairs in the landlord's apartment. There was no sign of Lamar.

Rodney showed up just as it was turning dark. He told my mother to pack some things and that she could stay with him. My mother called Nana and told her the story. Nana said to bring me to her house. My mother and Rodney went downstairs to pack, and I stayed upstairs and watched them from the landlord's window. My mother and Rodney were downstairs for about half an hour, and all that time, I stayed in the window. All of a sudden, I saw Lamar going into the basement apartment.

My heart was beating so fast. I saw my mother run out of the apartment, and ten seconds after that, Rodney came running out with a long, metal object in his hand and assumed a defensive position. My mother came upstairs, screaming, "The blood! The blood! There's so much blood!"

Lamar exited the apartment, covered in blood from his head to his toes. It was pouring down his face like a waterfall from the top of his head. He was begging Rodney, "Man, please don't hit me again!"

He tried to grab the metal object. Rodney struck him in the head, and then on the legs. Lamar ran out into the middle of the street. Rodney followed and struck Lamar again as he kept trying to grab the metal object. Both men were in the middle of the street, bringing traffic to a standstill as drivers stopped to witness the gory, bloody onslaught. Rodney was striking Lamar with the metal object again and again, and even kicked him a couple times.

I watched everything from the window. My mother told me, "Go in the back. You shouldn't be seeing this."

I stayed anyway. Maybe at seven years old, I shouldn't have been seeing it, but I felt that after all Lamar had put me through, and the way I saw him beat my mother, I deserved to watch him get his just desserts. In my heart, I was hoping that Rodney would kill him. It gave me joy to see him begging Rodney not to hit him anymore— the same way I was begging that security guard to help my mother. I wanted Rodney to show Lamar the same amount of sympathy he showed my mother that day. I wanted Rodney to kill him so that I would never have to see him again.

The police arrived for the third time, now with four cop cars and two detective cars. Lamar collapsed in the cops' arms. A police officer told Rodney to drop his weapon.

Rodney refused and told the officer, "I'm not going to drop this until you arrest that man."

The police officer pulled out his revolver from his side holster and pointed the gun at Rodney. "I said drop it now!"

Rodney followed the command and the officer's partner hand-cuffed him. My mother ran out to tell them that Rodney was just defending her. The police officer asked if she was going to press charges against Lamar. If not, Rodney was going to jail.

"Yes," my mother said.

The police officer came upstairs into the landlord's house and sat down with my mother as she told the whole story. She told the officer that she and Rodney were downstairs packing some things to leave. She said Lamar came into the apartment and cornered her, and that Rodney was hiding behind the door. She said Lamar grabbed her, and then Rodney hit him with the metal side rail from a bed frame that had been behind the door. That's when she ran out of the apartment.

Rodney was now in the back of the police car, handcuffed, and Lamar had been taken to the hospital by an ambulance. After my mother finished telling the story, the police released Rodney from custody.

That night, my mother and Rodney dropped me off at Nana's. I was in my old room; I was with my Nana. That night, I felt safe again. That night, I was home. I overheard Nana talking on the phone. The police arrested Lamar at the hospital. I heard that he had to have thirty-six stitches to close his face.

I said to myself, "Good for that muthafucker."

chapter FIVE

T he first thing Nana did was register me in the local public school, Benjamin Banneker, PS 156. It was January, so I was coming into the class mid-term. Most of the kids knew each other from the local housing projects, the Mahalia Jackson City Housing Projects. Also, they had been in class with each other for six months already. When Nana went to register me, I was to start class the same day. The principal escorted Nana and me to my new second-grade classroom. When we arrived, the principal called the teacher out of the room. Her name was Miss Diamond. She was a petite white lady with sandy brown hair. The principal introduced me and said, "This is your teacher."

Miss Diamond led me into the classroom as Nana stood outside and watched through the glass window of the door. Miss Diamond said, "Class, we have a new student."

The whole class booed in unison. Miss Diamond escorted me to my seat. I was tall, but not the tallest kid in the class. I could feel the boys sizing me up. They didn't know me. I wasn't from the Jackson Projects. Most of them grew up together and played on the housing projects' playground together. I was an outsider.

"Where you from?" asked this short black kid named John. "What building you live in? You from JP?"

I told him, "No, I'm from the Grand Concourse."

This didn't fly with them. The Jackson Projects were on Van Courtland Avenue. I only lived about five blocks away, but that didn't matter. These were kids from single-parent homes and, like me, they probably saw things they shouldn't have at their age. Still, I was the outsider. After school, about six of them jumped me. I ran back into the school to get away.

When I was sure they all left, I ran home to Nana and told her what had happened. I told her that the class booed when the teacher introduced me. She told me that she had heard them outside the door. I said I didn't want to go back, that they were going to beat me up again and that I was scared.

Nana said to me, "Oh, you're going back, alright."

I asked her if she was coming with me to tell the teacher to make them stop. She said, "No."

I was surprised. What was I going to do? I told her that there were at least six of them. In truth, there may have been more. I was being hit and punched from every direction. The only person I could make out was John, the one who had been questioning me.

Nana said, "Look, Malik, I'm not going to be around to fight your battles for you all the time. You have to learn to stick up for yourself."

I asked her what I should do, because I couldn't fight all of them at the same time.

Nana said, "Do whatever you have to. Get them one at a time. Throw a chair across the classroom, if you have to. Let them know you're crazy. You may not win every fight, but let them know that when they mess with you, there is going to be a fight. Don't lay down for anybody. If you let them pick on you and get away with it, they'll keep on doing it."

"Wouldn't I get in trouble for fighting?"

"That's when I'll come to your school," Nana replied. "Now, go clean yourself up and tomorrow, you go to school and handle your business."

The next day, I was on a mission. I didn't know what I was going to do, but Nana's words kept repeating in my head.

When I walked into the class, the kids that had jumped me were laughing at me. They were pounding their fists into their other hands, letting me know that there was going to be another beating. I froze. I didn't say anything. At lunchtime, in the cafeteria, they taunted me about what they were going to do after school. The taunting continued back in the classroom. John was the ringleader.

As I sat at my desk being taunted, fearing the next beating from the project thugs. I thought about every beating I had received—the beatings from Emma, the kids at the house jumping me, the scar over my right eye, the beatings my mother gave me, the beating my mother received from Lamar. As I thought about all these things, the fear in me became rage.

Without warning, I jumped up from my desk while Miss Diamond was in the middle of her lesson. I picked up my chair and threw it across the classroom at John, hitting him right in the face. I followed the chair and jumped on top of him before Miss Diamond could comprehend what was going on. I rained down on him with a hail of punches until Miss Diamond pulled me off. John's face was bloody, and I think his nose was broken from the chair hitting him in the face. The next time I saw him, he had two black eyes.

I was immediately taken to the principal's office; John was taken to the nurse's office. Nana was called and told to come to the school. My blood was still pumping with rage when Nana arrived. Something was unleashed in me. I had a lot of scores to settle.

When Nana arrived, the principal told her what happened, and that I was going to be suspended. He said I had injured the boy very severely. Nana jumped to my defense immediately.

"What about the boys that jumped him yesterday?" she asked. "What's going to happen to them?" The principal had no idea what had taken place so Nana explained everything. She wanted to know what he was going to do about it.

The principal was speechless, and the suspension was off the table. I went home that afternoon and couldn't wait to get back to school and enact my revenge.

I had a fight almost every day. Some I won, some I lost, but I was fighting everybody, taking on all comers. Some were justified, and some weren't. Nana never punished me for them. I was a boy living in the ghetto without a father to teach me how to be a man. They ended up putting me in another class. I had a reputation among the second graders, from all the fights I got into in the cafeteria.

One day, my mother came to school to get some papers for the welfare office and saw me acting up in class. I hadn't seen her for almost two months. When she saw me, I walked up to the classroom door as she was talking to the teacher. She looked at me and said, "I'm going to beat your ass."

The teacher was telling her all that had happened in the last couple of months, and she couldn't wait to deliver punishment. She left the school without me, and when I got home, I told Nana what my mother had said and that she was going to beat me. Not long after that, my mother arrived at Nana's, eager to inflict her punishment. I heard Nana talking to her, and then she came into the room and started to beat me the same way she had beat me before, with anger in every strike.

I escaped a prolonged beating by hiding under the bed, and then Nana came in and said, "That's enough."

My mother left right after that. I asked Nana why she let her beat me. She told me that my mother said she saw me acting up in class and that she was my mother. That's what she wanted to do. Then, Nana gave me a snack and comforted me.

I saw my mother again about a month later. She had a one-bedroom apartment on the fifth floor, on 175th Street and the Grand Concourse. It was a mile away from where Nana and I lived, on 158th Street and the Grand Concourse. Nana made it a point that my mother picked me up on the weekends, since I was living with her now. The apartment was much better than the basement in Queens. The neighborhood was a different story. It was drug-infested. That didn't matter to my mother. She would send me to the store by myself to get her cigarettes or whatever else she wanted. We didn't do anything special when I was over there. I would sit in the living room while she and her friend sat around smoking marijuana.

I never spent the night. I would just spend the day, usually a Saturday, and return the same night. One Saturday, Nana and Granddaddy had plans for the evening. Nana told my mother that I would have to spend the night. My mother also had plans that evening. She was going roller-skating with Rodney and Sandy. My mother decided to let Sandy's son Carrie watch me. I didn't care, since I wanted to look at his comic books.

When Nana and I would go to the movies, she would take me to see every black exploitation movie that was playing. I defined being a man by the way I saw Jim Brown, Fred Williamson, Richard Roundtree, Ron O'Neil, and many other black exploitation stars of the early 1970s. My profane vocabulary also increased extensively. I was eight years old by this time, and at this point, a young, hardened ghetto bastard.

When my mother and I arrived, Carrie was there with a friend of his. He was a dark-skinned boy who looked about fifteen years old. He had this funny look on his face when he looked at me. He made me feel uncomfortable. However, he left when my mother and Sandy left. I started to look at the comic books for a little while, and then Carrie said to me, "Hey, you want to play a game?"

I said, "Sure. What game?"

He said, "The undress game."

"What's that?"

"Well, we wrestle and take each other's cloths off. But you can't tear them off, you have to unbutton the shirt and unbuckle the belt from the pants, all the way down to the underwear. You know that guy that just left? I played that game with him a couple of times. Hey, what do you think if two men played that game, and when the guy's clothes were off the one guy had a hard-on?"

I said, "If two guys played that game and one had a hard on then he's a faggot, muthafucker."

"What if only one guy had a hard-on?"

I told him, "I don't care who had the hard-on. To me, they both faggot muthafuckers and we ain't playing that game."

He dropped the subject, and I continued to read the comic books with little conversation, until my mother came to pick me up. I was only eight, but I knew what Carrie was trying to do.

One time, my mother took me on the train with her to Brooklyn. We walked a couple of blocks and went into this taxicab stand. The lady behind the booth was Lamar's sister, the heavyset lady from before. I thought, *What the hell are we doing here?* My mother and I went into the booth with the lady, and they started talking about what happened with Lamar and Rodney. The sister wasn't mad. She said that he deserved it. From what I got from the conversation, the police agreed to drop the charges if Lamar didn't press charges on Rodney. My mother and his sister were having a good ole time.

Then I looked up, and there was Lamar, staring at us through the window. My heart stopped, and he ran off as if he was going to get something. The lady called one of the cabs, and my mother and I were whisked away before he came back. That was the last time I saw Lamar, but it wasn't the last time I heard about him.

All of a sudden, my mother just stopped coming by to pick me up on Saturdays. I didn't care, since I didn't want to go anyway. I asked Nana what happened, and she said that my mother had moved to Washington, D.C. She didn't tell me why, but Grammy and Pete came by to talk to Nana, and I overheard the details of why she moved. It was because of Lamar.

From what I gathered, Lamar followed my mother from Hostos College one day and somehow got into her apartment. My uncle, Maurice, was there. He and Lamar got into a fight. My mother had managed to call Grammy and Pete before the altercation. Lamar sprayed my uncle with mace. Maurice ran into the bathroom to get away, because Lamar had a knife. Lamar was trying to kick in the bathroom door while my mother ran out the front. Lamar locked the door behind her and went back to kicking the bathroom door, knife in hand. My uncle was holding his body against the door. Pete and Grammy arrived and tried to get into the apartment to help my uncle, but couldn't. Pete had a gun. He went up to the roof and came back down the fire escape. Pete climbed into the window, and Lamar saw him. Pete shot at Lamar, hitting the doorframe. Lamar ran out of the front door, past my mother and Grammy. I never heard about him again.

After that, my mother moved away. I didn't see her for a long time. However, about a month after the Lamar incident, she called Nana's to speak to me. She wanted me to move to D.C. with her. She must have thought I was crazy. She didn't want me there because she wanted to be a mother to her son, or that she loved and missed me so much—she just wanted a meal ticket. With me there, she could run the same welfare scam she had in New York. She could get her rent paid and get food stamps. The six months I lived with her have scarred me for the rest of my life. I'm now in my mid-forties, and still remember. I can see everything clearly in my mind, as if it were yesterday. If I had any say in the decision, I would never live with my mother again.

The next couple of years, I only saw my mother twice a year—Thanksgiving and some unannounced time when she came up to see her friends and hang out. During Thanksgiving, Nana always had a big dinner. My mother came for that, since all of the family was there. She never came just to see me. When she came by to hang out with her friends, she would stop at Nana's to see her for about an hour, but not to spend time with me in particular. I didn't mind.

The school situation didn't get any better. I was always fighting and always getting in trouble. However, I was getting good grades. The downside was that Nana had to keep coming to the school. Like I said, some fights were justified, and some were not. Nana had to spank me a few times, but when she spanked me, you could tell the difference from when my mother and Emma beat me. Nana even tried to put me back in St. Angeles for the fourth grade, but I was acting up so much, they wanted to put me on Ritalin. Nana would have none of that. She knew why I behaved that way. She knew all that I had gone through.

I remember when I first started to live with her. Once, I had to go to the bathroom, but I couldn't hold it, and ended up defecating in my pants while in the bathroom. I went crazy. I was crying hysterically. I didn't know Nana that well, and I thought she was like Emma. I thought that this woman would give me an even harsher beating for defecating in my pants. Nana came into the bathroom and told me to calm down. She took my clothes off and put me in the bathtub. She wasn't mad at all. Later, I heard her talking to someone on the phone about my accident. She said, "This boy must have really been through some stuff. By the way he reacted, you would think I was going to kill him."

Nana understood me. Nana understood why I was acting out. Nana loved me. The solution she came up with was to send me to boarding school. I understood why. The fights I was getting into were fistfights, but as I got older in the ghetto, they would soon become knife and gun fights.

chapter **SIX**

ana chose a Catholic boarding school called Sacred Heart
School for Boys in Kearney, New Jersey, about forty-five
minutes from the Bronx. The school used to be an orphanage.
During the interview process for admission, Grammy was there
with us. The nun that interviewed Nana and me was named Sister
Hyacinth. She was the most racist bitch I've ever known in my life.

Sister Hyacinth was a fat, white lady in her early forties. From
the very beginning, she and Nana got off on the wrong foot. Sister
Hyacinth couldn't believe I could have such good grades, since I
had behavior problems. Although I was accepted to the school, she
had it out for me from day one. When Nana explained that I had a
bed-wetting problem, Sister Hyacinth said, "We have accommodations for that."

The sleeping area was set up in a dormitory-type fashion. There
were four rows of five beds on two sides, with the fifth and sixth
graders on one side, and seventh and eighth graders on the other,
separated by lockers. There were four toilet bowls with no doors,
and one shower with six showerheads. There were two round, stain-
less steel basins to wash up in. Showers were Tuesdays and Thurs-
days. The boarding was from Monday to Friday, and we would go
home on Friday and return on Sunday night.

The place was like jail. It was the same routine every day. Wake
up at 7:00 a.m., a half-hour to get washed up, brush your teeth, and
get dressed. At 7:30 a.m., we would go downstairs to eat. 8:00 a.m.
chores and 8:30 a.m. school. At 2:30 p.m., school was out. We got

to play from 2:30 to 3:30, and from 3:30 to 5:00 p.m., we did home-work in the classrooms. At 5:00, we had dinner, and by 5:30, we were back upstairs to get ready for showers. At 7:30 p.m., we all sat in front of one television, watching whatever Sister Hyacinth wanted to watch. Usually, it was something like *Little House on the Prairie, The Waltons*, or baseball—she loved baseball. That was the routine every single day.

The accommodations Sister Hyacinth made for my bed-wetting was to yell out on the first morning, in front of everybody, "Is that bed wet?" For some reason, I finally stopped wetting the bed. Em-barrassment, I guess.

The classes were very small. There were six kids in mine, so it wasn't hard for me to stick out. Like any male-dominated environ-ment, all the boys had to show who the alpha male was. I was one of the youngest, at ten years old. Most everyone else was around twelve, thirteen, fourteen, and some fifteen. The older kids used to pick on the new and younger kids, but true to form, I didn't lay down for anybody. I got into fights, and to tell the truth, I lost most of them. Here are the ones that stand out the most.

The first fight was with this guy named Austin. He was thirteen, big, black, and ugly. Austin and I got into it in the gym. The coun-selor let us fight—or should I say, he let Austin beat the shit out of me for fifteen minutes. Almost all the kids in the gym were waiting for me to cry or give up, but I wouldn't. I kept on coming. I kept taking my beating, and finally, I think Austin just got tired. After that everyone understood that if they had to fight me, it was going to take a while, and like all bullies, they wanted an easy target.

The next notable scrap was with Edson, this big half-Spanish, half-white kid. Edson called me nigger so many times I lost count. When we were in the gym, he had been picking on me. So, I picked up a stickball bat and threatened him with it.

He said, "What you gonna do with that, you little nigger?"

He tried to take it away from me. That was a big mistake. I struck Edson with the bat multiple times, and he ended up having to go to the hospital. I didn't get in trouble that time, because Edson was so much bigger than me that the nuns couldn't justify punishing me for defending myself.

The first week, I knew I didn't want to stay there. I was miserable. A few of the other new kids felt the same way. We all told each other that when we went home, we weren't coming back. The seasoned kids would laugh at us and say, "Sure, we heard that bullshit before. You muthafuckers will be back."

When Nana picked me up on Friday, I told her on the bus ride home that I didn't want to go back. I told her that I hated it there.

Nana said, "Malik, I spent a lot of money for your clothes and the down payment for the tuition." The clothes were $350, and the tuition was $167 a month. "Now, if you don't want to go back, you have two choices. You can go live with Grammy, or you can go live with your mother in Washington, D.C."

I didn't want to live with anyone but Nana. I understand why she gave me that ultimatum. She was getting older, and didn't have the strength to deal with the nonsense of running back and forth to the school for my behavior. Besides, all that money she came up with wasn't easy to do on a waitress's salary. I chose to return to Sacred Heart. The older boys were right.

Nana got this guy with a van to pick me up to drive me to the school. He would also bring me home on Fridays, along with other kids from the school. His name was Ray. He was a short Spanish guy. His brother went to the school, as well.

One weekend when I came home, Granddaddy's room was empty. Nana told me that he moved out. Things started to get hard for her financially then. For the first time in my life with Nana, I realized something: we were poor. I knew we weren't rich. We would shop at Gimbals basement, and the sneakers I wore were called Skippy's. The kids used to sing, "Skippy's, they cost a $1.99. Skippy's, they make your feet feel fine." I didn't care until I went to boarding school and realized the other kids were well-off. You had to wear a suit every Friday and Sunday, and I always wore the same one. The other kids always made fun of me.

Once, I had to do a science project and brought a used iron from home. The objective of the project was to take the iron apart. When I did, there were dead cockroaches in it. Everyone made such a big deal about the roaches. I thought everybody had roaches. I used to play with them in the bathtub on my little boat. I thought it was normal.

While at boarding school, I learned that well-off kids were spoiled. So, I developed a small hustle. The nuns would make us eat everything on our plates at mealtimes. They would stand at the garbage can to watch us scrape our plates. The kids would pay me to eat their food. If they didn't want to pay me, they would try to throw it away by being sneaky. In that case, I would threaten to tell on them. I cleared about $10 to $20 a week doing that.

As I said, on Thanksgiving, Nana would always have a big dinner. This was one of the few times I would see my mother. Every year, she would have a new boyfriend. This time, it was a man named Wesley. He was short, husky, and light-skinned. He had been a boxer while in the military, but now he was a welder. He was nice enough, but given the track record of my mother, I knew it would only be a matter of time before they broke up.

The first year at the school was miserable, but I figured anything was better than living with my mother again. Then, all of a sudden, Grammy came up with this bright idea that I should start spending the summers with her so we could build a relationship. The first summer I went down to Washington, D.C., I was eleven. I knew this was another trap, like before. I'd stayed for the summer, then she decided to keep me.

Wesley and my mother lived in a one-bedroom apartment. I slept on the sofa bed. I remember my first night there. I was watching television when Wesley came out of the bedroom to talk to me. I just started to cry uncontrollably. He asked me what was wrong, and I told him that I wanted to go home. He tried to comfort me, but he didn't understand about the last time I stayed with my mother. He soon came to appreciate why I didn't want to be there.

One evening, while my mother was sleeping, Wesley asked if I wanted to go to the 7-Eleven to get a couple of slushies. When Wesley and I returned to the apartment, my mother was awake and asked where we were. Wesley told her. She asked if we brought her anything back. I was in a playful mood, since Wesley and I were joking around. I said to my mother, in a playful manner, "We wouldn't do something like that."

My mother began her verbal assault on me. "Why you playing fucking games with me? I see the slushy behind your back."

I told her I was just playing.

She said, "I don't want to play your little fucking kid games. And you know what? I don't like you very much, and by the time you leave here, I have a feeling you're not going to like me very much, either!"

She turned around and went to her bedroom, slamming the door. Wesley stood there with a look of shock on his face. I began to cry, I'm not even sure why. I guess everything I ever thought about the way she felt toward me was confirmed at that moment. Wesley went into the room to talk to my mother, and then she came out and gave me some fake-ass hug.

During that summer, Nana called and said that she had gotten fired from her job, so my mother would have to pay for boarding school. Also, the tuition had gone up from $160 a month to $180. My mother had a fit. I could hear her talking to Wesley, saying, "Why he gotta go to boarding school? Why can't he go to regular school like everyone else? She acts like he's special or something."

My mother never gave Nana a dime in child support. I was seven when she left to go to Washington, D.C. For the next four years, she never sent a dime, or even clothes for me to wear. The only person she had to take care of was herself. She was actually insulted that Nana suggested that she take care of me financially. My mother had to come up with $300 for uniforms and the first month's tuition. I heard all about how much it cost, and she let me know constantly how much she didn't want to do it. However, she also enjoyed not having the responsibility of taking care of an eleven-year-old. One hundred and eighty dollars was a bargain price.

The return to boarding school was just as miserable as spending the summers with my mother. Sister Hyacinth would look for every opportunity to get on my case, slap me, or embarrass me among my peers. She verbally, physically, emotionally, and mentally abused me whenever she could. But what could she do to me that hadn't been done already? What could she say to me that would make me feel any lower than when my mother would talk down to me? She didn't know what I had been through. Dealing with Sister Hyacinth was a cakewalk in comparison.

The next summer, I returned to Washington, D.C. My mother and Wesley were broken up by then, and she was unemployed. She pulled the same scheme she did in New York, using me as a meal ticket. She was collecting unemployment benefits, and she enrolled me in a local school. Then, she applied for food stamps. I was only there for six weeks, but she was able to keep getting food stamps and the cash benefit for six months. Back then, they didn't have the computer systems like they do now, so it was easy to get away with.

My mother always cried broke when it came to my school, but at the same time, she always had enough money to buy her marijuana. Once, when she was out, I went into her stash and tried to roll a joint. It was poorly rolled, but I tried to smoke it anyway. I didn't know what I was doing, because I didn't know how to inhale the smoke. I was twelve years old. Fortunately, my mother never found out. I guess the smell was gone by the time she got back.

chapter **SEVEN**

T hat summer, my mother brought me back to New York before Grammy came down by train to visit her and pick me up. My mother had something up her sleeve, but I didn't know what. She and Grammy drove me to Jamaica, Queens, to a very small house. The area was bad— some parts were just as bad as the South Bronx. I walked up and looked inside through the screen door. My mother told me to ask for Miss Mary. Inside were two young kids, a boy and a girl. The boy looked to be about a year younger than I was, and the girl looked about two years younger. I asked the boy if Miss Mary was there, and he called out, "Grandma! Someone's here to see you!" He was smiling like he recognized me.

When Miss Mary came to the door, she called out my name and said, "Oh, Malik! I'm so happy to see you!" She told the young man, whose name was Gregory, to go call his father and tell him his son is here. This was my grandmother on my father's side. The boy and the girl were my brother and sister.

My mother, Grammy, and I stepped into the house. My mother hadn't even told me I was meeting my father for the first time. I was anxious to see what he looked like. What he was like? Would he love me? We waited in the small living room. About ten minutes later, the man walked in. He was tall, about 6'1", and he was big, about 225 pounds. He was much darker than I was, and he had this big smile on his face. He yelled, "Hot damn!" and gave me a hug. He told me to follow him, and we went to the back room with my grandmother. My father said to her, "Momma, give the boy a hundred dollars."

"Leroy, you can't be giving that young boy all that money," my grandmother said.

"Okay, give him fifty."

My grandmother reached in her purse and gave me two twenties and a ten.

My father asked my mother if he could take me for a ride. She said yes.

I thought, *What's up her sleeve?* This was the first time I met my father, and he lived in New York all this time. Why didn't she take me to see him when I lived in Queens with her? Why not any other time?

My father and I left the house. He asked me if I knew how to drive. I told him a little, even though I had never driven a car in my life. He threw me the key to his big, black El Dorado, and told me to drive. He helped me from the passenger side, and we were off.

The first place he took me was a spot on Jamaica Avenue, where some nefarious black men were hanging out. We went inside, and there was a pool table and a bar. A big picture of six men, with my father in the middle, hung on the wall. My father proudly introduced me to the men as his son. The only person's name that I remembered was a fat guy named Cornbread.

Next, my father took me to a beauty parlor. We went past everyone to a door where we were buzzed in. Inside was a lady sitting at a desk, taking phone calls. My father told her I was his son, and the lady commented how handsome I was. My father asked her a few questions, and then we left.

We returned to the house. My father told me that he had a softball game tonight, and wanted to know if I could stay over. My mother was okay with it, but when my father asked her, she and Grammy looked at each other funny, as if Nana would not agree with the decision. I ended up staying, and my father took me, my brother, and sister to the softball game with him.

My father had a girlfriend whose name was Troy. She was a very beautiful, dark-skinned black woman with a body that matched. When the song "Brick House" came out, they must have been talking about her. She had all kinds of jewelry on. Rings, bracelets, gold chains—you name it, she had it. The odd thing was that everything either had my father's initials (LV) or his name, Leroy Vann. Her watch had "Leroy" on the inside of it, as if to say she was his. It wasn't his jewelry, because he had his own. I wondered what he did for a living.

My father played center field. He introduced me to everyone, who all seemed to know him and gave him a lot of respect. Everything seemed to revolve around him. Later, my brother, sister, and I stayed up all night talking. I found out they didn't live with my grandmother. They just came over on the weekend. I also found out that my father owned a couple of number spots and a couple of afterhours gambling spots. He was a street hustler. I later found out that he also dealt in heroin. He was a major player—that's why Nana didn't want me around him.

My father picked me up the next day in a black Corvette. We went for a ride, him and me. I asked how many cars he had. He told me he had three—an El Dorado, a Corvette, and a Mercedes-Benz. For the next hour, he told me about how I came to be. "All these years, you probably heard a lot of bullshit. But now, I'm gonna tell you my side of the story."

I told my father that I never heard anything about him. So, he began his story.

My father put all questions to rest. Until that point, I thought he had left my mother. I thought they were married and we were a family. The way he told it, my father was a high school basketball star. He was so good that he was invited to the 1969 Boston Celtics training camp. He didn't make it, but it was an honor to even be invited. He met my mother at a pool party. They were both sixteen. My mother had a boyfriend at the time. His name was Malik. She and my father messed around on the side, behind Malik's back. My father called my mother one day to hook up, and she said she couldn't because she was pregnant. She didn't say that it was his. Even still, my father started to calculate the last time they had sex and concluded that the baby could be his. Malik had no idea of the situation, and automatically thought he was the father. When I was born, my mother continued to allow Malik to think that. It wasn't until a couple of months later that my father started to protest about me being his son. From my understanding, the situation became very heated, and at times, the police had to be called. He even tried to kidnap me from Emma's when I was a baby.

My father continued to let me know how much of a bitch Grammy was to him because, in his words, "She just didn't want to accept the fact that her daughter was fucking two niggers."

When I was six months old, my father said he went to jail for one year for a robbery he didn't commit. When he was released, he started to hustle. He had wanted to be a police officer, but the jail internment ruined that. He went on to say how he resented my mother because I was his firstborn, but some other nigger's name was on my birth certificate. I told him that no father's name was on my birth certificate. When he dropped me back at his mother's house, he said that maybe we could try to hook up from time to time, now that we knew each other. I was looking forward to that.

When Nana found out where I was, she was very upset at my mother. She knew all about my father—what he was, what he did—and she didn't want that kind of influence around me. My mother, on the other hand, insisted that I be able to see him.

Later on, I was at Grammy and Pete's. I overheard Pete arguing on the phone with Miss Mary. When he got off, I asked him what had happened. As he and my mother didn't get along too well, he was all too willing to tell me. He also filled in the gaps that my father didn't know. He said that my mother told miss Mary she was going to ask Leroy to help pay for my boarding school. (This was the plan she had up her sleeve.) Miss Mary asked her not to do that. My father would be very resentful, since it had been twelve years without so much as a peep from her, and now when she finally bought me around, she was asking for money. She said Leroy wasn't the kind of guy you could play like that. She told my mother to at least let my father and me get to know each other better first.

Pete was upset at my mother for doing this, but also because of how Miss Mary was responding to the request. He told her that I did fine without my father's money all these years, and that I could continue to do so. He also apologized for my mother's actions. I asked Pete about the guy that my father told me about, Malik. I wanted to know where he was. Pete was more than happy to tell me the whole dirty story.

As it went, my mother was seeing two guys. When she first got pregnant, everyone thought I was Malik's baby, and that was why she named me after him. But as I grew older, there was no question that I wasn't his child. I asked what had happened to him. This was another story completely. Pete loved to brag about his hustling and the money he made, even to a kid.

One of his hustles was dealing heroin. He used to hide the heroin in the back of the television. According to him, my mother and everyone in the house knew this. One day when he and Grammy returned home, they found blood on the television. They also noticed that the television had been tampered with. Pete and Grammy looked inside, and the heroin was gone. They immediately knew it was my mother, because she was a user. It was over sixty thousand dollars' worth of uncut heroin that Pete had gotten on consignment from the Colombians he knew. The Colombians wanted to kill him and the whole family, but since he had a good relationship with them, he was allowed to pay them off over a course of time. He told me that Malik had run off with the drugs and was somewhere in Florida.

This kind of explains my mother's dislike for me, I thought.

I don't know if my mother ever asked my father for money or not, but the next few times I saw him, he was acting a little bit differently toward me. The first time he was supposed to pick me up, he was to come at 6:00 p.m. I waited all night, and finally went to sleep. My father eventually came to pick me up at six in the morning. Nana wasn't happy. He took me to an all-night diner. We sat in the back, and he had his back to the wall, facing the entrance. We talked, and being young and impressionable, with all the jewelry and fancy cars he had, I asked him, when he died, would I inherit some of those things?

He was very offended. "Muthafucker! What you talking about me dying for? Right now, if I die, you ain't gonna get shit, nigger. The only muthafuckers that gonna get shit is the muthafuckers with the same last name as me." I said that it wasn't my fault I didn't have the same last name as him, and he replied, "Ain't my fault. Talk to your mother."

This wasn't the same guy who was glad to see me just about a month earlier. I felt something had happened, and I knew it had to do with my mother.

Later that day, we went to another one of his softball games. His girlfriend, Troy, was with us. While he was playing, Troy started to talk to me. I found out that she was going to medical school, and didn't work. My father took care of her. She asked me about my life and where I lived. The topic got us to Nana, and how she didn't want me around my father. To my surprise, Troy said, "She's right. Stay away from him. He's no good for you. You can get hurt around him. He's evil. Listen to your grandmother."

I asked her why was she around him, and she replied, "I'm going to school. I'm going to be a doctor, and he takes care of me. I don't love him or anything, and he knows that. I'm just his trophy bitch."

I was shocked to hear this, but by the way she was telling this to me, I knew it was the truth.

When the game was over, my father dropped me off at his mother's house and left. He later returned with another woman. The three of us went to McDonald's, and then he brought me right back to his mother's. He told me he would be back to take me back to Nana's. He returned at 3:00 a.m. and drove me.

ot happy about this, either. I heard her talking on the phone to Grammy, telling her about the odd hours he picked me up and dropped me off. She was emphasizing the point of his chosen profession, and that this was what to expect from him.

I didn't see my father for a while after that, but at least I knew I had a father. And I knew a little more about myself that no one else had told me. I was a ghetto bastard. My mother was a pregnant teenager and a heroin user. My father was a street hustler. Grammy was a working woman—she worked for the telephone company—and Pete was also a street hustler, and neither had time to take care of a baby.

I found out that Grammy had also been a pregnant teen. She got pregnant when she was eighteen by Nana's son, my grandfather. In those days, people got married; but also in those days, the marriage didn't work out. My grandfather left, and Grammy was on her own with two kids. She couldn't afford to keep her children and work, so she farmed them out to Nana, Emma's mother. That's how my mother knew Nana and Emma. She just repeated the cycle, and with the same people.

During my mother's pregnancy, she used all kinds of drugs. Many times during her get high sessions, I would hear her tell people about how she was surprised and lucky that I wasn't born with some kind of birth defect because of it. I started to understand that my mother didn't care about me from the time I was inside her. To her, I was interfering with her life. I was her shame, her mistake. I wasn't a child conceived in love. If anything, I was just going to be her meal ticket. Like many unmarried teenage girls in the ghetto that get pregnant, the first thing she did was get on welfare.

Every year, Uncle Maurice would come to New York for Nana's Thanksgiving dinner. He always had a new woman on his arm, and he always had money. He would wear fur coats, and so did the women with him. He had a BMW, and everyone would talk about how much money he had. He would always throw me a twenty or

50

so when he saw me, and he had a personality that was the life of the party. I admired him. He was tall, handsome, and rich. I asked if I could visit him in Milwaukee for the summer, instead of going to Washington, D.C. Nana said she would think about it.

Springtime, when I was twelve, Grammy took me to one of her weekend-at-the-YMCA trips and told me that my mother was getting married. She was marrying this short guy named Ernest. When I say short, I mean shorter than me. By age twelve, I was about 5'10"; he was about 5'5". Grammy took me to Washington for the wedding. It was held at one of Nana's cousins' houses. I had a feeling this marriage was some kind of scheme, because my mother only knew the guy for six months or so. I then found out that she married him so that he could get a green card. He was from an island in the Caribbean.

chapter EIGHT

I was thirteen. Nana said I could go to Wisconsin to see Uncle Maurice for the summer. I loved my uncle. Besides Nana, he treated me better than anybody else. Even though his name was Maurice, my mother called him Reesy. So, I called him Uncle Reesy, too. I couldn't wait to go to Milwaukee. I took a plane there that Uncle Reesy paid for. When I arrived at the airport, he picked me up and took me to his place. He lived in the upscale part of Milwaukee, in a duplex apartment. I'd never seen a two-story apartment before. He was living with a woman named Brenda. I knew her from the couple of times she came with him to New York.

My uncle took me across town to the ghetto to see his daughter from his ex-girlfriend, Lynn. I also knew her from one of his visits to New York. She had two other kids that were my age, but they were not my uncle's. My uncle figured her kid could keep me company while he worked nights.

The first few days were great. We went out to eat every day. My uncle and I were about the same size, so he would let me wear his clothes and leather sneakers. He had about twenty pairs of them. Up until this point, I never had a pair of leather sneakers; I only wore Skippy's. I was living the life. I asked my uncle what he did for a living. He told me he worked at a nightclub, was very popular, and that the club paid him to be there. That was why he had to go out at night.

More and more, my uncle would drop me off at Lynn's house and leave me there for longer periods of time. Once, he left me there and didn't come back for a whole day. Lynn was about ten years older than my uncle, who was about twenty-seven. As time went on, Lynn and I started to talk more, since I was there a lot. She was a little bitter against him. She complained about him leaving me there all the time. I came to his defense, saying that he had to work at the club at night. She said, "What club?"

I told her that I didn't know the name of it, and that I was just telling her what he told me.

Lynn started to laugh. She said, "Your uncle's been lying to you. Well, he does work at a club sometimes, but he doesn't work at the club."

I asked her what she meant by that.

She acted surprised that I didn't know what she was saying, so I asked her straight out, "Well, what does he do, then?"

She replied with definitiveness in her voice, "He's a dope dealer. He deals cocaine, and he's one of the biggest dealers in Milwaukee."

At first, I was taken aback, but that explained all the money, fancy clothes, and fur coats.

Later that day, my uncle picked me up. During the ride to his house, I asked him if it was true. He said yes. He said he didn't want to tell me, because he didn't want me to tell Nana—his grandmother. From the time I started to live with Nana, she was very much against drugs. When we would go to see the Blaxploitation movies, most of them were about crooked cops, dope dealers, and dope fiends. When there was a scene of a junky going through withdrawal, she would always say, "See what that dope will do to you?" I told my uncle that I wouldn't say anything to Nana.

From that day on, everything was out in the open. My uncle would cut the cocaine up and bag it in front of me. When he was out, I would take orders over the phone for him. When people would come to the apartment to pick up the cocaine, I would open the door for them. Most were wealthy white people. He also introduced me to his street-level dealers, who came to pick up their co-caine when they ran out. I was still living the life. I felt great, like I was respected. I felt like my uncle really loved me.

During my stay, I would hear about the goings on in Washing-ton, D.C., between my mother and her new husband. I was glad I wasn't down there.

I would hang out with my uncle and his friends while they talked about freebasing. I didn't know what that was. I was there for six weeks, having the time of my life. I felt like I was grown.

After the six weeks, I had to go to finish the rest of the summer with my mother. The night before I left my uncle and Brenda, they took me out to dinner. When we got home, Brenda went to sleep, and I went into my room to watch television. Around midnight, I went downstairs to get something to drink. My uncle was sitting on the living room couch with a big pile of cocaine in front of him. He was sniffing it with a card that said "cocaine" on it. He had several various colors.

I sat down with him and asked if everything was okay.

"Yeah," he said. Then, he put some cocaine on the card and offered it to me. I sniffed it. I knew this wasn't right, and that it would disappoint Nana if she ever found out. But this was my Uncle Reesy, and if he offered it to me, then hey, why not? I mean, he loved me. He wouldn't do anything to hurt me. He was treating me like a grownup. He and I stayed up all night, sniffing cocaine. I had to catch a plane to Washington the next day at 10:00 a.m. We sniffed until 6:00 a.m. I started to tell my uncle how much I felt like I was a burden, and that I felt that my mother hated me, and all kinds of babbling from the high I was having.

When my uncle woke me up to get ready to go to the airport, he told me not to tell anybody about last night. I wouldn't; he was my Uncle Reesy, and I loved him with all my heart. The day before I was to go to Washington, D.C., Uncle Reesy bought me a whole wardrobe of new clothes to wear to school. He took me to the air-port and reiterated not to tell anybody about sniffing cocaine. This was our secret, and I wouldn't tell anybody. In fact, I wanted to be just like my uncle and my father when I grew up. They had money, cars, pretty women, and respect. Yeah! I wanted to be just like them.

When I returned to D.C., it was the same old story—my mother was unemployed and a miserable bitch. She was always crying that she was broke and talking about me having to go to boarding school. The only difference was she was seeing this new guy named Briggs. He was a much older man, maybe twenty years older than my mother. She was about thirty-one at that time. Briggs was wealthy. He had nice cars and nice clothes. He had a construction business. He also had a wife.

Yes—my mother was seeing a married man this time. Briggs would come by in the morning, and they would go into the bedroom for a couple of hours. Then, he would leave. A couple of times, when his wife was away on a trip or something, he would take us out. Briggs treated me the best out of all the men my mother went out with. He would buy me clothes. When he was taking my mother somewhere, he insisted I go, even if my mother wanted to leave me home. Briggs bought me my first pair of leather sneakers; they were Pumas, white leather with a suede emblem on the side. Briggs also took me out without my mother a few times.

I returned to boarding school for my final year. It was like jail—the same thing every hour, every day, every year. I almost got kicked out this time. One of the kids brought a pocketknife to school. I was playing with it when this kid tried to grab it from me, but grabbed the blade part instead of the handle. I pulled the knife away and cut him between his thumb and forefinger. It was an accident, but of course, I was the hoodlum from the Bronx. Grammy and Pete came to the school and begged them not to kick me out. Instead, I had an in-school suspension, so everyone could see me with my desk in the hallway. I would be humiliated every day for two weeks. After that, the days were pretty lame. Same crap, different day.

55

I spent two weeks in D.C. for Easter vacation. This time, my mother was living in the basement of the house of Nana's cousin, where she had gotten married. She was working now, so I would stay in the house by myself. I couldn't wait to see Briggs. He was such a father figure to me. This was a man who actually worked for a living, and treated me with respect. My mother said she wasn't seeing him anymore, but that he called sometimes. He did call, and he came by the house to see me. I ran and gave him a big hug. My mother walked out of the house and barely acknowledged him. Briggs took me out and said he would come back tomorrow to get me. When we got home, my mother wouldn't even let him in, and spoke to him with such disrespect. Briggs left, and I never saw him again. I tried to look up his company in the phone book and called information, but I couldn't find him.

My mother was just using him. When she didn't need him anymore, she treated him like shit. She didn't care that I loved him, or that he treated me kindly. She got what she wanted, and as I heard her tell people when she would talk about him, "Fuck him! I got a job now."

I returned for my last semester of boarding school. I took the test to get into Cardinal Hayes High School and passed. Nana was so proud of me. My mother didn't give a crap. She just figured she wouldn't have to pay what was now $200 a month anymore. I graduated from Sacred Heart and, like always, I went to Washington, D.C. for my final summer. My mother didn't really want me down there anymore because, for two months, she would have to take care of me and feed me. I was fourteen by this time. My mother had a friend who had a brother about my age, and they lived in the ghetto of Washington, D.C. (If you think New York ghettos are bad, you should see the ones in D.C.) My mother had a new boyfriend, too. His name was Bill. He was white and a car salesman. He always drove nice cars, but they always had the stickers on them. He didn't pay me any special attention, and the only time I really saw him was when he was picking up or dropping off my mother.

56

Finally, the summer was over. Thank God. Nana wanted to have a meeting with my mother and Grammy about Cardinal Hayes and the tuition. We were all sitting in Nana's living room as she began telling my mother it was $100 a month. My mother was so happy it was so little. She was going to send the $100 and nothing else.

"He's going to need clothes, and shoes, and other things," Nana said.

My mother said, "You really gonna find a way to make me spend this extra hundred dollars, aren't you?"

Nana told her that these were things I needed. With all that, my mother still didn't send any extra money. She didn't care what I looked like; she was fine.

Cardinal Hayes was an all-boys Catholic school. It was on 151st Street and the Grand Concourse. I loved it. It had sports, and the teachers were respectful to the students. I knew a lot of the kids, because I went to grade school with them. I tried out for the cross-county track team, but I needed to buy a pair of track shoes. I dared not ask my mother for anything. So, I just stopped trying out for things. But I still enjoyed the environment, and I was with Nana all the time now.

One bad element about the school was that many of the kids' parents were drug dealers. The dealers would send them to better schools because they could afford something beyond public school. These kids thought they were little gangsters—not all of them, just a few. They were around a lot of their parents' activities, and on occasion, would bring drugs they stole to sell to high school kids. They were bigshots and bullies.

Since I was back in the city all the time now, I would sometimes walk over to see my cousin, Mitchell. He only lived about four blocks away. Mitchell was a young thug. He was only thirteen, but he had much more experience in the hood than I did. While I was away at boarding school, he was hanging in the streets. His mother was something like mine, except she loved him. However, she got

57

high and hung out a lot. When she was out, Mitchell ran the streets all hours of the night.

One time when I went to see him, Mitchell was playing handball against the curb. A police car drove by, and when it passed, Mitchell hit the trunk of the car with his hand. The car stopped immediately, and a short, redheaded cop jumped out with his partner. The cop grabbed Mitchell and pinned him against the car, the same way Lamar pinned my mother up against the iron fence at the hospital, with his elbow under Mitchell's neck.

The cop said, "You think you bad in front of your boys? I'm going to kick your little nigger ass, and they ain't going to do shit about it. Next time you hit my car, I'm going to fuck you up, and then run your little piece-of-shit ass in."

I never had any trouble with the police, but from watching all those Blaxploitation movies, I knew you didn't fuck with them. When the cop finished threatening Mitchell, he got back in his car and drove off. Mitchell started to cry, but quickly pulled himself together. By the time the incident was over, many people from his block had gathered around. He was known as a tough guy, and knew that showing weakness would not be tolerated. That was the last time I saw Mitchell alive.

When I was growing up, Nana never muttered a single racist word. I would hear all kinds of racist stuff from Pete, my mother, my father, and my uncle Maurice. They would say stuff like, "Fuck them redneck muthafuckers!" and "The white man is the devil," and "Don't trust white people," even though my uncle was doing business with white people. My mother was with a white man. They still preached black racist ideology to me.

Something else Nana wouldn't do was help me with my homework, because she couldn't. In time, I found out the reasons for both of these things. Nana had gotten pregnant when she was fourteen years old and had to drop out of school. She got pregnant again at sixteen. Furthermore, she had gotten pregnant by a white Italian gangster in the 1920s. She was seventeen years old, raising two bi-racial kids. It must have been hard. My grandfather and his sister were half-white. That's why their skin, as well as my mother's and uncle's, was so light. Nana was very dark, and my father was dark. I was more of a caramel color, a mixture of all of them.

In school, everything was going well. But as always, in an all-male environment, the alpha males had to show their dominance. I tried to keep a low profile, but I was tall. Bullies tend to try to chump the bigger guys first; the smaller ones usually fall right into place. The first time I was approached by a bully was in homeroom. The class had a substitute teacher that day, so everyone just sat any-where. This big Dominican guy came up to me and said, "Get the fuck out my seat, muthafucker." This was in front of the whole class. Everyone stopped to look at what I was going to do.

I said, "We can sit anywhere today."

"Fuck that! I want to sit in my seat, bitch."

The substitute teacher saw the verbal exchange and ordered eve-ryone to their assigned seats. I escaped that situation without a phys-ical altercation, but now the guy viewed me as a sucker. It was just a matter of time before he tested me again. Not to mention that the other wannabe alpha males were looking at me as if I were weak. I didn't want to get in any fights with the tough guys, because most of them had reputations for having guns in school. I didn't even know where to get a gun.

The lunchroom was the most popular place for the bullies to flex their intimidation toward "the weak people." The bullies would stay away from each other because, like all bullies, they wanted an easy target.

Every day, I would come home, say hi to Nana, then go into my room to do my homework. One day, Nana followed me into my room. This was strange, because she usually sat in the front room and would stay there. She said, "I gotta talk to you."

I remember this so well because I was in a good mood that day. Not for any particular reason—I was just happy. Life was going well.

Nana said, "Mitchell's dead."

I couldn't believe what I was hearing. "What?"

"He was shot outside his school at 1:00 today. He's dead. He died at the hospital."

How could this happen? I thought. *He was only thirteen. Who would want to kill him?*

Nana didn't seem sad about it. She knew the kind of kid Mitchell was, and I guess she expected it sooner or later. Still, I think she would have liked it later rather than sooner. I told Nana that I was going over to his house to find out what happened.

When I arrived, his mother, Jewel, answered the door with tears in her eyes. I couldn't even speak.

"It's a kick in the head, ain't it?" she said.

I just smiled and said, "Yeah," and we hugged each other.

I thought about how much I loved Mitchell. He wasn't blood, but we had known each other for as long as I could remember. Nana used to put us in the bathtub together when I was four and he was three. For some reason, I wasn't able to cry. I felt overwhelming sadness, but I didn't cry.

In Jewel's house, there were several people over to give her moral support. Three women, Lori, Jazz, and Maria stuck out because they were calling her Frida instead of Jewel.

I asked Jewel what happened. She told me that it was over a girl. The shooter was a Spanish kid. Mitchell was seeing the girl. The Spanish kid and Mitchell had some words over it. The Spanish kid didn't even go to the school. He came around the school at lunchtime, while Mitchell and a friend were outside, and they had some more words. The boy pulled out a gun and started to shoot at Mitchell's friend, who dove for cover behind a car, Mitchell just stood there. He didn't run, he didn't hide—he just stood there.

I mentioned before that Mitchell was a thug. He wasn't scared of anything or anyone. The thing about thugs, though, is that they think everyone is scared of them. They think they're invincible.

As the shooter pointed the gun at Mitchell, he hesitated for a moment. Mitchell said to the kid, "If you gonna shoot, then shoot, muthafucker."

Then the boy shot Mitchell twice in the chest. Mitchell fell to the ground, and the boy fled. The other kids ran back into the school, and an ambulance was called to take Mitchell to the hospital. He was still alive. He died on the operating table.

I went home later that night, thinking about everything. I wanted revenge for my cousin, but what did I know about revenge? I couldn't kill anybody. I remembered the movies that made it look so easy. The only thing was, this wasn't a movie. There was no music and there were no reruns. Mitchell was dead. I would never see him again.

When Mitchell was killed, a reality came over me. You could die at any time in these streets. If someone threatened you, strike first, because you may not have the time to prepare for the enemy's strike. You might not survive it. Deal with your enemies before they deal with you. It was like some of the thugness that Mitchell had was a part of me now, and I wasn't going to end up like him. My worst nightmare of the ghetto was to be shot dead in the street. I would be another ghetto bastard, shot down just like that. A statistic.

The shooting made the six o'clock news. There was even a candlelight vigil around the school. I saw Granddaddy and Mitchell's father, big Mitchell, at the funeral. Nana didn't come. Like all deaths in the ghetto, when all the fanfare is gone, you're just another dead youth struck down by urban violence.

I started to hang around Jewel's more often, and came to understand Mitchell's life. The three women—Lori, Jazz, and Maria—were Jewel's hangout girls. They would hang at an afterhours club called the Recovery Room. The place was a cocaine den. I know this because Jazz and I became close. I had a little crush on her. She was a very pretty woman, but what was a fourteen-year-old virgin—me—going to do with a twenty-two-year-old woman? Jazz was a hairdresser and worked at a beauty salon on the eighth floor of Lincoln Hospital, right around the corner from Cardinal Hayes. After school, I would go to see her and we would talk about Mitchell. Sometimes, I would get a free haircut.

Jazz had some baggage of her own. Her six-year-old son was in foster care in Long Island. She got pregnant when she was sixteen, and was unable to take care of her baby. The foster family allowed her to maintain a relationship with him, but she wasn't able to see him much due to her lifestyle. She rented a room from some lady who sold weed from the apartment. She was also a slut; when she and the girls were at Jewel's house, she would brag about how she loved to fuck. I think she was looking for a father figure. She told me that she didn't know who her father was, and that her brother had murdered her mother and cut her eyes out when he was high on PCP. Jazz was Puerto Rican, but couldn't speak Spanish and was born and raised in the South Bronx. She definitely had issues.

Lori was a heavyset, medium-complexion woman who worked for the city. She hung out with the other women to get high and stuff. The only unusual thing about her was that she would always comment on how handsome I was. I knew her from Jewel's.

Maria worked at the post office and, to my surprise, was Jewel's lesbian lover. I found out that Jewel was bisexual. Her boyfriend, Ron, lived with her. I guess Jewel would allow him to partake in the action sometimes, because he and Maria were a little touchy-feely at times. Hey, to each his own.

When I would hang around Jewel, she would allow me to drink alcohol. I would make drinks right in front of her and the rest of her crowd. No one would say a thing. Sometimes, they would tell me to fix them a drink. This must have been Mitchell's life. He was able to do whatever he wanted. He had no supervision. They would sniff cocaine and smoke weed right in front of me. Again, I felt grown, like when I was visiting my uncle.

The women would brag about leaving the Recovery Room at 8:00 and 9:00 in the morning, after a whole night of sniffing cocaine. When Jewel was doing this, who was watching Mitchell? I started to feed into the mindset that Mitchell had. I could do whatever I wanted around them. I could only imagine the things he saw.

I remembered that his mother was also a heroin user when he was younger. If I had stayed with my mother, this could have been me. The difference was Mitchell's mother loved him. She wasn't the best mother, but she kept him. Of course, she played the welfare game, also.

Soon, my grades started to suffer. I would go to Jewel's—who I now called Frida—after school to hang out. It was like I was taking Mitchell's place. When my report card came, the grades were bad, but not the worst. Grammy and Pete decided they were going to have me live with them in their one-bedroom apartment as punishment until my grades improved.

I slept on one couch, and Grammy's bother slept on the other in their small living room. Her brother's name was Rudy, and he was an alcoholic. He had a wife that died, and as a result, he crawled into the bottle and never came out. They let him stay there sometimes to make sure he was taking care of himself. I thought, *What kind of dumb shit is this? When I was a baby, nobody wanted to take care of me. But to punish me, now you want me in your apartment that doesn't even have room for me?*

Their justification was that Nana was getting older and couldn't handle me anymore. Therefore, Pete was going to straighten me out. How could Pete straighten me out? What kind of role model was he? He must have thought I forgot about the story he told me about my mother and Malik taking the heroin behind the television.

I played along. They would clock my time down to the minute from when I left for school until I came home. Before, I could walk to school from Nana's. Now, I had to take two buses to get to school and two buses to get back. Yeah, this was going to make me get better grades, alright.

Well, like always, when things got bad, they got worse. I had a music class where I played the trumpet. One day while in class, I was playing around with a couple of my friends, and this Spanish guy pushed the trumpet into my mouth. He was in my homeroom class, also. He must have seen the verbal altercation I had with that Dominican guy. This guy wasn't as big, but he perceived me as weak. I was pissed off and cursed him out.

He said, "What the fuck you gonna do about it?"

I invited him to an ass-whooping after school. Just as I said it, the Dominican guy was passing by, and evidently, was a friend of his. They spoke some Spanish to each other, and then the Dominican guy, whose name was Carl, said, "Why don't you fight me, you fucking pussy?"

I wasn't the same guy from a couple of months ago, but still, I didn't want some dumb muthafucker bringing a gun to school and shooting me.

As I was about to respond to Carl, a teacher walked by and told us to move along. Carl told me, "I'll see you later, muthafucker."

At lunchtime, I sat at the nobody table. We weren't troublemakers, and we weren't tough guys. Carl came over with a couple of his goons and stood right over me. The rest of the guys at the table gave him some room so as not to become the target of his wrath. He told me I needed to be taught a lesson. He said after school, my ass was his. I'd had it with this asshole. I told him that I would fight him, but I needed to go home right after school.

He and his boys started to laugh. They thought I was chickening out. Not by a long shot! I told him that if he wanted to fight, I would meet him across the street from the school, at the bus stop, before school started. School started at 8:15 a.m. I told him that I would be there at 7:45.

He seemed even more angered that I wasn't backing down this time, especially in front of his boys. He must have been telling them what a punk I was, and now, here I was scheduling a fight.

64

He said, "Alright, muthafucker! In the morning, I'm gonna fuck you up!"

Then I started to talk shit to him. I said, "Maybe you the one that's going to get fucked up!"

You could see the rage in his eyes. "You talking shit, muthafucker? We can do it right now!"

I got cocky. "Look, bitch, if you want to fight, it's going to have to be in the morning. If we fight right now, the staff is going to break it up, and I don't want anyone to stop me from kicking your ass."

Carl was enraged. After school, I saw him and his boys, and he said, "In the morning, muthafucker!"

I said, "I'll be there!"

He told me, "Don't bitch up!" and walked away with his boys. There were about five of them altogether.

When I went home that night, I didn't say anything to Grammy and Pete, but I did tell Uncle Rudy what had happened. He asked me what I was going to do. I told him I had to fight, because if I didn't, the guy would keep fucking with me and that I couldn't take it anymore. Uncle Rudy asked me if I thought I could beat him. I said I might not be able to, and he may kick my ass, but he was going to know that he was in a fight. I was concerned about maybe being jumped by his boys.

That night, I thought of a plan. Before we would fight, I would try to talk to him and say stuff like, "Hey, man. We don't really need to do this." I hoped that since there wasn't the lunchroom crowd, I could eat a little crow and he could save face. I also thought about when Grammy used to take me to the YMCA with her. I used to take karate lessons. I started to remember some basic tips, like don't be the aggressor, and defend yourself. That was a good plan, because if he was attacking me, he would leave himself open for me to strike. It had been a while since I practiced karate. This all sounded good in theory, but let's see what happens in a real fight.

65

That morning, there was snow on the ground, so I had boots on—not the ideal footwear to fight in. When I got on the bus, every thought was about the fight, and the worry of Carl's boys possibly jumping me. I had to take two buses, the 36 bus to Tremont Avenue and the Grand Concourse, then catch the number 1 bus that stopped across the street from the school. When I got on the number 1, I walked to the back and saw this guy I knew named Greg. Not a friend, but we would say, "What's up?" to each other at school. He was with some other guys. He was also loud, and the center of attention.

I said, "What's up? Hey, you want to see a fight?"

And of course, what fifteen-year-old wouldn't? I told him what was going down. Greg told the guys that were with him, "Hey! Y'all want to see a fight?" They were all game. My thought was that if I got off the bus with these guys, Carl and his boys wouldn't know if they were there to back me up or what, so at least it would be a fair fight.

When the bus got to our stop, Carl was waiting with six guys. At least the same number got off the bus with me. Carl said, "You ready for your asskicking, muthafucker?"

I said, "You ready?"

The bus stop was in front of Frane Sigal Park. We decided to go up into the park so that the school officials couldn't see us. We stood in two groups. The guys with Carl were on his side, and the guys who got off the bus with me were on mine. I knew one of the guys with Carl. He came over and apologized for being there. He told me that he didn't know it was me that his boy had some beef with.

I said, "Don't worry about it. No hard feelings."

The two of us prepared for combat. I took my jacket off and rolled up my sleeves. I had on a white button-down dress shirt and boots. Carl, on the other hand, brought a change of clothes. He put on a t-shirt, changed into a pair of sneakers, and then began to wrap his fists with Ace bandages. One of the guys with me said, "That muthafucker wants to kick your ass real bad." After Carl finished changing, we were ready to fight.

We both walked toward each other as the other guys stayed behind us. We met in the middle, and I started to say, "Hey! We—" and before another word came out my mouth, he swung with a haymaker to my head. I ducked and hit him multiple times. He dropped to the ground in front of me, so I stepped back into a defensive position. Everyone looked on in amazement as he jumped up and had a small smirk on his face, as if it were a just a lucky shot.

He charged me and swung again with all his force. This met with the same result, only he didn't jump up as fast. You could hear the "Oooohs" and "Ahhhs" from the spectators as the fight continued. I was beating him like a drum. He was able to graze me in the face, so I had a small cut, but it was nothing I could feel. As the fight went on, my confidence increased, and he became fatigued from the beating.

Finally, I stood in front of him, toe to toe. His face was swollen, and his eyes were shut. I struck one last decisive blow to the middle of his face that opened up a floodgate of blood. In the process, I slipped on the ground and he jumped on top of me. As he was so badly beaten, he couldn't do anything, so I kept striking him in the face. He was bleeding all over my white shirt. Finally, his boys pulled him off and carried him away.

I knew I couldn't walk into the school like this, so I ran the seven blocks to Nana's house. It looked like I had murdered somebody. Here I am, running down the street with this blood-soaked shirt. When I got to Nana's, I rang the bell. When she opened the door, she gasped in horror as if I were hurt. I immediately said, "It's not my blood."

Then she started to laugh. I told her the story as I was changing, and she just had this look of pride on her face.

When I got to school, people were patting me on my back as we waited in the hallway for class to start. News was all around the freshmen classes—Carl didn't make it to school. His friends carried him into the school and he said that he got jumped by six guys on the train. At least he didn't snitch. They took him to the hospital by ambulance. The kids were looking at me differently now. People wanted to be my friend all of a sudden. I learned something that day: people respect strength.

But I also learned something else. It was something that Pete once said: "The strong take from the weak, and the wise take from them all." I thought about how wise it was to have those guys with me from the bus, or else, when I was getting the best of Carl, his boys may have jumped me. I also learned something from the guy I knew that was with Carl. He told me that under Carl's Ace bandage wrapping, he had a set of brass knuckles on each hand.

When I got home, Uncle Rudy opened the door and said, "Well, I don't see no blood." I told him there was blood, but it wasn't mine. He was happy for me. I heard Grammy talking to Nana on the phone. She and Pete asked me what happened, but it didn't seem like a big deal to them. It was a big deal to me.

I had to deal with two things now—the aftermath of kicking this guy's ass, and how he was going to try to seek revenge. Also, I had to consider that every Tom, Dick, and Asshole tough guy would want to take a shot at the title. Every bully thought I had just gotten lucky, and would try to goad me into stupid fights. But I was smart. I already proved myself. If they wanted to fight, I told them that all they had to do was lay their hands on me, and they would have a fight. A lot of them talked shit, but few took the bait.

That semester, I didn't do any better in school. Grammy and Pete were pissed off and sent me back to Nana's. I started doing the same things as before. I hung out at Frida's house. Jazz had disappeared for a while, but Lori was around. She had a dog, a big Great Dane. She asked if I would mind coming by to walk it after school and said she would pay me. I started to go by every day to walk her dog.

Lori, as I mentioned, was a big-boned woman. As time went by, we started to hang out more. One day when I was at Frida's, her boyfriend, Ron, was bagging up some nickel bags of marijuana to sell. I stole about five and went to Lori's house to smoke them with her. I didn't know what I was doing. I couldn't even inhale right. I just wanted to seem grown. When I went back to Frida's, she and Ron were laughing about what I did.

I started to walk Lori's dog more often. I noticed that the outfits she wore around the house were becoming a little more revealing. One time when I came by, she was in her panties and bra, as if it were nothing. I was only fourteen, so my hormones were raging. I liked seeing her in her more revealing outfits, but acted like I was cool and it didn't matter.

The next time I went by Frida's, Jazz was there. She told me that she was living there now. She was six months pregnant, and didn't have a place to stay. Word was she brought an undercover cop to the house she was staying at, where the owner sold marijuana.

As time went on, I stayed at Lori's more often. She was twenty-seven. Our conversations became more sexually oriented, and I began to want to have sex with her. She was sending me mixed signals. Sometimes, she would ask me to massage her back while wearing just a towel. Other times, she would take a shower and leave the door open. She knew what she was doing.

On this particular day, I was massaging her as she lay on her bed. She then took her towel off and turned to lay on her back, buck-naked. I climbed on top of her and entered her. This was it. I was losing my virginity. It was February of 1983. It didn't last that long, but I felt like a man. This twenty-seven-year-old woman wanted me.

We had sex every day after that. I would leave for school early in the morning, go by her house, have sex, go to school, then go back to have more sex. She would call my house sometimes, so Nana started to ask me who she was. I told Nana everything. She wasn't mad, and she didn't say much. She did have a look of disapproval, though.

Jazz had her baby. It was a boy, and she named him Alex. I introduced Jazz to Nana, and Nana would babysit sometimes. Often, Nana would ask me if Alex was mine, considering the current relationship I was in.

School was going the same, the tough guys trying to test me. There had been a lot of fights, so the school developed a zero tolerance policy. If you were caught fighting in school, it would mean a two-day suspension. I was in gym one time, and this kid and I got into some words. He bragged about how good he was in karate. I think he was just selling wolf tickets. So, he and I started to shove each other when no teachers were around. He was doing some crap he called karate, and I was giving him straight blows to the face. Blood flowed the same way it did with Carl. My fighting techniques were becoming well-defined. I hit to hurt, and wasn't worried about looking good. After the fight was broken up by other students, they whisked him away to the locker room so as not to be detected by the gym staff. It was the last period of the day, so he was able to get out of the school with his facial wounds undetected. I went to Lori's house and had sex, feeling good about myself.

The next day when I got to school, the Dean of Discipline called me down to his office. He was a tall man, a priest, and had a mean disposition. He said, "Hey! You got something you want to tell me, mister?"

"No."

He said, "What about that fight you had yesterday during last period?"

I told him it was a small altercation, and I wouldn't really call it a fight.

"Oh yeah?" he said. "Well tell that to his mother. When he went home last night, half his face was hanging off and he had to go to the hospital. That sounds like a fight to me." He then told me that since the kid and I weren't caught in the school, he wasn't going to suspend me, but we each had a week of detention.

70

I thought, *This is really going to mess up my sex life.* That was the last fight I had in that school. The other kids didn't want to chance getting the beatdowns I was becoming popular for.

During the school year, my mother never sent any extra money to Nana for me. My sneakers had holes in them, and my jeans were high waters. One day, I went to Grammy's job at the telephone company on 125th Street. She was a service representative, and sat at the desk as you walked into the building. Grammy was embarrassed by my appearance, especially in front of her coworkers. I sat down at her desk, and she told me if I needed a new pair of sneakers, I should have called her. Then she gave me $30 to buy a new pair. She told me that I should call my mother in Washington, D.C. to ask her for some kind of allowance.

That night, I told Nana what Grammy said earlier, and Nana agreed. She did a little babysitting here and there, but she was just getting by. I called my mother that night, and she cursed me out. "That's what you called me for, muthafucker? You don't call me any other time, and I ain't got it, so fuck you!"

Then she hung up the phone. I couldn't wait until the time I wouldn't have to ask her for anything. Lori would give me a couple of dollars here and there, so I had some money in my pocket, but nothing to brag about.

I went to Lori's house one morning, and she let me in. There was an album cover on her dining room table. I picked it up and put it away. She went ballistic.

"What you doing, nigger?"

I said "What? I just put the record away."

"That shit had cocaine on it, and you spilled it on the floor."

Oh, yeah. I forgot that she sniffed cocaine with Frida, Jazz, and the rest of the girls. She threw me out of the apartment that day.

chapter **NINE**

My birthday came and went. I was fifteen now. I wasn't doing too well in school, but I was passing. I may have been failing two classes—algebra and physics. I was hanging out in the park when I saw a kid I knew from school named Eric walking around with another guy. He saw me and asked if I wanted to hang out with him and the other guy, Hector.

Eric lived on 167th Street and the Grand Concourse. When we got to the block, he introduced me to a couple of guys who lived around the block. Hector began talking to a skinny Spanish girl who was looking out of the first-floor window. There was this other girl in the window with her, a tall, skinny black girl. When Hector was done, I asked him who he was talking to. He said it was his girl-friend, Joann, but she was on punishment, so she couldn't come outside. The other girl was Joann's best friend, Denise.

Hector was eighteen years old and didn't go to school. Joann was sixteen, and Denise was turning seventeen in a couple of months. When Joann and Denise would walk to the store, Hector would meet them around the corner so that he and Joann could spend some time together.

I was with Hector one day, and I saw Joann and Denise walking up 167th Street. I hadn't really noticed Denise before, just that she was in the window with Joann and that she wore these big glasses. When I saw her outside, she was tall, slim, and walked with class about her. She wasn't like…how should I say it…the other hood rats. When Hector introduced me to Denise, she said hi, but had this "oh, brother" attitude about her. A little stuck up, but not bad. More like she didn't feel like meeting a new boy.

I said, "What's up?" And then Hector and I went on about our business.

Later that night, I went over to Frida's to find that she was pissed. She told me that she knew all about what's been going on. I didn't know what she was talking about. What happened was that Lori had been running her mouth to Frida's lover, Maria, about screwing me, and then Maria finally told Frida. Frida was livid. To her, it could have been Mitchell Lori was having sex with. They told me that Lori was over earlier and told them everything.

I was upset. I went to Lori's house and asked her why she admitted to it, and why was she running her mouth to Maria. She was defiant and said, "Fuck them bitches! It's not like I'm fucking somebody else's man. Fuck them!"

I told her I never wanted Frida to know, and left the apartment.

I went to hang out with Hector that night. He told me that Joann was off punishment. He said that he, Joann, and Denise were going to the movies later, and Denise had asked if I wanted to go so that she wouldn't be a third wheel. I said yes, but that I needed to check with my grandmother. I really wanted to borrow the money from Nana to pay for it. She gave me enough to go to the movies.

Denise looked very cute that night, even with her big glasses. The four of us went to see *Superman 3* at the Valentine Theater on Fordham Road. While watching the movie, Joann and Hector were all over each other.

I said to Denise, "May I put my arm around you?"
"Sure."

Denise snuggled up next to me. I made sure to not make any inappropriate moves.

We all took a cab back to 167th Street that night and hung out for a little bit before I had to be home at eleven. I would always tell everyone that I had something to do when I was leaving. I was the youngest among all of us, but I told everybody that I was seventeen.

I started to hang on the block a little more. One day, Denise asked me to walk her upstairs to her apartment. When we got to her parents' door, she took her glasses off and started to make out with me. She was the first girl that I kissed. I had sex with Lori, but there was never kissing involved.

That night, I was on top of the world. I had a girlfriend, someone my age, someone I could relate to. I told her all about Lori, and she told me we could hang out, but that she just broke up with this boy named Patrick and wasn't really looking for a boyfriend. I was cool with that.

The next day, I went by Lori's. I was still a little upset with her about what had happened with Frida. Lori opened the door and said, "Long time no see, nigger. What you here to do? Give me my walking papers?"

I told her that I met this girl and that I didn't want to do this anymore. She wasn't happy, and she didn't believe me. She even tried to have sex with me again to show me that she was in control, but I didn't want to. I wanted to be with Denise. Lori then said, "Then get the fuck out my house nigger!" I left without any further incident.

I went over to Frida's and told her that I broke up with Lori. She said that she wasn't mad at me; she was mad at Lori because she was twenty-seven and I was jailbait. Frida said Lori molested me. I didn't care, I liked it.

Grammy got me enrolled in a summer youth job. It was a program that the City had for underprivileged kids so they could work for the summer. Really, it was urban programs that would get funding from the City. All we did was sit around all day from 8:30 to 4:30 doing nothing.

I was going to see Denise every day. We would just hang outside of her building, talking. We told each other everything. There was no jealousy, just two friends talking about life.

Denise was a lot different from me. She had two parents in a working household. They bought her whatever she needed. Her parents loved her. I would go up in her room and play with the toys she had in her closet that she had outgrown. She would look at me like I was crazy. I only did it because I didn't grow up with nice toys like she did. Then I told her that I was only fifteen.

She replied "Oh! That explains it." I asked her what she meant by that and she said, "I was wondering why you were acting so immature."

The end of the school year came, and I had failed two classes. In Cardinal Hayes, if you failed any classes, you would have to go to summer school to make them up. No one was left behind. Everyone had to stay on the same track. The summer school cost $75 per class. I had failed two. Nana told me to call and tell my mother how much it would cost.

When I called, she said to me, "Well, if you ain't got it, you ain't going." She then hung up.

Nana didn't call her back, and neither did I. If you didn't go to summer school, you were automatically expelled. I was glad. I didn't want to ask my mother for anything else for the rest of my life. This was it. She didn't call back, and that was it.

Later, the school sent an official letter saying I was expelled. I would have to go to public school in the fall, and this was just what my mother wanted. This way, she wouldn't have to pay for school anymore.

That summer, I was assigned to the Harlem section of the summer youth jobs. Harlem was right across the bridge from where I lived. The kids in the program were local, from the area around 145th Street and Adam Clayton Powell Blvd. They didn't like a guy from the Bronx too much, but since I was so close by, it wasn't a big problem. We got paid $3.35 per hour from Monday to Thursday. Every two weeks, I would have about $300. However, Nana needed that money, because my mother wasn't sending her a dime. So, Nana would tell me not to cash my check until I got home. She would take me to the check-cashing place, and then take a good amount. I was a little upset because she didn't tell me what her plans were, and I had my own plans for my money.

Later that summer, Nana got cataracts in her eyes and had to go to the hospital for an operation. She made arrangements for me to stay with her daughter, Aunt Shirley. She was my grandfather's sister. I decided I would sneak back to Nana's house. I climbed through the window of my room and then opened the door. I would have a couple of guys from Denise's block over, and we would hang out there smoking marijuana and drinking.

Hector said, "Hey! Let's have a jam here! Just a few people, nothing big."

Being high and drunk, I said, "Alright."

Hector invited a few people he knew. Some of them were part of this local gang called the Flying Dragons, and their leader was this short guy named Little Man. The party, of course, got out of hand. The next thing I knew, there were about sixty people in Nana's house, playing loud music, drinking, and smoking weed. I didn't know any of them. I actually got really drunk that night, so Hector called my Aunt Shirley to let her know that I wasn't going to be able to come home that night.

The party ended, and I was able to clean the house up pretty well. Nana was still in the hospital and was going to be back in a couple of days. Aunt Shirley didn't know that I had a party at the house, because she had the only key.

I went back to Aunt Shirley's the next morning. She lived in the Dykeman City Housing Projects, located in Upper Manhattan. She wasn't too happy, but she didn't make a big deal about it. I guess she figured boys will be boys.

It was time for Nana to come home. Aunt Shirley and I picked her up from the hospital and brought her home in a cab. When we arrived at Nana's apartment, we had trouble with the lock on the door. Nana told me to go around and climb through the window to let her in. When I went around to the back of the building, the kitchen window was boarded up with plywood. I knew something was wrong right away. I crawled in through my bedroom window. When I got in, I saw that it had been ransacked. It looked like a tornado had blown through the apartment.

I opened the door, and Nana's heart sank. She was a very private person, and the thought of people in her house like that was a lot for her to bear. The superintendent came shortly after we opened the door. He told Nana he was walking by the apartment and heard some kids tearing it up. He told the kids he was going to call the police, which made the kids run out. As it turned out, it was the kids from the party. They came back when I was gone and tried to burglarize the place. I felt lower than a piece of dog crap. Here was Nana, just out of the hospital, with a patch on her eye, and she had to come home to a place that was destroyed, and it was entirely my fault.

Some people from the Flying Dragons were responsible, and I knew where they hung out. I was going to seek revenge.

I left the apartment and went to where the Dragons hung out, a public swimming pool on Jerome Avenue called Mulally's. I was by myself, but I wasn't scared. When I walked into the pool area, I stood out because I didn't have a bathing suit on. I saw the Dragons hanging out in a corner, Little Man in the middle of a crowd. I proceeded toward the gang, and they saw me. As I got closer, a couple of them stood in front of Little Man.

One walked up to me and said, "You got a problem?"

I said, "Yeah, I got a problem. I threw a party the other night, and some of your people broke into my grandmother's house and ransacked it."

He went over to Little Man and spoke in his ear. When he was done talking, he waved me over. Little Man said to me, "What's this shit about?" He said he never gave an order to break into anybody's house.

Another member stepped up and told Little Man, "It wasn't us. It was this bitch that hangs out with us sometimes, but she's not part of the crew." He also told Little Man that another member fucks her sometimes. The other member pointed to the pool and said, "There she is—Princess."

Princess was swimming in the pool. I recognized her from the party. She was with about three other girls, and Hector knew her.

Little Man said, "Well, go slam the bitch and take her with you. I don't give a fuck."

I told him, "If I do that, what about your boy who's fucking her? I don't want any beef with him, because then I got beef with you."

Little Man said, "True that." He ordered six of his soldiers to grab the girl and take her to my house. The gang member walked up to her and pulled her out the pool, along with two of her friends. The gang members questioned them about the break in, and all the girls sold each other out, blaming each other. Then, they dragged the girls to Nana's house, with me leading the way. When I walked into the building complex, people were looking at me like "Look what he did. He went out and got the people who broke into his house that quick." They also recognized the Flying Dragons from their gang patches. When I came into the apartment, Nana was upset, but the house was cleaned up a little. Her marble coffee table was broken into two pieces.

As the gang members walked into the living room, my Aunt Shirley came in to talk with them. Nana was pissed, and she didn't want them in the house. Aunt Shirley tried to explain why they were there. Nana didn't care. She just wanted them out.

When Aunt Shirley came back into the living room, one of the gang members spoke up on their behalf and offered apologies for what happened. He said to the rest of the gang, "Hey! Homeboy was cool enough to throw a jam, and look what happened."

Now, Aunt Shirley knew I had a party and looked at me through the corners of her eyes.

The gang members said they would make the girls bring money by every week to pay for the broken coffee table and apologized again before leaving.

Nana was very upset with me that night, and told Aunt Shirley to take me home with her for a couple of days. I felt bad. To me, she was the only person who loved me.

Two days later, Nana sent for me to come home. She and I went for a walk to the supermarket. On our way, she asked me about what happened. She also wanted to confirm a few things that the neighbors had told her. I confessed to everything, and told her that things got out of hand and that I was very sorry. She wasn't mad anymore, and told me that she knew I didn't mean for those girls to break into the house. She also said one of the girls came by to give her some money, but she told her that it was okay.

Nana not only forgave me, she forgave the girls that broke into the house. It was like nothing ever happened. Nana was like that. When something would happen with family, she didn't stop loving you because you messed up. She told me about when she got pregnant, how she and her father went to war, so to speak, and how that led to her leaving the house. He later contacted her and told her to come home. She said family sticks together. Maybe that's why she raised me and never asked my mother for any money. She didn't even argue about money with my mother for me.

Things went back to normal. I would go to the summer job during the day, and go see Denise in the evening. I would see her every day. We would talk for hours at a time. She wasn't like these other girls from the ghetto. Denise did have one issue, and that was that she was still hung up on this guy named Patrick. I guess he cheated on her and maybe broke off the relationship, so she kept insisting that we weren't boyfriend and girlfriend. We were just kissing friends, in a sense. I thought, *If that's the case, why do we see each other every day?*

She said we could see other people, but I didn't want to see other people. I even brought her a gold chain with the letter "D" on it when I got paid from my summer job. The same day, she went out on a date with some guy she met at a club called The Roxy. She even told me about it. So, I guess that meant we weren't boyfriend and girlfriend. I didn't go by as much after that. I hung out with the guys from her block, but didn't pay as much attention to her as before.

There were plenty of girls at the summer job, and all we did was sit around all day and do nothing. So when I saw this pretty girl I liked, I started to talk to her. Her name was Pam. She was shorter than Denise, and didn't have the same class, but she was very pretty. She lived in a housing project on 155th Street and Amsterdam Avenue. I went to her house a couple of times, but she was a real ghetto rat. She liked me, but she was all hood, and I didn't want any of that. I did tell Denise about her, and as soon as she knew I had another female interested in me, all of a sudden Denise wanted to be boyfriend and girlfriend. So now, we were officially a couple.

Problems started to develop at the job. It was just a matter of time when 100 ghetto kids were left sitting around all day doing nothing. Most of the kids hung out with people they knew. I hung out with four guys who weren't troublemakers. We were there just working the program and getting paid. There was me, Lester, Warren, Greg, and Pedro, the only Spanish kid. Greg was eighteen and had four kids. The rest of us were fifteen.

There was a crew of four, a small-time gang called the Funky Crew. I had never heard of them, but the local Harlem kids knew them, and they were troublemakers. Their leader was this guy named K.C., who was short, loudmouthed, and liked to pick on people. The four of these guys were always together, and they were known for jumping people. They also had their hands in some small-time drug operation. They were bad news.

Of course, I couldn't just lay low, mind my business, not stand out, let the bigmouths be bigmouths, and eat a little humble pie. No, I had to end up tangling with these assholes. One day, when I was walking Pam home, we passed K.C. He was sitting on a car with his boys and saw me with Pam. I guess he wanted to test me, so he got loud with Pam and said, "Fuck you looking at, bitch?" He looked right at me when he said it. I didn't know Pam well enough to be getting my ass kicked defending her honor, so we just ignored him and kept walking. I asked her what that was about. She said that K.C. had tried to rap to her, and she blew him off. Since he saw me with her, he was going to try me. She told me that I did the right thing, because his crew doesn't fight fair.

That was fine for her, but for what K.C. just did, I didn't like him. I knew he would think I was weak. I had been through this before. He had to be handled. I knew he was with his boys all the time. I was also sure that they had access to guns. I definitely didn't want to end up like Mitchell. I had to bring K.C. down in front of a lot of people, so if he retaliated, he would look like a punk and lose all respect. I had a plan.

Now, the counselors were just as ghetto as the kids in the summer youth program. They liked to stir things up just as much, even though they were older. They would smoke marijuana on their breaks and come back with bloodshot eyes, smiling from ear to ear. They would even buy the marijuana from K.C. and his boys sometimes.

There's this sport in the ghetto that few outside know about. It's called slap boxing. Young boys would do it to show their fighting skills without having to kill each other afterward. The object was to slap your opponent in the face as much as possible without getting hit by bobbing and weaving. The faster person usually won. It wasn't unusual for someone to end up with a bloody nose or a busted lip, and there was always a crowd to watch.

One day, while all of the summer youth kids were sitting around doing nothing, I told one of the counselors that I wanted to slap box K.C. The counselor walked over to K.C. and his boys, whispered in K.C.'s ear, and pointed at me. K.C. jumped up all loud, causing a scene so everyone could see and hear him. "What? This muthafucker want to slap box me? Let's go!"

He took the bait. What K.C. didn't know was that I was fast as lightning with my hands. I had found that out from past fights.

The kids made a ring of bodies, and then K.C. and I squared off in the middle, with the counselor as the referee. There are two types of slap boxers: one who wants to look all pretty and fancy, and one who just wants to box. K.C. wanted to look fancy for the crowd. I just wanted to kick his ass and embarrass him in front of everyone, to get him back. I did just that. I slapped him all over the place, and he never touched me. When the contest was over, he had a busted lip. The counselor stepped in because K.C. wanted to fight for real now. I walked away hearing the whispered admirations from the crowd.

K.C. and his boys later walked up to me and told me that I cheated. That was why he had a busted lip, he said. This was just an excuse to fight me so his boys could get in it. He knew if he couldn't beat me slap boxing, there was no way he was going to beat me in a fistfight. They all told me that they would see me after work. The rest of the crowd heard him and started to call him out. Greg knew K.C. from the neighborhood. He said, "K.C.! You know it was a fair fight, so why you trying to fight the brother? You gonna look like a punk if you do that dumb shit."

K.C. and his boys changed their minds.

Good, because it was a long run to the bridge to the Bronx. I never had a problem with K.C. and the Funky Crew after that.

The biggest problem with the summer youth program was payday. Everyone in the Harlem area of the summer youth jobs would get paid at the armory on 142nd Street and Park Avenue. Every two weeks, hundreds of kid would pick up their $300 paychecks, and everyone knew it, even the stickup boys. What made it worse was that a lot of the stickup boys worked with you. If they didn't stick you up, they set you up to get stuck up. I heard all the time on the Monday after payday how it happened to someone in our section. They wouldn't use a gun; they would walk around with a trained pit bull and jump you. I would see these guys walking around outside the armory. They'd prowl like lions circling a herd of wildebeests. Everyone knew who they were and what they were doing there; they didn't try to hide it. You just hoped you weren't the next victim. The guys I hung out with would pick up our checks together. We figured there was strength in numbers.

The second time we went, everything seemed fine. Three of us got ours and then headed over to the local check-cashing place. Once we had our money, we started to walk up 8th Avenue toward the Polo Ground Towers, a Hugh Housing Project with thirty-story buildings. Lester and Warren lived there. It was right across the bridge from the Bronx, close to the Grand Concourse.

When it came time for me to separate from Lester and Warren, there were five guys waiting by the bridge. I didn't even notice them. Lester and Warren said, "Hey Malik! Don't go that way. Those guys look a little shady." I continued to walk with Lester and Warren as the shady guys started to follow us. We didn't walk any faster, but we started discussing the situation.

All of a sudden, they were in front of us. One of them said to us, "Up it, niggers."

Warren started to panic and say, "Oh boy, oh boy. It's a stickup!"

I was ready to fight for mine and said, "Fuck that! You gonna have to take it!" Which they were prepared to do. I thought, *There are only five of them, and they don't look that tough to me.*

Now, what surprised me was Lester. He was always a low-key guy, and never seemed hard in any way. I knew he grew up in Harlem, but he never acted like a tough guy. He said to Warren and me, "Now, calm down." He then addressed the stickup boys, "Look here, fellows. Why you got to do this shit? We black like you guys. Why don't you go downtown and stickup white people?"

One of the stickup guys said, "We ain't going downtown. We here to rob you."

I thought it was on. I was ready to start swinging. Lester then said, "Look here, muthafuckers. My name is Les, and I'm from the

Towers. You fuck around, and I'll be back with fifty niggers to handle this shit. So if you know what's good for you, you best step the fuck off. You better ask around about me. Remember, Les from the Towers."

One of the stickup guys said, "Fuck that shit."

But one of the leaders said, "No. Leave them." They walked off.

Come to find out that Lester had a brother who was well-known in Harlem.

When I got home, I told Nana what happened, and she said not to cash my check in Harlem anymore. She also asked me for some money, and we got into a small disagreement because I had plans for my check. I didn't realize that she was also depending on that money. That Monday when I went to work, people were talking about the attempted robbery. I didn't think it was a big deal. I figured the worst thing that was going to happen was a fight. I didn't know the whole story. One of the guys who was with them filled me in.

He told me, "There weren't five guys, there were twelve guys. We were behind you. If you started to fight, we were going to come up behind you."

I thought, *Wow! I never did look behind me when all that stuff was going on.* Thank God for Lester that day.

Later on when I came home, Nana was getting the mail. I said hi and went into the apartment. Nana came in and sat in her room, opening up her mail. It looked like there was a check in one of the envelopes.

When Nana opened it, she said, "These people…. They just keep doing this crap to me."

I didn't know what she was talking about, but what I saw broke my heart. Nana started to cry. I hadn't seen Nana cry since her mother had died when I was four. I asked her what was wrong, and with tears in her eyes and a breaking voice, she said that the check wasn't what she thought it was going to be. She had to pay some bills, and she didn't have the money. I felt so bad. I thought about how just a couple of days ago, I was arguing with her about giving her some money. I begged Nana not to cry. I even started to cry with her.

I said, "Nana, please don't cry. I'll give you my whole check. You can have whatever you want. Please don't cry."

She soon composed herself and said, "Everything's okay." She told me to calm down.

I never realized how poor we were. I knew I didn't have a lot of clothes, and that we shopped at Gimbals basement store, but I had love. To me, I had everything, but I learned one thing for sure that day, something I would know for the rest of my life: Love don't pay the bills.

The summer went by quickly, and I did give most of my last check to Nana. Denise and I were growing closer than ever. I was in love, and so was she. We would spend hours talking on the phone, and whenever I had the chance, I would go to see her. Her father was sick of seeing me. He told her, "You're starting to look like Joann and Hector," because we were spending so much time together. I had introduced Denise to Frida and Jazz. Sometimes, Denise and I would even babysit for Jazz.

When the summer was over, Nana had to enroll me in a public high school. The closest one to us was William Howard Taft on 171st and Sheridan. Let me tell you, it was no Cardinal Hayes. The school was a four-story, square building with gates on the first two floors of windows. The kids weren't in uniforms, and there was a policeman named Officer Gallagher roaming the school. Before school, the kids would hang outside the back of the building, smoking weed and playing dice or whatever other bad habits they developed. Kids hung out in the bathrooms all the time, smoking weed or using angel dust, which was popular at that time. This school was just warehousing kids. They didn't care if you cut class or not.

William Howard Taft was a whole new world. I soon realized that if you went to homeroom class, which was the fourth period, you were marked present for the day. All the troublemakers hung out at the back of the school until fourth period, and then went in and left the school at fifth period. I didn't stand out in class. I had old clothes and an old jacket that I wore all the time. Some kids had nice things to wear, some kids didn't. The only time it became an issue was if you got into a disagreement with someone. Then, they would point out your raggedy clothes.

Most of the time, I didn't have any money in my pocket. Denise went to Brooklyn Technical High school. Her parents would give her money for lunch, and then she would give me a couple of dollars. I didn't have any money to take her anywhere or to buy her anything. She didn't care about all of that. She loved me for me, and I was grateful for the couple of dollars.

Nana was struggling to make ends meet. It was like my mother felt that since I wasn't going to Cardinal Hayes, I didn't need anything else like food and clothes.

During the week, I would walk nine blocks just to see Denise for five minutes, when she went to the store for her parents. We weren't really allowed to see each other on weeknights during school time. She was my world, along with Nana. I felt they were the only people who gave a crap about me. There was no word from Grammy or Pete. My uncle lived a thousand miles away, and I hadn't heard from my father in a while, either. Really, the only time I heard from him was if I called him myself. I could have been dead and buried, and none of these people would have known or cared.

I soon conformed to the new school, just like any other kid with no supervision. I wasn't getting high, but I wasn't going to all my classes. In the few classes I did go to, I was a disruption.

I hung out with a couple of classmates at lunchtime, but they weren't really friends or anything like that. I had a printing class, and in it was this loudmouthed kid with a jerry curl. His name was Jason. He and I hit it off. There is an old saying that Nana would repeat to me: "Birds of a feather flock together." I think that's why Jason and I became friends.

Jason lived with his aunt and two cousins. His mother had died, and he didn't know who his father was except for the fact that he had been white. He had several brothers and sisters, but they were all grown and no longer lived at the aunt's house. He would tell me how his aunt didn't like him very much. He had to spend a week in Spofford Juvenile Facility because he was picked up by the police for jumping the turnstile. His aunt told the police to keep him.

Jason had to share a small bedroom with two of his cousins, and the only time he went home was to sleep. I remember how we became friends. He was having some trouble with this guy on his block over some girl, and asked me to walk with him to his house. That way, if the guy saw that he was with someone, he wouldn't bother him. It worked.

Jason was also a punk. He wore nice clothes, but his aunt didn't buy them, even though she was getting public assistance for him. Jason had a part-time job after school working for Saga, the food service for Fordham University on Webster Avenue.

I was starting to meet more people—not friends, just associates. I met this guy named Darryl. I came to find out that he and Mitchell had been running buddies. When he met me, I was walking down the street with Frida and she introduced us. Whenever I saw him in school, I would just say, "What's up?" He was part of some small-time gang that dealt drugs and had a couple of guns, so people feared him somewhat. He had a sidekick named Ant, who was a weightlifter. They always hung out together, doing their dirt.

I had a couple of small-time fights in school, but they were nothing serious. Nothing to get killed over. I was conforming to public school life very well. I didn't go to class. I didn't even bring books to school anymore. I didn't care about grades, and just hung out all day. I was still broke and didn't have decent clothes, but Nana and I got by.

One evening, Nana came in my room and said, "Listen, I applied for welfare last week, and they're going to be sending us $110 every two weeks. We can go and get you some clothes from Gim-bals and some new sneakers this weekend, because they sent me one back check."

I was glad to hear that.

The next day, she came in my room again and said, "Malik, I'm sorry. I just can't do it."

I said, "Do what?" She told me that welfare had sent her two checks for me, not one. But she needed the money, so she told me that there was only one check. I told her that I didn't care, and that if she needed it, she could take both checks. It was for both of us, anyway.

She said, "I just wanted to tell you because I felt bad about it." Nana sacrificed for me all the time, and she was worried about tak-ing from me. She wasn't using me as a meal ticket like my mother was. She saw how I dressed. I was wearing the clothes I bought from my summer youth job.

It was report card time, and I failed every single class, of course, since I didn't go to any of them. Nana was very disappointed and called my mother to tell her. Not to talk about the bad grades, but to let her know the effect public school was having on me, and to basically blame her for not paying the $150 for the Cardinal Hayes summer school. When Nana finished talking to my mother, she gave me the phone. I hadn't talked to my mother since the summer school conversation. I never gave her a second thought.

For some reason, my mother felt like she had to threaten me about getting bad grades. She said, "Look here, muthafucker. I don't know what your problem is, but I'll come down there and kick your fucking ass and bring you down here to live with me. I can still do that, you know. I never legally gave you up. You understand?"

I said, "Yes," but I was thinking, *Who is she to talk to me like that? I'm fifteen now, not seven. And it's her fault I'm in this school doing these things, anyway. I got decent grades when I was in Cardinal Hayes.*

She hung up the phone on me, and that was that.

88

I knew I wanted to be on my own. I wanted to be out from under her thumb. Welfare was helping, but it wasn't enough. Nana was still struggling to make ends meet.

One day, Jason asked me if I was interested in a job, because they were hiring in the dish room at the college. I said, "Sure." I thought this would be great. I could make my own money. I could help Nana out a little, and I could finally buy Denise something and take her to a movie. Up until now, we just hung out at her house or at Nana's.

I went to the place and filled out the application, with Jason as a reference. They said I could start the next day. The hours were from 4:00 to 8:00 p.m., working in the dish room, and I would be making $3.35 an hour. I couldn't wait to get home to tell Nana.

When I did, she was livid. Nana told me that I couldn't go to work. I didn't understand why. I just wanted to make some money to be able help out. She didn't want to hear it, and forbid me to go. I loved Nana, but this was something I had to do.

I went to work the next day and got home about 8:30, so Nana knew I had gone. She was mad, but not furious.

I said, "I'm tired of not having anything. My mother ain't sending nothing, and the welfare isn't enough." Then it hit me why Nana was so against me working—it was the welfare. My social security number would show up, and it would look like she was committing welfare fraud.

So Nana dropped the cash assistance, but kept the Medicaid, and I was working every day. When I got paid, I would give Nana some money, and with the few dollars I had left over, Denise and I would go out. I was able to buy a couple of things to wear. The job was only part-time, but it was better than nothing. I was in control of my money, and Nana didn't have to ask my mother or anybody else for anything for me.

I was still doing the same things in school. My mother knew that I was working. I would hear Nana talking to her over the phone, telling her how every time I got paid, I would give her some money.

One good thing about the job was that, in the summer, you could work fulltime.

chapter **TEN**

The end of the school year came, and out of nowhere, I started to hear talk about me going down to Washington, D.C. for the summer. I was sixteen now, and my mother lived in an efficiency apartment—no room for me whatsoever. I was trying to figure out what the angle on this was. There were two. The first was that I had failed all my classes again, and my mother convinced Nana that if I came down there for the summer, she would straighten me out. The other was since I was able to work, my mother figured I could get a job down there and help her with her bills. She actually believed that.

I told Nana that I didn't want to go, and then Grammy and Pete put their two cents in it. Where were they when Nana and I needed money or I needed clothes? The plan was that I would leave in July.

What about Denise? We had been together for a year now, and we were more in love now than ever. We spent hours on the phone. We saw each other every chance we got, and now people thought they could just separate us like that.

It was June, so I still had some time. When the school year was over, I started to work fulltime at the college and save some of my money. I still gave Nana some, but didn't buy anything.

At the college, they were having an alumni dinner and needed the staff to work long hours for a few days. They gave us keys to an old dorm that they were going to tear down so we could stay over for those days. The dorms had furniture and working bathrooms and showers.

July came quickly, and Pete came to pick me up from Nana's as if he were a police officer escorting a prisoner. The biggest fear I had was that my mother would try to keep me. I knew no one cared about how I felt. I hated my mother for all the things she ever said and did to me. I hadn't forgotten anything. I knew this was not going to be a pleasant trip.

Pete put me on the train, and all I could think about the whole ride was how much I loved Denise and how much I was going to miss her. When I arrived in Washington, my mother picked me up at the train station. She was in a foul mood, as always, and took me to her new apartment.

It was so small. She made room for me on the floor in the living room. There was only one room, a bathroom, and a kitchen. The bedroom and living room were one and the same.

The first night I was there, my mother started with her threats and setting the rules about how things were going to be. "I don't know what kind of shit you been playing in New York, but I'll kick your ass. I'm not Nana, and if you talk any smart shit to me, I'll slap you in your fucking mouth. Now, tell me what kind of shit you been pulling in New York."

I said, "Nothing. I'm not doing nothing."

"Bullshit! All I know is, if I let you go back to New York, we all gonna sit down—you, me, Nana, and Grammy—and find out what the fuck is going on. And if you get smart with anybody, you gonna get fucked up."

Well, I listened to her run on, and then I lay on the floor in the corner and pretended I was asleep. I heard her talking to Grammy, telling her how she told me it was going to be, and so on.

What she, Grammy, and Pete didn't know was that I had money on me. I had $50, and the bus to New York only cost $25. I knew I was going to get out of here. But where would I go, and how would I get away without my mother noticing? I thought about it all that night.

When morning came, I waited for her to leave for work. I knew that she might come back for lunch in three hours, since she didn't work far from her apartment. Otherwise, she wouldn't be back until after five. I didn't want to take any chances, so when I heard her leave, I got up and packed my bag right away. I wrote a note telling her that I didn't appreciate the things she said to me, and that if I couldn't live with Nana, I wasn't going to live with anybody. I left it on her dinette table and left. The apartment had a slam lock, so once the door was closed, there was no turning back.

I walked to the bus station and bought a one-way ticket to New York City. I didn't know what I was going to do when I got there, but I'd figure that out then, as long as I was back in New York. The bus ride was three hours, and by the time I got there, I figured my mother would just be getting home to find out I was gone.

It worked out perfectly. When I got to New York, the first thing I did was call Nana to let her know that I was alright. I knew I couldn't go to Nana's, because Pete would try to make me go back to my mother's by force. I felt like a runaway slave. Nana told me everyone knew and asked me what I was going to do. I told her I didn't know, but I would call and keep her posted, and that I knew one thing: I was not going back to Washington, D.C.

The second person I called was Denise. She was happy to hear from me, but she was also worried.

The first night, I slept on the staircase to the roof in Denise's building. Pete called Denise's parents and informed them of the situation. Denise snuck out and met me two blocks away, just in case Pete or the police were looking for me. She was scared for me, but I was determined.

I went by Jason's house and asked him if he still had the keys to the dorms at Fordham University. He said, "Yes, but they're demolishing the building." He gave me the key, and I still had my work ID, so I was able to get past the security guards without any problems. The only problem was that I only had the key to the dorm room, not the building. So, I had to break into a window to get to the room.

When I got to the building, the rooms were still intact. The construction men would get there at 6:00 a.m., so I had to be out before then, and I didn't come back until 11:00 p.m. so as not to be noticed climbing into the window.

I didn't have any money left for food. I called Nana and asked her if I could come by to get something to eat. I knew she wouldn't betray me to Pete or my mother. When I came to Nana's, she asked me to call Grammy and Pete, just to talk to them. I did what Nana asked, and of course, they said everything I knew they would. Pete said that if I didn't go back to Washington, they were going to call the police and send me to Spofford Juvenile Facility, and that they were going to fuck me in my ass up in there. I told him I wasn't going back, so call the police. I said if they sent me back, I would get off the bus or train before it got to Washington. If I couldn't live with Nana, I was going to take my chances on my own. I hung up the phone on Pete.

Nana heard the whole conversation. She gave me some food, and when I finished, I gave her a big hug and a kiss and left.

I stayed at the dorm room for about a week, getting up early and coming back late. I almost got caught twice. Once, someone reported someone climbing into a window. The other time I woke up late, and the men were already working on the building. I left in a hurry and forgot my wallet with my ID, so I had to go back into the building to get it. Those were two close calls. I knew if I had gotten caught, the police would have been called.

Pete did all he could to make it hard for me to see Denise. He even called her parents again and told them I was committing crimes so that they would be against me. He also asked them to call him if they saw me.

I would go by Nana's every other day to get some food, and Denise would buy me food as well. One day, when I went by

Nana's, she said, "Okay, that's enough of this crap. It's time for you to come home."

I said, "What about Grammy, Pete, and my mother?"

"This has gone too far, and gotten out of hand. This is your home, so you can stop running."

She told me to go take a shower and to get some rest. I didn't even realize that I hadn't taken a shower in two weeks. Nana called Pete and Grammy and told them I was home and staying there. She also called my mother and told her the same. I called Denise to let her know that I was home for good, and then Nana spoke to her parents to let them know all was well. I took a shower that night and lay down in my bed. I was home and I was safe. For the first time in two weeks, I got a decent night's sleep. Once again, Nana had saved me. She was my guardian angel.

That summer, I worked fulltime at the college. Denise graduated from Brooklyn Tech and started to work at the college, too.

I learned a new form of racism at Fordham University. When I was in boarding school, the worst thing I was called was nigger, so I was used to that word. When the kids called you nigger, it was because they were taught that word, or they heard it from somewhere else. They were children. When Nana would take me to see the Blaxploitation movies, I would see the white people in the movies openly saying racist remarks to the black actors on screen. That gave me a kind of perception about how racist people behaved— that they were always upfront with their intolerance.

Jason and I worked in the dish room. The white head manager, Dave, called one of the employees a porch monkey. Jason and I thought that saying was funny, so we started calling each other and other people porch monkeys. Soon, most of the guys in the dish room were doing it. When the head manager saw this, he got a kick out of it and would laugh with us. He would say things like, "Hurry up and get done, porch monkeys," and we would all have a big laugh.

There was another manager named Jim, who was also white. He would look at us with such disgust when we were calling each other this term. After about two weeks, Jim yelled at Jason and me.

"Stop saying that shit. Do you know what a porch monkey is?"

We both responded, "No."

"You ever see those lawn jockeys in front of people's houses that hold the lanterns?"

We said, "Yes," even though we never saw them in the ghetto; we saw them in pictures.

Jim said, "Well, did you ever see the black one? That's what racist people call a porch monkey. So he's calling you black people monkeys, and you guys are running around calling each other monkeys."

Jason and I looked at each other like we were the dumbest guys on the planet. I learned some important things that day—not all white people are racist, and sometimes, racist people smile in your face. They're not always angry. Jason and I never used that term again. The funny thing was, we never heard it in the ghetto. I guess, outside of the ghetto, white racists had a whole lot of names they called black people that we were not aware of.

The company was short on employees, and asked Jason and me if we knew anyone that wanted to work for the summer. I knew this short, stocky guy named Al, who lived in Denise's building. He wasn't a friend, but I would say, "What's up?" to him when I would go by and see Denise. He was an older guy, about twenty-three or twenty-four. When I dropped Denise off one day, I asked him if he was looking for a job. Since he was in front of the building all the time, I assumed he didn't have one. He told me yes, so I took him in to fill out an application. He had a criminal record, but they didn't care, since it was the dish room. Al got the job and started work right away.

Since Al was older, he taught Jason and me a few scams that we were able to pull off working for the food service. The biggest one was when the managers would open the alcohol refrigerator and tell us to pack certain items for a banquet, we would take a few bottles, put them in garbage bags, and go back later to retrieve the alcohol. At first, I didn't understand why they locked up the alcohol, but then I realized that it was because of people like us. Soon, it wasn't only limited to alcohol. We would steal some food. We did it little by little, so the managers wouldn't notice. They didn't keep good inventory.

When we got paid, Jason, Denise, and I would buy clothes and things like that, but Al was married and had two kids. He would have to take his money home to his wife, but not before he bought himself a gram of cocaine. Al ended up getting fired from that job. I would still see him in front of Denise's building, but now, I considered him a friend. I figured he appreciated me hooking him up with the job, even though it was short-term.

The summer was over, and Jason and I went back to working part-time. Denise was able to stay on fulltime, since she had graduated from school. Jason and I had gotten used to making more money than part-time was paying. I learned that the more money you make, the more you spend. By the end of the summer, we were just as broke as we were in the beginning. Sure, we had a couple of clothing items, but not enough cash.

We returned to Taft, and the school year was just like the last one. Jason and I would hang out in the back of the school with all the troublemakers until fourth period. We became pretty tight. Jason knew more people than I did because he grew up in the neighborhood. He would take me around his old neighborhood on 171st and Gerald Avenue, right off of the Grand Concourse. There, he introduced me to this lady, Julie. She was an obese Puerto Rican lady in her early forties with long black hair. She used to be a nurse, but had lost her license. I'm not sure why, but it was drug-related. She lived in the same complex as Jason's sister, Mavis.

Julie lived in a two-bedroom apartment with her husband, Denin, who was a scam artist. He would scam the tourists in Times

Square with three-card monte. Others in the apartment were her son, Bengi, who was a dope fiend; her father-in-law, who was bedridden, blind, and senile; her grandson, Bengi Jr.; and her husband's three sons, George the ex-con, Justin the crackhead, and Franco the window washer and part-time photographer. Franco had his own room in the back, because he was the only one working and contributed the most to the household on a regular basis. Julie, her husband, her father-in-law, and Bengi Jr. stayed in the second bedroom. George, Justin, and Bengi slept in the living room. Julie's husband and his sons were Cuban.

Julie liked to sniff cocaine and drink, and partook in a lot of illegal activities. Even so, she would give you the shirt off her back if you needed it. If you needed a place to stay, Julie made room. If you needed something to eat, Julie made you a plate with a pork chop and some rice and beans. If you needed a prescription and didn't have one from a doctor, Julie could get it for you. Everyone in the neighborhood knew Julie. In time, I would come to love her like a mother, second only to Nana.

Since Jason and I were always hanging out in the back of the school, we always heard the young dealers bragging about how much money they made selling drugs. They always wore nice clothes and had money in their pockets, so we thought it must have been true. Jason and I came up with the idea that we would sell drugs so that we could have a lot of money, too. I thought I could be like my uncle and father.

We decided to sell cocaine. I believed I had a little knowledge about it from sniffing it with my uncle. The first thing we needed was a contact. We dared not asked Julie, because she would kick our asses. We were only sixteen years old; Julie knew the drug game was a dirty business, and she wouldn't want us involved. She knew what could happen. Remember, her son was a dope fiend.

The only other person I knew I could ask was my friend, Al. When I saw Al, I asked him if he wanted to make some money, and if he knew anyone who would sell us some weight in high-quality cocaine. Of course he did; he sniffed coke. I also asked if he wanted to put some money in to be down with Jason and me, and I said we would all be partners. Al said he didn't have any money; he wasn't working.

So, the plan was on. When Jason and I got paid, we each put up $100, and from what we understood, the more cocaine you bought, the better the price and quality you got. That way, it could be mixed with more cut—additive mixed in to multiply it—and therefore, more money could be made. At that time, a gram of cocaine would cost $50. We had $200, so my thinking was that we would be able to get four grams of coke, add the cut to it, and double our money.

When payday came, Jason backed out, saying he had something else to do with the money. I was pissed off. I had a plan in place, and he was messing it up.

Lo and behold, I had another person who was willing to put up the other hundred dollars. This person was present through all of the planning and knew exactly what I had in mind. It was Denise. We had only been together for a little more than a year, and she was a good girl from a good family, but she was my ride or die chick.

That night, we met up with Al. I told him we had $200 and asked him to get us four grams. I gave him ten crisp $20 bills. Denise and I walked with Al around the corner from her building to another, and Al said, "Wait here. I'll be right back." He went in.

First lesson/first mistake I made: when buying drugs, never let the money leave your sight.

Al came back and said, "Alright, we got four grams of pure rock cocaine."

Next, we went to buy the cut—lactose—and small bottles to pack the cocaine at a local bodega. I noticed that when we bought the lactose, Al paid for it with a crisp $20 bill that he peeled off of a couple others. I recalled that earlier, he had told me he didn't have any money. And I knew he didn't work, so how did he have this money on him?

Second lesson/second mistake: go with your gut instincts.

I didn't say anything because I wanted the deal to go through, and I didn't know the ratio of cocaine to lactose to mix.

Third lesson/third mistake: know how to run your own business.

Denise, Al, and I went to his apartment. Al put the cocaine on a plate and said, "There it is—four grams of pure rock cocaine."

Al cut the cocaine, and we packed it in small bottles. Al was going to go to a bar that he hung out at to sell it.

Fourth lesson/fourth mistake: don't give all your drugs to someone who uses that same drug.

Two days passed, and I went by Al's house to find out how much money we made—it should have been $400. He had a hare-brained excuse that there was a cop at the bar, and he had to run into the bathroom to dump the coke in the toilet. My gut told me that he was full of shit, but I tried it once again with him, this time to test him.

I gave him $100 and told him to buy two grams of cocaine. I told him that Denise and I would be by later to help bottle it up. Denise and I went out that night and bought the cut, but we also bought a small scale to weigh the cocaine.

When we arrived at Al's house that night, he had the cocaine sitting on the table and said to us, "There it is—two grams of pure rock cocaine."

Then, I pulled out the scale.

Al had a look of surprise on his face as I said, "Let's weigh it."

When we weighed the cocaine, it was only half a gram, or $25 worth. I asked him where the rest of it was. His excuse was that he left it on the table, and his wife must have taken some. He knew I wouldn't step to his wife about it. I knew this wasn't going to work.

We bottled what we had, but again the next day, Al said that when he was at the bar, people were complaining about the cocaine, saying that it burned their noses. I was out $300 and had nothing to show for it. I was only sixteen, and I thought I could be Scarface. The truth was, if you wanted to be a successful drug dealer, people had to fear you, and you had to be willing to kill for your money. Drugs are a dirty business, and people will always test you. Al was twenty-five years old and an ex-con. He knew the game. When I let him get away with that bullshit excuse the first time, he knew he had a sucker on the hook.

There was some cocaine left over, so I gave it to this kid at school named Wayne, who said he could sell it for me. He ended up sniffing it. When I tried to collect, rumors were going around that he and his boys were going to try and kill me, so I let that go, too. I wasn't a gangster, and I wasn't willing to kill for the drugs. Also, I didn't have the muscle behind me to back me up. Al and Wayne were seasoned in the art of hustling. For now, I decided to give up trying to hustle.

The job at the college ended, and even Denise got a better job, working downtown at some department store. I was broke like before, but was able to land a part-time gig down in Manhattan at the Sea Port as a grill cook. Jason got a job as a messenger.

Jason and I were hanging in the back of the school one morning, as usual, and we heard people talking about Darryl, the one who knew my cousin Mitchell. I heard that, during the summer, he was playing around and tried to jump over this fence, but didn't make it. The pole of the fence ended up impaling his anus. He needed surgery and had to wear a colostomy bag. I knew I hadn't seen him in a while, but we weren't friends, just acquaintances. Darryl returned to school and told everyone that he had gotten shot.

One day, while in the lunchroom, the gym teacher was talking to me and Jason, and the subject of Darryl came up. The teacher was telling us what a tough guy Darryl was and all, and how during the summer he had gotten shot and lived. Jason and I countered that he didn't get shot; he got a pole stuck up his ass trying to jump a fence. As we were talking, I looked over at the cafeteria table next to us. Darryl's sidekick, Ant, was there, looking at us with an evil eye, shaking his head back and forth. Ant got up from the table and stormed away. I knew this stare—this was going to be a problem.

Darryl and his boys were a bad crew to mess with. They had guns and were in the drug trade. It was just a matter of time before they retaliated. Jason and I had violated the number one rule in the ghetto: Mind your fucking business.

A couple of days went by and nothing happened. I just about forgot about the incident. Then, after school, Jason and I were coming out of the building and saw Darryl. He was in some verbal confrontation with another guy, so we went about our business. Darryl finished with that person, then looked in my direction and said, "Somebody's gonna get shot." He started to walk away.

I knew if someone said you're going to get shot and they didn't shoot you on the spot, that meant they had to go and get the gun. I wasn't going to let him get the gun—I was going to strike now. I figured he must have feared me a little, because if he was so upset, he would have tried to beat me down on the spot. Or maybe he didn't want to try it because Jason was there.

I started to follow Darryl up the block to the Grand Concourse. I was yelling at him, "Who you gonna shoot, muthafucker? If you a bad muthafucker, handle your shit now."

Darryl kept walking, saying, "Yeah! You wait and see, muthafucker. You gonna get yours."

Jason was following us. "Hey, Malik! Let it go, man. Let's get out of here."

"Fuck that! You think I'm gonna let the nigger get a gun? I'm gonna handle this shit now."

I kept following Darryl, and we came to the corner of 170th and the Grand Concourse. There was his sidekick, Ant, and Ant's brother, standing on the corner. Darryl was a skinny guy, but Ant was a little bigger because he lifted weights. His brother was a small guy. I continued to mouth off as Jason caught up. Darryl stood near Ant.

Ant started to chime in. "What the fuck you gonna do, muthafucker? You just talking shit. That's your fucking problem. You always talking shit. You need to learn how to mind your fucking business."

My adrenaline was pumping, and I knew there was going to be some action. I was ready, but I wanted to fight Darryl. He was the leader, and if I whooped his ass bad enough, the others would step back. However, things didn't always go according to plan. Jason stood there silently as I ran my mouth to Ant, "Look here, muthafucker, if you want to deal with me, wait your turn. After I whoop his ass, then I'll fuck you up."

Ant looked at me with surprise at my boldness and confidence considering his size, which most people feared. He replied, "Oh yeah? And who's gonna help you, this muthafucker?" As he said that, he slapped Jason's hat off his head. Jason's dumb ass bent down to pick it up, and the action began.

Ant grabbed Jason in a headlock and started to twist his neck. I was still a good distance away from them and started to take my coat off while I surveyed the situation. Was it a fight between Jason and Ant? I watched Darryl and Ant's brother to see what they were going to do, and it was clear that it was a jump. They both started to stomp Jason's head into the ground.

I dropped my jacket and ran toward the commotion. I struck Darryl in the jaw. He fell back, and that drew the attention of Ant and Ant's brother. They had the eyes of wild predators. All of their attention was now on me. They left Jason, and I started fighting all three of them at the same time.

I was winning. I grabbed the top of a garbage can and began swinging it. I was kicking, punching, dancing around, and making contact.

Jason was still on the ground, recovering from the beatdown and yelling to some people he knew, "Somebody help him!"

Jason later told me someone said to him, "He don't need no help."

A police car pulled up. The cops remained in their car, laughing at how I was fighting these three guys off. Soon, the three got frustrated and turned their attention back to Jason. They all ran at him, so he started to run down the block, toward Julie's house. He stopped at a sandwich shop halfway down and ran in. He knew a couple of guys from the block that worked there.

So now, the three of them were chasing Jason, and I was chasing them. When they saw me, they ran into the street in front of the sandwich shop to take defensive positions against me, but I ran into the shop also. The guys in the shop were asking what had happened. Jason was yelling out of the store to the three guys, "I'm going to go get a gun."

The three guys left, saying, "This shit ain't over."

Jason kept yelling, "Yeah! I'm gonna get a gun from my brother-in-law."

I was down. I said, "Let's go."

Jason and I walked to his sister's house, which was about a block away. When we went into the complex, Julie, whose window was in front, saw us coming in.

Jason was still filled with rage and shouting, "I'm gonna kill these muthafuckers." Julie asked what happened, and he said, "We got jumped!" He entered his sister's building, not even stopping to address Julie.

I just followed along. I was down for whatever. Get them before they get me. "Yeah, let me have a gun, I'll show them!"

When we got to the apartment, Jason banged on the door. This tall, slim man opened it. It was Mavis's boyfriend. I was confident now that we were going to get a gun and handle some business. Jason said to the guy, "Hey, we got jumped!"

The guy went to the living room window, pulled the curtain back, looked out the window and said, with fear in his voice, "They didn't follow you here, did they?"

Jason was full of shit. This guy didn't have a gun. This guy was scared that we brought the trouble to his house.

I thought, *Oh boy. We're really in some shit now.* Jason put it out there that he was going to get a gun, and Darryl and the others already had guns, so it was just a matter of time before some bullets started to fly.

I was pissed. I told Jason that he fucked up. He said he knew, but he was pissed off back there. I had to come up with a plan, and I had to come up with one fast.

I asked Jason if he could get some boys together to watch his back. He told me he could call his cousin Maurice and the crew he ran with. I told Jason to go home, and just make sure he got those guys tonight. I would call him later.

I walked home, and on the way, I stopped by Denise's to tell her what happened. I saw Al in front of her building and asked him if he would come and watch my back. He said, "Yeah." I figured that was the least he could do, since he ripped me off for $300. I told him I would meet up with him later that night.

I told Denise what happened, and that I was going out later to find the guys and handle my business. She was scared that I would get killed, since there was talk about guns, or that I was going to kill someone and go to jail.

I went home and told Nana about it. I told her everything when it came to me getting into fights and stuff like that. She asked me what I was going to do. I told her that I had my friend getting some guys together, and I was going to go look for the three guys. She didn't try to stop me. She knew where we lived, and she knew the rules—you either hunt or you get hunted.

When I called Jason that night, he told me that he had gotten ahold of his cousin, Maurice. I told him to meet me in front of Denise's building about nine. Then I called Al and told him to meet me downstairs at nine as well.

As I left Nana's house, she told me to be careful. When I showed up at Denise's building, Al was downstairs waiting. I thought, *Okay, that's one guy. Let's hope Jason comes through.* I was worried, since now I knew he could be full of shit. About five minutes later, I looked down the block and saw a group of six rough-looking fellows coming down the street. It was Jason and his boys. Even I was a little intimidated.

A tall, skinny, dark-skinned fellow with a big, combed-back afro was leading the group. Jason introduced him as his cousin, Maurice. Maurice said, "You know where these muthafuckers live?" As he said this, he pulled out a blackjack and slapped his hand with it. "We got something for their asses."

The rest of his crew murmured in support. I told him that I didn't know where they lived, but I knew a way to find out.

Maurice said, "Well, let's go, then."

At that moment, I became their leader. The group of thugs followed me to whatever destination I chose, without question. There were eight of us altogether. We roamed the streets like a pack of wolves. The conversations consisted of what we were going to do to the guys if we caught them. These guys were hungry for blood; you would have thought they were the ones who got jumped.

The first stop was a pool hall where the local hustlers hung out. I saw a couple of guys I knew from school and asked them if they had seen Darryl. I also inquired about where he lived. No one would even dare speak in his defense, considering the manpower I had with me. Every place we went, we walked in like we owned it, waiting for someone to mouth off so we could make an example out of him.

After we hit about three or four spots, someone told us where Darryl lived and that Ant and his brother lived in the same building. The informant even gave us Darryl's floor and apartment number. The thugs I was with could smell blood. They didn't want to knock on the door; they wanted to kick it in. They wanted to do a home invasion.

The hunt was on. Our destination was determined. As we walked toward Darryl house, I had to develop a game plan. All too often, a group of people engaged in nefarious activities end up testifying against each other. I realized I didn't even know the thugs. I only knew Al—who I already didn't trust—and Jason. If someone died or got seriously hurt that night, these thugs had no loyalty to me, and I didn't know what their relationship was with Jason or Maurice.

As we arrived in front of Darryl's building, I instructed Jason and his boys to wait in front, just in case Darryl saw us coming and got past me. That way, Jason could recognize him. I took Al with me, since I could control his actions so that things wouldn't get out of hand. My plan was to get Darryl downstairs and have a fair fight. I was going to kick his ass one on one.

If I did that, combined with the fact that I brought eight people to his house, it meant that we all knew where he lived, and he didn't know who these other people were. The worst position you can be in when you have trouble with an enemy is that he knows where to find you, but you don't know where to find him. It's terrifying.

Al and I walked up the stairs to the fifth floor. I had Al stay on the staircase one floor below. Darryl's apartment was right by the staircase, so Al could hear everything and come to my aid if I needed him. I knocked on the door aggressively. I saw someone look through the peephole and walk away from the door. I knocked again, more aggressively. I wasn't thinking about his mother, or if he had any brothers or sisters. My aim was to instill fear at the door for whoever opened it. I heard the lock disengage, and the door opened slowly. It was a female about my age. She said, "How you doing, Malik?"

I didn't recognize her. "Do I know you?"

She said, "You don't remember me from Mitchell's funeral?"

I didn't, but acted like I did.

She said, "You trying to hurt my brother? I heard what happened, and it sounds like it was a fair fight to me."

I corrected her and told her that Darryl and his boy, Ant, jumped me and my boy. She said that it looked like I was fine, so what was I going to do? I told her to tell her brother to come out, and he and I would settle it right now.

She said, "What about those niggers downstairs? I saw you guys coming down the block."

I told her that it would be one on one. She said that Darryl wasn't here. I knew she was lying, but if he was there, he was probably armed and scared to death.

"You tell him this shit better be over. If anything happens to me or Jason, the niggers downstairs are coming back without us, and the next time, no one is going to be knocking on the door." She asked me if that was a threat, and I said, "No, it's a guarantee."

I told her to also relay the message to Ant, then turned around and walked down the steps. She watched me and saw Al join me on the lower level. I walked out of the building and told the thugs that Darryl wasn't there. I was lying, but I didn't want things to go any further.

As we walked down the street, I could see someone peeking out from behind the curtains. I knew my point had been made, so I just kept walking with the thugs. Later that night, we all drank and smoked some marijuana together, joking about what would have happened if we had caught Darryl and Ant.

I was glad things turned out the way that they did. I wasn't going to kill anyone, but if we hurt one of them, they were going to seek revenge, and the cycle would have kept going until someone was dead. I went to Denise's that night to let her know I was okay. When I went home, Nana saw I was okay and didn't ask any questions about the night's activities. She asked me was I going to school the next day, and I told her yes, because if I didn't, people in school would think I was scared.

That night, when I went to sleep, I felt like I accomplished something. I felt a little bit of power, but I also felt wise because I made my point and didn't have to kill anybody. The next day, I would see if my plan worked.

When I woke up and got out of bed, I had a sore ankle and was walking with a limp. I must have hurt it during the fight, but with my adrenaline flowing all that day, I never felt a thing. I felt a little vulnerable since I wasn't at my best. I thought if I ran into Darryl, or Ant, or both, I would not be able to fight them off like before.

When I got to school, I didn't hang out in the back like before. As I went from class to class, there was no sign of Darryl or Ant. There was also no sign of Jason. I went the whole day and saw no one. People were all talking about the fight, and it also got around that I brought some boys to Darryl's house. People looked at me differently.

Later that day when I got home, I called Jason and asked him why he didn't come to school. He said he was dropping out. I couldn't believe it. He was scared to come back to school. Now I was there by myself, and even though I knew Darryl and Ant were scared, I also knew it was just a matter of time before we bumped heads again.

As time went on, I saw Darryl and Ant a couple of times in the hallways, but neither one ever said anything to me. I knew if they had the chance to, they would do me in. I made it a point to always walk in a crowd during class movements and never hang out in the back of the school anymore.

Public school was nothing like Cardinal Hayes. Every fight seemed like a life or death situation. I was becoming irritated with the school. I knew, sooner or later, something bad was going to happen.

I went by Frida's house, and when she opened the door to let me in, she gave me an earful. She heard about the move I made at Darryl's house. His mother had called Frida and asked her to talk to me because of the thugs. Darryl's mother was very upset, and feared for her son's safety. I told Frida that Darryl and his boy had jumped me and my friend. Frida said she talked to Darryl and told him to cut the dumb shit, and now she was telling me the same. She said Darryl was a punk without his boys, and if Mitchell were here, he would know better than to be fucking around with me. I had no doubt in my mind that what she was saying was true. I told her that it was over.

I decided to drop out of school. I didn't feel safe at all. I would see Darryl and Ant in the hallways, and I knew in the back of their minds, they were waiting for the opportunity to get me. Jason wasn't there anymore, and they knew that. All it would take was the right place at the right time, and I would be another statistic like Mitchell. Also, Wayne and his boys were still talking shit about trying to kill me over the cocaine incident.

I told Nana I wasn't going back to school and gave my reasons. She didn't say much. I knew she was disappointed, but she understood that I could end up just like Mitchell. This was the reason she had sent me to boarding school. She knew as I got older, fistfights often turned into gunfights in the ghetto.

Here I was, sixteen, and now a high school dropout. My job at the Sea Port was over, since the place closed down. So that meant I was an unemployed sixteen-year-old high-school dropout. I had no money. I was the epitome of the ghetto black youth stereotype.

Denise decided to go to business school and was working at some job. I knew it was just a matter of time before she would outgrow me. She was a high school graduate, I was a dropout. She had a job, I was unemployed. She was furthering her education; I was sitting at home with no game plan. I loved Denise. She, Nana, and Frida were all I had. I didn't talk to anyone else in the family very often, and I hadn't spoken to Grammy, Pete, or my mother since I had run away. I didn't even know where to start looking for a job. I knew my mother was getting a good laugh knowing that I dropped out of school. Now, she could say to people, "I knew he wasn't going be shit. That's why I didn't want to send his ass to private school." Me becoming just another statistic would give her justification for all her actions.

chapter **ELEVEN**

I was walking to Denise's one day and saw this kid named Thomas that I recognized from Taft High School. He had a tool belt on, so I asked him if he was working. He told me he had dropped out of school, too, and that he enrolled in this job training program called Youth Energy Corps. He went to work from 8:00 a.m. to noon, and went to school from 1:00 to 4:00 p.m. to get his GED. He told me it was all part of the same program, and he was on his way there at the moment. I asked if I could come with to ask the people about the program, and he let me tag along.

Thomas took me to a building down the block from Denise's house that was sort of a community center with various programs in it. Thomas introduced me to a counselor named Dan, who explained the program. It was designed to train at-risk urban teens. The work part consisted of installing replacement windows in low-income housing; the school part was located at a middle school building in Manhattan, on 116th Street and Columbus Avenue. If you didn't go to school, you couldn't work. Dan told me that if I was interested to bring my parent in to register me. He gave me the paperwork and told me that there was an opening, but he didn't know how long it would be vacant.

This program would be perfect for me; I could work and still get my GED. I ran home and told Nana about it, and she came along the next day to register me. I started work the following week.

The first building I went to work on was located in lower Manhattan, in Alphabet City. I worked with a crew of about six guys.

They were all like me, high school dropouts, and some had trouble with the law.

The building was rundown, with low-income people living in it. At noon, I followed the rest of the guys to the train station, and we took the train up to 116th Street. We entered through the side of the middle school and went right up to a large classroom on the third floor. The goal of this class was to get us ready to take our GEDs.

There were two teachers, a white lady named Sheila who had some kind of dreadlocks in her hair, and a heavyset black woman named Pam. There was also a black guidance counselor named Chuck. The first thing the teachers did was test me to see what level I was on. I didn't take the test very seriously and blew through it. The test indicated that I was on a fourth grade academic level. The teachers gave me work that was beneath me. I felt like an idiot. I knew that, at this rate, it would take forever to get my GED. I asked if I would be able to retake the test, and I was allowed. I scored well in my range, and was now given work to prepare for my GED.

I went to work and school every day. I wasn't making much money, but it was better than nothing. Denise had a fulltime job, so she would give me a couple of dollars sometimes.

Thanksgiving was coming up; it was time for Nana's yearly dinner. All of the family would come, even Uncle Maurice. Of course, my mother would be there, as well as Grammy and Pete. I hadn't talked to my mother since I ran away from Washington, and I wasn't going to. Denise was coming over for the dinner, and had never met my mother. I wasn't going to introduce them, either. Denise knew everything that had happened, and knew I hated my mother.

When the day came, I went to pick up Denise. She was a bit nervous. When I got back to Nana's, my mother was there. Grammy and Pete were there, also, and I spoke to them. Grammy and Pete had met Denise before. I didn't say a word to my mother at all. I didn't introduce Denise to her, and everyone knew I wasn't speaking to her. It was fine with me if I never had to talk to her another day in my life. Near the end of the evening, Grammy came up to

112

me and started to cry. She said that it hurt her to see me treat my mother that way, and begged me to introduce Denise to my mother. I granted her request.

My mother answered with a smug "Nice to meet you," and walked away in a huff. That was it.

I didn't need her. I had Nana, Denise, Frida, and Jazz, who were cool with me. From time to time, Denise and I would watch Jazz's son, Alex. Jazz moved out of Frida's into her own place, and sometimes would let Denise and I use it so we could be together in private.

Things were going well. I was getting close to getting my GED. I was going to work every day. I always gave Nana a couple of dollars when I got paid. I was doing what I had to do. Denise was doing well in school, and she got a job at a place called Ticketmaster. She even made a couple of new friends. She started hanging out a lot with this girl, Tara, who went to Blake Business School with her. The girl was from Brooklyn, streetwise, and sort of a hood rat. Tara lived in city housing and had a couple of boyfriends. She was even seeing one of her teachers at the school. I thought Denise and Tara made an odd set of friends, but who was I to judge?

I would pick Denise up from school sometimes, because she didn't get out until 9:00 p.m. Occasionally, I would come to get her by surprise and she wouldn't be there. I'd call her later, and she would tell me that she had to work late or some other story. Sometimes, she would tell me that she and Tara were hanging out. Funny thing was, Tara wasn't there, either.

116th Street and Columbus Avenue was a highly Dominican-populated area. In the late afternoon, a lot of the locals would come to the middle school gym to play basketball. Most were low-level drug dealers. One day after class, a couple of the guys from work and I went into the gym to play basketball. Most, if not all of the people in the gym, were Spanish. The guys I was with were all black.

We got into a game with the locals and were beating them. It started to get very physical, and a lot of elbows started to get thrown. The other guys were speaking Spanish, so we didn't know what they were saying.

Out of nowhere, one hauled off and took a swing at me. I dodged the punch and jumped back. He was very angry about the ballgame, but I didn't know what he was saying. He was a short, stocky guy with a beard who looked to be in his early twenties. He ran toward the exit vestibule and motioned for me to come in and fight. I didn't know this guy from Adam, and he wanted to fight me—for what? I knew the basketball game was getting a little rough, but that always happened in street ball.

I was full of adrenaline from the swing he had taken, so I followed him into the vestibule to engage in combat. When I entered, a bunch of the other locals followed, and so did the guys I worked with. The Spanish guy ran and tried to hit me with a flying kick. I thought, *What the hell is this guy is doing?* I knew one thing—the guys he was with weren't just going to stand around for long after I started to kick his ass.

I moved out of the way of the kick, hooked him by the throat as he went by, and threw him to the ground. I grabbed his neck when he fell and started to choke him from behind. I laid on the floor on my back, and he was on top of me. I did this so that his boys wouldn't be able to stomp me in the head while I was on the ground. I was choking the guy, and he started to bleed from his eyes. I could hear his boys saying, "Let him go, you're killing him!"

Oh, now these muthafuckers speak English. I wasn't going to let go. I saw the blood from his eyes running down his face, but I didn't care. I knew if I let him go, his boys were going to jump me. The guys I worked with weren't friends or anything. And besides, there were only five of us. There were about twenty of them.

I saw a guy that seemed a little older than the rest. He was in a white shirt and looked like a weightlifter. He appeared white, not Spanish. He was the security guard.

He made his way to the center of the crowd surrounding me and told everyone to clear out. He yelled at me to let go of the guy's neck. I released the guy. There was blood all over his face, and he was gasping for air as some of his boys carried him out of the building.

The security guard brought me and the guys I was with into an office and asked what happened. Then he asked if I knew who the guy was. I said no.

By this time, a tall black man came into the office. He said that my friends and I had to get out of there in a hurry. He was the director of the gym, and said the guy I was fighting was the leader of the local drug gang, and was rounding the troops to come and get me.

We followed the man to the back exit. He opened the door, and the four other guys and I walked out. It was about three blocks to the train station, and maybe four or five blocks to Harlem. If the Spanish guys started to chase us, we knew they wouldn't follow us into Harlem and try to beat up a black guy. We definitely didn't want to get caught waiting on the train platform. We were contemplating all options while walking out the door. However, as soon as we stepped out, all options went right out the window.

All we could see was the whole block lined up with Spanish guys waiting for us—or should I say, waiting for me. By the time I noticed the people in the street, the door closed behind me. And locked. The people were just standing there, as if waiting for orders. I didn't see the guy I had the fight with.

I walked away from the door and proceeded down the block. I saw him when I rounded the corner. Three of the four guys I was with took off running. Will stood with me; I knew him from around Denise's way. He sold marijuana on one of the street corners of Sheridan Avenue. The guy I had fought with went into a garbage can and pulled out a glass bottle, and then broke it on the sidewalk. That's when I noticed that all of the guys standing around had large, empty bottles in their hands. There had to be at least fifty of them. This wasn't going to be good. My adrenaline was pumping, and I was young and full of piss and vinegar.

The guy charged me and tried to stab me in the face with the broken bottle. I started punching him in the face while slipping from his jabs. I was getting the best of him once again. I started to become confident that I would beat him without getting hurt, but I forgot about his boys surrounding me. I was too focused on not getting stabbed with the broken bottle.

Then it happened. I felt a bottle crash into the back of my head, then another one. His boys were throwing bottles at me and running up to crash them into my head. My adrenaline was pumping, so I didn't really feel too many of them. I did feel some, and I knew I had to get away.

I started to run back toward the locked door. Will was standing by the door, banging for someone to open it.

The guy I was fighting with was right on me, trying to stab me in my back as I ran. I spun around and hit him with an elbow to the face. He was able to stab me in the chest with the broken bottle. I didn't even feel it, but I did start to feel more of the empty bottles hitting the back of my head. He stabbed me three times as I was fighting him off. I was weakening from all the shots I was taking from the bottles crashing into my head. I ran toward the closed door, not knowing what to do. I was cornered like a wild animal. The bottles were flying, and he was still trying to stab me. I thought this was it. There was no way out. I was going die here in the street—over a basketball game.

Will kept banging on the door for someone to let us in. The crowd wasn't attacking him, but since I ran to the door, the bottles were headed in the same direction. The door opened, and it was the director of the gym. As the door opened, I was so stunned from all the blows to the head that I collapsed in his arms. I heard him yell "No!" to the crowd as the bottles kept flying. I heard the bottles crashing and breaking against the wall inside of the school.

Will slammed the door behind me. He and the security guard helped me upstairs to an office. I had hurt my ankle during the altercation and was walking with a limp. The director had called the police while I was fighting outside. When I got to the office, they saw the stab wounds to my chest. An ambulance was called and arrived at the school. The crowd outside disappeared as the police arrived.

When the medics came upstairs, they saw the blood on my shirt and cut a section away where the stab wounds were. They examined the wound and pulled out a pair of tweezers. At this point, I hadn't felt the stab wounds. They weren't bleeding. I just saw that my shirt was bloody. The medic took the tweezers and pulled out two long pieces of glass from my wounds. Pieces had broken off inside of my chest every time he stabbed me. The medic said that I needed to go to the hospital to get a shot in case of an infection, since the glass came from the garbage.

The police took statements from me and from the director, who gave them all of the guy's information. The police also seemed to know who he was. They said that he was on probation, and had been on their radar for a while. They also commented that I was lucky to be alive. A detective would be calling me at home. The medics escorted me to the ambulance. Will rode with me to the hospital and stayed with me in the emergency room.

The ER was crowded, and the hospital was only about five blocks from the incident. The first thing that crossed my mind was, *What if one of the gang members stayed and watched the ambulance leave?* They would know I was in the emergency room and might wait for me to leave. Will had the same thought. When the medics dropped us off and did the paperwork, it started to get dark outside, so Will and I decided to sneak out of the hospital from the side entrance.

As Will and I walked to the train, we kept a sharp eye out for anyone following us. We made it to the station and took the train to 167th Street. Will lived around there, and so did Denise. I was safe, and my adrenaline level started to come down. I thanked Will for watching my back. He didn't have to stay with me and put his life in danger. He could have run off with the rest of the guys. It wasn't like we were friends or anything.

After Will and I separated, I went to Denise's house. It was late. They didn't have cellphones back then, and I didn't want to stop and use a payphone, in case I was being followed. Denise was worried because she hadn't heard from me, and I told her what had happened. She was clearly upset, and concerned about what was going to happen next. I didn't even know. I was just glad to be alive and wanted to go home.

It was about 10:00 p.m. when I left Denise's. Nana was also upset that I wasn't home at my regular time, which was 4:30 p.m. I told her what had happened, and she was just relieved that I was alive. She didn't hug me and say, "Poor baby, you alright?" She didn't ask me what I was going to do. She just asked if I wanted something to eat, and nothing else was said about it.

The next day, I didn't go back to work or school. I didn't know what I was going to do. I was close to taking my GED, and this was my job. The phone rang; it was the principal of the school. He asked me what my intentions were about my schooling. He also asked me to come to the school, because he wanted to have a sit-down with me and one of the gang members—not the one I was fighting with, but a spokesman for them. The principal asked if I would be willing. I told him I would. The meeting was set up for two days later.

Later that day, a detective called me about the incident. He told me the name of the guy that fought with me was Pedro. He had an extensive criminal record and was on probation. The detective said that if I wanted to press charges, I would need to come down to the station to fill out paperwork, and then they would pick him up on a parole violation and press new charges. I would also need to testify in court at a later date. The police officer didn't sound to convincing over the phone.

I had to take into consideration a couple of options. If I pressed charges against Pedro, then I couldn't go back to school or work because of the threat of retaliation by gang members. His lawyer could get my information—name, telephone number, address. These were the things the detective wasn't telling me. These were the things that could get Nana and Denise hurt if they had a lock on me.

I knew how things worked. To the detective, it was just a job; to me, it was my life. I told him I wasn't going to press charges, and that I only wanted the situation to be done with. The detective said to call him if I changed my mind.

Two days later, I went back to the school and into the principal's office. In there was a Spanish guy sitting in a chair. I recognized him as one of the guys throwing bottles. The principal stated that this was a call for peace. He thought I was rallying the troops to seek revenge at a later date. That thought never crossed my mind. This was a serious gang, not some high schoolers wanting to be gang members. I wasn't trying to go head to head with them.

The Spanish guy explained their position. He said that Pedro was upset over the basketball game and wanted to fight. Once Pedro realized he couldn't beat me, he had called in help. The gang member said Pedro figured if he couldn't take me with his hands, then they would just jump me. He also said that Pedro felt I was trying to kill him because I didn't let him go when I saw the blood.

When it was my turn to speak, I just said, "Hey, it was just a basketball game. The guy wanted to fight me. I only know one way to fight, and that's to win." I told him the real reason I didn't let go wasn't because I was trying to kill him, but because I knew that if I let him go, the rest were going to try and jump me. I let him know that the police did call and ask if I wanted to press charges, and I declined. I also told him that I had no intentions of seeking revenge—what's done is done. If they say it's over, then I say it's over. The gang member agreed, and we both stood up and shook hands.

The next day, I went back to work and back to school as if nothing had happened. The only thing that was different now was that I had the scars from three stab wounds on my chest.

I had learned the window trade well. The leader for my crew was Spanish, and his name was Joey. He was from the Bronx. In

119

fact, he lived close to me. He taught me everything he knew about windows, and he did a little side work as well. Joey liked me. I never gave him any problems, and he knew I did good work.

There was another crew leader named Joe, and he was a militant black guy that was always talking about how the white man was bringing minorities down. Joe was in charge of a different crew, but sometimes we worked with his crew when there were big projects.

By the summer of 1985, before I turned seventeen, I had taken my GED and passed it. I didn't know what was next. There was no more use for the program.

The program had what they called junior crew leaders. They weren't paid as much as regular crew leaders, but more like assistants. The position paid $5.50 an hour, and was fulltime. The administration of Y.E.C. was very impressed with how quickly I had gotten my GED and with my work ethic. They were also so impressed with how I had handled myself with the stabbing incident that they offered me a position as a junior crew leader. I accepted.

chapter **TWELVE**

The summer of 1985 started off great. I was working fulltime, and was able to give Nana more money. Denise and I were getting along great. We had been together for about two years now and were becoming very close. The only drawback was that because she went to school and had a fulltime job, we weren't spending as much time together as we used to.

In the evenings after work, she was at school, so I started to hang out with Jason more often. He had moved into the same complex as Julie and his sister, Mavis. He had a roommate whose name was Eddie. The apartment was really Eddie's mother's, but she moved and just let them stay there as long as they paid the rent. It was a real rat hole. Eddie had a sister named Cindy that would also stay there from time to time. Jason was about eighteen, and Eddie was my age. They had their own place and no adult supervision.

By now, Jason had developed a taste for marijuana. He smoked every day. I would smoke on occasion, but it was always somebody else lighting up and passing to me. At seventeen, I didn't even know how to roll a joint. The more I hung out with Jason, the more marijuana I smoked. I would go over to Jason's just to smoke, and sometimes would ask him to roll me a joint so I could take it home and smoke it there. I would go up to the roof of Nana's building to smoke it before I went in.

Denise was getting annoyed that I was hanging out with Jason so much. She knew he was trouble, and that I was smoking marijuana more and more. I didn't really listen to her. What was I supposed to do? Stay home and do nothing while she was at school all week?

Sometimes, even when Denise wasn't at school, she was hanging out with Tara, going here and there. It was girl stuff, I guess, so I didn't really ask too many questions. I was fine with going over to Jason's and hanging out.

Once, Denise and I went to Tara's house in Brooklyn. She lived with her mother. I met Tara's boyfriend, Reg. He seemed like a decent guy. I thought, *If he only knew how his girl was playing him.* Oh well, that was their business. They seemed to get along fine.

I was still hanging with Jason. We really didn't do much but hang out at his place and smoke. One time when I went over, he told me that his cousin, Maurice, had been arrested for robbing a gas station. Maurice and Ace, one of the other guys that were with us that night we went looking for Darryl, were locked up in New Jersey. Maurice used to work at the gas station and cased the place from the inside, but one of the co-conspirators snitched on him before the robbery. The police were there waiting for them when they left the gas station. Maurice pleaded guilty so that he wouldn't have to go to trial and receive a longer sentence. He was given three years.

That same night, Maurice came by. He had to report to the jail in a couple of days. I liked Maurice, and I have always been grateful for the way he rolled with me that night. When he arrived, he was in a somber mood and talked about seeing us soon. We all sat around drinking alcohol and smoking marijuana. Later, Jason and I gave Maurice a hug, and he went on his way for his three-year bid.

By now, Jason had taught me how to roll a joint. I would have him buy me a bag and give it to me when I came over. I would take it home and roll it myself. I started to get more daring, and would smoke it in Nana's house. I saved the bag, and after work, I would come home and take a shower. There was a window in the shower. I would run the water hot so the steam would flow out the window,

as well as the smoke. The smell and the smoke would go out undetected.

Soon, I was smoking every day. But to me, it didn't seem like a
habit. I was just doing something that made me feel good.

Denise wasn't really with smoking anything because she had
asthma. Her thing was a couple of drinks, but nothing beyond alcohol. Once in a blue moon, she may have taken a drag, but that was
as rare as a four-leaf clover. There came a point that she was very
upset at my smoking habit and I saw her disapproval.

Denise had gotten a new job and met a couple of new girls.
Their names were Rosemary and Christine. Denise and I were going
to go to the movies, but she wanted to have a bite to eat with Rosemary, Christine, and Christine's boyfriend, Eric, and another couple
before the movie. I met them at the restaurant, and we all seemed
to hit it off pretty well. The other couple seemed just a little older. I
knew we were going straight to the movies after the restaurant, so
while Denise and the other couples were getting ready, I went outside—we were downtown in Manhattan—and smoked a joint on
the street.

When the group came outside, I was done already. Christine and
Eric had a car, so they gave us a ride to the movies. The marijuana
smell all over me consumed the car, but Eric and Christine were
joking about it. Denise didn't find it amusing at all. When we got
out of the car, she was yelling at me for embarrassing her in front
of her friends. I told her I didn't see what the big deal was, that they
seemed to be alright with it. She wasn't concerned about what they
were alright with, it wasn't alright with her, and I didn't consider
that. The night didn't end well.

In 1985, Denise was nineteen, and I was seventeen. It was obvious that we had different types of friends, and we were spending
more time with our friends than with each other. We were young,
and young people needed attention. We were slowly drifting apart,
but we loved each other and didn't want to admit it to ourselves.

One day, Nana told me that Uncle Maurice was coming to town, and so was my mother. She said that he was going to take the family out to dinner. I called him at Grammy and Pete's when he arrived and asked if I could bring Denise. Denise had never met him, although she knew a lot about him from everything I told her, including that I loved him. He said sure, and that he was with a new woman that he wanted me to meet. Her name was Michelle.

We were going to Tavern on the Green, which was a high-class restaurant in Central Park. When Denise and I arrived at Grammy and Pete's, my uncle and Michelle were lying down on the couch. Both got up, and then my uncle introduced me to Michelle, and I introduced Denise to them. My mother came into the living room, and I ignored her like she was a piece of furniture. Denise didn't even say anything to her. I continued my conversation with my uncle without interruption. I didn't even look in my mother's direction. She got the message and went back toward the bedroom area.

Grammy was upset with my behavior when she saw this. I didn't care. She came over to me and asked me to sit down to talk with her. I sat down while my uncle entertained Denise and his new girlfriend.

Grammy started to make her plea. She spoke with tears in her eyes, like before at the Thanksgiving dinner. "Malik, please don't treat your mother like that. We all make mistakes, and she loves you very much. She's in the room crying because you wouldn't speak to her. She wouldn't be crying if she didn't love you, so please stop acting the way you're acting. You're hurting me and your mother. You know that's my daughter, and when she hurts, I hurt."

I didn't feel any different, but I did have some respect for Grammy, and I knew that she wouldn't let up. So for the sake of keeping the peace, I started to talk to my mother again.

I didn't believe what Grammy was saying, though. My mother was crying because she was embarrassed that her only child couldn't stand her, and everybody knew it. She cared about how other people saw her. She wanted people to like her. The funny thing was that most people did like her, until they got to know her. She knew how to put on a good front. I figured I would only have to talk to her at family functions, because I wasn't going to start calling her or making nice with her. I was just going to be respectful.

I was doing a good job as a junior crew leader, and soon they promoted me to a full crew leader. I wasn't making as much money as the other crew leaders, but it was more than $5.50 an hour. I was buying nicer clothes and had some money in my pocket. I had a better job than Jason. He was some kind of messenger, and was only making minimum wage, which was $3.35.

I was always looking to do things out of the blue, so the thought came to me that I hadn't spoken to my father in at least two years. I didn't even have his phone number anymore. I didn't want to ask my mother so she wouldn't know my business. I did remember the street number of the house that my grandmother, Miss Mary, lived in. It was 155th street and 112th Avenue in Jamaica, Queens.

I set out to Queens. I took the E train and got off at Sutphin Blvd. I looked at the street signs and just followed the numbers upward. I was in the general area, but I couldn't find the house. I also remembered the place on Jamaica Avenue that my father had taken me to when I first met him. I walked to Jamaica Avenue and found the spot.

There was this big, older, fat guy sitting on a chair in front of the store. I walked up to him and said, "Excuse me. Do you know Leroy?"

The man looked at me with extreme caution.

I said, "I'm his son, and I'm trying to find my grandmother's house."

The last time I was in the area, I was about twelve. Now I was seventeen, and to hustlers, I could be anybody. I could even be a hit man. The fat man waved over two other men, and they both stood on each side of me at close proximity and guided me into the storefront. Yeah, I remembered this place, and the same picture was hanging on the wall, with my father in the middle of a group of men. The fat man said, "Point him out."

So, I pointed to my father in the picture and said, "That's him, right there." I understood why they did what they did. In the underworld, people can put a contract out on your life. The hit man trying to fill the contract doesn't know what you look like, so they ask around about you until someone points you out. The men were just being cautious. It wasn't inconceivable that a contract was out on my father's life, considering the line of work he was in.

The fat man made a phone call, and in about a minute, a Lincoln Town Car pulled up to the storefront. The fat man told me to get in the backseat while he got in the front seat. He directed the man driving to take him to Ms. Mary's house. When we arrived, the man let me out of the car, pointed, and said, "That's the house right there." The men stayed until my grandmother opened the door.

When she did, she gave me a big hug and said, "Malik! I'm so glad to see you!" and waved to the men in the car. They drove off. My grandmother and I sat down, and I told her how I had gotten lost looking for the house, but I had remembered the spot. That was why I went there. She told me the fat man's name was Cornbread, and he was one of my father's partners. I asked her where my father was, and she said "Oh! Your father's in jail. He's been locked up for about three years now."

No wonder I hadn't heard anything from him for a while. My father was arrested for pulling a gun out on an FBI agent. It was an undercover operation, and he was caught driving with $100,000 in cash from New York to Georgia. The FBI agent offered him a deal if he would testify against the other people he was working with, but my father knew if he did, his life wouldn't be worth a nickel.

When I asked about my brother and sister, my grandmother gave me their phone numbers. They lived in Amityville, Long Island. I asked her if I could visit my father in prison, but she said that he didn't want any visitors because he didn't want people to see him like that. She did give me an address so I could write to him. I said my goodbyes and told my grandmother that I would visit more often.

I called my brother and sister. Denise and I hooked up with them in Long Island. I introduced Gregory and Crystal (my sister) to Denise. They lived in the bad part of Amityville, in a small, two-bedroom ranch house. It looked like a shack to me. Their mother, Judy, was a short, dark-skinned, skinny woman, and a recovering heroin addict. She looked like it. When Judy saw me, she gave me a hug and said, "I babysat you a couple of times."

Judy also had two other sons, named Tyrone and Darryl. Both guys were about five years older than me. Darryl had a regular job, but Tyrone was a drug dealer in the neighborhood. I found out that my father was married to this woman, so Tyrone and Darryl considered him their father, and me their stepbrother. They all gave me a warm welcome.

Denise and I hung out with them a couple of times, but they also hung around with some shady people. Being out there and around those kinds of people—people I didn't know—made me uncomfortable.

When I visited my grandmother again, she gave me the scoop on Judy and my stepbrothers. She told me that my father and Judy were boyfriend and girlfriend around the time I was born. Judy was a little older than him and had two kids already. She told me that they had gotten married and were selling heroin together. They had gotten busted by the police. Judy's aunt was a local politician, and was able to get Judy off with probation, but my father had to do a year in jail. My grandmother told me that when my father got out of jail the first time, he and Judy didn't get along too well. My father had wanted to be a police officer, but the drug conviction ruined all of that. That's when he became a fulltime hustler. My grandmother even showed me the newspaper article from the arrest. It was big news at the time. She said that my father should be out of jail in about a year.

I wrote to him several times, trying to develop some sort of relationship with him while he was in prison. I hoped that he and I would bond when he got out.

chapter THIRTEEN

M y job as a window installer was going well. The only problem
I had was that sometimes funding for the program ran short,
or work would be slow, so I would get laid off for a couple
of months. The good thing was that I had a trade, and the window
replacement business was booming.

Most of the window companies were run by underworld figures
that would rig the bids for a job. That didn't matter to me; I was just
hired help, a plain old window installer. The first window job I had
outside of Youth Energy Corps (Y.E.C.) was with a company called
New York Window, working with white people. The job was simply
to install windows. I wasn't in charge of anyone but myself. It paid
$10 an hour, and I was living the dream. This was the most money
I ever made in my life. It was 1986. I was making money, Denise
was making money, and all was well.

Denise and I were hanging out less, but I was still in love with
her. Even at seventeen, I was talking about marrying her and being
together for the rest of our lives. We both lived at home, so when
we wanted to have privacy, we would rent a hotel room. We always
had to leave each other at the end of the night.

Even though I didn't know it, the less time we spent together,
the further apart we grew. I loved her with all my heart, but it
seemed like we were becoming good friends with benefits. Denise
was hanging out with older professional people, and I was hanging
out with marijuana-smoking, cocaine-sniffing, and alcohol-drinking
people. Our classes of friends were very different. I could hang

around the new friends she made, but the friends I had were like
Jason—other street people he would introduce me to.

Sometimes, if I had nothing to do, I would hang out at Jazz's
beauty salon. She would give me free haircuts. One day I was there,
this older lady, around her mid-forties, was getting her hair done.
Her name was Pat. I was telling Jazz about my window work. Pat
said that the following week, she was having her windows installed
and wanted to know if I would mind watching the installation to
make sure the installers didn't cut any corners. She would pay me.
She gave me her phone number, and I met her at her house the
following week. She lived right across the street from me.

I watched the window installers do their work. Pat and I talked
while the men worked. When they were finished, I checked the windows. She gave me a few dollars and asked me for my phone number. She said it was just in case she needed some work done around
the house. I had the feeling she was looking for a boy toy, not a
handyman. I told Jazz about what I was thinking, and she said it
could be. Jazz said she really didn't know the lady, that she only did
her hair.

Pat wasn't bad looking, and I had been with an older woman
before (Lori). But the mid-forties was way up there to me.

One day, Pat called and asked if I knew a woman named T. I
told her that I didn't. This woman lived in my complex and was
having trouble with her lock. Pat asked if I would come with her to
take a look and see if I could fix it.

The woman lived in Building 10, and I lived in Building 5. I had
never seen her around, because when I left Nana's house, I never
hung around where I lived. I would always hang out on Jason's
block. I would say, "What's up?" to a couple of people I knew from
when I went to Taft, but that was the extent of any socializing I did
where I lived.

I met Pat in front of T's building, and Pat escorted me up to the
fifth floor where the woman lived. Pat knocked on the door, and
this short, pregnant woman with a scarf on her head opened the

130

door. The apartment looked old and needed a paint job. Her furniture was aged and dirty, and she was dressed in maternity clothes that didn't match. She had two kids running around. One seemed to be about five, and the other maybe two. Pat introduced us and told the lady that I would look at the lock for her. T agreed, but had a very nasty attitude and about her. She also had bad teeth. This woman was your classic ghetto rat.

As I tried to fix the lock, the woman stood over me, telling me that I was fixing it wrong. Finally, I gave up because she was getting on my nerves. I figured if she knew what she was doing, she should fix the lock her damn self.

Pat and I left, and I walked Pat home across the street. When we got in front of her building, I stopped and asked her what was up with that woman and how she knew her. I was trying to make conversation so as not to have to go upstairs with her. Pat seemed to have a lot of class, and that woman seemed like a bum. Pat told me that when she would pass by my complex, T would say hi to her, and sometimes complimented her on her attire. Soon after, Pat started speaking with the lady more often, and a few times lent her a couple of dollars when she was short on funds. The woman had the two kids by different fathers and was pregnant with her third, from yet a different man. She was on welfare, so Pat felt sorry for her and would sometimes bring her old clothes and food for the kids. I thought the woman was a real bitch.

Denise and I would go by to see Grammy and Pete sometimes. I was glad to always be able to brag about my job and the trade I learned. Pete always had some new information to tell us that he had heard on the news. One day, he said to Denise and me, "You know they got this new drug out called crack? It's highly addictive, and it's spreading like wildfire around the poorer neighborhoods." Then he told us about this new disease called AIDS. He said gay people were getting it, and they were dropping like flies. I had heard of crack, but not AIDS. Denise and I listened, like always, and left.

131

I knew about crack because a few of the people Jason hung out with were crack dealers. Pete was right when he said it was highly addictive. People would come around trying to sell their televisions for $5 or $10 just for a hit. I never saw anything like it. Women would sell their bodies or give oral sex for the same amount. To my understanding, it was just cocaine freebased in a smaller form, but more affordable.

Poor people could afford to freebase now. Before, you would need to spend $300 or $400 to do that. The problem was the high only lasted five minutes. Crackheads were springing up all over the place. This was an epidemic in the ghetto. You would see people you went to school with walking around trying to steal, rob, or sell something they stole, just to get a hit of crack.

Julie's stepson, Justin, was a crackhead. Sometimes, Jason and I would see Justin walking the street with what we called the "on a mission" look in his eyes—meaning, on a mission to get a hit of crack. Crackheads walked around like they had no souls.

Even at my job at New York Window, some of the guys smoked crack. I remember many times riding with a coworker to a job site. The driver would stop to pick up crack to smoke before work. Many times, I was offered a hit. But to me, that would make me lose my soul, and I didn't want that. My coworker would steal material from the job site and sell it for crack money. I would see them making pipes out of plastic Pepsi bottles.

The people Jason knew that were selling crack were making a bundle of money. On 171st Street, where we hung out, everybody sold. Some sold for someone else, some sold for themselves, and some sold to support their own crack habits. Jason and I didn't touch the stuff, but Mavis did.

New York Window Company went out of business. It was no wonder, with crackheads working for them and stealing all the time. Fortunately, Y.E.C. was back in business, and hired me again so that I didn't have any downtime.

There was a new player in the game this time. His name was Walter Cook, but people just called him Cook. He was an ex-cop, tall and burly, standing about six feet six inches and weighing easily three hundred pounds. He had a disposition to match his size.

Cook had a contract with the City to manage ten low-income apartment buildings. If he managed them successfully, he would then become the owner of all the properties. Most of the buildings were rundown and drug-infested. The City gave Cook money to replace the windows and do other necessary repairs. Cook gave the contract to Y.E.C.; therefore, Y.E.C. had plenty of work now.

I got to know Cook a little more than the others because Joe, the black crew leader, had a side deal with Cook to order windows for his house with those for his buildings, since he got them cheaper at a bulk rate. Joe had me install the windows in Cook's house. Cook liked me and my professionalism, so he offered me some side work repairing broken windows in his buildings. From time to time, he would give me a call, and I would do the work for him. What I didn't know was that Joe was doing some side work for him also, and wanted it all to himself.

Cook had a notorious reputation among drug dealers; he was determined to rid his building of them by any means necessary. Since he was an ex-cop, he was allowed to carry a gun legally, and that gave him an upper hand. If he ended up shooting a drug dealer, chances were the dealer would have a record. I didn't think it was beneath him to plant a knife or a gun on his victim. He was an old-school cop.

One story comes to mind when I think about how notorious his reputation was among the drug dealers. One particular dealer would sell out of one of Cook's buildings, right off of University Avenue. Cook would see the dealer and his crew outside of the building. The leader of the crew would often give Cook the middle finger and curse him out in front of people to make Cook look stupid and weak. The dealer was not in the building, so there was little Cook could do to stop the disrespect.

133

At night, the dealer would use one of Cook's vacant apartments to bag up his drugs while Cook wasn't around. Cook had a couple of tenants that he paid for information, and this got back to Cook. The informant even gave Cook the apartment numbers.

For about a week, Cook would survey the place at night, coming around 3:00 or 4:00 a.m., unseen. Once he gathered all the information he needed, he made his move.

Besides carrying a gun, Cook also carried an ax handle without the ax on it. The gun was concealed; the ax handle wasn't.

Cook arrived early one morning, about 3:00 a.m., snuck up to the vacant apartment where the dealer was packing his drugs and kicked in the door. The dealer was there with two other guys that weren't part of his crew, just workers packing the drugs. When Cook busted into the apartment, the workers took off running out the window and door while Cook commenced beating the drug dealer mercilessly with the ax handle.

After Cook finished beating the dealer to a bloody pulp, he dragged him by his shirt collar down five flights of stairs and outside the front of the building. As the dealer lay bloody on the ground, Cook went into the building and rang all the tenants' buzzers, waking them up and telling them to look out of the window.

This was 3:30 a.m. He had the whole building awake and looking out of the windows. When he was sure he had enough of an audience, he yelled at the top of his voice, "You see this muthafucker here? Well, he sells drugs in my building, and this is what I do to drug dealers who sell shit in my building."

Cook then unzipped his pants, pulled out his penis, and began to urinate on the drug dealer. Once he finished pissing on him, Cook told the dealer, "If I ever see you in my building again, muthafucker, I'll kill you."

With that, Cook got in his car and drove away. Needless to say, that drug dealer never showed his face again, and the word got out not to fuck with Walter Cook.

134

One day, Pat gave me a call and said that the woman had had her baby, and that she was going to drop some things off for her. She wanted to know if I could help her carry them. I met her at her house and carried the items across the street.

This time, when the woman opened the door, she wasn't pregnant, and the newborn was lying on her dirty couch, wrapped in a blanket. The lady seemed in a little better mood. She smiled at Pat with her bad teeth, thanking her for her donation. After that, I would see the woman more often when I was leaving my complex.

T was one of those hood rats that was outside all the time, in everybody's business. I would say, "Hi" and keep on going. Once, she stopped me and said, "I didn't know you lived in the complex. I just thought you were a friend of Pat's. I never seen you around."

I just nodded my head to her conversation, and then she asked me if I was interested in modeling. I told her I was. I asked her why people called her T, and what her real name was. She said her real name was Teresa, and that people called her T. I asked her where she was from, and she said, "The University housing projects." She was twenty-seven years old.

Now, every time I saw T, she wanted to stop and talk to me like we were good friends or something.

As time went on, Jason started seeing some girl, so when I came around, I would be the third wheel. Denise was always in school or hanging out with Tara or her new friends from work, so I had a lot of time on my hands. One day, when I was walking out of my housing complex, T stopped me again and started talking to me. I had nothing to do, so I asked her if she wanted to go to the movies with me. I wasn't thinking anything romantic; I just wanted some company. She said, "Sure," but she needed to pay for a babysitter. I asked her how much, and she said $20. I thought that was pretty cheap for three kids and offered to pay for the sitter. When I picked her up, we took a cab to the babysitter's house. The babysitter was her mother. I thought, *She has to pay her mother to watch her grandkids?* I should have turned and run right then.

It was a Friday night, and I had to go to work the next day for some overtime at Y.E.C. T and I took the train downtown to 42nd Street and saw some movie. I don't even remember what it was. On the train ride back, I was asking her questions about herself. She had no problem talking; she loved to run her mouth. She also loved being the center of attention.

I asked about her kids, and she told me that all three kids had different fathers. The first boy, who was getting ready to turn six, was named Ben. He was a Jr. T and his father had been married for about two years. Ben's father was in the Air Force, and they had gotten married because she had become pregnant. She said the marriage was over before it got started, but Ben's father sent $100 a month for his son.

The second child's name was Cordell. T got pregnant with him from a guy she was messing with, but it wasn't anything serious. The guy was no good, never sent a dime for Cordell, and only ever saw him once.

The last child was a girl named Gennie, and her father was a bus driver named Steve that T was seeing. She was one of his side girls. Her exact words were, "He was my lover." From what she was telling me, Steve had been very upset that she was having the baby, since they were not serious—and he was married.

After hearing all of the sordid details of her life, I thought, *This is one dumb bitch, and she's nothing but trouble.* I should have followed my gut instincts. Because I didn't, this woman almost ruined my whole life.

That night, T and I went to her apartment and drank a bottle of wine. I told her about Denise, and she told me all about her sordid love affairs. I left her apartment about 4:00 in the morning. There wasn't anything romantic about the evening. She was just someone to hang out with.

The next morning, I overslept and didn't go to work. At 9:00 a.m., T knocked on my door and asked me to go with her to pick up her kids. I didn't have anything else to do, so I went. Her mother,

Ella, lived in a one-bedroom apartment with T's younger sister, Rain, who was about ten years old. Ella slept in the living room, which had two sofas in it. I sat down on one, and Ella sat across from me. She asked me if I was a cop. Then, she pulled out a plastic bag containing an ounce of marijuana and began to roll herself a joint.

Ella was a light-skinned woman, about the same complexion as T, in her late forties. She had the same disposition—she was a bitch. Ella had a very dysfunctional background herself. She was raised by her father, Harold, who molested and raped her from about the ages of eight to fourteen, until her grandmother took possession of her. At age nineteen, Ella became pregnant with T, and left T to be raised by her grandmother. At twenty, Ella became pregnant again with another girl, who she named Lisa, and left that child too. At twenty-two, Ella became pregnant with Tyrone. She left him to the same fate as her other two children. All three children were raised by their great-grandmother on welfare in a city housing project.

Things were innocent at the beginning between T and me. I was just looking for company. T was the classic ghetto rat. She was a master manipulator, and I was her next victim. Every moment, she was thinking about her next hustle. I would talk about Denise, and T was sucking it all in, to use against me when the time was right.

She started out slowly, by borrowing money from me some-times. Trying to be macho, I wouldn't ask for it back. That right there should have been a sign. T would come by my worksite to hang out and wait for me to get off. She had nothing else to do, since she didn't have a job. She was stalking her prey. T knew I had a good job, and that I was a generous person. I always had money in my pocket, and I had nice clothes.

I felt sorry for her young son, since he had to sleep on a urine-stained mattress. I offered to buy him a twin mattress to sleep on. T said that she had a set of bunk beds on layaway and asked if I would get them instead, so that she wouldn't lose the down pay-ment. I thought that was okay, since she already had money on it and made it seem like it was almost paid off already. I figured I would spend about $75 on a mattress.

When T and I went to the store and she handed over the receipt for the layaway to the salesperson, the balance was $250. T had only put $5 on the bunk bed set. I, being young, dumb, and prideful, didn't want to withdraw my offer. If I had been smart, I would have said, "Bitch, are you crazy? I ain't buying no $250 bunk beds! They ain't my kids!" But, of course, what came out was "Okay." I was even proud that I was able to afford the beds.

As time went on, T was tightening her trap. On my paydays, she would always—by coincidence—be in the courtyard of the building complex when I came home. When I turned eighteen, I made the ultimate mistake and had sex with her. It wasn't that she had any outstanding beauty traits. It was just new pussy, and as the saying goes, there's nothing more appealing to a man.

Afterward, I felt bad about betraying Denise. I loved her with all my heart and made a big mistake. Once the deed was done, T started to play her mind games, at which she was a master. I didn't see her for the next couple of days. Then, she called me on the phone and said it was a big mistake, that she was too old for me. I agreed and jumped at the opportunity to get out of the situation. I thought, *Okay, you fucked up, but it was a one-time thing. Since she's talking this "It was a mistake" shit, fine! Let it be over with.* I was going to try to distance myself from her as much as possible.

It was like Adam realizing he was naked after he ate the apple. I saw with open eyes that I was jeopardizing what I had with Denise by sleeping with this ghetto, three-kids-having, welfare bitch. That was my plan—but like I said, T was playing mind games. Her plan was a bit more sinister.

Afterward, I didn't speak to T for about a week. Denise and I went out a few times, and I appreciated her more than ever before. I saw the difference between the two women like night and day. Denise had class. She was a smart and independent woman. She didn't look for me to buy her things; she would buy me things. She wasn't out to use me or see what she could get from me. She loved me.

The disadvantage T had over Denise was that Denise and I lived at home—her with her parents and me with Nana. I had to leave Denise at night to go home. T's apartment was facing the courtyard, and she would spot me coming in, late at night sometimes, and invite me up. Even though she was saying it was a mistake that we had sex, she was still offering it to me. I was only eighteen, and didn't have the control or willpower to dismiss her, so I would wind up sleeping with her.

T was now singing a different tune. She would say it was alright that I had a girl; she just wanted to have sex with me. I thought I could have my cake and eat it too. I didn't want T to be my girlfriend. I was young and dumb, and she was cold and calculating.

As time went on, I was having sex with T on a regular basis. I was also giving her more money when I got paid. When she would ask me for some money and I'd refuse, she would often remind me that I was having sex with her. T started to show her true colors. She'd often make scenes in public to embarrass me, and sometimes we'd get into physical altercations.

While all these things were going on, I was trying to keep it secret from Denise. T used this to her advantage, as she would sometimes threaten to reveal our relationship to Denise. She had me trapped in a corner. I loved Denise, and T knew it. I was a coward, and T knew it.

There came a point when Denise started to become conscious that something was going on. She would call my house after I left her, and I wouldn't be home. This would happen very often, and when she would inquire about where I was, I would tell her that I was at Jason's. But it happened one too many times, and she started to demand answers. I was too much of a coward to admit to her what was going on, but she knew.

chapter FOURTEEN

My father got out of jail and was on parole for about a year. He would conduct his illegal operations during the day and report to a halfway house at night. I'd head down to Queens on the weekend to ride around with him while he conducted business. His new ventures were after-hour nightclubs and gambling spots. I saw why he was a good businessman by the way he dictated how he wanted things set up to the construction workers. I would hear him ordering materials and alcohol and talking to his partners about the layout and design of the clubs.

During the daytime, he looked like a man with money. But at night, when it was time to go to the halfway house, he would change his clothes and look like someone in need. It became a routine for me. It was the same thing every weekend. Business during the day, and then he and I would go to the house of his new girl, Eleanor. She was a big-boned, light-skinned woman that lived in a small ranch house near my grandmother. Eleanor would cook us both something to eat, and then my father and I would ride the train to downtown Manhattan, where his halfway house was. He would get off downtown, and I would ride the train up to the Bronx.

My job was going well. Y.E.C. had plenty of work, and Cook was still giving me work. The funny thing was, I was making more money, but juggling two women always left me broke. Together, Denise and I had a decent amount of money. We both lived at home, so there wasn't any rent to pay. I would give Nana a few dollars, but then T was always around, leeching off me.

I started to act like I was Gennie's father, and the little girl even started to call me Daddy. I fell for it, hook, line, and sinker. I was buying T's kids clothes because she had them looking like bums when I walked around with them in the street. It was embarrassing. I think she did it on purpose, knowing that I was vain.

Jason and I started to hang out more because he had broken up with the girl he had been with. Jason didn't live with Eddie anymore. He lived with his sister, Mavis, and she was a crackhead. Jason didn't have a well-paying job, and he didn't have any kind of dress clothes.

One day, Jason was hanging out with me at T's house, and one of her hood rat friends named Jerry was there. T was having a birthday party for one of her kids. Jerry was just like T—three kids, on welfare, and older than Jason and me. She liked to sniff cocaine. Jason liked to also, and would usually have some on him. So, Jason and Jerry hit it off, of course. Also, Jerry thought that Jason was like me; therefore, she hit pay dirt with some young sucker, too. But Jason wasn't like me. He talked a good game, but he had a job that sucked, and he lived in his crackhead sister's living room.

T and I decided to double date with Jason and Jerry. It was wintertime, and Jason didn't have a winter dress coat. I had a couple, an overcoat and a three-quarter leather coat with fur on the collar. It was very expensive, but I let Jason wear it so he could look nice for the evening. That night, I took them to this high-class bar at a hotel. The bar had a rotating floor with a view overlooking Times Square. I knew about the place because when my uncle came to town, he would stay at this same hotel to go to the bar.

T, Jason, and Jerry were impressed with the majesty of the bar. We sat down and drank for a couple of hours, enjoying the motion and the view. I learned something that night: never take a classless person to a classy place. By the end of it, Jerry was a staggering drunk and throwing ice across the bar. It was embarrassing. Security almost had to remove us, but I was calm and collected, and was able to convince them to allow us to leave on our own.

The three of them thought it was so funny. Jerry was roaring drunk as we took a cab to T's house. I went into the bedroom with T, while Jason and Jerry stayed in the living room. T was upset that they were in the house because she knew Jerry was a slut, and most likely having sex with Jason out there. She demanded that I tell them to go to Jerry's house, which was in the same complex. When I went into the living room, Jerry was naked on the sofa, but Jason still had his pants on. Jerry invited me to join them in a sex act, but I knew T was already upset about them being there. I didn't want to take the chance of her walking in on us. I declined, but the offer was tempting. Unlike T, Jerry was a good-looking woman with a big ass. And there she was, fully naked, inviting me in.

Jason got Jerry dressed and went over to her place. The only thing was that her kids were there, and they were a little older than T's. They were used to their mother bringing strange men over. Jason left wearing my leather coat and called me the next day to tell me what a wild fuck Jerry was. The following weekend, Denise and I were getting together, and I wanted my leather coat back. I went over to Jason's sister's house and knocked. Jason opened the door, and I said, "Hey, man. I need my coat."

Jason replied, "You need it more than you think." I asked him what he was talking about. Jason told me that when he went to get the coat out of the closet earlier when I had called him, it was missing. Jason told me that his sister, Mavis, had stolen it and sold it to this crack dealer on 170th Street. I was furious and confronted Mavis, but she was high on crack and mumbling. I told Mavis I was going to come back that night for her to take me to the crack dealer, because I was going to get my shit back. I had to go to pick up Denise, and I figured the later I came around, the better the chances were that I would find the guy, since crack dealers mostly sold at night.

I picked up Denise and told her what had happened. We went out with some friends of hers, and she and I were going to go to a hotel after. Denise could see my mind was on the situation that I was going to have to handle later. She suggested we put off going to a hotel and find out what was going on with my coat. I didn't want her to go with me, but she insisted. She wanted to be by my side.

When we showed up at Mavis's house, she had sobered up. I forced her to take me to where she had sold my coat. It was about 2:00 in the morning. Jason, Denise, and I followed Mavis to 170th Street and Sheridan Avenue. No one was around but crackheads looking for a hit. I told Mavis to point the guy out, but he wasn't around. I asked a few crackheads if they had seen him, and some said he was going to be back in a minute. About five minutes later, I saw this guy walking down the street with my coat on like he was the cock of the stroll. Mavis said, "There he is." I walked up with Mavis and told him that the coat he was wearing was mine, and that I knew he bought it from Mavis. I said I would pay him what he paid her for it.

The crack dealer gave me a puzzled look and said, "Wait a minute." He went into this afterhours spot on 170th street. I saw him pull a curtain back and point to me. Jason, Denise, and I were standing outside the door, waiting for him to come back out. If he didn't take my offer, I was going to take the coat from him.

I felt the situation could become dangerous and told Denise to get a cab home. She refused. I demanded that she leave. I wouldn't be able to focus my full attention on the situation because I would be concerned about her. I didn't know what the guy was planning.

Denise said in a definitive voice, "I'm not going anywhere."

I knew she was serious and wasn't going to leave. I didn't want her caught in the middle of anything, and I couldn't take the chance of her getting hurt, so I said, "Let's go." We left. I told Jason he would have to pay me for the jacket, and he was cool with that. This just reinforced how much Denise had my back and how much she loved me. She was my ride or die chick.

When I saw T the next day and told her that Jason's sister had stolen my coat, she seemed to get a big laugh out of it. She was like that. She found joy in other people's misery.

The situation with T was getting deeper and more complicated. She was trying to be my woman, and now her objective was to damage my relationship with Denise. I didn't love T. I didn't even like her. I think the reason I would have sex with her was because I was angry.

As I said, Denise had her suspicions about another woman, but she didn't bring it up. Later, I would find out why not.

For a while, T stayed in her place as the side chick. She would cause me hell around my house, but that was it. Then, she decided to take it up a notch. One day, Denise and I had planned a trip to Virginia for Grammy's family reunion. I met Denise in front of her house, and we called a cab. As we waited for the cab in front of the building, I heard someone yell out, "Malik!" It was T. She was standing across the street. She yelled, "I want to talk to you."

Denise was calm and ladylike. She didn't know T, but she knew who T was.

I crossed the street, angry, and said to her, "What the fuck are you doing here, bitch?"

She ignored my question and my disrespect. "Where you going?"

"None of your fucking business. Get the fuck out of here, bitch."

Denise was watching the whole exchange from across the street. Just like a true ghetto rat, T was making a scene in the middle of the street to make me look like an idiot. She was hoping the situation would get physical, so as to cause even more of a scene. She screamed, "You think you can just fuck me anytime you want and then go away with this bitch? You think you can just treat me like a piece of shit, you muthafucker?"

I just ignored her rant, and when I saw the cab pull up in front of Denise's building, I walked away and got in. T didn't dare follow.

144

She didn't know how Denise was. T wouldn't fight a woman over you; she would make the woman leave, and then pick up the pieces.

The cab ride was quiet, and so was the plane ride, but Denise didn't seem furious. I mean, she was upset about the scene, but she wasn't furious like I would have been if the shoe were on the other foot. I didn't know what to say. I was waiting for her to speak first. For the first time in my life that I could remember, I didn't have the words.

When we got to the hotel and were alone, Denise made the comment, "So, that's her, huh?" I just nodded. It was all up front and center now, but being the class act that Denise was, she said, "We'll talk about it when we get back to New York."

I wasn't looking forward to the conversation, but I was becoming ever so curious about how calm she was with everything. I mean, she was cool with me the whole trip. No attitude, no wisecracks. Just Denise.

When we got back to New York, Denise and I sat down and had a long talk. She had a lot of questions, and I was ready to answer her and tell the truth. She asked how long the relationship had been going on. I told her, "About a year." She asked me if I loved T and I told her, "Hell, no!"

When she got the answers she wanted, she hit me with a bombshell. She said, "Well, I've been seeing people, too."

My heart sank and my anger rose. I know it seems hypocritical, but I was insanely jealous. I wanted to know who, what, when, where, why, and how. I never even had a hint that she might have been seeing anyone else. I guess I was so busy trying to be sneaky that I didn't pay enough attention. And she didn't say person—she said "people."

She told me that she was seeing this guy at Blake Business School, and another at her job. I'm sure there were others, but I think she realized she made her point that if I could do it, she could do it, too.

I didn't dare ask her if she was having sex with them, because I was already furious and knew I didn't have a leg to stand on. I still didn't want to break up. I didn't want to lose her. I got played at my own game. Everything I thought I had was an illusion. Denise was smart not to tell me about the guy from her school, because I would have gone there to kick his ass. Yes, I was the type to fight over a woman. By the time she told me about him, she had already graduated. The funny thing was, she was seeing him even before I started to see T. That was why she was always out with Tara or hanging out—she was on dates. I felt like a sucker. But then again, I felt like I was getting what I deserved.

Denise and I came to an understanding that we loved each other, but we were young and had become very serious very quickly. We thought that maybe we should slow things down. We weren't breaking up. I guess we would be doing what we were already doing, but now it was out in the open.

When I left her that night, I felt like I couldn't trust anyone— no one but Nana. For the past four years, I trusted Denise without question. If she had said the sky was purple, I would have believed her. But now, even though I still loved her, I didn't trust her like I used to. I knew she wouldn't do anything to hurt me on purpose, but I was destroyed from the revelation that she wasn't devoted and committed to me alone. I knew I had never considered what I was doing, but in retrospect, I understood why I was the way I was.

When I was growing up, there was no one to show me how to be a man. There was my uncle, who had a different woman every time I saw him, and who had four kids by three different women. There was my father, who also had many women and had six kids by five different women. Really, there was no one to teach me about love, commitment, and devotion to a woman. My role models were the movie stars from the Blaxploitation movies like Jim Brown (*Black Gunn*), Fred Williamson (*Hell Up in Harlem*), Richard Roundtree (*Shaft*), and Ron O'Neal (*Superfly*), among others. There were many more, all with the same image. Nana took me to see all those movies, and in them, the stars had money, guns, and multiple women. This was what being a man was to me. I was just imitating, the same reason I had no hang ups about drugs.

I tell you, when it rains, it pours. Denise and I basically had an open relationship. We would now see each other, but we didn't ask each other too many questions about what we were doing when we weren't together. I saw T outside in the courtyard of my complex about three days after that stunt she pulled, and she again said, "I need to talk to you." I was through with her. I told her to fuck off. She had caused me enough problems already. She said, "Is that what you're going to tell your baby? I'm pregnant." I just looked at her with an evil stare. I hated her for everything she was doing to me. I just walked away and didn't say anything. She loved to spring shit on people to shock them and catch them off-guard.

I went home and thought, *This is it. Denise is going to leave me for sure now. I just became a ghetto statistic, having a baby with a woman I'm not married to, that had kids from other men. I just impregnated a ghetto rat with another ghetto bastard like me. The cycle is repeating itself. I am going to have a baby with a woman I don't love. A woman I don't even want to be with. A woman I don't even like.*

A woman I began to hate.

I went to see my father that weekend and told him my situation. He didn't comment much on it, but he knew the type of woman I was dealing with. By this time, he was off parole, and he drove me back to the Bronx. But first, he drove me by Denise's, and I introduced her. Then he drove me home, and I introduced him to T. My father didn't say much, but he seemed pleased about having a grandchild.

Later, I talked to T on the phone after I had calmed down, and she told me she was about two months along in her pregnancy. I didn't tell Denise. I wanted to hold on to her as long as possible. I knew this would absolutely drive her into the arms of another man for good, and I had a pain in my heart just thinking about it.

About another three weeks went by, and my father wanted to take T and me out to celebrate the pregnancy. I wasn't in the celebrating mood, but I felt like maybe this would be an opportunity for my father and me to become closer. I still felt a void between us that I didn't understand.

T and I took the train to my grandmother's house in Queens. My father and Eleanor picked us up from there. My father was dressed up in a gray suit with a pink shirt. Few men can sport a pink shirt and still look masculine; he was one of them. My father drove us in one of his many cars to a busy restaurant. The people there seemed to know him, and all greeted him with respect. He introduced T and me, and the waiter led us to a table. I felt like I was special that night. People were showing me respect because I was with him. Everyone that passed by the table acknowledged my father.

About a half-hour later, T said that she wasn't feeling well and wanted to go home. I was pissed at her, because for once, I didn't feel the void between my father and me. For once, I felt like I was his son. My father put us in a cab back to the Bronx and paid the cab driver. I didn't talk to T the whole ride. I didn't give a crap about her. I wasn't celebrating her pregnancy; I was dreading it. I was only happy to be a part of my father's environment.

When we got back to the Bronx, I just went home to Nana's. The next day, T called and said she needed to go to the hospital because she still didn't feel well. I told her to go the fuck ahead. She came down to Nana's and threatened to act a fool if I didn't escort her. When we got to the hospital, the staff performed a bunch of tests and admitted her.

My father and Eleanor came to the hospital a couple of days later to see T. I would go after work, but I wasn't doing any bedside vigil. T ended up having a miscarriage. I don't know what the reason was, but I felt like I dodged a bullet. When she came home a couple of days later, we went to her mother's house for some reason. While we were talking about the miscarriage, T went into the bathroom.

148

Her mother said to me in a sly manner, "Mama's baby, papa's maybe."

I thought, *What the hell does that mean?* Later, I understood—it meant that just because she was pregnant, who's to say it was my baby? If Denise could cheat on me, why wouldn't this ghetto rat? Besides being a master manipulator, she was also a skilled liar. To be honest, I didn't care about her enough to be jealous. I would have been pissed that I was being played, taking care of someone else's baby, but I was doing that anyway with her daughter.

Around that time, T's great-grandmother died. Her sister, Lisa, had her in the project apartment they were raised in, living with her husband and two kids while paying $30 a month rent. The apartment was in the grandmother's name, so the rent was cheap. They were also collecting her Social Security checks. The woman belonged in a home, but they kept her there, in diapers, in a room on a hospital bed for years. Sometimes, you could smell her when you walked into the apartment. T was bad, but her sister was a real piece of work.

T's mother was scared that Harold was going to attend the funeral because it was his mother who died. The whole family was scared to death of this guy. T begged me to be there, and asked if I could come strapped so the family would feel safe. I really didn't care about her family, but I did feel empathy for the old woman that died—the way T's sister and family used her. I felt that she at least deserved to have a decent funeral. I thought about how Nana had taken in a four-year-old in her later life, when her child-rearing years were long past. It was the same way this old lady rescued her granddaughter from a monster—her son—and then raised her three great-grandchildren. After all she had sacrificed, all she was to her great-granddaughter was a meal ticket. Yeah, this lady deserved a decent burial, without a bunch of bullshit. So, I agreed to be there with some help.

I knew this guy named Burgess from my job. I went to Taft with him, and he ended up at Y.E.C. also. In school, he was a real thug and hung out with some real hoodlums. Maurice was in jail, so I asked Burgess if he would watch my back. He agreed, but said he couldn't get his hands on a gun. I told T and her mother that I had someone coming and everything was good to go. I didn't tell them that I got a gun, but I let them think I had one.

The day of the funeral, Burgess had a long steak knife and waited on the corner. I met T's family in front of the funeral home and acted like I had a gun. I met her brother for the first time that day. He was in and out of jail, a petty criminal, and he looked it. When they got out of the car, I motioned to Burgess, and he nodded so that they could see I was with someone. Then, I went inside with them.

The funeral went off without any problems. When it was over, I went outside and stood by Burgess on the corner. The family got into the limousine and waited for a few minutes. T's brother came up to me and asked, "Is that your boy?"

I said "Yeah." It looked like he was trying to see the gun I pretended to have. I quickly dismissed him and walked away to get in the limousine with the rest of the family. As we pulled away and passed by Burgess, I rolled down the window and said, "Thanks, man. I'll hook up with you later."

"No problem."

To everyone, I was the thug hero for the day. They thought I was ready to kill for them, if necessary. Boy, were they wrong. In the car, Tyrone asked to see the gun. I told him that I gave it to Burgess. I didn't even know this guy. Who was he to ask to see my gun?

Later on, I hooked up with Burgess and we smoked marijuana together. He pulled out some cocaine and took a sniff. He offered me some, but I declined. He started to talk about this woman he knew in New Jersey that was a dispatcher for a cab service, and that the cab drivers were always looking for some cocaine to stay awake on the night shift. So, he and I decided to get into the business. I had learned a few things when I tried to sell cocaine with Al, so I thought I could handle myself better this time.

Burgess said his next-door neighbor, Ron, knew some Dominicans in Fort Washington that sold some pure shit. He introduced me to the guy. Burgess and I decided I would put up the money, and he would have the woman in Jersey sell the cocaine from the cabstand.

Burgess brought his neighbor to my house, and the three of us took a cab to 142nd Street and Broadway. When we got out, Ron called over a Spanish guy that was standing on the corner. They seemed to know each other. The Spanish guy led the three of us up to an apartment in a nearby building. He knocked on the door with some sort of code, and the door opened.

Inside were three other Spanish guys, standing around the room with guns drawn. The one we met outside ordered one of his men to search us. The three of us were patted down, and then the head Spanish guy asked us how much we wanted. I had $200, so he told us we could get four grams of pure rock cocaine for that much. I thought if the cocaine was as pure as he said it was, we could cut it with four grams of lactose and make $600 profit.

The Spanish man pulled out a scale, called a triple beam, and put the cocaine on it. He weighed out four grams. The cocaine was shiny and had little rocks in it. The Spanish man wrapped it up in tin foil and gave it to Ron. That's when we got up to leave.

As I approached the door, I reached to unlock it to leave, but the four Spanish men raised their guns and started to speak Spanish, very fast, as one of them put his gun to my head. Ron said, "Wait, wait, it's okay! He didn't know! He didn't know!"

The Spanish man took the gun from my head, but the other three still had their guns pointed at me, at close range. He looked out the peephole, and then opened the door to let us out. It closed quickly behind us.

I asked Ron what that was all about. He said, "That's how muthafuckers get robbed. Someone opens the door from the inside, and then the stickup men rush in. They don't know you, and you went to open the door. They thought it was a setup."

The three of us took a cab back to Ron's place, which was right across the hall from Burgess. I had purchased the packing equipment and the lactose earlier, so all we needed to do was cut the cocaine and pack it in the little bottles.

I still didn't know how to cut, so Ron and Burgess did it. Ron's apartment was rundown, dark, and dreary. His furniture was ragged, and the apartment smelled a little. I sat back and watched them. From my calculations, we should have had eighty bottles of cocaine. The bottles would sell for $10 apiece, so Burgess and I should have netted $600 profit. I didn't think about Ron or what he wanted. In the street, nobody does anything for nothing.

As Burgess and Ron cut and packed the cocaine, they were also sniffing it. They also rolled Cooleys, which was cocaine and a cigarette with the filter removed.

As the night went on, a friend of Ron's came by. He started to partake in the cocaine as well. My gut was telling me that this wasn't going to work out, either; you can't sell a drug that you use, and Burgess used cocaine. I didn't know he sniffed as much as he did. I had only seen him take that one hit in the past.

As they sniffed up the cocaine, they also began to talk. Cocaine makes you feel intellectual. I sat back and listened to both of them and Ron's friend; I wasn't sniffing anything, so I was stone cold sober.

Ron was an ex-con who got out of jail about a month earlier and was on probation. He was locked up for some drug-related crime, so I was already out of my league. By the end of the night, after the cutting and packing was done, there were only forty bottles. Burgess, Ron, and his friend had sniffed up half the profits. I didn't say anything. I chose not to confront three men that were high on cocaine—anything could have happened.

Burgess and I went over the plan; he was going to New Jersey the next day to drop off the cocaine to the lady at the cab stand. I didn't care about what Ron was going to get. I figured he sniffed away any monetary compensation. Burgess said that the forty bottles should go quickly, so I should call him in a couple of days. I thought since I put up $200 that I should make $400. If it worked out, we could just flip it. The only difference would be that someone else would cut it, because I already lost $400.

I called Burgess three days later and couldn't reach him. I knew that something wasn't right. One day, Ron showed up at my house unannounced. I didn't even know him like that. I asked him what he wanted, and he said he needed to talk to me about something. I let him in, and he sat down on the sofa in my room. He began to tell me that Burgess had fucked up the money from the cocaine and sniffed up most of it. He never went to New Jersey. Ron also said he could sell cocaine for me at a club he hung out at. He told me to just give him another $200 and he would do all the work. I told Ron I would think about it. I wanted to catch up with Burgess first to see what he had to say. I gave Ron my phone number and told him to never come by my house unannounced again.

Two days later was Thanksgiving, and the whole family was by Nana's house, as usual. During the meal, the phone rang, and someone said it was for me. It was Ron. I told him now wasn't a good time, and I still hadn't talked to Burgess yet. Ron was being very persistent about making it happen that day. It was a party night, and the cocaine would go fast. He wouldn't take no for an answer. I finally said, "Look, I'll let you know!" and hung up the phone. I was getting a bad feeling about the guy.

The next day, he showed up at my house, unannounced, again. This time, he was with someone I didn't even know. Denise was in my room waiting for me, and the guy asked could he come in. I had to get ghetto on him now, because I had Nana and Denise in the house. The second he asked if he could come in, I asked him what the fuck was he doing here. I reiterated that I told him to never come by my fucking house unannounced again. He tried to talk, and I cut him off and said, "Look, muthafucker, I don't know you like that, and I don't know this muthafucker." I pointed to the man that was with him. "I don't want to do business with you. I don't trust you. So lose my number, muthafucker!" I slammed the door shut.

I still hadn't heard from Burgess, so I figured it was a loss, considering what Ron had told me. I wasn't going to try and collect my money. Burgess hung out with a rough crew, and I wasn't about to try and go to war with him over $200. I just took it as another lesson learned.

About two days later, Burgess called, pissed off. I thought, *I haven't heard from this muthafucker for over a week, and he's calling pissed off at me?*

I asked him what was up with the package, and he said, "Fuck that package, muthafucker! What's this shit I hear about you coming to my house with some niggers to fuck me up?"

I told him I didn't know what he was talking about. "I haven't been by your house since that night we brought the cocaine."

"You a lying muthafucker. Ron told me he saw you."

I said Ron was full of shit.

Burgess said, "Why would he lie?"

I told him what went on with Ron and me during the past week, and that Ron had told me that he—Burgess—had fucked up the package and sniffed the cocaine. I said I didn't know why Ron was telling him that shit, but I could prove that I wasn't planning on trying to hurt him in any way. I was just going to take it as a loss.

Burgess wanted to know how I was going to prove it. I told him that I would call Ron on a three-way call, and for him to talk to Ron and ask him about the alleged night I brought people by his house while I listened on the other line. Burgess agreed. I dialed Ron's number and listened on the line. Ron reiterated that I was by the house with three guys looking for Burgess; he even told Burgess that I knocked on his door, asking about him.

When Ron was done speaking, I yelled over the phone, "You lying muthafucker!" You could hear a pin drop over the phone. I said, "What the fuck is your problem, muthafucker? What the fuck you telling him that shit for?"

Ron stayed quiet. Burgess was listening carefully as I cursed Ron out for being a piece of shit. I told Ron he better tell Burgess the truth, or I was going to be by his house to fuck his shit up. He told Burgess that he was lying, and before he finished, I said to Burgess, "Now this shit is done. You two deserve each other." I hung up. That was the last of our dealings.

T's sister, Lisa, and I didn't get along at all. There were always some issues between us. I thought Lisa was always being condescending toward me because I was younger, and she was married to a man that she walked all over. She was on welfare, just like T, and her husband worked, so she was the same kind of ghetto rat that T was, scamming the system. But Lisa was what you would call "ghetto fabulous." She had a few more dollars than most people living in the housing projects because of her scams—receiving her dead great-grandmother's Social Security checks, being on welfare, her husband working, and only paying about $30 a month for rent. She thought that because of this, she was better than everybody else.

The relationship between Lisa and me was so volatile that I wouldn't speak to her if she was in the same room. I had no problem cursing her out in a heartbeat, and her husband didn't have a thug bone in his body. He worked for some rental car place, and wouldn't dare try to defend her honor by fighting me. Besides, he knew she was a bitch.

I think T instigated a lot of the arguments that Lisa and I had, because she liked that kind of stuff. I think she was also a little jealous of her sister, so seeing her get knocked off her high horse once in a while gave her great pleasure.

At my job, Joe, the black crew leader, became the crew leader supervisor. He was now my boss. One day at a worksite on 116th Street, Joe approached me and said, "I want to talk to you in private." There was another guy who helped me out when I did side work for Cook there also, and Joe pointed to him and said, "And you, too, in private. Let's go." Joe led us to an empty stairwell and inquired if I was doing work for Walter Cook.

I said, "Yeah, he calls me from time to time to do some repair work for him."

Joe was angry. He said that it was his side work, and told me to keep away from Cook. His exact words were that Cook was "his meal ticket." Howard, the director of the program, told us that any employees of Y.E.C. were not to engage in side work with customers of Y.E.C. So, what Joe should have been telling me was not to engage with Y.E.C. customers. But since he was doing it too, he was coming at me from a personal perspective, not a supervisor quoting company policy.

I asked Joe why I couldn't make extra money, too. Cook had plenty of work for the both of us. Joe told me, "Fuck that. I told you already that's my meal ticket. Got it?"

I tried to break it down for him again, to let him see that he was being unreasonable. I said, "Let me understand you correctly. What you're saying is that there's this big pie, and there's enough for both of us to have a slice, but you want the pie all to yourself?"

"That's right."

I was nineteen, and Joe was about thirty, or a little older. I would have expected that dumbass answer from someone my age, but I thought an older man would have been wiser. I saw that Joe wasn't going to be reasonable, so I became ignorant with him. I said, "Well, fuck that shit, muthafucker. Who the fuck made you king? If Cook wants me to do work for him, then I'm going to make the extra money."

Joe tried to act like my boss now, and he said, "Well, you're not supposed to be working for Y.E.C. customers anyway."

I cut him off and said, "Fuck that shit. You ain't supposed to be working for him either, so if I go down for working for him, then so do you."

Joe was upset that he was unable to bully me. "So what you're saying is that you're willing to take your chances with me."

I said, "Fuck you. Who the fuck are you? What chances you talking about? You threatening me, muthafucker?"

"I'm not threatening you," Joe said. "I'm just saying, if you want to go on with working for Cook, you'll be takin' your chances."

"Well, I'll just take my chances." And I walked away. I knew now that I had to do everything right on the job, because Joe would take any chance he had to fire me. I did notice something odd when this whole conversation was taking place: Joe was scratching his arm a lot.

Denise and I were seeing each other less and less. However, when we saw each other, we always had a good time. She had made new friends that we would hang out with, older people from work. One woman she worked with, Rosemary, was seeing two guys. Sometimes when I was with Denise, Rosemary was with Dwayne, and sometimes she was with Greg. I couldn't help but wonder if Denise was doing the same thing with me. Rosemary and Dwayne had an open relationship, and they both knew that they were seeing other people, but kept it on the down low.

Dwayne liked to get high. Once, I was hanging out at his house and became drunk on some corn liqueur he had, and when I talked to him, I would call him Greg. Every time I did this, Rosemary was horrified. I kept doing it all night. Dwayne didn't get upset. He knew Rosemary was seeing someone else, as was he. Later, Denise and I left Dwayne's apartment together. I was so apologetic to Rosemary, but she was still upset.

The relationship between T and me was a miserable one. On more than one occasion, she called Denise and told her things we did in an attempt to get Denise to leave me. This did cause more friction between Denise and me, but she would just curse T out and hang up the phone.

Once, T and I got into a fight in her apartment and it became physical. I wasn't beating her or anything, but she would come at me and I would push her away; she was the aggressor. One time, she ran out the house into the courtyard. She left her kids inside. I just left behind her and went to hang out with Jason.

Jason lived at Julie's, now. His sister had become a full-blown crackhead and lost her apartment. Julie's house was already crowded, but she never turned away a person in need. Besides everyone else that was living there now, she had Jason and her best friend, Helen, living there. Helen was a redheaded white woman who lived in the ghetto. She had a daughter from this Spanish guy, and she liked hanging out with minorities. In the ghetto, we don't care what color you are; we're all in the same boat together. Helen's daughter, Judy, was about my age.

At Julie's house, you could smoke marijuana, sniff cocaine, and drink in the open, but there were always people there to help you do it at your expense. The other thing you could get at Julie's was a plate of food. You may only get one pork chop or piece of chicken, but you would always get a full plate of rice and beans.

I walked home that night feeling good. I was on the Grand Concourse around 3:00 a.m. Some guy was walking in the opposite direction, toward me, and as he got closer, he started to look familiar. It was Will. Happy to see him, I said, "Hey, man!" I hadn't seen Will since that day he stayed with me when those guys tried to kill me over the game of basketball.

He said, "Hey, Russ! How you doing?" I thought it was strange that he was out there this time of the morning, and he looked different. He and I made small talk, and then he said, "Hey Russ, could you do me a favor?"

I said, "Sure. What is it?"

"Can you let me have five dollars?"

I knew the second he asked me for the five dollars, and he knew I knew. I looked at him with empathy. I remembered that Will was one of the popular guys that got along with everybody. As I looked at Will a little more closely, I noticed that his clothes were dirty, his hair was uncombed, and he had this look in his eyes. I'd seen that look before. Will was a crackhead. I felt bad for him, but I could never forget how he stood with me that day, so I went in my pocket and I pulled out a twenty-dollar bill. I said, "Here, man."

I never saw Will again, but that night, I went to sleep with a heavy heart. I realized if this crack shit could happen to him, it could happen to anybody.

About a week had passed since that incident with T. I hadn't heard from her, and I was glad. Then, T came knocking on Nana's door, and I answered it. She was standing there with two of her kids and this stupid-ass grin on her face. She said, "What's up?" as if nothing happened. I asked her what she wanted, and she said, "Come outside with me. I want to talk to you." I told her to get lost, that I wasn't in the mood for her dumb shit. She left Nana's door, went to her apartment, and called me from there. She threatened to act a fool in front of Nana's apartment if I didn't come up to her place to talk to her.

So, I went up, and T started to talk about the reason we were fighting that night. She was upset because she had made one of her troublemaking calls to Denise, and Denise basically told her to go to hell.

As T and I were talking, there was a knock at the door, and T ran to open it. It was two police officers. She said to them, "I have a restraining order I need served."

She had called the cops before I came upstairs. T handed the officers the paper. They looked at it, looked at me, and said, "Are you Malik Russell?"

"Yes."

They handed me the paper and said, "You are served."

I thought they were going to arrest me, but they said it was just a summons to appear in court. It was a temporary restraining order, and I needed to answer the allegations. The officers then left, and T was standing there with a big smile on her face like, "I showed you."

159

I couldn't believe this bitch was taking me to court over this dumb shit. I bet if I had stayed that night, she would have had me arrested.

The real messed up part was that she was the aggressor. She was coming at me. She was pissed off that Denise made her feel stupid, and she was going to make me pay. This was some real hood rat shit. She had all the time in the world to go to the courthouse and file this bullshit paperwork because she didn't have a job.

I was in disbelief about what was going on. I felt trapped in my situation. Every time I came home from seeing Denise or hanging out with Jason, she would be waiting. When I ignored her, she would threaten to act out in front of Nana's door. This wasn't an empty threat, because sometimes when I came home and ignored her calling me from her window, she would come and bang on Nana's door in the wee hours of the morning, or yell at my window in the middle of the night.

I went to the court appearance and told the judge my story. T lied, of course, and the judge gave her a thirty-day restraining order. T loved this, because she could start a fight and then have the police remove me from the apartment with the threat of arrest.

My anger was becoming a liability. Once, while T, her three kids, and I were walking down the street, T and I were arguing. She said something that enraged me, and I pushed her in the back of her neck. The jerk knocked her unconscious, and she fell to the ground in front of her kids. I panicked and dragged her into an alley so that no one would see her lying in the street. She was unresponsive while two of her kids cried uncontrollably. This brought back memories of Lamar, my mother, and the beating at the hospital. I thought, *Am I like Lamar?* But I wasn't; this was an accident. Nevertheless, her kids were witnesses to this, the same way I was a witness to the beating my mother took. I slapped T's face a couple of times and she didn't even know what happened. We got in a cab and went to her house. I thought she was going to call the police again, but she found the whole thing funny.

T started following me, and when I would leave Denise's house, she would pull up in a cab, jump out, and start to fight with me in the street, causing a scene.

Nana hated T. She knew what kind of woman she was from the very beginning, but always let me be. I guess she figured everyone is entitled to their mistakes, and you either learn from them or you keep making the same ones. The final straw was so severe that from that point on, I was willing to do anything to cause T the same misery and humiliation she had caused me for the past year.

During an argument over the phone, I was just fed up and told her, "I'm done with you, bitch, and I don't care what the fuck you do."

Nana would babysit sometimes for extra money. On this day, she had a little girl that lived across the hall. Nana's building had a wired glass door entrance, and the girl's apartment was right next to it. Her parents were still home. I was in my room and I heard a bang on the door. Nana went to open the door, and T started yelling, "Tell that muthafucker to come out here." Nana told her to leave, and then T tried to push past Nana to come into the apartment. I was still in my room when I heard the commotion. I went to the door and saw T trying to shove Nana out of the way. I was furious that this bitch would disrespect my grandmother that way. I ran to the door and got in between them. T saw the rage in my eyes and said, "Yeah, muthafucker, what you gonna do? This shit ain't done till I say it's done." I went to chase her, and she ran out in front of the building and picked up a huge rock.

By this time, the parents of the little girl that Nana was watching heard all the yelling. They opened their apartment door and saw where the commotion was coming from. I was standing inside the building by the glass door, and T was threatening to throw the huge rock. The little girl's father touched my arm and said, "Hey, man. Don't do anything stupid."

I just pushed his hand away. I was waiting for her to throw the rock, and then I was going to kick her ass.

I could hear Nana yelling my name, but I was so filled with anger that it sounded muffled. I was focused on one thing: getting that bitch.

T threw the rock, and it shattered the glass door all over the hallway. The sound was like an explosion. I covered my face from the flying pieces, pulled the door open, and grabbed T. I threw her to the ground and dragged her by her shirt collar from in front of the building into Nana's apartment. All the while, Nana was yelling, "Malik! Malik! Stop, Malik! Stop!"

I dragged T all the way through the hallway, into the back room of the apartment. When I got her there, she lay on the floor. I stood over her, ready to strike her with my fist when I heard Nana yell with an urgent tone and her hands clenched, "Malik, no!"

This time, I heard her and snapped out of the rage. T jumped up and ran out of the apartment.

The little girl from next door was a witness to everything. Her parents came right over to get her. I heard Nana telling them how sorry she was. I started to realize the damage that had been done. T just cost Nana money; those people would never let Nana watch their child again. Through the whole altercation, I didn't even realize the little girl was there. I understood her parents' actions. I would feel the same way. I apologized to Nana numerous times. Still, Nana wasn't as upset with me as she was with T. She saw the whole thing.

During the altercation, someone had called the police on T, and they had gone to T's apartment. The police didn't do anything. To add insult to injury, T had the nerve to call Nana's, and when I picked up the phone, she said, "You called the cops on me, mutha-fucker?" I told her I didn't, but she had the nerve to talk about calling cops after the restraining order incident? I told her how the little girl was in the apartment and how she cost Nana money. Her response: "I don't give a fuck."

I knew at that point that this woman had no pride, no class, no civility whatsoever about her. She thought this was funny.

That night, I thought long and hard about my life. Denise was hanging on by a string, and was most likely seeing someone else; the signs were all there. We used to call each other every day, and now three times a week was a lot. We used to talk on the phone for an hour or more about plans for our future. Now, it was just to make plans to get together. And when we were together, there was a pink elephant in the room all the time. We weren't best friends anymore, people who could tell each other anything. We couldn't tell each other what was going on in our lives when we weren't together. I still loved her with all my heart. I thought, *How did all of this get so out of hand? How did I ever get mixed up with this ghetto bitch?*

Here I had the perfect girl for me. She was smart. She was beautiful. She had class, and she treated me with respect. In the four years that Denise and I were together, I never laid my hands on her. I mean, we would have arguments, but never to the point that I wanted to strike or hurt her. But now, we didn't even trust each other. We loved each other, but there was no trust. I knew I had a big role to play in this situation. I was responsible for my own actions. Still, I couldn't help but think to myself that T was a twenty-seven-year-old woman from the streets. By this time, she was twenty-nine. She could run circles around me and Denise, especially since she had no class, no self-esteem, and no self-respect about her. It was just a matter of time before Denise was going to leave me. It was inevitable. The thought of it hurt me to the core, but I needed to do something even though I knew in the long run, it was going to cost me the only other person in the world I loved besides Nana.

T thought she had me trapped, but she didn't know anything about me. All she knew was I had a job and I lived with my grandmother. We never talked like Denise and I did. T didn't understand that I was abused by people all my life. It stated from the earliest time I could remember. She didn't know about the physical abuse from Emma, the mental abuse from Guy, the verbal abuse from my mother and Sister Hyacinth. T didn't know that I wasn't ever going to be put in a corner again. She didn't know that, at nineteen, my heart had become very hard, and the only softness in there was for Denise. And since I had just about lost her, my heart was harder. I had developed a vindictive disposition. If you hurt me or anyone I loved, I would seek revenge and get it, no matter the cost.

chapter FIFTEEN

I thought, *What can I do to hurt this woman the way she hurt Denise and me, the way she disrespected Nana, and the way she humiliated me in court? What can I do to a woman who has no shame, no conscience, no respect, and no moral integrity?*

It came to me fast and hard—the way a bolt of lightning snaps a tree in half. Up to this point in T's life, all the men she had been with were bums. All she had were sexual relationships with them, but none of them wanted her. They were her age, and they knew what kind of bitch she was (the fuck 'em and leave 'em kind). T didn't have a father, and she grew up watching her mother have three different kids by three different men, treating each with disrespect.

Yes, I had a master plan for revenge. Up to this point, the relationship with T was sexual for me and financial for her. I didn't even like her. She was just someone that was easy to have sex with. At eighteen, I didn't understand the magnitude of my actions. To T, I was a young sucker that she could pussy whip and suck dry financially.

Now, I was going to change the dynamic of the relationship. I was going to make her fall in love with me. I was going to treat her better than any man she ever knew. I was going to treat her better than she deserved. I was going to make her feel that the sun rose and set when she opened her eyes. I was going to make her think I loved her—that she had won, and Denise had lost.

However, as the saying goes, "When setting out on the road to revenge, you may as well dig two graves."

The plan was in motion, and I didn't tell anyone, not even Jason. I started to treat T better and pay more attention to her. In the process, I was paying less attention to Denise. I was extra nice to T's children, buying them clothes and taking them places. I brought T nice clothes and leather jackets to wear. I made her look better than she ever looked in her whole life. I even moved in with her. I kept my stuff at Nana's, but I had a couple of thing at T's house. I still saw Denise, but when I left her, I would go to T. Of course, there would be a fight about where I was, but T was being treated so good at this point that she didn't argue as much.

Then a new plot came into play, one not planned, but that would enhance the humility I would bring on her. One day, T needed to find her birth certificate, so she went down to the hall of records. The certificate had her birthdate, but it had her sister's name on it. T took the birth certificate and later asked her mother about it. Ella said that she was going to originally name her Lisa, but changed her mind, and the hospital people never changed it on the birth certificate. Just like any ghetto rat, this was T's chance to pull off some hustle.

The first thing she did was to go to the Social Security office to get a Social Security number for that card. Now, she had two Social Security numbers; one still had her sister's name on it. T suggested that we get married "in name only" so that the other Social Security card would say Lisa Russell. Then, she could use it without her sister finding out. That is, if some mail happened to go to her sister by mistake.

She did everything to sell me on this idea. I figured what the hell. I would only be ensnaring her more into my confidence. The marriage wouldn't be real anyhow, because she would be using false identification. She was still going by and using her other name. She

was also collecting welfare in that name, so what she was really doing was committing identity fraud. I thought, *Good. This is even more
to have on her when it's time to make my move.*

T and I went to get a license, and then to a friend's church,
where she asked the preacher to marry us. The preacher looked at
her very funny, like he knew something strange was going on. He
found it odd that no one from her family or my family was there,
and he also noticed the age difference. She showed him the marriage
license and he agreed, but it was with much hesitation.

The ceremony was odd, to say the least. There were no vows or
exchanging of any rings; he just took a cloth, tied it around our arms,
and said, "Okay, you're married." It was like he knew it was all bullshit.

T couldn't wait to start her new hustle. She started to get credit
cards in her new name, and she also started to do something else—
telling people in my building complex that we were married, as if it
were all legit. She even called Denise to tell her we were married,
but Denise blew her off and hung up the phone.

I confronted her about telling people, and she said, "They don't
know it's fake." I reminded her that she had said no one would
know. She responded, "Well, I lied."

She even told Nana behind my back. This wasn't exactly how I
planned it, but it was going to be just fine. Here she was, a woman
marrying a boy ten years her junior, and bragging about it like I really
cared for her or something. This, of course, was a dumb move on
my part, but I was driven by pure revenge. I let her think she had
the upper hand at all times. I didn't count on her telling everyone
that we were married, least of all Denise. But Denise was going to
leave me sooner or later, especially now that she was seeing other
people. I knew that until I was rid of T, she and I would never have
peace. T would do everything to destroy Denise and me, because
she figured with Denise out the picture, T would just pick up all the
pieces.

At nineteen, I couldn't see it, but my life was spiraling out of control. I thought I could handle it all on my terms, but like all young teenagers, I didn't know anything. Life was about to show me what a true fool I really was.

The job was going fine, and there was plenty of work. I had to keep my eye on Joe, because he was waiting for me to screw up so that he could take my job. I had been with the company for about three years now. I had my own crew and got along pretty well with the bosses. One day at a worksite, after we finished, one of the tenants of the building came out and gave the crew a six pack of beer. This was after work. I saw one of the guys drinking his can, but he was on his way home, so I didn't say anything to him. At that exact moment, Joe pulled up in the company van and spotted the worker drinking the beer. Joe asked the guy where he got the beer from, and the guy said a tenant gave it to him. The worker said, "It's afterhours anyway. What's the beef?" I was walking up to them, and Joe watched me while he was talking to the worker.

Joe said with a grin on his face, "The beef is you're underage to be drinking that beer, and your supervisor is standing right there letting you." He then got in the van and drove away. I knew he was going to take this and run with it.

A couple of days later, I was at another worksite and my pager went off. It was the main office. I called, and Joe answered. He said, "Remember when you said you would take your chances? Well, report to the office."

When I got there, Joe was sitting at the conference table with the director, Howard. Howard said, "Malik, I like you a lot, and you've done good work for us at Y.E.C., but with the information Joe told me, I'm going to have to let you go."

I couldn't believe it. I was fired. Howard gave me a check for two weeks' pay and told me he had no objections to me filing for unemployment. That was it. I was unemployed. Three years of hard work down the drain, but that still wasn't the end of it.

I went upstairs to the human resources office and got my check. When I came back down, Howard was sitting at the conference table by himself. I asked if I could have a word with him alone, and he said, "Sure."

I said, "Howard, I know what I did was wrong, but I feel Joe had an ulterior motive for relaying the information to you." I told him that Joe and I were doing side work for Walter Cook, that Joe had threatened me earlier about working for Cook, and all the rest.

Howard asked me if I would mind coming by the next day and confronting Joe in front of him. The next day, I came into the office, and Howard and Joe were sitting at the conference table again. I sat down to join them. Howard asked me to repeat to him what I had told him the previous day, and I did. Howard asked Joe if he was working for Walter Cook, and Joe said, "Yes." He fired Joe right there on the spot. I got up with a smile on my face and bid them farewell. Like I said before—when it rains, it pours.

I had no job now, and when I got home, T told me she was pregnant. This wasn't in my master plan.

I went on unemployment, and I was still doing some work for Cook. T really started to show her ass now. Her actions became bolder. I was still seeing Denise. T was going to try to put the nail in the coffin regarding our relationship. But before she did, she was going to blackmail me.

T asked me to babysit while she went out with some friends. I agreed, since I didn't have a job, and all I would do was sit around the house and smoke Marijuana. It was about 3:00 a.m., and she still hadn't returned. I was looking out the window when I saw this car pull up to the side of the building, and then drive out of my view. About five seconds later, I saw T coming around the corner. I recognized the car. It was Gennie's father, Steve—T's old lover. When T came upstairs, I said, "Where the fuck was you?" I wasn't upset that she was with someone else; I was pissed off that she was playing me by having me watch her kids while she was doing this. Also, Gennie's father never gave T any money—that's what she told me,

169

anyway. He may have, and she just said that he didn't. I figured, hey, if this bitch was doing this kind of shit, then who's to say that baby she was having was mine? Mother's baby, papa's maybe.

I told her, "Fuck you, bitch! Good luck with your baby, and good luck with your life. I'm outta here."

She said, "So, you leaving? Why?"

"I saw you, bitch. I saw you get out Steve's car."

"Alright. You can leave, but first, I'm telling Denise everything. The marriage, the pregnancy, the whole nine yards. And then you can leave, muthafucker."

"Why?"

"You think you just gonna walk away scot-free? Hell no! You want to go, fine, but Denise is going to know what kind of fucked up nigger you really are."

I just went to Nana's and stayed the night.

I went on with T, trying to put off the inevitable, as usual. I knew sooner or later, Denise was going to find out about everything, but I was a coward. I didn't want to feel the pain of losing her. I realized I loved her more than ever now, and she was slipping away. The threat continued every time I said I was done with T. She would even draft letters to Denise, along with a copy of the marriage license, and show them to me.

I was able to find another window job with one of the largest window companies in New York, Ecker Windows. This company was very professional, and I was making good money. I went to work every day and had a good reputation among my bosses. I was with them for about four months, and then my life came to a complete halt.

I was just tired of T's shit. I told her to go ahead and tell Denise, that I didn't give a fuck. I was at Denise's house one day, and there was a knock at the door. Denise answered. It was the security guard from downstairs. He wanted to talk to me.

I went to the door, and the security guard said there was a woman downstairs ringing all the buzzers, and that he stopped her.

She said that her husband was upstairs with another woman, and she wasn't leaving until I came downstairs. I just said to Denise that I needed to go downstairs for a minute. I headed straight out of the building and down the block. T was yelling and cursing at me, so I wanted to get her away from Denise's building. There were people that Denise knew out there, and I didn't want to embarrass her.

T followed me to her house and was throwing stuff at me in the street. She was telling me, "Yeah, muthafucker! This is how it's going to be until you tell her what's up."

I went to Nana's house and called Denise. I told her that T was acting a fool in front of her building, so I led her away so that people wouldn't see her and me fighting. Denise said, "Look, just come clean. Tell me what's going on. We can work it out."

But I was so ashamed of my actions and so cowardly, I just couldn't. I could hear the frustration in Denise's voice, but I just didn't have the courage to tell her.

T kept harassing me. Finally, I called her bluff and hung up the phone on her. That night, T called Denise and asked her to meet her downstairs. Denise did and saw right away that T was pregnant. T also said to her that we were, indeed, married—of course, she didn't tell her the details of the marriage. Then, they came to Nana's house to confront me.

There was a knock on the door. I looked through the peephole and saw Denise. I opened the door and saw T standing next to her, in the corner. Denise said to come outside so she could talk to me. I tried to get her to come in so that I could talk to her alone, but she and T had become allies. They wanted me to confront them at the same time, so that I couldn't lie my way out of anything.

That night, everything came out. I was pissed off at T and told her to get the fuck out of there. Denise and I walked across the street and sat on the courthouse steps while she cried. I was apologetic, but it didn't help. Denise demanded that I get an annulment, and said that we could work it out. I was glad to see that she just didn't dump me, but she was only talking off the top of her head. It was over. I wondered how it was going to end.

I took Denise home, and when I got back to Nana's, I sat down on my sofa, and everything hit me like a ton of bricks. I was thinking about the past two years and the way I hurt Denise. I knew she loved me, but how could she ever forgive me for all of this? My master plan for revenge was turning on me. I needed to talk to someone, so I called my uncle in Wisconsin. Instead of him answering the phone, it was his new girlfriend, Michelle. I told Michelle that T had brought Denise to my house and told her everything, and then for some reason, I just broke down and started to cry like a baby. Michelle told me that my uncle wasn't there, but he would call me back. He never did. I cried for about a half-hour, and then I pulled myself together. I thought, *At least T doesn't have anything over my head anymore.*

I stayed away from T after that and I was hanging out with Jason. Denise and I were talking, but it just wasn't the same. We were even intimate, but the pink elephant was always in the room.

I hung out at Jazz's house sometimes, because she let me smoke marijuana inside. I brought Jason with me a couple of times. He and Jazz would get high on cocaine and have sex. Jazz wouldn't let Jason come by the apartment by himself. The sex was usually followed by drug use. As time went on, Jason would always beg me to take him to Jazz's house, so I'd take him.

A couple times, I stood up Denise to take Jason over to Jazz's. One day, I called her to cancel a date that we had, and she said over the phone, "I'm done." She thought I was still seeing T, but I wasn't. I went by her house that night, and we talked. I tried to convince her to stay with me, that I was sorry for everything. But she said she was done. We could make love one last time, and then it would be over between us. I didn't believe her. Why would she have sex with me and then leave me for good? We made love, then she walked me to the front, said goodbye, and closed the door.

A couple of weeks went by, and then the Jason and Jazz thing faded out. I called Denise, since I hadn't spoken to her in a couple of weeks. I thought I would give her some time to cool off and get her thoughts together. When we spoke, she seemed a bit distant. I was trying to force a conversation, and asked her the big question: "Are you seeing anyone else?" She avoided it. I kept asking her, and she kept avoiding it, until finally I said, "Will you just answer my question?"

She said with a venomous tone in her voice, "Do you really want to know?"

"Yes."

"Yes. I'm seeing someone else."

I asked how long she had been seeing this guy, and she told me for a couple of weeks. I was just torturing myself at this point, but I asked her if it was serious and she said, "Yes." I asked her the final, tormenting question that every man wants to know. I asked her if she had slept with him, and again she answered with that venomous tone, "Do you really want to know?"

"I wouldn't ask if I didn't. So, did you?"

"Yeah. I slept with him a few times." My heart dropped, and she continued, "So, how does it feel?"

With every syllable she spoke, it was as if she were stabbing me with a dagger. It was as if she were getting her revenge for every ounce of pain I had caused her in the past two years, drop by drop.

I begged and pleaded with her over the phone for us not to be over. I cried to her, "Please! I'm sorry for everything! Please don't do this to me!"

She just kept saying, "It's too late." I even threatened to kill myself, but she knew I was bluffing. She knew I wasn't that kind of person. Finally, Denise said she had to go and hung up the phone. I was still crying my eyes out. I even called Grammy, crying and telling her that Denise was seeing someone else. Everyone in my family knew the situation, and Grammy just said that in life, sometimes these things happen. That wasn't any kind of comfort to me at all.

For several days, I tried to call Denise at her job. She was now working at New York University with her friend Tara. The answer was still no. I went into a state of depression. I didn't go to work. The bosses were calling me, telling me I still had a job if I wanted it, even though I hadn't shown up or called for two weeks. I couldn't go back to work. They finally fired me. I didn't want to leave the house. I was like a zombie. All I could think about was another man touching Denise, and her letting him. I thought about how we made all kinds of plans together, how much I loved her, how much we loved each other, and now I had no one to love and no one to love me. I was all alone.

My master plan for revenge didn't seem to be working out like I planned. At this point, the only person suffering was me. I had no job. I had no woman. I had a baby on the way with a woman I hated. I was depressed and had no plan to get out of the situation I was in.

This was the kind of situation T lived for. Everything she was hoping Denise would do was happening. Now, all T had to do was lie back and pick up the broken pieces. She would use the baby to the best of her ability to reel me in like a big fish on her hook.

was a broken man. For a couple of weeks, I would just sit at Nana's and think and think. I thought about Denise and her boyfriend. I thought about the baby that was coming. I thought about how I was going to make money. I called my father and asked him for a job. I knew it would be something illegal, but I didn't have any money, and I thought he would look out for me. My father knew I had a baby on the way, so he said, "Yeah. I got something you can do. Be out here at eight a.m. Saturday morning."

I caught the train out to Queens that Saturday and met my father at my grandmother's house. He told me I was going to be writing numbers for him at a numbers spot. He drove me up the block to a candy store on Sutphin Avenue, and we both walked in. There was a guy with glasses behind the counter, whose name was Vernon. My father told Vernon to buzz us in. Vernon reached under the counter, pressed a button, and the door to his left buzzed open. My father and I walked through the door, to the back of the store. There was a space with two glass windows and another door. Eleanor, my father's girlfriend, was behind the windows. She buzzed my father and me into another door that led us behind the glass.

My father said to Eleanor, "Show him what to do." Then, he turned around and left. Eleanor explained to me how the numbers racket worked and how to take the bets. The first thing was that a person could bet on a single number, a double number, or a triple-digit number. She gave me a long white sheet of paper and wrote down the numbers zero through nine across the sheet, each in its own box. She told me that when a person came in to bet, I would mark down how much money was on that number. The morning people would bet on the three-digit number, because that one didn't come out until the end of the day, and the bets needed to be in before 12:00 p.m. The single and double numbers would come out during the course of the day, one at 12:00 and the other at 2:00 p.m. The numbers came from the racetrack, and they were the last three numbers from the amount of money the track took in that day. I didn't know who was on the other end of the call. They just said the number.

Eleanor only covered the single action—that's what they called one- and two-digit numbers. She would drop off the betting slips for the three-digit number bet because the single action paid six-to-one odds, but the three-digit number paid 600 to one.

Eleanor stood by and watched me take bets from people throughout the course of the day. They would come in, and if Vernon knew them, he would buzz them into the room in front of the glass windows, where I took their bets. It seemed like pretty easy stuff.

At the end of the day, the phone rang. Eleanor answered it, and I heard her say, "Okay, okay." She hung up. She said that it was my father. I would be paid $30 a day, and only be on the weekends.

I thought, *That's only $60 a week!* He knew I needed money, especially since I had a baby on the way. Besides, this was illegal gambling. The police raided these places from time to time, so there was a chance that I could go to jail for doing this. Also, illegal gambling spots were prime targets for stickup men since they dealt in cash, so you couldn't go to the police. $30 a day felt like a slap in the face. And my father just had his woman tell me.

I didn't complain about it, though. I just said, "Okay" and thought, *This is better than nothing, but I have to do something else.*

Jason was working at some minimum wage security job, and I was hanging out with him during the week. Since he lived with Julie now, we were at her house. We would drink and smoke marijuana at the dining room table. The building complex and the block that Julie lived on became infested with crackheads and dealers. There were two crack-dealing gangs, and one lone wolf dealer by the name of Nesto. A man named Jose ran one gang, and a man named Danny ran the other. The crack each one sold had different colored caps on the bottles. Nesto had red caps, Danny had blue caps, and Jose had yellow caps. That way, the crackheads knew who they were buying from. However, if one group ran out, to an addict, crack was crack. It was like a deadly plague in the ghetto. People I knew from high school were crackheads. It made zombies out of people. Women sold their bodies for $5 or $10. Mothers were selling their kids' food. Fathers were stealing their children's televisions. It was ridiculous. You could buy a television for $10 on the right night. Everyone and their grandmothers were trying to sell crack. Very often, Jason and I would laugh at someone getting beaten down on the block for trying to sell crack on Jose, Nesto, and Danny's territory. Like I said before, drugs are a dirty business.

Soon, Jose and Danny's gangs went to war over territory, and it got ugly. As a result, one of Danny's boys was killed. In retaliation, Danny's gang burned down the apartment where Jose packed drugs. In the end, they both had to leave the block. It was too high profile now, due to the killing, so both of them left the area. That left an opening, and guess who filled it.

Jason and I decided to sell crack on the block. People already knew us. Jason had grown up with Nesto, so there wasn't going to be any beef with us. The customers were already there. All we had to do was supply the demand. There were two things wrong with this strategy: I didn't have a cocaine hookup, and neither Jason nor I knew how to cook crack.

First order of business was to get the cocaine hookup. We spoke to Nesto and told him what we wanted to do. He didn't have a problem with it. It was better that people he knew came in and tried to sell crack instead of strangers. Strangers would try to take him out of the game. Nesto knew if he helped us get started, he would also have us to watch his back. Up to this point, Nesto just packed up the crack and had the crackheads sell it for a commission of $1 a bottle. The bottles were $5, so Nesto made $4 a bottle and sold about 300 a day. He said that he would hook us up with his connection, but he wouldn't cook the cocaine for us.

Nesto gave us a telephone number and told us to call it the next day. He would tell the guy we were calling. When we did, the guy knew who we were and asked us how much we wanted. I was thinking that the cocaine was going to cost us at least $50 a gram, but that was for low-level street people who wanted to sniff it; we were going to sell it. The guy told us it would cost us $100 for four grams of pure cocaine, and he would deliver it to our location. I thought, *Oh shit! This really is a hookup.* All we needed was someone to cook it for us.

Julie had a crackhead brother named John. He knew how to cook. He was more than willing, since he knew he could get some free crack out of it. Just like that, we were in the crack business. Jason made the call, and the guy pulled up in a beat-up car, dressed very low-key. He delivered four grams of pure cocaine, shiny and rocky. We only bought that much because we wanted to start off slow and get the hang of things before we put any big money into it.

Jason called John, and we went over to his house. John smoked crack, but he wasn't a full-blown crackhead yet, so he had a nice apartment and was married. His wife wasn't home. Jason and I brought two large bottles to cook the cocaine in. We also brought fifty small plastic bottles with red caps to pack the crack in. Last but not least, we brought baking soda to use for the cooking.

We watched John as he put some cocaine in the large bottle, then mixed it with some baking soda and a little water. John put the mixture over a small flame on his stove and started to shake the bottle as the mixture agitated from the heat. After about a minute, the mixture turned into a round, hard ball. John emptied the hard-ball onto a paper towel. The ball was called a rock, and this was crack. Now, we had to cut it up with a razor and pack it.

Most crack dealers were selling $5 bottles. Sometimes, the crackheads were short on funds and would offer to pay in different ways, like oral sex. Our plan was to sell $3 bottles. We would sell them one for $3 or two for $5. Jason and I packed all fifty bottles at $3 each—that would make us $150. After buying the cocaine and the cooking and packing materials, we would break even.

John's wife came home just as we were finishing up, and she gave Jason and me a deadly stare. She knew who we were and what we were doing there. She also knew her husband smoked crack sometimes. John and his wife started to argue in Spanish, and it got loud. She went into the bedroom and slammed the door behind her. Jason and I just asked if everything was cool, and John said, "Everything is cool, but you guys can't cook here anymore." With that said, John pulled out a crack pipe and started to smoke some of the leftover after we filled the bottles. That was his fee for cooking it for us.

Jason and I went back to Julie's block that night and started to sell the crack. The bottles were selling like hotcakes. We ran out in fifteen minutes. We had the location, we had the hookup, and we had the customers. We were now officially crack dealers.

I waited until after the weekend, when I made my $60 from working at my father's number spot. Jason and I pooled our money together again, and this time spent $200. We were able to get ten grams this time. The more we bought, the cheaper the price per gram. We had a guy named Phil cook it in his apartment for us. Phil was a full-blown crackhead, and so was his wife. We let Phil cook it, and we would allow him to sell for us at $1 a bottle. We were now selling $5 bottles. We had 125, and we gave him fifty. That way, he would make $50, and we would walk away with about $550. We would make about $325 profit after everything. That's how drug dealing works—you work your way up. The more you buy, the more you get and the more you sell. Drug Dealing 101.

That night, the whole batch sold in about two hours. Jason and I knew if we had a big enough package, we could start to make some real money. The next order we made was for twenty-five grams. We figured that we could make our money back and pocket $400. After that, we would spend $500 and get even more.

After we received the twenty-five grams from our contact, we needed another place to cook. Phil was a big-time crackhead, and it was only a matter of time before he set us up to be robbed when the package got big enough. Jason knew this guy named Teddy from back when they were kids, and I would see Teddy around the block now and then. Teddy was a tall, skinny Puerto Rican. He told us that he knew a place we could cook at whenever we wanted, and would even cook for us if we let him have some crack. This sounded good for two reasons. First, the place was around Mt. Eden Avenue, away from where we sold; and second, we would have a stable place to cook, rather than having to go from house to house.

Jason and I decided to take Teddy up on his offer. We bought 300 bottles, and already had the cooking bottles, so we met Teddy on Mt. Eden and the Grand Concourse. Teddy was with this guy named Tito. He was also Puerto Rican, and I knew him from around the block. The four of us walked about two blocks toward Jerome Avenue, and Teddy led us into this apartment building. He rang the buzzer, and when a man answered, Teddy said, "It's me." Then, we were buzzed into the building. The four of us took the elevator to the fifth floor and got off. Teddy led us to an apartment down the hall and knocked on the door.

A short, fat, Puerto Rican man opened the door and said, "Come in." I was on full alert, since I didn't know this guy or Teddy that well. This could have been a setup, so I was ready for anything. The new guy's name was Jose. He lived there with his wife, but she wasn't there at the time. Jose told us that he smoked crack, but it wasn't out of hand. He continued to run at the mouth about how we could cook there anytime. I cut the conversation short and said, "Let's get down to business."

Jason and Jose began to cook the crack, and Teddy and Tito helped me pack it. We ended up packing 310 bottles. We left some crack for Jose, and the four of us left the apartment. Jason held the drugs. I was smart enough to know not to carry large amounts of drugs on me, in case the cops caught me selling. With just a little, I could say it was for personal use. It would only be a possession charge, instead of possession with intent to distribute. Jason had a bag with 300 bottles in his jacket pocket and ten bottles in his pants pocket. The ten were samples we could give new potential customers.

The four of us—Teddy, Jason, Tito, and me—walked toward the Grand Concourse. Jason and I stopped at a small bodega (a Spanish grocery store) to buy something to drink, and we were excited about the money we were going to make from this package: $1,000 profit.

Jason and I walked out of the store and headed up the hill with Teddy and Tito behind us. Halfway up the block, everything seemed to go into slow motion. I didn't understand what was happening, and then I heard, "Don't move, or I'll blow your fucking head off. Put your hands over your heads slowly and move towards the side of the building."

Jason and I followed the orders.

"Now put your hands on the wall and spread your legs."

We continued to comply. There were four white men, and two of them took Jason a few feet away from me and began talking to him. These were cops. I first thought they were stickup men, and that we were set up by Jose. The cop kicked my legs further apart to keep me off balance and patted me down for any weapons. He said, "Don't you move, or I'll blow your brains all over that wall. It'll be my third this week, and all it's going to cost me is some paperwork."

After about a minute, the two cops talking to Jason came over to me and asked, "Do you got some drugs on you like your buddy over there?"

I told them, "No."

They brought Jason and me together. We were told that we fit the descriptions of two men that were committing some cab robberies in the area. The cops called over the walkie-talkies, and a police car passed by. A person in the backseat looked at us, shook his head no, and the police car drove away.

I just knew we were going to jail that night. I was about to become another statistic—another black man sent to jail for selling drugs. I could just hear my mother now: "I knew he was nothing but trouble." Or Sister Hyacinth saying, "I knew he would be in jail one day." The loudest voice I could hear was Nana's. She told me a long time ago, "If you get caught doing something wrong and go to jail, don't call me to get you out."

It was all over. Another victim swallowed up by the ghetto.

Then, with all the things going on in my mind, I heard one of the cops say, "Well, fellas, this looks like your lucky day. We're not narcotics, we're robbery." He held up the bag of 300 bottles and said to Jason, "Now, what you're going to do is take this bag and throw it down the sewer."

The cop led Jason to the sewer. Jason threw $1,500 worth of crack down the drain.

Then the cop said, "Now, you guys could just go start over. At least you're not going to jail tonight." The four cops got into their unmarked police car and drove away.

Teddy and Tito came running up to us after they left. They said they saw the cops looking at us, so they stopped walking with us. They saw Jason throw the bag of crack into the sewer and asked us what the cops had said. We told them.

Jason and I left Teddy and Tito and went back to Julie's house. On the way, Jason realized that the cops didn't feel the ten bottles of crack that were in his pocket, so when we got to Julie's block, we sold the ten bottles before we went up to her apartment. When we got upstairs, we told her what had happened, and she told us how lucky we were. We didn't feel that lucky. That night, with the $50 we made, Jason and I bought some marijuana and beer, then got high and laughed about the whole thing. We figured we were out of the crack business for a while, since all our money was down in the sewer.

Everyone on the block heard what had happened to us. There was now an opening for some newcomers to sell on the block. Teddy was one of them. He was selling crack bottled with white tops. Jason and I saw Teddy and asked him who he was selling for. We knew he didn't have any drug connections. Teddy told us it was a Spanish lady who lived in his building on Mt. Eden. Jason and I were cool with it, since we didn't have anything to sell. More power to him, we thought.

That weekend, I went to work again for my father at the number hole and collected my $60. I thought, *I could end up in jail just as fast for doing this as for selling crack*. I felt like I was being cheated, and so I started to steal from the gambling money. This was not an easy task. If there's one thing about criminals, it's that they count their money very closely. I had figured out a way to pocket some money through Eleanor's laziness. When I first started to work there, she would check how much money was bet on the single number twice a day, before the numbers came out. She would call after the numbers came out and ask how much was bet on that number and what the payout was. I would simply wait until the number came out, make a fake receipt slip for that number, and take that money. When Eleanor called, I would tell her that there were more bets on that number, and then put that much in my pocket.

To make sure I had all my ends covered, I had to get Vernon on board, and I did it in a most straightforward fashion. I called Vernon to the back one day, after one of the numbers had come out, and I said, "Hey, pick a number." He said eight. I then handed him $20 and said, "Congratulations, you just hit the single number."

Vernon knew exactly what I meant, without any questions asked. I would walk away with about $200 every weekend, and Vernon with an extra $50. This went on for a couple of months.

One weekend, when I was done at the number hole, I went to hang out with Jason. He told me that crackhead, Jose, whose house we had cooked the crack at the last time, wanted to tell us something.

I asked, "Why didn't he just tell you what he had to say?"

"Jose said he wanted to tell us both at the same time."

We met with Jose at Julie's house. He had a bag with him, and he said what he's going to tell us should be worth something. I gave him a twenty-dollar bill and told him to say what the fuck he had to say.

Jose reached into the bag and pulled out two bottles—the ones we would use to cook the crack in. I said, "Big deal, cooking bottles. Give me my money back."

He said, "Wait! These are your bottles."

I started to listen as Jose told us that the night we were at his apartment, Teddy came by later, by himself, with a bag full of crack bottles with red caps on them and changed the caps to white. Teddy told him that later on, Teddy had gone back and fished the bag out. Jose said the crack Teddy was selling on the block was ours.

Jason and I knew it was true, because Jose had too many details about the police stopping us—he wasn't there. We asked him why he was telling us this. Wasn't he Teddy's friend?

He said, "Fuck Teddy! He didn't even give me some of the crack to smoke." Also, if we found out later, Jose didn't want us to think he was a part of it—since Teddy repacked it in his house—and then have us seek revenge on him. Jose gave us the two cooking bottles and left.

Jason and I saw Teddy selling in front of a building down the block, with two girls hanging around him. Jason asked what I wanted to do. I said, "We're going to handle our business. That's $1,500 worth of our shit that muthafucker's got."

184

GHETTO BASTARD

I was full of rage knowing that this punk was selling our crack and making us look like suckers. I told Jason to just follow me and bring the two cooking bottles with him. On the way to the building Teddy was selling out of, I saw one of our customers, Mack. He was fresh out of jail, so he was a rather big guy. I told Mack to come with me, and there would be a couple of bottles of crack in it for him. Mack was more than willing to assist, no questions asked, as long as he got some crack for it. I wanted Mack along in case Teddy had some boys with him.

Jason and I walked toward the building with Mack in tow. We saw Teddy go inside and followed him. Teddy saw us and greeted us in a friendly manner. "What's up, guys? What's going on?"

I said to the girls that were with him, "Beat it, get lost!"

They walked outside the building and looked in.

We were all in the lobby area. Jason pulled the two cooking bottles out of his pocket and said, "Hey, what's this?"

"Cooking bottles. So what?"

"Do they look familiar?"

Teddy said, "No." But the look in his eyes told it all. "What are you getting at?"

Before Jason could answer, I said, "Fuck all this back and forth bullshit, muthafucker. You know what's up."

Teddy acted like he didn't know what we were talking about. I told him Jose told us everything. Teddy tried to deny it, but this wasn't a court of law, and I didn't need proof beyond a reasonable doubt. So I said to Teddy, "Fuck all this bullshit. Run your shit, muthafucker."

Teddy said, "You ripping me off?"

"Run your shit. Empty your pockets."

He had about 100 bottles of crack on him. Mack was standing there, and I could see his eyes open wide at the site of so much. Now I had to worry about Mack ripping Jason and me off after we got the crack from Teddy.

185

I said to Teddy, "You're a piece of shit." I told him to run the rest of his shit. He asked me what I meant, and I told him to strip down to his underwear. It was the dead of winter. He couldn't believe I was making him do this, but he knew if he didn't, he was going to get a beatdown. Teddy stripped down, and the girls that were looking at us started to laugh.

I said, "Now get the fuck out of here, and don't let me see you around this block again, or next time I'll make you walk home naked."

Teddy exited the building in his underwear, and people were laughing at him as he walked down the block. As he got to the end of the block, he yelled out to Jason and me that there were going to be consequences for all of this, and then ran out of sight.

Mack stood there, waiting to see what he was going to get. He really didn't do anything, but I gave him five bottles of crack to keep him at bay. I was ready to fight him if necessary, but he just said thanks and left to smoke.

Jason and I went up to the roof of Julie's building to watch the block, just in case Teddy came back with a gun or some people. He didn't. That night, we sold the rest of the crack and had about $500. That was it for us in the crack game. We knew sooner or later, we were going to get caught by the police, or going to have to kill someone, or someone was going to kill us.

That weekend, when I went to the numbers spot, Vernon had some news for me. He told me that my father and Eleanor caught him stealing. I thought he was talking about what he and I were doing, and that I was exposed, too. I was wrong. Vernon was running his own scam with the triple digit numbers. The chances of someone winning the triple were low. It did happen, but it was few and far between.

Like the gambling saying goes, "The house always wins." Vernon's luck ran out. Someone had hit the number, and they had hit it big. A man that owned a bar down the block played the same number every day for $10; the man was owed $6,000. Vernon was off the day he came to collect, so the man went to Eleanor. He showed her the slip, and she didn't have a record of it. The man said he'd been playing that same number for the past year, and he had the slips to prove it. Eleanor called my father, and he paid the guy.

When Vernon returned to work, Eleanor pulled a gun on him and said, "You think I won't shoot you, muthafucker?" She cocked the gun and put it to his head.

My father stopped her and was sympathetic toward Vernon, saying to Eleanor, "The boy was just trying to run his own bank." My father said that from now on, Vernon would be working for free until he paid off the debt. I think he was getting paid the same thing I was—$30 a day—so that meant he was basically a slave to my father and Eleanor.

When Eleanor came into the number spot, she came right to the back and told me what happened. She also apologized to me. She told me that Vernon was making me look bad, because she noticed that since I started to work there, the money coming in on the weekend was not as much as it used to be. She had thought I was stealing. I acted surprised that she would even think that, but the gig was up. Now I had to think of something else to do, because T was about six months pregnant, and I didn't have any money for a baby.

I needed to get a job during the week. It was evident that my father wasn't going to do right by me. He was basically paying me minimum wage, and I was risking being incarcerated. Having a criminal record, I thought he would look out for me better, but that was a fairy tale. I ended up getting a security job working for a company called Integrity. This was a low-rate company that paid minimum wage. They put you in the most dangerous job sites, patrolling low-income housing buildings. The first place they assigned me was around Hunts Point in the South Bronx. This area, even to this day, is infested with drug dealers, heroin addicts, and crackheads. The company would hire anybody. I got paid in cash on Fridays. That should have told me something right there. The other security guards I worked with were bad. One was an ex-con, another was an undercover crackhead, and the third was a thief. To tell the truth, the complex needed to hire security for the security.

Everyone in the complex had a gun. If any of the security guards tried to intercede in anything, the residents and drug dealers had no problem pulling guns out and telling us to mind our fucking business. I almost lost my life there for some nonsense an undercover crackhead pulled. I came to work on a Monday after working at the number spot. I had my uniform on, and when I arrived at the security office, there were three guys standing in front of the building. I recognized one of them as the resident crack dealer. He was a tall guy, about two inches taller than me. The undercover crackhead's name was John. The dealer said to me as I walked up to the building, "Hey, you down with John?"

I didn't understand what he was referring to. I thought he meant was I working with him, so I said, "Yes, I'm down with John." Just then, the guy reached into his jacket and pulled a gun on me. I stood there in shock.

Then, out of nowhere, this fat guy I used to know in Taft High School named Laurence appeared. (We called him Rerun, from the old 70s TV show *What's Happening!!*) He said, "Clayborn, he ain't down with that shit."

The guy looked me up and down, put his gun back inside his jacket, and walked away like nothing happened.

I said, "What's up, Rerun? What you doing around here?" He said he hung out with a girl in the building. I thanked him for interceding, and asked him what it was all about. He told me the undercover crackhead, John, wasn't so undercover anymore, and the day before he and Clayborn got into some words. John had pulled a gun on Clayborn and pulled the trigger, but the gun jammed. When Clayborn asked me if I was down with John, he meant if I was watching his back.

I told Rerun that I just knew the guy from work. "I ain't down with shit. I don't even like the muthafucker."

Rerun started laughing and said, "Man, you almost got killed for some dumb shit." He then pulled out a joint. "You want to smoke?" I turned him down and told him that I get off at 1:00 a.m.

After work, Rerun and I hung out for a while. I came to find out that he knew my cousin, Mitchell. Rerun told me that Mitchell was a bad muthafucker, and he was there when he got shot. He said Mitchell could have gotten away, but when the guy pointed the gun at Mitchell, he just looked him right in his eyes and said, "If you gonna shoot, muthafucker, then shoot." As the night ended, Rerun told me to be careful around the area, because dudes were having shootouts all the time, and the security guard uniform didn't mean shit to them. I took his words to heart.

After that night, the other security guards and I decided we were not going to risk our lives for minimum wage, and we became part of the problem. We started to hang out with the female residents in the buildings. I was twenty years old. We would go and buy liquor while on duty and have little parties in the security office. I even had sex with two roommates. I would switch off day by day with another guard. I was doing all this while on duty. Women love a man in uniform.

Soon, word got out about us, and they transferred me to another low-income housing building on 149th Street and Morris Avenue. This time, it was in a more controlled environment. I was at a desk right at the entrance of the building, in view of the management office. Management left at 4:00 p.m., and then I was doing crazy stuff like drying wet marijuana in the facility laundry. The other guard and I would drink alcohol in the back office, and like before, I got familiar with some of the residents and had sex with one of them

Then, I was moved to a different location again. It was a Burger King right across the street from Union Station. Working there was worse than in the South Bronx. I had to deal with the after-club partiers, the homeless, and the thieves working there. The employees were all running hustles, and the homeless people would come in and harass the tourists, begging for money, and some just wanted to stay there all night. I didn't care about people's hustles. I just let them do their thing. I did have to fight a couple of homeless guys to get them to stop harassing customers, but they were mostly the drug-addict homeless. There were two kinds: one was homeless because they were junkies, and the others were homeless because they were crazy. I found this out from a particular incident. This black woman would come into Burger King, stay for about two hours, and drink a cup of coffee. The woman had a hat on and never caused a problem. She wasn't bad-looking, so I would let her sit there. I started to talk to her one day, and her conversation seemed normal enough. And then she said, "You have to be careful what you say. You know they're always listening." I asked who she was talking about, and she put her finger to her lips. She removed her hat and showed me the inside of it. It was lined with tinfoil. That was the last conversation I had with that lady.

One time, this tall guy walked in, and I recognized him from when I used to work in the dish room at Fordham University. His name was A.J., and he recognized me as well. I gave him some free coffee and told him to sit down. He was homeless. I asked what had happened to him. Why was he homeless? He told me all the sordid details. He started to smoke crack, and from the first hit he took, he was hooked and kept chasing that first hit. He lived in the tunnel under Union Station— it was like a little city down there. Most of the residents were either crackheads or heroin addicts, and it was a warm place to sleep. He offered to give me a tour of the underground city so I could see for myself. I took him up on his offer; I was curious.

After work, A.J. led me around Union Station and pointed out the many hustles that the homeless people were doing. Then he took me to the entrance of the underground city and asked if I wanted to go in. I saw the homeless people going in and out of this tunnel opening. I thought, *Nana didn't raise no fool. If this guy thinks I'm*

going in that tunnel with a bunch of homeless crackheads and junkies, then he's
both of the homeless types put together—a crazy junkie.

I told A.J., "No thanks." I mean, it wasn't like he was my friend
or anything. It wasn't inconceivable to think that he could be setting
me up to rob me. Being a former seller of crack, I knew he would
do anything for money. I told A.J., "Thank you, but I'm going to
take off."

Before I left, he asked me for some money. I gave him $10 and
never saw him again. He never came back to Burger King. I thought
he would show up just to ask me for more money, but he didn't.

I was working as a security guard for minimum wage, working
at an illegal gambling spot on the weekends, and I had a baby that
was due, by a woman I hated, in about six weeks, and the only
woman I ever loved in my whole life was with another man. There
was a lot on my shoulders at the age of twenty.

I started to hang around T more, because I knew this baby thing
was going to happen soon. I didn't want to be like my mother and
father were to me. I never went to any doctor appointments with T.
She and I were fighting just like always, usually about some manipulative stuff she was trying to pull. She knew I was going to be a
good father to my child just by the way I treated her daughter. How
much better would I treat my own child?

T was always doing things to try to make people think I was
some kind of monster and she was the victim. I can remember one
incident in particular, when she was eight months pregnant. I'm not
particularly proud of it, but it did happen—just not the way she told
people.

One evening, she and I were arguing about something, and I
went to sleep. I was lying on my back, and as any woman I've ever
slept with would tell you, I'm a very jumpy sleeper. I react in a defensive manner when awakened suddenly, and T knew this. I was
asleep and lying on my back when she attacked me. I jumped up
swinging, and I struck her in the face three times. She fell on the

bed and started crying. I yelled at her, "What the fuck are you doing?" She just lay there crying, so I got dressed and left the apartment. I thought she might try calling the cops again.

I went to Nana's. The next day, T's mother called me and said, "Why you got to go beat T up like that?" Her mother said her face was all swelled up and bruised. I hung up the phone. One, it was none of her business; and two, I didn't beat T up. Nevertheless, she was going around telling people that I kicked her ass. The situation looked especially bad because she was eight months pregnant.

That passed, and I was back at her apartment because she was still pulling the "I'm going to act a fool in front of your grandmother's house if you don't come up to my house" shit. I was still hanging on the block with Jason, even though we weren't selling crack there anymore. I was there a lot more; anything was better than going home to T and fighting with her. I remember during one of our fights, she said to me, "If this is a boy, I'm really going to fuck you over."

Jason and I were hanging on the block, and just like we knew it would happen, there were people who stepped up to take our place selling crack. It was like the Wild West around there. Every day, you'd see someone getting beat down because they were trying to sell on Nesto's territory. There were a couple of guys that Nesto didn't mess with because there were too many. He learned from Danny and Jose's gang war.

One day, Jason and I were just sitting around Julie's. I looked out the window, and on the corner, I saw about five guys standing around, hanging out. They weren't selling drugs or anything. On closer observation, I noticed that one of them was Teddy. I called Jason to the window, and he said he knew one or two from around the way.

I told Jason to follow me, that I thought I saw Teddy. We walked up to the five guys on the corner, and it was a positive ID. Teddy saw us coming, but didn't seem scared in the least bit. I thought that maybe he had a gun or something, but at the time, I was very young and stupid. I didn't care if he had a gun. If he didn't have it pulled out by the time I got close to him, he wasn't going to get it out.

Jason and I walked right into the middle of the group and just started laughing. The four other guys looked at us, confused. One said, "What's so funny?"

I stepped up and said, "This muthafucker is funny," pointing to Teddy. I looked at Teddy and said, "Didn't I tell you not to let me see you around here anymore, muthafucker?"

Teddy seemed to have gone and found some courage somewhere. "Who the fuck are you to tell me where I can go? You don't own this block, muthafucker. I can go wherever the fuck I want to."

Just as Teddy finished that sentence, I balled up my fist and struck him in the middle of his face as hard as I could, knocking him to the ground. The other four guys moved out the way. I stood over Teddy and said, "What did you say to me, muthafucker?" I kicked him in the ass. "Stand up, so I can knock your ass out, muthafucker."

I stepped back and allowed Teddy room to get up. He ran for his life. I chased him halfway up the block, until he was out of sight. The four guys he was with were all laughing at him. Teddy never— and I mean *never*—showed his face on that block again.

Jason walked up to me and said, "Russ, you're fucking crazy." By this time, everyone in the street called me Russell. In fact, the only people that would call me Malik were family members. It was like I had a whole separate identity.

chapter **SEVENTEEN**

I t was February 21, 1989. Jason and I were hanging out as usual. By this time, I had graduated from smoking joints to smoking blunts. Blunts are marijuana rolled up in a Philly cigar paper. Jason had taught me to remove the tobacco from the cigar and just use the tobacco leaf to roll the marijuana. After he and I rolled a blunt and smoked it, we went up to T's apartment. She was in the shower. I opened the door to let her know that I was there with Jason, and to make sure she was dressed when she came out. She said, "Malik, it's time. I'm in labor."

I told Jason, and we both started to laugh. We were both very high.

T came out of the shower and said, "Call a cab." I called, and Jason and I were still grinning and laughing at T while she was having labor pains. She got a little upset and said to both of us, "What the fuck is so funny? This shit ain't no fucking joke." Jason and I continued laughing and joking until the cab arrived.

When we reached the hospital, we all went right to the maternity department, and T put on a gown. Jason waited for me in the waiting room, and I went into the delivery waiting room with T. She wasn't acting like she was in all that much pain. I mean, this was her fourth child, and believe me, she was a pro at this.

The labor only lasted four hours from the time we left the apartment until it was time for her to deliver the baby. I went into the delivery room with T, and the nurses prepped her. I could hear the doctors and the nurses saying that it would be real soon now, and that T was dilated about nine centimeters.

While all of this was going on, I just stood there thinking about Denise. It had been about four months since I had spoken to her. Four months since I found out she had given her heart to another man. I know that I fucked up sleeping with T, but I never loved her. I never gave her my heart. I just couldn't stop thinking, while I was in that delivery room, that this should have been Denise. This should have been us sharing this moment. I heard the doctor tell T to push, and she pushed about three times. The baby came out with ease. I couldn't see what gender the baby was. As the nurses took the baby and put it on a table to clean it up, I saw it was a boy. I looked at T and said with excitement, "It's a boy!"

I had a son. I promised myself that I would do all I could for him. I would never treat him the way my parents treated me. I would give him the world. At that point, I was a proud father. All hate and animosity for anyone was gone. I was going to start over. I had a son now, and all I wanted to do was give him all the love my parents didn't give me.

The doctors wrapped the baby and gave him to T. They moved her to a room, and I went to the waiting room to tell Jason that I had a son. We were both overcome with joy.

I left T at the hospital, and Jason and I returned the next day. When we arrived, T's sister Lisa was there. I decided to talk to her. I was going to let the past be the past. I pretended that I forgot about all the dirty stuff Lisa tried to do, and I was kind to her for the sake of my son.

My father and Eleanor came to see T and the baby at the hospital. They were there when it was time to name the baby. I decided on Malik Leroy Russell. I gave the baby the middle name Leroy, hoping it was a gesture that would bring my father and me closer together. That somehow he would love me for doing it. At the time, he seemed flattered.

That day, I went to T's apartment and cleaned it spotless. She was a pig, and I didn't want my son coming into a dirty home. I went down to Nana's apartment and told her the good news. She was happy for me. Then, I went to the store and bought large packs of Pampers and some onesies for the baby. On the third day, I went to the store and bought balloons that said, "It's a boy!" Jason and I picked T and the baby up from the hospital in a cab. The first place I took the baby was Nana's.

I made a choice to try to have a normal relationship with T, for the sake of my son. I didn't want him to be me—another fatherless ghetto bastard in this world, left for the merciless streets to raise. I went to work, and I spent all my money on my son. I would have just enough after I got paid to get to work. I was still a security guard during the week and at the number spot on the weekend.

T saw how much I loved my son, and she saw the difference in the way I was treating her. Just like any ghetto rat, she took full advantage. T would demand that I buy my son things that I knew he didn't need at two months old. She insisted that I buy him a $500 crib. What did he need a $500 crib for? But I mean, it was nice. It was the type that would turn into a toddler bed later on, and it had drawers. I brought the crib. There wasn't anything I wouldn't do for my son.

T started to play games almost immediately. She would say she was going to the store and not come back for hours. She would come back with Jerry, smelling like alcohol. If I complained, she would say, "It's your baby. You can watch him. And since you're going to be here, you can watch the other kids, too." I didn't even try to protest. I just smoked a blunt and took care of my son. To argue with T was useless. All she did was use my love for my son against me.

The few times I could get away, I would hang out on the block with Jason. I'd tell Julie all the stuff that T was doing, and she would tell me that T was going to play on my feelings toward my son for everything that she could. I knew it was true, but I owed it to my son to have a chance.

The baby was about two months old when I called Denise to give her the news. To my surprise, she wanted to see the baby. I made arrangements with her to meet at the park on Jerome Avenue, while T was away. I took my son to the park in his stroller and sat on a bench while I waited for Denise. My heart was beating so fast. It had been six months since I last saw her, and I was more in love with her than ever.

I saw Denise walking through the park toward me. She was more beautiful to me than ever. I guess it's true how the saying goes: "Absence makes the heart grow fonder." Denise sat next to me and looked down into the stroller at my son.

She looked up at me, smiled, and said, "So this is what you and I have come to. This is the reason both of us are with someone else. Let me ask you something, Malik. Was it all worth it? Was it worth us?"

My heart sank; she was right. I couldn't even answer her. I knew I loved her with all my heart, but now I had someone else to love with all my heart, also.

Denise got up, kissed me on the cheek, and said, "Goodbye."

As she walked away, tears started to run down my face. Some even fell on my son's forehead. The way she walked away gave me the feeling that she was walking out my life forever. It was as if she was saying we couldn't even be friends.

I went home that night. I was living with T. I only had some things at her house, the bulk of my stuff still at Nana's. I smoked a blunt every day before I went home, just to be able to tolerate her. However, as long I knew my son was safe, it was bearable.

Most of the times I got away from her, Jason and I would just hang out on the corner, smoking blunts and drinking forty ounces of malt liquor. Old English 800 was our preferred; we called it Old

E. The block was just as wild and crazy as when he and I were hustling. We just sat back and enjoyed the show. He and I figured we weren't doing anything but hanging out, so what could happen?

Plenty.

One day, Jason, Tito, and I were hanging out on the corner of 171st and the Grand Concourse, drinking and smoking marijuana, minding our own business. Just having a good old time. Four Spanish guys walked up to us and started talking. Jason and Tito knew two of them from Julie's building. I had seen two of them around, but I didn't know them. Two were brothers. The four guys were talking about a confrontation that they had the day before with some black guys from across the Concourse. One bragged about how he pulled out his gun, and even pistol-whipped one. Jason, Tito, and I were just listening and drinking, not really caring about what they were saying. Two of the guys said to the brothers, "Hey! We're going across the street to the store to get a forty."

I remember thinking, *Why are these guys going across the Concourse to the store when there was one on this side, especially since they just finished telling us that they had the trouble with the black guys from across the street?*

The two Spanish guys started to walk across the street without a care in mind. I watched them, and for some reason, everything started to move in slow motion. As I looked more intensely, I started to see people come from the other side of the Concourse. They were coming from behind parked cars like shadows, creeping very slowly, until I was able to see them fully.

Then I heard one of them yell out, "What's up now, nigger?"

I saw the flash of a gun, and then the bullets rang out. I started running toward Julie's building. I could feel bullets whizzing by my head. I slipped and fell to the ground, but I kept moving, running for cover. Jason and Tito took off just the same, the three of us running in our own directions. The groups of guys were advancing across the Concourse as they were shooting at us.

One of the Spanish brothers pulled out an automatic .45 and started to return fire. By this time, Jason, Tito, and I were at the other end of the block, hiding behind the side of Julie's building and watching the situation unfold. As one of the brothers returned fire, the black guys from across the street started to retreat back across the Concourse. When the gunfire stopped, miraculously, nobody was dead. The four Spanish guys disappeared quickly, knowing the police would be around soon due to the gunfire. Jason, Tito, and I stood there laughing about what had just happened, not realizing how close all of us had come to death or becoming paralyzed from a bullet to the back, since we were running away from the situation. In fact, I think if I had not slipped and fallen, I would have been hit.

I noticed a young black kid walking down the street toward us. I pointed him out to Jason, and he said, "Oh, that's James. He lives on the third floor."

James walked up to us and said, "What's up?" He asked us if we were the guys that were standing with the four Spanish guys.

We said, "Yeah. Why?"

"Hey, sorry about that. We were after the Spanish guys. You guys were just at the wrong place at the wrong time." James was only about seventeen. He continued to tell us that he and his boys had trouble with the Spanish guys, and had been tracking them for about an hour before the shootout, just waiting for the right time to strike. He and his boys saw them talking to us and weren't going to do anything. But when the two guys started to cross the Concourse, the black guys felt they could kill them easily. James apologized again and began to walk away. He stopped and turned around, then said, "Hey! Who was the guy who fell?"

We all just started to laugh. I guess it was the adrenaline running through our blood, because in reality, there was nothing funny about what had happened.

That night, when I went home, I hugged my son and kissed him. I almost died that night. I almost broke my promise to him. I almost made him a statistic, a fatherless urban baby with a mother on welfare with four kids by four different fathers. I thought, *I need to get a gun.*

199

I didn't tell anybody else about what happened that night. I realized that the streets can get you killed, and bullets don't have names on them.

I needed to make some extra money. T was bleeding me dry. I thought it was funny that, with her other three kids, she had enough stuff, but with my son, she never had enough. She was also getting extra money in her welfare check, but that was for her, not for my son.

I gave Walter Cook a call and asked him if he needed any work done. He said to come by the office; he had a couple of repair jobs for me. I went to his office on Woodycrest Avenue, but he wasn't there. So, I waited for him.

Cook soon arrived and gave me a few repairs to make. There wasn't a lot of work, because he now had Y.E.C. doing a lot of his repairs. He was just throwing me some work to keep me afloat.

Even though Cook was throwing me some work, it wasn't steady, and money was still tight. Still, my son had everything he needed. Then one day, out the blue, Nana called me at T's and said that a man named Howard called about a job and left a number to call him back. I thought, *A job? I haven't filled out any job applications.* I got the number from Nana and called. It was for Y.E.C., my old job. I asked to speak to Howard, and the person said, "Hey, Russ, how you doing?" I told him I was okay and got straight to the point. I asked why he called me.

He said, "I'm not the president of Y.E.C. anymore, but now, I'm a consultant for them. They're in a little bit of a jam. There's a state contract that they need to finish, and they don't have the labor force to do it. I was wondering if you were interested in some temporary work installing windows for us. We'll pay you $10 a window."

I could install at least ten windows a day. I told Howard, "Sure. No problem."

Howard asked me how soon I could start and said that time was of the essence. I told him I could start the next day, and that I didn't work my guard job until 10:00 p.m., so I had plenty of time to do both.

When I went to the Y.E.C. office the next day, it was at a different location and an entirely different staff. Joey, the Spanish crew leader, wasn't there anymore. And of course, Joe, the guy that got me fired, wasn't there. The company now rented space out of a drug rehab center called Argus Community Center. Argus had a charter school located in the building, which Y.E.C. used for their work-study program.

The only person I recognized when I walked into the office was a guy named Vinnie. I knew him from when I first started to work at Y.E.C. a couple of years ago in the work-study program. I said, "Hey, what's up?" and we talked a little, reminiscing. Vinnie was a little older than I was, about twenty-two at the time. He was with Y.E.C before I started there, and he was there when I got fired. Vinnie stood out all the time because he was tall, white, and living in the ghetto. He was into heavy punk rock, and his dress was usually jeans, an old t-shirt, and a bandana around his head. But he sure knew his way around installing windows. In the ghetto, we're all on the same sinking boat, trying to get out of it.

Vinnie was now the boss, the crew leader supervisor. He had Joe's job. There was one other thing different now: there weren't any crew leaders. Vinnie told me that Y.E.C. was on the brink of closing down. He said Joey, the Spanish crew leader, started doing window repairs on his own and had a small shop in a storefront. If Y.E.C. didn't finish the contract for the state, they're going to close down due to a lack of funds.

As Vinnie was talking to me, Howard came out of his office. He said hello and greeted me with a smile and a handshake. He told me to come in and have a seat.

"First of all, Russell, I want to say I'm sorry about the way I had to let you go before. But I had no other choice with what was involved."

I told Howard there weren't any hard feelings, and that I understood. Howard explained the urgency of completing the project at hand. There were 400 windows that needed to be installed within two weeks, and he called a few other guys that graduated from Y.E.C. to help. The students that they currently had were not up to the task. I was anxious to get started.

Vinnie drove me out to the worksite on 183rd Street and Bathgate Avenue. It was a six-story building, and no work had been started on it at all. Later, a couple of other guys that used to work for Y.E.C. showed up. We were all anxious and ready to make some money.

The next day, the trainees arrived. There were about fifteen kids, but they were different from when the other guys and I were trainees. Back then, Joey would have us do the work and learn as we go. These new guys didn't know anything. They just wanted to hang out and play. The other guys and I didn't care; we were getting paid by the window, so we really just used them for garbage removal and as gophers.

About the fourth day into the work, there were rumors about what everyone was getting paid. I asked Vinnie, since he was the supervisor, and he said he didn't know. Howard and this guy named Steve handled the money. Vinnie just handled the worksites. He said he would call Howard at the office and clear things up. When Vinnie returned, he relayed that we were getting $300 a week. The other guys and I stopped work immediately. We stated that we were told $10 a window, and that Y.E.C. couldn't change up the terms on us now. The reason we were all working so hard and so fast was because we knew the harder we worked, the more we got paid. Vinnie called the office again and said that Howard and Steve were both coming to the worksite later on that day. They would straighten things out then.

We all agreed to go back to work until Howard and Steve arrived. Later that day, Vinnie called the crew downstairs and said Steve and Howard would be at the worksite in about five minutes. We all stood in front of the building, talking about what we were going to do if they tried to go back on the deal that Howard originally offered. Some said they were going to quit; some said they would stay and finish the work anyway. I was going to stay and finish the work no matter what they said, because I needed the money.

Soon, this old two-door car pulled up to the worksite. It was a red 1980 Datsun 210 hatchback. Two men got out of the car. One was Howard, who was short, brown-skinned, bald, in his early sixties, and wearing glasses. The other man was tall, skinny, light-skinned, about six feet tall, had a small afro, wore glasses, and looked to be about fifty—that was Steve.

When Steve stepped out of the car, before anyone could say anything, he smiled and announced, "Everyone is going to get the money they were promised."

That statement immediately eased the tension that had built inside us. Steve went on to say that he was sorry for the miscommunication, but it was urgent that we finish this building on time.

Later, Vinnie informed me what had happened and the new dynamics of Y.E.C. He said that the board members had made Howard step down as president because he wasn't running it properly. But since he had been there so long, they didn't want to just leave him out in the cold. Walter Cook was one of the board members. Steve was now the president of Y.E.C. Howard just wanted to get the job done; it was like his last hurrah before he left the company for good, so he wasn't promising anything to anybody but to complete the building. Steve didn't know about any arrangements that Howard had made with the workforce he assembled. Steve reprimanded Howard for making promises that he didn't intend to keep. Steve was an honorable man; Howard was more a politician.

Steve was a former college professor. He was black, but he spoke fluent Spanish. He wasn't from the ghetto, and his knowledge of it was slim to none. But he had this job running a company that dealt with high school dropouts, troubled, at-risk teens, working on low-income housing in low-income neighborhoods, and with a staff that was mostly compiled from former drug addicts funneled down to the program from the rehab that Y.E.C. rented their operational space from. This job was going to be his college on ghetto life and the people that lived in it. I was going to be his professor, because I had a PhD in ghettonomics.

(Well, maybe not a PhD; more like a master's degree. Jason had the PhD, but I would get it later in life, and Julie would award it to me.)

We were able to complete the building on time, and Y.E.C. got their funding from the state for the next year. I was very professional in my work. I came every day, on time, and respected authority. Steve took a liking to me, and Howard recommended Steve hire me fulltime, even though the position was originally supposed to be temporary. I had my old job back. Vinnie was my boss and we got along great.

Howard retired after that job, and Vinnie and I were the only two remaining Y.E.C. people there. Except Steve, the rest were from the rehab program, and no one but Vinnie and I knew the window business.

After the first building was completed, the company's state contract increased. Originally, it was a $100,000 contract; now, it was $200,000. It would have been more, but since the company completed the last one by the skin its teeth, the state wanted to make sure it was up to the task. The contract money included salaries, and every time Y.E.C. finished weatherizing a building and all the documents were submitted, the state would reimburse the company for materials and manpower. The company was nonprofit.

The new staff consisted of Steve, the president; a program supervisor named Linda, who was an ex-dope-fiend; a job developer named Roland, who was also an ex-dope-fiend; a bookkeeper named Willie; a secretary named Mira; Vinnie; me; and about thirty at-risk teens between the ages of sixteen and nineteen. Mira was a heavyset, pretty, Spanish woman, about twenty-five. She was not a past drug user, nor was Willie. Linda and Roland were not qualified for their jobs. They were just funneled down into their positions because they graduated from the rehab program, and Y.E.C. did the program a favor in hiring them. In return, Y.E.C. rented the space for cheap. So, in a sense, Linda and Roland were just glorified counselors telling the at-risk teens the path of destruction that drug addiction can lead you down. I had come to find out that while people stopped using dope, some still had what I called the "dope-fiend mentality." It's hard to describe. You have to witness it to understand, but I'll try my best.

A drug addict is someone who has been on drugs for an extensive amount of time. They hit rock bottom, go to rehab, and recover. However, during the time they were in their addiction, they schemed and scammed and hustled to get their drug money. They lived their lives manipulating and stealing from friends, family, and anyone who would trust them. They did this for months, and sometimes even years. This was the only form of living for the drug addict, because they couldn't hold down a job. Getting the drug of choice was their mission in life. Even though it's called a dope-fiend mentality, it doesn't only pertain to heroin. It could be crack, cocaine, or any other highly addictive drug. Marijuana users usually don't fall under this category.

After the addict has recovered, they have a feeling of entitlement. They think since they were able to kick the addiction they may have been on for years, and are now living life like the rest of the world, that they have done something special. In reality, they didn't do anything special. The addict got to drop out of the world and get high all day, while the rest of the human race went to work every day and took care of their responsibilities. Now that they decided to stop wasting their lives getting high and rejoin the world, the world is supposed to put them on a pedestal for not getting high anymore?

What often happens after rehab is that the addict will refer to themselves as recovering, meaning that they still crave the drug, but fight the temptations to use. Now, the reason I label them with dope-fiend mentality is because they bring the same scamming, scheming, and manipulating they mastered while on drugs into the workplace or relationships, even to the point of bragging. You may hear a recovering addict say, "I had a $200 a day habit" and then glorify some past scheme that they pulled off. Often, a recovering addict can easily find a job counseling other recovering addicts, because let's just say game knows game.

Linda and Roland fit this description right down to the last detail.

Vinnie and I were responsible for going out and measuring the windows for projects and assessing the buildings' other weatherization needs, like weather stripping or boiler replacement. Vinnie would order the windows and other materials, and price the cost of the projects. Once everything was delivered to a job site, Vinnie and I were responsible for training the teens in the program to make sure the job was completed and quality was assured.

Since I had this job fulltime now, and it was paying me about $14 an hour, I let the weekend job at my father's number spot go. I didn't want to take the chance of getting arrested and losing this job again. After a couple of weeks more, I let the security guard job go as well, but I still did some side work for Cook.

Money started to come in, and things were looking up for me in my professional life. As far as my personal life was concerned, I was at rock bottom. I was with a woman I didn't love, much less like. The woman I loved was with another man. And I had no strategy for my life whatsoever. I was still dedicated to my son, and the more money I made, the more things T would find to spend it on. Of course, I never saw any of the things that T said the baby needed so desperately.

After work, I wouldn't even go home to T's; I would go and hang out with Jason at Julie's. We would smoke and drink our forties. Jason had gotten this new job as an undercover detective working at the Woolworth's chain. The stores were like mini Wal-Mart's with counter diners inside of them. Jason walked around in plainclothes and caught shoplifters. After work, we would laugh about all the people he caught that day.

Jason was seeing Jerry sometimes, and the four of us—Jerry, Jason, T, and I—would go hang out at a local bar or something. I wouldn't take the women anyplace classy after the episode they pulled at the rotating bar. It was strictly ghetto bars for the ghetto rats. Jerry was like T. They were ghetto best friends, but their relationship was based on both being on welfare, having several children, and having no jobs. They were the women that sat in front of the building complex, getting in everyone else's business. They would talk about everyone else, and then, when they were with other people, they would talk about each other. These women were older than Jason and me. I was twenty-one, Jason twenty-two; T thirty-one, and Jerry about the same.

I did notice something odd about Jerry when she was drunk: she was somewhat touchy-feely with me. It wasn't something that would stand out, but I remember when the four of us were drinking at some bar on 149th Street and Walton Avenue with T's mother. Jerry was drunk and doing the touchy-feely thing, and I heard Ella say to T, "You better watch your man" as she looked at Jerry.

Jason bought Jerry some keepsake bracelet to wear. It was nothing expensive, but to a ghetto rat, if a man spent money on her for something other than alcohol or drugs, they thought the man was hooked. Jason wasn't hooked; he was just making her think that way so he could keep having sex with her without having to buy her drinks or cocaine.

During this period, I wasn't seeing any other woman. I was just in limbo, as far as T was concerned. I didn't want to do anything to jeopardize being with my son. However, T didn't feel the same way.

She thought she was going to play me. There were a couple of incidents that stood out, and I knew afterward that it was just a matter of time before everything would come to an end.

One day, T told me that she was going out and asked if I could watch her three children; she was taking my son with her. I said that was cool. T left, and about an hour later, I got dressed to go buy some marijuana. This was in the middle of the afternoon, and the kids were watching television, so I told them I would be right back and not to answer the door. I never asked T where she was going, and I really didn't care. I was just going to be in the bedroom smoking and relaxing.

Up to this point, from when my son was born about six or seven months ago, I was the ideal man. I wouldn't come home straight from work, but I didn't mess around with other women. I came home every day. When I got paid, I would buy groceries and give T some money. I wasn't a happy man, but I was the best man that woman ever had. I was the type of man she would brag about to the other ghetto rat friends of hers, whose own men had no jobs and were waiting to get their welfare checks and food stamps.

I left the house and walked to the marijuana spot on 149th and Walton Avenue, which was about nine blocks from the apartment. I bought three dime bags and headed back to the apartment. I walked down Walton, and about five blocks down, I looked across to the other side of the street and saw a hatchback stopped on the corner. This guy was leaning against the car with a woman that had a baby stroller. She was standing in a flirtatious manner. They were talking and smiling at each other in their own little world. As I got closer and their images became more defined, I realized it was T and Gennie's father, Steve.

It took a minute to comprehend what I was seeing. I stood across the street, watching them for a minute to see how they were acting around each other. Up to this point, T always told me what a piece of shit Steve was, and that he never wanted to give her any money for Gennie. I started to believe that maybe he was giving her money, and she was lying, all the while asking me for money for Gennie. The real disturbing part was that she had this little three-year-old girl calling me Daddy. So many thoughts came to my mind, but none of jealousy. I thought, *Why is she out here with my son, talking with this guy? Why didn't she just bring Gennie?* The other erroneous part of this situation was that I loved that little girl.

They had no idea I was there. I started to cross the street to confront the two of them—not to fight, but to get the real story. T wasn't worth fighting for. Who did she think she was, Denise? When Steve saw me, he jumped in his car and sped off with his tires spinning. I looked at T, and she had this grin on her face like it was funny. I just looked at her, said, "You are one fucked up bitch," and walked away. When I got back to the apartment, I rolled a blunt and smoked it. I wasn't mad; I felt like a fool.

T came home about an hour later and said that she was walking from her mother's when Steve drove by, stopped the car, and got out to talk to her about Gennie. T didn't realize that I had been watching them for about ten minutes and knew that the conversation wasn't about Gennie.

I played it off like I wasn't upset, to give her a false sense of security. I wanted her to think I loved her. She tried to reassure me, saying, "You know I love you, right baby?" What T didn't realize was that I wasn't the eighteen-year-old she manipulated three years ago. I was twenty-one now, and a little more seasoned in the habits of the ghetto rat.

I didn't want to lose my son. I didn't want him calling another man Daddy. I didn't want him not to grow up around me. I was hoping that I could withstand all of T's degenerate ways so that my son would grow old enough for him and me to have a relationship. Right now, he was only about seven months old, and he didn't know me from Tom, Dick, or Steve.

The second incident was more cunning than the first. I let the other one go. All I wanted was to be able to love my son. A couple of months had passed, and the job was still going well. I was doing my same routine. I would go hang out at Julie's with Jason after work and smoke and drink. I noticed that Jason had been acting strangely with me for about a week. Finally, I said, "Yo, mutha-fucker! What's up with you?"

Jason said to me, "She didn't tell you?"

"She who?"

"T didn't tell you what happened?"

"Tell me what?"

Jason said, "Sit down. I need to tell you something." I sat down at the table in Julie's vestibule area and listened to what he had to say. Jason lit a cigarette and started to speak. "When I was at work, T walked into the store with another man. She didn't see me, and I followed her and the guy around the store. Then, she and the guy sat down at the food counter and ordered something to eat. When they were almost done, I walked up to the counter and said hi to her. She tried to play it off, but she did have a surprised look in her eyes. She introduced the guy as her godfather, but she didn't know that I had been following them around the store and saw the way they were acting. They were being very flirtatious and smiling in each other's face."

I asked Jason when this happened, and he said about two weeks ago.

"Two weeks! Why the fuck didn't you tell me?"

Jason said he was trying to give her the opportunity to tell me herself, since she knew he saw her. "I was waiting for you to say something and then talk about it with you, but you never said any-thing and time passed. I knew if she told you, you would have said something. Since you didn't, I just had to let you know."

I said, "Okay, thanks man. But next time some shit like that happens, you let me know what the fuck is going on." I thought, *What a foul bitch. She didn't even show a hint of guilt being caught by my best friend.* I hadn't even suspected, in the past two weeks, that something had happened. The only thing was that Jason and Julie were acting strangely.

210

I wasn't jealous, I was angry. All I do for this bitch and her kids, and this bitch is running around during the day, making me look like a fool in front of my friends and where I live. I say that last part because the other ghetto rats were doing the same things to their men. While some of their men were at work, the ghetto rats had all day to do their dirt because they didn't have jobs and their kids were at school. I didn't even want to argue with T about the incident. She must have figured that if Jason didn't tell me that night, he wasn't going to say anything at all, and neither would she.

chapter **EIGHTEEN**

I called Nana and asked her if I could come back home. I needed a break. Nana said, "Sure," and while T was out, I packed what few things I had at T's and went down to Nana's. I didn't even say anything to T. When she got home, I was just gone. She didn't know I took my stuff, so it took a day of me not coming home for her to call Nana's looking for me.

The phone rang and I picked it up. T wanted to know where my stuff was and what was going on. I told her to figure it out, and she acted dumbfounded. "Figure what out?"

I said, "Look, bitch! I'm not playing your fucking mind games. If you can't figure it out, why don't you go ask that muthafucker you was having lunch with."

She paused for a moment and said, "That fucking Jason. He's a troublemaker. I'm going to curse his fucking ass out. He needs to mind his fucking business."

Just like this manipulative ghetto rat, trying to take the attention off her actions.

T continued with her tirade, saying, "He knows how you are. Why would he tell you that shit? Fuck that muthafucker. Wait until I see him, just wait."

"Whatever, bitch. Just leave my ass alone. I'm tired of your bull-shit." I hung up the phone on her. I didn't even ask her who the guy was; I didn't really care. The only things I cared about were her making a fool out of me and my son. If I broke up with her now, what would it be like with him? I knew she would use him as a weapon against me. She knew how much I loved him, and he was her meal ticket.

I called Jason as soon as I hung up the phone and told him what T had said. I told him to just curse her ass out if she called. Fuck her. But Jason wasn't that type of guy to curse out another man's woman. I was, but he wasn't.

That happened at the beginning of the week, and payday Friday was coming up. Staying back at Nana's was a break. I was able to rest mentally and gather my thoughts. T didn't call or bother me, but I knew by Friday, she would be calling or showing up in front of Nana's door and starting her same old bullshit. Then, out of the blue, the thought came to me to call Denise. It had been at least six months since I had spoken to her or seen her. In fact, the last time was when she kissed me on the cheek and walked away in the park. I dialed her number, and when she answered the phone, her voice was like a breath of fresh air. We started to talk, and it was like old times. It was like when we first met.

Then the question just came from her mouth: "Do you want to get away for the weekend?" She told me that she had gotten her driver's license, and she could rent a car and go somewhere.

I thought *Hell yeah*. Then I thought *What about her boyfriend?* But I really didn't care. *Fuck him!*

That Friday, Denise rented a car, and we went away to Rye, New York for the weekend. I met her at her house, and she let me drive. When I saw her, she was more beautiful than ever. She seemed a little more mature and a little more confident. We stayed at this hotel called the Courtyard Inn by Marriott. That weekend, we went out to eat, we made love, and we talked like we were best of friends. Not once did Denise or I mention the other people in our lives. I knew the other person was still in her life, because she didn't say she was single.

During our many conversations that weekend, Denise mentioned some trouble she was having. She wasn't asking me for any help; she was just telling me about the situation. Tara had gotten her caught up in this pyramid scheme, and Denise borrowed $800 from her job. When it was time to receive her portion of the money, the woman whose turn it was to give up the money started to act shady and refused to give Denise anything back. Tara knew the lady, but Denise never met her. When Denise called to ask about the money, the lady became very indignant with her. Now, she was out $800 and still had to pay her job back. I asked if she had the woman's address. She didn't, but Tara did. I told Denise that when we got back, I would call her to see if I could help her out. I thought, *Her new boyfriend must be a punk, because if she was still my woman, she would have her money back already.*

The weekend was over too fast, and I knew we had to part soon. I asked Denise if we could do this again, because I had a wonderful time and I missed her. She said that we could. I told her how much I loved her and that I never stopped. I told her I was sorry for anything and everything that I ever did to hurt her, but without mentioning T. I looked in her eyes and could see that she believed me. I could see that she still loved me, but it was like a double-edged sword, because I knew she also loved another. I thought that this was a start. She didn't hate me, and she still had some love for me.

When that weekend was over and I had to part with her, it was like losing her all over again. The thoughts of her with another man were unbearable. For the past six months, I had thought about her, but not about her being with another man. It was renewed torture.

When I got back to Nana's, she told me that T had been calling all weekend and had come by looking for me. Nana lied and said she didn't know where I was. Nana knew everything, because she was the one taking my messages, and I told her that I was going away with Denise for the weekend. Nana liked Denise. At first, she just didn't like T. But after that incident when she threw the rock, broke the hallway door, and cost her that babysitting gig, Nana hated her. She never showed it or said anything, but I knew.

That Monday, when I got home, there was a knock at the door. It was T. She had seen me from her window going to Nana's. When

214

I opened the door, she started her shit right away, trying to swing at my head when the door opened. "Where you been all weekend, muthafucker?"

I told her, "None of your fucking business."

"We're married, muthafucker. You just don't disappear and not let me know where you're going."

I said, "Married? Bitch, you must be falling for your own bullshit. You know that marriage bullshit is just that. If we're married, why isn't the name on my son's birth certificate Lisa Russell?" I had her there. She was able to pull the married card with Denise because Denise didn't know the details, but I knew that she was committing identity fraud and the marriage was invalid. My son was a ghetto bastard, just like I was.

T said, "So what? Your son's supposed to do without now?"

She still hadn't said who the guy was that Jason saw her with. So I said, "Why don't you ask that muthafucker that you were with for some money? Or better yet, why don't you go and meet Steve somewhere and have him give you a few dollars, bitch?"

T was furious, and she told me again that she was going to let Jason know what's up. But she still wouldn't say who that guy was.

I told her that I wasn't giving her any more cash. I also told her to let me know what my son needed, and that I would buy it myself. She tried to argue that she wanted the cash because sometimes she didn't know what he needed—she would just buy it as she saw it.

"Too bad. That's the way it's going to be from now on."

She stormed away from Nana's door. "Alright! We'll see, muthafucker."

I knew it was just a matter of time before she came back with some other bullshit. But for now, I was just relishing the weekend that I had with Denise.

I called Denise the next day to follow up with her about that situation she was having. I asked her if there was any progress, and she said there wasn't. I asked for Tara's phone number and told her I would get back to her. I called Tara the next day. I knew she was a more streetwise person than Denise, and if this woman had any affiliation with Tara, the likelihood was that she was streetwise as well. And by streetwise, I mean a ghetto bitch.

Tara told me that she spoke with the woman, and the woman took the money from everybody when it was her turn. But when it was her turn to give back the money, she said she didn't want to do it anymore and she was keeping it. If you don't know what a pyramid scheme is, it relies on everybody staying in the scheme and bringing more people into the group. I remember Denise taking me somewhere with Tara before we broke up. It was a pyramid thing, but of course, they don't call it a pyramid scheme. It's played out like some kind of foolproof investment, but the one thing I remember about this meeting was that a fight broke out. I figured if people were fighting about money, then it wasn't foolproof. I remember telling Denise that we weren't going to do it, but I guess when we broke up, she decided otherwise.

I asked Tara if she had the woman's address. She gave it to me along, with her phone number. Then I asked Tara if she knew where the woman worked and if she had her job number. Tara gave me all the information I requested. I think the woman's name was Janet. I called Janet and told her I was an acquaintance of Denise's. I asked her about the money situation, and she played dumb and acted like she didn't know what I was talking about. She even acted like she didn't know who Denise was. I asked her if she knew Tara, and she said she did, but she didn't know Denise. She said she didn't owe anybody any money. I told her I would be calling her back as soon as I got more information, but I didn't tell her my name.

I called Tara back that night. Tara, being her ghetto self, said, "Look, Russ, this bitch knows what the fuck is going on."

I told Tara, "Okay. That was all I needed to know."

I had given Janet the benefit of the doubt and a chance to do the right thing. But like all ghetto rats, she thought she could manipulate everybody.

216

I called Denise the next day and asked her if she had ever met the woman. Denise said she had. So that was another lie the woman told me. Besides, if she met Denise, she knew that Denise wasn't a ghetto bitch. She must have figured Denise wouldn't do anything about it. I knew just how to handle this bitch. I waited a couple more days, so that Janet would get a false sense of security.

I called her again and got right to the point. "This is Denise's acquaintance."

She said, "So what do you want? I already told you I don't owe anybody any money." She had an attitude in her voice like she didn't feel like being bothered with me.

I spoke to her in a way that ghetto rats understand. "Look, bitch, I want you to listen. I want to make sure you understand me loud and clear, because there ain't gonna be no more phone calls. That money Denise gave you was my money, and I ain't gonna let some lowlife bitch like you rip me off. I know where you live. I know where you work. In fact, I know everything I need to know about you, so if Denise don't have that $800 you owe her by Friday, your ass is going to be in the hospital on Saturday. When you get out of the hospital, if she don't get her money, you gonna be making a return trip. I don't care who you tell. You can tell your boyfriend. You can tell your daddy, or you can call the cops if you want. But if anybody goes near Denise about this, you're not going to be going to the hospital—you're going to be going to the morgue. I know you. You know nothing about me. Now, you have until Friday, and like I said, there will be no more phone calls. If Denise doesn't have her money by Friday, you won't even see it coming. You'll just wake up in the hospital. Now, try me, bitch. I don't care about anybody else's money. You keep that shit, bitch, but Denise better get hers."

I hung up the phone.

I didn't call Denise or Tara back. I gave the woman until Friday so she could get a paycheck, in case she had spent the money. I

hoped the lady didn't think I was bluffing, because I wasn't. If anybody did anything to Denise, I would have had no problem putting
them in the ground.

Denise called me on Saturday and asked what I said to the
woman. I asked her, "Why? Did you get your money?"

Denise said the woman gave her the $800 and was so apologetic.
Denise even apologized to the woman about me. That's how Denise
was—humble. She knew I probably used some thug tactics. She
didn't want to have to resort to that, but it got the job done.

My job was growing, but it was in its infancy compared to when
I started as a trainee. Y.E.C. didn't even have a company vehicle at
this point. Staff would use their personal vehicles, and the company
would reimburse them for gas. The students would take the train to
the job site, and so did the crew leaders. The only staffers that had
cars were Linda and Steve. Linda would take the reimbursement,
but Steve wouldn't. Linda and Roland didn't have to come to the
worksites much, because they didn't know anything about installing
windows. They would show up once in a while to say they observed
the students in their job training environment. This was a perfect
arrangement, because by this time, I was smoking marijuana every
day before I went to work. I didn't need to be walking into the rehab
center, having the recovering addicts saying, "I smell weed."

Y.E.C. had a big job coming up. The building was on Weeks
Avenue in the Bronx. In fact, it was on the same block that my
mother lived on before she moved to Washington, D.C. The building had 500 windows to be installed. Vinnie and I measured the
windows and broke them down according to sizes and the apartments that they went to, then ordered them. Steve even hired another crew leader named Bumpy, who was a short, fat, Jamaican
man about twenty-eight years old, to help with installing. Bumpy
wasn't very smart, but he could install windows. This was going to
be a big reimbursement from the state, so the job was critical. It was
about three months into my return. From what I saw, Vinnie was

218

the construction part of the program. He did everything regarding the installation of the windows—ordering the materials, making sure the jobs were complete. He was good at his job.

The construction part was the lifeline of Y.E.C. Without it, there was no job training, and therefore, no Y.E.C. No one else in the office knew anything about the windows except for how much they cost and whether they showed up at the job site. The only other person who knew about the whole operation from beginning to end was me.

Vinnie had been irritable about not getting paid enough for all the work and responsibility that he had. He wanted a raise, but he was looking for the perfect time to ask for one. Up until this point, he was lucky to have a job, since Y.E.C. had finished that last contract by the skin of its teeth. Since there was a new contract, Vinnie felt he was owed his due. He wasn't going to ask for a raise; he was going to demand one.

He decided this would be a perfect time, since the building we were starting was a critical start for Y.E.C. This was the company's time to shine, to let the state know that the old regime was gone and this new one would go above and beyond expectations. Vinnie told me about his idea and asked me what I thought. I told Vinnie that I understood what he was saying, but people don't like to be put in compromising positions at critical moments. It makes them feel like they're being extorted.

I thought, *After what I've been through the past year, working a minimum wage job, working in a number hole with the chance of being busted, and selling drugs to make some decent money, I'm just happy to have a decent job.*

Vinnie said he was going to call Steve the day the windows got delivered to demand a raise, and if he didn't get one, he would threaten to quit. Vinnie knew that Steve was new and didn't know anything about the window business. Vinnie had ordered everything and knew the breakdown of the whole job. He knew if this job didn't get done on time, Y.E.C. was finished. The whole operation depended on Vinnie.

The day came, and 500 windows were delivered. There were fifteen students there, and Bumpy, Vinnie, and I were unloading the windows from the truck. When the windows were unloaded and packed away, Vinnie said, "I'm going to call Steve." I heard Vinnie on the phone, demanding a raise and threatening to quit. Then I heard Vinnie say, "Okay." He hung up the phone.

I asked Vinnie what Steve said; Steve was coming to the worksite to talk to him. Vinnie was confident that he had Steve over a barrel and was going to get what he wanted.

Vinnie, Bumpy, and I were standing in front of the building when Steve arrived. Steve got out of the car, greeted us, and said, "Vinnie, I wish you would reconsider what you're asking. Now is not a good time for Y.E.C., and if you're patient, we can work something out later."

Vinnie was inflexible. He wanted a raise immediately, or else he was going to quit right there on the spot.

Steve said, "Well, I guess this is it. I can't give you a raise, so thanks for your service here." Steve told Bumpy and me to close up the worksite and report to the office. Steve got in his car and drove away.

Vinnie just stood there, dumbfounded. He just knew the company couldn't survive without him. He couldn't believe that Steve called his bluff. Vinnie packed up his tools, looked at Bumpy and me, and said, "Good luck, guys."

Bumpy and I looked at each other like "What are we going to do?" This could mean we were both soon going to be out of a job. Vinnie didn't even give any details about the job for us to follow up with since he was gone. I think he did this on purpose, hoping the project would fall behind so Steve would have to beg him to come back and offer him anything he wanted.

Bumpy and I closed the worksite and reported to the office. Steve had an emergency meeting that day and informed the staff of what happened. Everyone was concerned for their job. It was just a matter of time.

I thought, *What's the big deal? I can do this.* I helped Vinnie measure the windows, I was there when he ordered them, I knew which windows went to what apartments, and I knew how to run a job site. I said to Steve, "I can complete the project."

Everyone looked at me with surprise, but also with skepticism. Up to this point, everyone thought I was just a window installer, a dime a dozen. They didn't think that I could run things.

Steve said, "Russ, are you sure you can pull this off?"

"Yes, under one condition. "

"And what's that?"

"I get Vinnie's job."

chapter NINETEEN

W hile my professional life was taking a turn for the better, my personal life was heading in the opposite direction, as always, downhill. I was still living at Nana's, and T was doing all she could to make it a living hell. She would often come by my bedroom window in the early hours of the morning, yelling and throwing rocks in an attempt to break it. She would show up at my office and threaten to act a fool in an attempt to embarrass me. Every time she would perform her ignorant behavior, it was always under the guise of "your son needs this" or "your son needs that." She even sent the police to Nana's house one time, telling them that I was threatening her over the phone.

It got so unbearable that it was just easier to move back in with her. However, I didn't move all my stuff back to her place, just a couple of changes of clothes and a toothbrush. I still felt bad about the incident at Nana's with her losing her babysitting job, so I wanted to cause the least amount of trouble at Nana's door as possible.

Denise and I hooked up a couple more times, and I thought that maybe this was a chance at reconciliation. But when I mentioned the possibility of us getting back together, she made it clear that she didn't want to be in a relationship with me; she just wanted to have sex with me. When she told me this, I became a broken man again. The few times we got together were wonderful, and I started to have high hopes, but I guess they were. Denise hadn't forgiven me. She just wanted me to be her boy toy and nothing else. Her heart now belonged to another man.

Even though I was living with T, I tried to spend the least amount of time there as possible. In fact, the only reason I ever came home was to enjoy my son. It was always bittersweet to spend time with him, so I would pretend that I was in a good relationship with T. As far as T was concerned, she had won, she had broken me.

I had no place to go but Nana's, and T knew where I worked. I hung out with Jason more and more, and she would even come by Julie's sometimes and act a fool. Jason and I had to start hanging out at other places, like Frida's. Frida was a street bitch, too, so T knew better than to act a fool around Frida's house, because she might have kicked T's ass.

Jason and I would also hang out with Jerry sometimes, but T wasn't invited anymore. One night, the three of us were hanging out, and we all got pretty drunk and ended up in the park across from where T lived. Jerry was a very attractive woman, and she had a big ass, something I liked in women. She was also very sexy—a ghetto rat, but sexy. I had wanted to have sex with her ever since we went on that double date and I saw her naked in T's apartment. But I would never dare make a move on a woman so close to home.

That night was like the perfect storm, but I didn't make a move on Jerry because I didn't really know how Jason would react. I knew he wasn't in love with her or anything like that, but he did give her that bracelet.

As we continued to drink and smoke, Jerry became more touchy-feely. The three of us were sitting on a park bench. Jerry then took her hand and rubbed the outside of my pants, close to my groin area, right in front of Jason. She then grabbed my crotch, squeezed it, and said, "Do you want to fuck me, Russell?"

I was very aroused and looked over at Jason to see what his reaction was. Jason looked at Jerry and said, "Hey, bitch, what the fuck you talking about?"

Jerry ignored Jason. She got up from the bench, walked over to the next one, pulled her pants down, and lay on the bench with her legs spread, pleasuring herself as she kept saying, "Fuck me, Russell. Fuck me. You know you want to."

Jason and I looked at each other and said, "Oh, well."

We both had sex with her on the bench. Jason had intercourse with her while she performed oral sex on me, and she finished the job. When we were done, the reality of what I just did hit me. I just had sex with my friend's girlfriend and T's friend.

The second we finished and started to walk home, Jason said to Jerry, "Wait a minute." He snapped the bracelet he had given her from her wrist, took it, and said, "Thank you."

Jerry looked at him. "Is something wrong?"

Jason just ignored her and said, "Let's go, Russ."

I said, "Yo, man, don't treat her like that. She might start acting funky, and remember, she lives in my complex."

"Man, fuck that bitch. She wanted you all the time. She was just using me to get to you. That's all. She don't give a shit about me. She got what she wanted."

I asked Jason what he was talking about, and he said, "Man, please! I saw how she was always touchy-feely with you. I was just counting the days and fucking her for as long as I could, but fuck that now. That bitch just swallowed your load."

Jason and I laughed and watched Jerry cross the street to go home.

I was a little concerned about my next move. I didn't feel guilty; I just didn't want any more drama where I lived. I saw Jerry a couple of days later, and she acted as if nothing happened. I thought either she was that drunk, or she knew how to keep a secret. I think it was a little of both. After that night, I saw Jerry a lot when she would hang out with T, but she never mentioned it or tried to come back for seconds, and neither did I.

Jason was cool with it. He was hard on women. His attitude was that they were there for the pleasure of man, and that's it. Jason was the definition of a street person. Everything I ever learned about the street, I learned from him, and when it came to the exploitation of women, he was the master.

The first thing Jason introduced me to in that regard was strip clubs, and I liked it. The first strip club I ever went to was called El Coucha, on Hunts Point Avenue. It was a small place, and thinking back to all the clubs I've been to since, it was very modest. El Coucha only had one stage, and the strippers were mostly Spanish women. They were not that great looking. That was the first place I learned how to smoke cigarettes, also compliments of Jason.

I can remember it like it was yesterday, even though it was more than twenty-five years ago. Jason had picked me up from my security guard job. We went to the liquor store and bought a large bottle of this cheap, cherry-flavored wine called Cisco. Jason and I bought the wine so that we would feel nice and wouldn't have to buy a bunch of drinks at the bar. We walked to the strip club, downing the Cisco and smoking a blunt. When we got there, I was feeling no pain. I sat at the bar, and we both ordered Heinekens. I was feeling very high, and Jason said, "Here, man, have a cigarette."

I said, "No. I remember the last time I tried to smoke a cigarette was with Lori when I was fourteen, and I had a choking fit."

"Man, that was years ago. You smoke blunts, don't ya?"

That was true. I guess the experience was so bad that it scared me off from cigarettes.

Jason handed me a Newport. I lit the cigarette and Jason said, "Now, drag it slowly."

I pulled on the cigarette very slowly. I could feel the thick smoke flowing down my throat and filling my lungs. The smoke was much thicker than smoke from marijuana blunts. When my lungs filled to capacity, I quickly exhaled and watched the smoke exit my mouth and fill the dimly lit club, flowing past the naked woman dancing onstage.

That was my first successful drag of a cigarette. After that, I kept dragging as if I were a kid with a new toy. Jason encouraged me.

Now we had something else we could share in. The reason that night was so memorable and so vivid in my mind was not because of the cigarettes, but because of what happened afterward.

As I sat there at the bar, watching this naked woman dance on an elevated stage and playing with my new toy, I got up to go to the bathroom. When I sat back down next to Jason, the next thing I noticed was that the room started to spin very slowly.

Jason looked at me and said, "Are you okay, man?"

I turned to say something, but threw up all over the bar instead. Everyone was looking at me. I couldn't even walk. Jason had to help me up and half-carry me out of the club. Jason hailed a cab and took me to Julie's house. As he helped me up the stairs, I threw up again. Jason knocked on Julie's door; it was about five in the morning. Julie opened and asked what happened. Jason told her that I threw up at the bar and that I was out of it ever since. He took me to Julie's because she used to be a nurse, and she could tell us if it was something serious or if I was just drunk. I thought it had to be something else, because Jason had the same things I had and he was fine.

Jason laid me on the couch, and Julie asked about our activities during the evening. Jason told her about the strip club, us drinking a large bottle of cherry Cisco, and that I had a Heineken, but that was it. Julie asked if he was sure, if I did anything different that evening that I hadn't done before. Jason said the only thing I did was smoke a cigarette and Julie said, "Russell doesn't smoke." She asked Jason how many cigarettes, and he said he didn't know, but he saw a cigarette in my mouth all night.

Julie looked down at me on the couch and said in Spanish, "Bendito," which means "poor thing."

"He's just having a reaction to the nicotine in his body." Julie said that with the drinking and smoking, and probably the mixing of the cheap wine and the Heineken, and then introducing nicotine, my body was just rejecting so much at once. "He'll be alright; just let him sleep it off."

226

Then, Julie went into her room and brought a blanket out to cover me. I woke up about three hours later, and Julie was right there. She asked me how I was feeling and if I wanted something to eat. I told her I was feeling okay, and yes to the food. Jason had stayed also, and was just waking up as well. Julie fixed us both some toast and grits and gave us orange juice to drink. When we were finished, Jason and I thanked Julie for looking out for us and left.

As Jason and I walked to the street corner, we made plans to meet up later. I hailed a cab to go home. When one pulled up, I opened the door and said, "Later." I got in, rolled down the window, and called Jason back to the cab as he was walking away. I said, "Hey, you got a cigarette, man?"

When it came to strip clubs, Jason was a professional of sorts. He didn't just introduce me to strip clubs; he would find out about the underground places. At a regular establishment, there was minimal touching, and if you give the girl $5, maybe she would rub her breasts in your face. For $20, you could get a lap dance, where the naked woman would grind on your midsection for a couple of minutes, but you weren't allowed to touch them. The women were also encouraged by owners to get men to buy more drinks. To Jason, this was women manipulating men, so if he was going to give women money, he was going to get his money's worth.

At the underground strip clubs, all was permissible. I don't know how he knew about the different ones, but every now and then, he would say, "Hey, you got to check this place out with me."

The first underground club Jason took me to was a place he and I called the Tunnel. It didn't have a name. It was near an overpass on the Grand Concourse. To get to the Tunnel, you would have to go behind a building and know where you were going, because there weren't any markings to identify the club. From the outside, it looked like an abandoned building. But when you went inside, there were two bars, a large stage, booths that sat four people aligning the walls, and several tables and chairs in the middle floor area.

The place was very dimly lit. The only bright area was the stage, which was at ground level. The first thing that made me like this club was that you could get high right at your table. No going in the bathroom to take a hit of cocaine, or going outside to smoke a blunt—you could put the cocaine in tin foil right on the table, out in the open, and sniff at will, or roll a blunt and lay it in an ashtray. The only thing you couldn't do was bring your own liquor; you had to buy that. Jason and I would usually show up about two in the morning, and it was standing room only. If you wanted a booth, you would need to get there about midnight, when the place opened. There were usually six to eight women working the floor, and there would be a main show where one or two would pull a man out of the audience and perform sex acts on him while people threw money on the stage. It was not uncommon to look over and find one of the women that had been dancing on stage giving someone oral gratification in a corner booth.

The other place I liked was called the Goat. This place was much more out in the open. It was at the end of Hunts Point, right on the main avenue, but it didn't have a sign. It was much classier than the Tunnel. There were four bars, ten TVs, a dance floor, about forty half-naked or fully naked women running around, and it was brightly lit. The women at the Tunnel were okay, but those at the Goat were stunning. Every type of woman you could think of was walking around: black, white, Spanish, Asian, short, tall, skinny, thick, blonde, brunette, big ass, small ass, big tits, small tits, light-skinned, dark-skinned—you name it, they had it. One commonality of the two places was that you could get high right out in the open. However, at the Goat, any sex acts usually took place in a designated area. It was more a brothel/strip club combination. Even if you didn't have sex with any of the women, it was no problem to get a handful of derriere or breasts if you had a small tip for them. I have felt up almost every type of woman you can picture.

By the age of twenty, Jason had introduced me to the many corruptions of the street—drugs, cigarettes, strip clubs. The final one was something that when I was younger, I thought I would have never engaged in: prostitution. It started when we were selling drugs and progressed from there. It wasn't unusual for a crackhead to offer sexual favors in exchange for the drugs. However, that was once in a blue moon, and the clientele was not very appealing. But every now and then, you would run across some attractive female who was just losing control of her moral integrity.

At the Goat and the Tunnel, Jason and I never indulged in any sexual activities. It was too public and rushed. Actually, Jason did once. He showed me a more private form. He had a lot more time on his hands, so when I was with T and my son, Jason was sampling the goods. He would always introduce me to women that had their own places and turned tricks on the side. One of his regulars, who soon became mine, was this Spanish woman Jason called the Old Lady.

He told me one day, "I want you to meet this old lady I been fucking."

When he said this, I thought, *I don't know. Geriatrics are really not my thing.* But with Jason, anything was possible, because I knew he would have sex with anything that had a heartbeat, except a man.

Jason took me to a building on 170th and Walton Avenue. He led me up to the fifth floor, to a door that had two doorknobs on it, and knocked. I didn't know what to expect. The term "old lady" kept sticking in my head. I was only twenty or twenty-one at the time. When the door opened, there stood a very attractive Spanish woman in her mid- to late-thirties. There was nothing old about her.

She spoke broken English and said to Jason, "Hey, papi. You brought a friend. He's cute." She told us to come in and have a seat. The apartment was a one-bedroom, and was kept decently. "Who's first?"

Jason laughed and pointed to me. "He is, and give him the special."

The woman led me to her bedroom. Inside was a queen-size bed. I stood and watched her undress, admiring her curved shape and the firmness of her body. While she was undressing, I thought about how worn and battered T's body was, with her sagging breasts and stretchmarks from having four children. This woman didn't have a mark on her. She told me to undress, and even helped me. She wasn't rushing me; she was even making small conversation as we went along. I had never done this before, so I didn't know what to expect. The only thing I knew about paying for sex was what I saw on TV, with hookers on the street.

The woman performed excellently. She did anything I wanted without question, and there was no stigma about it. No performance issues, just submissive, fun sex, and my pleasure was her only concern. When we were done, the woman got up, went to her bathroom, and took a shower.

I got dressed and went into the living room, where Jason was watching TV. He smiled and said, "All done?"

"Yes." I was smiling as well. I asked him how much to pay her, and Jason told me this one was on him. She usually charged $20, but once you got to know her, she'd even let you get some on credit. Jason then went into the lady's bedroom and waited for her.

She came out of the bathroom in a towel and smiled at me on her way into the bedroom. I could hear them laughing and the headboard banging. After a few minutes, Jason emerged from the room with the naked lady. He pulled some money out of his pocket and gave it to her. I don't know how much, because she didn't count it. She opened the door and as we walked out, she said to me, "Don't be a stranger."

I wasn't.

By now, I hated my life at home, but I was always hanging out, and now, women were literally a dime a dozen. When I was home, I took care of business and played the role well. As always, my personal life was headed down a spiral of depravity while my professional life was taking off like a rocket. But, by chance, there was a strange course of events where the two intertwined for a brief moment in time.

I had finished the job that Vinnie abandoned and completed a couple of other jobs, so Steve finally gave me Vinnie's position. I now had the title of crew leader supervisor, the job of the man—Black Joe—who had gotten me fired about a year earlier. I started to get to know a few people that worked in the building, but not for Y.E.C. There was a lady named Belinda, and she was some sort of job placement counselor for the recovering addicts. And there was the secretary, Kim. They were two heavyset black women that would go for happy hour after work, almost every day. (They weren't recovering addicts.) Sometimes, they would invite me to drink with them. There wasn't anything sexual about it. We were just hanging out. Sometimes, Willie, the bookkeeper, would come with us, because he was trying to get in Kim's pants.

I soon came to learn that all of them—Belinda, Kim, and Willie—sniffed cocaine and smoked marijuana. I introduced Jason to all of them, and we would all hang out sometimes. I came to find out Willie's live-in girlfriend, Jeannette, was a cocaine dealer. All of us spent many nights getting high, and would see each other in the rehab center the next day like nothing had happened.

chapter TWENTY

O ne day, I went to Belinda's office to secure plans for later that evening, and there was another woman there. The woman was white, which, given the administration, wasn't out of the ordinary in a rehab center. But this one was different. She was the most beautiful woman I had ever seen in person. She looked like she walked off a movie set or the cover of a fashion magazine. She had a body to die for, well-proportioned in every area, long blonde hair down her back, bright, beautiful eyes, a pretty face, and a smile that lit up the room. She was dressed all in black and walked in six-inch heels like they were roller skates. She looked like she was around my age, and had just the right amount of makeup on. She looked like a young Pamela Anderson.

As I was talking to Belinda, the woman was putting some files away. "Does she work here?" I asked.

Belinda said, "No. Russell, this is my friend, Melanie."

I shook the woman's hand as I gazed into her eyes, still overwhelmed by her beauty. I confirmed our plans for after work and inquired if Melanie would be joining us. Belinda said she would. I said my goodbyes and left the office.

I couldn't keep myself from thinking about this woman all day. I knew that if she was a friend of Belinda's, she indulged in some sort of pharmaceutical recreation. I met up with Kim, Belinda, and Melanie after work, and we went to a bar. I paid a lot of attention to Melanie, which I was sure a woman of her beauty was no stranger to. In fact, I thought I was out of my league, but it wouldn't hurt to try. Melanie seemed really down to earth.

chapter TWENTY-ONE

After the bar, Kim caught a cab, and Belinda, Melanie, and I went to Belinda's house on White Plains Road. She lived in a beautiful high-rise building with a terrace in the North Bronx. The three of us smoked a blunt, and then Belinda went into her bedroom and left Melanie and me alone in the living room.

I made a move on Melanie, and she didn't reject me. The interaction was hot and passionate. I even got as far as getting her breasts out and my penis exposed, but she wouldn't go all the way. She said, "You didn't think it would be that easy, did you?"

I said, "No." I was surprised I had gotten that far.

"I think there are some things you should know about me before you try to fuck me."

I told her I knew all I needed to know, and that she was the most beautiful woman I had ever laid my eyes on. Then I tried to continue our interaction.

She pushed me away and said, "You can do better than that. Look, what you want to happen tonight ain't gonna happen. I'm not saying it ain't gonna happen, but it ain't gonna happen tonight." I was impressed that at least she wasn't a slut. Melanie said, "You have Belinda's phone number, don't you?"

I told her I did, and she asked for mine, then asked for a good time to call. I gave her Nana's number and told her to call me the next day at 6:00 p.m. I put my penis away, still aroused, and she put her breasts away. Then, we smoked another blunt together. I asked her what I needed to know, since the blood was back in my top head. She said she would tell me when we spoke the next day.

I could hardly keep my mind on work. I saw Melanie in the building, but we acted like we didn't know each other. Later, I went to Nana's and waited for her phone call. Nana was used to me getting phone calls from other women. Melanie called at 6:00 on the dot, and we made small talk. She told me that she liked me a lot, but was hesitant to tell me what she wanted to, out of fear I would run for the hills. I told her that as long as she didn't tell me she was a man, I was pretty open-minded. She asked me if I was sure, and I said, "Go ahead. Try me."

"Okay. Here it is: I'm a call girl."

"Call girl? What exactly does that mean?" I asked.

"Come on now. You know what a call girl is. I have sex with men for money. The only difference between me and a hooker is, she walks the street corner and I call men on the phone, make dates, and fuck them."

At first, I was speechless. Then I said, "That doesn't mean I have to pay you to fuck you, do I?" She replied that I didn't. I said, "Cool. What else you got?"

I asked her how she knew Belinda, and she told me that she didn't. Her pimp boyfriend knew Belinda, and they were staying with her for a while. I asked where he was that night, and she said she didn't know. He would disappear for days at a time. That's why she didn't want to have sex with me that night in the apartment, just in case he walked in.

I asked when we could hook up, and she said, "Let's shoot for the weekend."

That Saturday, I called, and it was a go. Linda, the counselor at Y.E.C., had invited me to a get-together she was having. So, I decided to fly by there that night and show off the beautiful woman I had with me.

That night, I got dressed up at Nana's, called a cab, and then waited in front of my building. The plan was to take the cab to a predetermined area that Melanie and I chose, then shoot by Julie's, and then Linda's. After that, we would see where the night took us—hopefully to a hotel.

While I was waiting for a cab, T just happened to walk out of the building with my son. She saw me and asked where I was going so dressed up. I told her that I was hanging out with Jason. Normally, I would have told her none of her fucking business, but I didn't want to screw up this opportunity. T waited with me for the cab to come, then I got in and said goodbye. I met Melanie at a small strip mall down the block from Belinda's. She got into the cab, and we headed to Julie's house.

All heads turned as we walked into the building complex. Once we were at Julie's, Jason couldn't keep his eyes off of Melanie. He loved white women. This was the first I was ever with, and I hadn't even had sex with her yet.

Julie was pleasant and offered her some food, and Melanie was right at home. I had already told Julie and Jason who she was.

After we finished eating, Melanie and I got ready to head to Linda's, and on the way out, Jason called me back in and said, "Hey! When you gonna let me fuck her?"

I said, "Nigger, I got to fuck her first," and walked off.

As Melanie and I walked to the corner, all eyes were on us again. She drew that kind of attention. We stopped by Linda's, but didn't stay long because it was a dull scene.

Melanie and I took a cab downtown to Times Square. During the ride, she said, "There's something else I need to tell you, since we're headed into the area."

"What's that?"

"I've only been with my boyfriend for about three weeks. I was teaching him the pimp game, and I guess he's out trying it with some other girls because he don't want me fucking other guys. But I ran away from a real pimp before that."

I asked her why she was telling me that now, and she said because this guy was bad news, and he was big-time. He had ten girls in his stable, and if a car were to pull up and some men grabbed her to pull her in, I shouldn't try to fight them. They would kill me without even thinking about it.

I thought about it while we headed downtown and said, "Cool. I'm with it. Let's go."

That night, Melanie and I walked around Times Square and took in the sights. I asked her how long she had been in the profession and how much she got paid. Melanie told me she had been a call girl for about five years, and that she made $500 a session. Sometimes, she would go on trips with men, and the price could go up to the thousands. She had just finished a trip to Puerto Rico with a guy for two weeks before she met her boyfriend, Orlando. Melanie said Orlando had been spending all of her money, thinking he was a pimp by doing so, but he didn't know anything about the pimp game. He was so jealous that he wouldn't let her make any money.

I asked her to tell me about the guy that was such bad news. Melanie said that she used to walk the street corner with about seven other girls. She made about $1,000 a night, and he got it all. He had three different locations downtown that brought him in about $10,000 a night, and he had a bunch of men that would beat the girls up for him. She ran away a couple of times, but he always found her. She said this had been the longest she's been away, but that downtown was a dangerous place because someone could recognize her and call him. I asked her how she transitioned from streetwalker to call girl. She said that when she would meet decent guys, she would ask them for a number and if they would be interested in a call service. She only made the offer to guys driving expensive cars. After that, all she did was call the guys. They would meet up in a hotel room, and she would make her money. She figured if she could do that, what the fuck did she need a pimp for?

The night ended with me putting Melanie in a cab home. I took a separate cab to 170th Street and Walton Avenue to see the old lady, and then I went home to T and my son.

That whole night, all I could think about was Melanie and how much I hated my life with T.

When I went back to work on Monday, I saw Melanie with Belinda. But again, we acted like we didn't know each other. A couple of times that week, we all went for happy hour at some bar, but parted afterward. One day, Nana called me and said that some woman named Belinda called. She wanted me to call back, and said it was an emergency. Nana always took messages for me from other women. I went downstairs to Nana's and called Belinda. When she answered, she sounded pained. Belinda said, in a rambling sentence, "I can't let this happen, I can't let him do this to her." She kept repeating herself. I told her to calm down and to tell me what was going on. Belinda said that Orlando was beating up on Melanie. Belinda got in between them, so Orlando left, but he was coming back.

I thought, *What the fuck does that have to do with me?* But it had everything to do with me. Belinda knew I liked Melanie. My nose was open for her, and I was the only one they could call.

I asked what she wanted me to do, because I wasn't going to fight anybody over a woman that wasn't mine. Belinda said she just wanted to get Melanie out of there, if I knew someplace she could stay. That, I could do. I told Belinda to be ready to go when I called back in two minutes.

I thought about Julie's, but the place was crowded already, and Jason would be trying to fuck Melanie. So I called the next best person I could think of, a person I knew didn't care who or what Melanie was as long as she was going to be able to make some money out of the deal. Besides, she had an extra bedroom that she wasn't using. I called Frida.

I told her a female friend of mine needed a place to stay. Frida asked me if I was fucking the chick, and I preemptively said, "Yes." Frida knew about T, but she also knew I wasn't committed. She looked at me like a son, now that Mitchell was dead. Frida said that

238

Melanie could stay, and that it would cost $75 a week. I told Frida that we would be over later that night. I called Belinda back and had her meet me at Frida's by cab. When they arrived, Belinda let Melanie out with a suitcase while she stayed in the cab. Belinda said to me, "Take care of her," closed the door, and the cab drove off.

Melanie stood there. Her face seemed a little swollen from being slapped, and her eyes were red from crying. Although she had no makeup on, she was still a beautiful girl. I put my arm around her, picked up her suitcase, and led her upstairs to Frida's. Frida let us in and greeted Melanie with a smile, welcoming her warmly. I took Melanie to Mitchell's old room and let her unpack while I went to talk to Frida.

I took care of Frida right away and gave her the $75 out of my own pocket. She started asking me about Melanie. Who was she? Where she was from? Why did she need a place to stay? By this time, Frida and I had more of a grownup relationship, and I told her not to worry about it as long as she was getting her money. Frida was an ex-dope-fiend and a current cocaine and crack user, so she was going to get as much as she could get out of the situation. I didn't want to tell her that Melanie was a call girl, because then she would try to hustle more money out of us. Frida left the subject alone for the moment as she and her new boyfriend, Dennis, went to spend the $75 I had just given her.

I went back into the bedroom with Melanie and made sure she was feeling comfortable, and then she and I went out to get some food. I asked her what happened, and she said that Orlando had spent all their money. He wanted her to go prostitute on Hunts Point and suck dick for $20 in parked cars. When she refused, he tried to beat her into submission.

Later that night, when we returned to Frida's, Melanie went to take a shower. While she was in there, Frida said to me, "Hey, take a walk with me while I walk the dog."

239

I accompanied Frida as she walked her large Doberman and made small talk, but I knew there was a point to her asking me to go with her.

She knew I had a decent job, and she saw that I had a few dollars on me when I paid her earlier that night. Finally, Frida said, "Do you mind giving me an advance for next week's rent?"

I jumped on the defensive. "What the fuck is this, a shakedown? I just gave you $75 an hour ago!"

"No. I just need a few dollars more."

I gave her another $20 and told her not to make a habit of this shit.

I knew this was going to be a problem, because crack and cocaine were both very expensive habits. Her boyfriend was doing the same. Dennis was about ten years younger than Frida, so she had him wrapped around her finger. He would spend his whole paycheck on her when he got paid, and most of that went toward getting high.

When I returned to the bedroom, Melanie was there. She was lying on the bed, naked, in a position that was welcoming me to partake. I didn't say anything. Neither did she. I undressed and joined her on the bed. I rolled a blunt, and we smoked it together. As I smoked, I admired her beautiful body. Melanie didn't have a mark on her. She was as attractive nude as she was with her clothes on, and she was comfortable in her nakedness.

When we finished smoking, she went to work on me without hesitation, and without instruction. I didn't have to say a word. She knew what to kiss, what to rub, what to suck, and didn't miss a spot. I didn't have to request anything; she did it before I could think to ask. She was a professional. That night, I saw the difference between her and all the other women I had ever had sex with. That night, I could feel her gratitude for helping her out. I could feel it in every kiss, every rub, and every word she whispered in my ear. After that night, my nose was wide open.

I would go to work during the day, and then go to Nana's to change my clothes to head right to Frida's. I would get Melanie, get her some food, and buy some weed. The nights would end like the first, with her screwing my brains out. I wasn't even going by T's house. It was like I just disappeared. T would call my work, looking for me. She would call Nana's, but I wasn't there. She had no idea what was going on, and I didn't care. I was all about Melanie.

One day, Melanie said to me, "Hey, I'm going to have to start making some calls so I can make some money for us." It had only been three days, and I had all but forgotten she was a call girl. I was even having sex with her without a condom.

I said, "Okay. What do you need me to do?"

Melanie would call the guys from the list that she had, and whichever one wanted a date, she would meet up with. She asked if I wanted to make some money also.

Up to this point, I hadn't realized that I was paying for all her food, drugs, and room and board. I had never asked her for anything. So, I said, "Sure. What do you need me to do?"

Melanie spelled out my role in this operation. She would make her call and set up a meeting area, and I would wait with her. When the client picked her up, I would be seen so that he knew she wasn't alone. I would take down his license plate number, just in case Melanie didn't return. Once Melanie and the client reached the motel, she would call me at a payphone to let me know where she was and that she was safe. The first time went like clockwork, as did the second and the third and so on.

This was easy money. After work, I would do my routine at Nana's, and then Melanie and I would go out to meet her dates. We did this about three times a week. Frida started to ask questions, now that she saw Melanie and me going out at night with me returning alone, then going back out to pick her up. Frida finally asked me if Melanie was a prostitute, and I told her she was. I could see the wheels spinning in Frida's head about how she could make more money from us, but Melanie wasn't turning tricks in her house, so

241

why would we give her more money? Not to mention, Melanie had been a street bitch, even though I forgot that for a while. She knew how to handle the likes of Frida.

One night, Melanie told me that she wanted some cocaine. It was about one in the morning. I told her that I didn't know of any place to get it. She said, "No problem. I'll just ask Frida."

I replied that it was sort of late to be knocking on Frida's bedroom door.

"It's no problem. Watch this." Melanie knocked and said, "Hey, Frida. I want to get some blow."

Frida opened the door and said, "I'll be dressed in a minute."

While I was at work in the daytime, Frida and Melanie had struck up a friendship based on their mutual interest in cocaine. Melanie was paying for it, and Frida was copping it and helping her snort it. This was how Melanie kept Frida at bay about our operation. Soon, Melanie asked me if I had a gun. I told her that I could get one, but she said, "No, your own gun. You may need it one day." She said that I should carry one when I was waiting for her, just in case a client was acting up and I needed to come to the motel. Melanie gave me $250 and told me to go and buy one. I knew just who to ask about buying a gun from the street: Jason.

I called and told him that I wanted a gun, and that I had $250. Jason said that it shouldn't be a problem. The next day, he had one for me. I went by Julie's and gave him the money, and he handed me a nickel-plated .25 automatic pistol. This was my first gun, and I felt powerful with it. The gun was small and easily hidden—it was perfect. I told Jason all about what I was doing with Melanie and the money we were making. Jason again inquired about when he was going to be able to fuck her, and I just brushed him off.

Jason said, "Hey, man! You not falling for this whore, are you?"

When he called her a whore, I was a little offended, but not angry. I said, "Why she got to be a whore?"

Jason said, "Because she is, muthafucker, and it looks like your nose is wide open."

I tried to deny it. He said he could prove my nose was open for her. I asked him how, and he said, "Because you won't let me fuck her. How many girls we done fucked together, and now this whore is off-limits? It's not like it's your woman or something, but you treating her like she is. She's a ho, muthafucker! A ho! You should know better than to treat her with respect. She goes out and fucks niggers for money, and you probably fucked her without a condom, didn't you, you stupid muthafucker?"

When it came to prostitutes, Jason was a pro. Even with the old lady, he didn't treat her with too much respect. He didn't disrespect her, but it was strictly business. No chitchat, no small talk. I, on the other hand, would go to the old lady's house, sit down, smoke a blunt with her, have a drink, and then get down to business. I would treat her like a person. Jason treated her like an object intended for his pleasure. The truth was Jason was right on the money regarding Melanie.

So I said to Jason, "Okay, muthafucker, I'll let you fuck her." I knew after that, my nose would close real quick, because I'd seen how Jason fucked women. He didn't respect them; he dogged them. Melanie would be the finest piece of ass he would ever have.

We were having this conversation right in front of Julie, and Julie said, "No, Jason. Don't do that. You know he really likes her."

Jason said, "But Julie, she's a ho! She fucks other niggers all the time, and he takes her to them."

Julie said, "But those men aren't his friends."

I left it at that, and told Jason I would get back to him.

I went back to Frida's, thinking about all the things Jason said, but I couldn't get past her beauty. She had me pussy-whipped by now. Every night, we had cocaine-fueled sex. I was snorting just because it was there. I still got up and went to work. I didn't really like cocaine, but somehow it was right for the sex we were having.

I hadn't been by T's for at least two weeks. I was always at a job site, not the office, so she couldn't pin me down. One afternoon, she was able to catch me on the phone at the office. Crying, she said, "I'm at the doctor's office and I'm ready to have this abortion."

I said to her in an instant, "Go ahead, bitch. What the fuck you telling me for if you at the office? That's what you there for, right?"

T said, "You coldhearted bastard. That's how you really feel, isn't it?"

"Hell yeah! I don't want no more fucking kids by you."

"Where you been muthafucker, with Denise?"

"None of your fucking business."

"Fuck you!" T hung up the phone.

Two thoughts came to mind. Either she was really pregnant, really getting an abortion, and wanted me to stop her; or she was just fucking with my head. Either way, I didn't want any more kids by her. I went by T's house after work to see my son, and to see if she was bullshitting me or not. T was sitting on the couch like she was in pain, and I felt no sorrow for her whatsoever.

T looked at me, the way I was playing with my son and not inquiring about her health. She said, "You don't really want to be here, do you?"

I said, "No."

"Go, then."

I left and went right to Melanie.

I saw Melanie every day, and every day, we got high. I was watching her back on her dates, and thought I was living the life. I thought I had it all going for me.

I saw Belinda at work, and she said to bring Melanie for the three of us to hang out together. That weekend, she invited Melanie and me to the Boston Road Ballroom. We got dressed and took a cab to the place.

When I walked in with Melanie, Belinda was sitting at a booth, close to the entrance. She got up and hugged Melanie, greeting both of us with great elation. As we sat down with Belinda, I could feel all eyes in the place on Melanie and me. The men were looking with jealousy, and the women were looking with animosity. Yes, I was that guy—the guy that brought the only white person into an all-black club in the middle of the South Bronx.

I didn't care. I felt like a rock star walking around with something other people wanted. When I would walk away to go to the bar, the men would roll up on Melanie to try to get her telephone number. If they saw me coming, they wouldn't stop talking to her. They wanted to test me. I think Melanie wanted to test me, as well.

I would notice the vultures from the bar. I would order an extra drink, a straight shot of 151 Bacardi rum. My intention was to throw it into someone's eyes, blinding them while I commenced kicking their ass, defending my white woman. I would just walk up to Melanie and whomever she was talking to, pull her toward me in the middle of the conversation, and wait for the guy to make his move. I didn't say anything; I just gave them the look of, "Is she worth getting fucked up, muthafucker?" No one ever made the move. Anywhere Melanie and I went, heads would turn, and not for me.

When Jason hung out with us, we would go downtown or someplace where there were white people. White men's heads would turn as if to say, "What is this beautiful white woman doing with these guys?"

Everything seemed to be going well. Melanie and I were talking more, and not about her dates or the drugs we were getting every night. She started to tell me about her family and where she was from. She said she was French Canadian, and her father owned a construction company. Her family was very wealthy, but that was as far as she would go. I could tell there was a deep, dark secret there that caused her much pain because dry tears would run down her face. This relationship had been going on for about a month, and she was making money and paying for everything. I even got a gun out of the deal. I thought, *I could get used to this shit.*

I was leading a double life. At twenty-one years old, during the day, I was a crew leader supervisor with approximately thirty at-risk teens under my supervision, working in rented space inside of a drug rehab center. At night, I was a marijuana-smoking, cocaine-sniffing pimp.

Yeah, I thought life was really good then. I was falling for Melanie really hard. I started to trust her. I was cool with her selling her body, as long as I didn't see the business transaction take place. I knew it was just business, and she came and spent the money on me. As always, when it comes to the street, all that glitters is not gold, and things aren't always what they appear to be. When you indulge in degenerate activities of the street and you're a virgin to the rules of the game, it's just like playing with fire. The only question is whether you're going to get third-degree burns, first-degree burns, or die in the fire.

One day, Jason came to pick me up at Frida's. Melanie stayed there, getting over a hangover from heavy partying the night before. It was about 4:00 p.m., and I told her we would be back to get her at about eleven. Jason and I were at Julie's when I ran out of money. I decided to drop by Frida's to pick up more and to check on Melanie.

When I got to Frida's house, Melanie wasn't there. I asked Frida where she was, and she said that Melanie left about an hour after I did. Frida assumed that she was going to meet me someplace. I thought it was odd, but really didn't think anything of it. I thought that maybe she hooked up a date for money, because we were spending the income as fast as she was making it. I went into the stash and took a couple of dollars, and then Jason and I left the apartment to head back to Julie's.

We were walking down the block, around the corner from Frida's, and at a distance, I saw this girl with two black guys. I didn't recognize them; they just stood out for some reason. The girl had long, blonde hair, but I was too far away to make out any facial features, and I didn't recognize the two black guys from any place. The only describable features about them were that they were tall. I was staring at them for some reason, like the girl didn't belong in the neighborhood. As Jason and I got a little closer—but still at a reasonable distance—I recognized Melanie.

Jason hadn't noticed the three individuals; I was observing them to myself. As we got closer, Jason saw them and said, "Hey, that looks like—"

Before he could finish, I said, "Yeah, I know, muthafucker. It looks like Melanie, and guess what it is?"

Jason said, "Let's go roll up on them and see what's up."

I had my gun on me, but I wanted to watch them for a while. I told Jason to chill out, that we'd just follow them from a distance until I could figure out what was going on.

Jason and I followed them to a park on the Grand Concourse, and they sat down on a bench. They were laughing and just hanging out. I was trying to cover all the angles in my head about what I was seeing. I was thinking about running up on the three of them, but what if one of the guys had a gun? I didn't want to end up in a shootout in the middle of the street in broad daylight. Only two things would have come out of that scenario: he would die, or I would.

Jason and I continued to watch when Melanie noticed us. Just like the professional hustler she was, she didn't skip a beat. She continued to laugh and joke with the two black guys and from time to time, looked in the direction of Jason and me. The two guys didn't notice a thing. After a while, the three of them started to walk toward 161st Street, and we followed.

They walked into a small pizza parlor, and we stood outside, still looking at them. Jason asked me what I was going to do. I was still thinking, and finally, the rage built up inside me. I was sizing the guys up all the while I was watching them, and decided to make my move. I swung open the pizza parlor door, drawing the attention of everyone in the place, and beelined straight toward Melanie and the two black guys. One had his arm around Melanie's shoulder. I stood right at the table they were sitting at, pointed to him, and said, "I want to see you outside, muthafucker."

I could see the fear in his eyes, and he could see the rage in mine. His eyes said, "Who the hell are you and what do you want with me?"

My eyes said, "Say the wrong thing or make a wrong move, and I'll kill you, muthafucker!"

The guy got up and walked out of the pizza parlor, with me behind him. The other black guy didn't make a move as Jason stood at the table.

When we got outside, I was fuming, but I wasn't upset with him. I said, "What the fuck is your name and how do you know Melanie?"

The guy could see the fire in my eyes and said, "Hey, man! I don't want any trouble. My name is Orlando, and she's my ex- girlfriend. She's been calling me all week, telling me how much she loved me and missed me. She called me today and told me where she lived, and I just came to hang out with her. I don't know who you are and nothing about you. I'm sorry, man."

His words pierced my heart as he spoke them. They did more damage than any gun or knife could. I just stood there in disbelief.

Then, I told the guy to go back inside the pizza shop, that I had no beef with him. I needed to talk to Melanie. Orlando went back inside, and then Jason and Melanie came out shortly after.

I wasn't yelling, but my voice was filled with rage. "How could you do this to me? Isn't this the guy you were running from, and that I protected you from? How could you humiliate me like this? If you were going to go and see him, why would you bring him around here, where everyone sees you with me?" I threw out the questions like a hail of bullets, never giving her a chance to respond.

When I was done spitting my venomous words, she said in a quiet voice, "You shouldn't have done this."

Again I berated her. "What do you mean I shouldn't have done this? You shouldn't have done this. You're a fucked up bitch, and this shit isn't over. I'll see you later." I stormed off, with Jason following.

As Jason and I were walking back to Frida's, I was fuming, thinking about what I was going to say to Melanie when I got her alone. I wondered if Frida knew anything about this, since it had been going on for about a week. Frida was my eyes and ears during the day, but I also knew her loyalty could easily be bought with the right amount of dollars or drugs.

When Jason and I got there, I knocked on the door, and Frida answered it. I walked into the apartment and started yelling. "Did you know about this shit?"

"Know about what?"

I told her what happened, and she denied knowing anything. She said that Melanie went out to the store a few times, but she never stayed out that long.

"Look here, muthafucker," Frida said. "Don't be coming into my house, talking shit to me about your white whore bitch."

I didn't respond. I walked away. I took all of Melanie's makeup and hid it, so if she came back to Frida's before I did, she would have to wait to find out where her stuff was. Her makeup was important to her—I mean really important. I hid all two boxes of it, and told Frida I would be back that night.

Jason and I went to Julie's, got high, and told her what happened. Julie didn't have anything bad to say about Melanie. She only told me to watch my temper and listen to what Melanie had to say. I went back to Frida's that night around 8:00 p.m. I had called Frida a couple of times while I was at Julie's, but Frida told me Melanie hadn't shown up.

I stayed up all night waiting in the bedroom for Melanie to come home. Around 4:00 a.m., Dennis came into the room and said to me, "Man, I don't think she's going to show up tonight. Why don't you get some sleep? Don't you have to go to work in the morning?"

I went to sleep and got up about 7:00 a.m. for work. I called Frida several times during the day. Frida told me that Melanie did show up, and took her things. I started to ask Frida a whole bunch of questions, and she told me to come by after work. She would tell me everything.

After work, I rushed over. Frida said that Melanie had shown up with two black dudes, and she thinks one of them had a gun. When Melanie knocked on the door, the two guys were right there with her. Dennis had stood at the door with Frida to ensure her safety, and he and one of the guys were gritting on each other. Melanie said to Frida, "All I want to do is get my stuff."

Frida told her she could come in, but she had to come in alone. When Melanie was gathering her things, Frida asked her why she brought those guys to her house. Melanie said that I seemed so upset that she knew I wasn't going to let her go.

When Melanie finished gathering all her things, she said to Frida, "Where's my makeup?" Frida told her that I had taken it.

Melanie stormed out of the house after that. Frida started to laugh after telling me what happened. I asked what was so funny, and Frida said, "You are a fucked up muthafucker. Out of all the shit that bitch had—clothes, jewelry, a nice radio—you go and take her makeup. You are a spiteful muthafucker. You had that bitch walking out of here looking like a fucking ghost."

Later, I went by Julie's and hung out with Jason. I told them what happened. Julie could see that I was more than a little depressed about the situation. In fact, I was heartbroken.

She said, "Russell, don't go looking for her. What's done is done. You had your fun. Now move on."

"I think I loved her."

Julie, being the street mother to me, and everyone who needed her, said, in the kindest possible way, "Look, you didn't love her. You just loved the pussy. You just wanted to fuck you a white bitch. You knew she was a whore. I don't judge anybody, you know that, but you are too kindhearted. There was no way you could have handled that woman. She was running circles around you. She needed a heartless bastard like Jason. She knew you couldn't hurt her, so she treated you like a trick and used you to her benefit. When she

250

was done using you, she threw you away. You can't be mad at her for that. You can't change her nature; she's a whore. Her job is to manipulate men, and you're only twenty-one. You're still a baby.

"I know it hurts now, and it's a hard pill to swallow, but you'll get over it. Just learn from this, because I love you like a son, and let me tell you this, women will take your kindness for weakness all the time. You need to learn not to fall for a pretty face. I can tell you right now that pretty women will be your weakness and your downfall if you don't learn to control that shit. Remember that there is no difference between a pretty bitch and an ugly bitch when it comes to fucking them, because if you turn them upside-down, they're all twins."

Julie was right, but it didn't make the pain in my heart feel any better. I was hurting. I was, once again, a broken man. Except this time, I was not only broken, I was humiliated as well. I thought, *How could I let myself fall for a whore?* I was the biggest trick of them all! I fell in love with a whore. I had thought I was a pimp, but the entire time, I was being pimped. I thought about what Julie had said, and how a pimp would have handled the situation when he saw Melanie with the two black guys. I think a real pimp would have walked into the pizza parlor, dragged Melanie out by her hair, and said fuck you to whatever the guy had to say.

Jason listened to what Julie had to say and put in his two cents.

"You know what the most fucked up thing is about all of this shit?"

Julie and I looked at Jason and said, "What's that?"

"I never got to fuck the bitch."

chapter **TWENTY-TWO**

As always, when I was at my lowest, T would be around to pick up the pieces. I was staying at Nana's again, ever since the Melanie thing. T was playing her same games, coming to Nana's door, starting nonsense. Always the baby needs this, the baby needs that. I always had my gun on me, in my right jacket pocket. One day, something told me to unload the gun before I put it in there. I don't know why; it was just a feeling, and I had never had this feeling before. I was walking out of Nana's, and T was standing in front of the building. She confronted me about where I was going. I told her I was going to hang out. I hadn't seen her for a couple of weeks. T was trying to persuade me to come to her house to have sex, but I wasn't with it. I knew it was a ploy.

T rubbed up on me and felt the gun in my side pocket. "What this?" she asked. I pulled the gun out to show her. She said to me, "Oh, you got money to buy a gun, but you ain't got money to give me for your son." I told her that I gave her enough money for my son, and the money was for him, not for her.

T complimented me on how pretty the gun was, and asked to hold it. I gave her the gun, and she played with it in her hand for a minute and said, "Oh, this is nice." She continued to play with the gun and then pointed it at me—right at my gut—and I could see this sinister look in her eyes. Then she pulled the trigger. I heard the pin of the gun click.

I said, "You fucking bitch! You could have shot me!"

T looked surprised that the gun didn't go off. She tried to play it off and say, "Man, I know you wouldn't give me a loaded gun."

"You didn't know shit, you fucking cunt. What the fuck is wrong with you?" I took the gun from her and walked away. I thought, *This bitch is really crazy in her mind. She probably thinks that if I died, my son would get my Social Security, and she would have more income.* You never know with bitches like her. She would tell the police that it was an accident. That we were arguing and struggling with the gun, and it went off. Then she would tell them about the prior order of protection she had. Yeah, T probably had it all planned in her head.

I had a routine every day, as always. I would get up in the morning, go to work, come home, take a shower while smoking a joint, get dressed, put on my jacket, pat my right pocket to feel for my gun, and then head over to Jason's. On this particular day, nothing seemed out of the ordinary. I came home, said hi to Nana, and she said hi back. Nana always sat in the front room by the front door, looking out the window. I went on about my daily routine. When I put on my jacket and patted my right side pocket, it was empty. I patted it again, since I was high—maybe I missed it. Again, it was empty. I patted my left side, thinking maybe I got off my routine and put it in my left pocket, but that was empty also. I looked in my dresser drawers, in case maybe I put it away. Still no gun. I knew I had it the night before. Where could it be? And then it came to me: Nana.

I walked to the front room, where she was sitting in her chair, looking out the window, like she didn't have a care in the world. I said, "Do you have something that belongs to me?"

Nana looked at me, got up from her chair, and walked into the kitchen. She sat down at the kitchen table and told me to sit down. I did. Nana began to speak. "Now Malik, I understand where we live and I understand why you have it, but you can't have it in this house. I have small children in this house sometimes, and I just can't risk it. Now, I'm going to give it back to you. But if I see it again, I'm going to call the police, and I wrote down the serial number. So, are we understood?"

I told Nana, "Yes," and she gave me back the gun. From then on, I let Jason hold it. I was so surprised at how calm Nana was about the gun, but she was pretty calm about most things. I had forgotten that she went through my stuff from time to time, so her going through my pockets wasn't unusual at all. There were times she would find wrapping paper and just leave it out on the dresser to let me know she found it; she never found marijuana.

A few weeks after the Melanie incident, Melanie called me at Nana's. By this time, things were cool with me. I wasn't feeling any anger toward her. I asked her how she was doing, and the first thing she asked was what happened to all her makeup. She gave me this long, sordid tale about the street life. Long story short, when she left me, she went with Orlando. He tried to pimp her downtown in the big city. Then a real pimp stole her from Orlando, and she ran away from the real pimp. The end.

Melanie asked if there were any hard feelings, and I told her that I was cool and that I understood. She explained that she was in love with Orlando. She said that I was a nice guy, but too nice. When she saw me act the way I did at the pizza parlor, she was scared to come home. Melanie told me, "You're no pimp, you respect women. When you're a pimp, you have an inner disrespect for women. A woman is nothing but a piece of meat, and a means to make money. A pimp has no feelings for his whores. His only concern with his ho is where his money is. You couldn't be like that with me. You had feelings for me. I could tell."

That was the last time I ever spoke to Melanie. The truth was, I was still a little smitten. But time had passed, and I was getting over her. I didn't want to open that Pandora's Box again by asking to see her, but to this day, I can remember her and that short time we spent together. I loved her.

254

Like before, my personal life sucked, but my professional life was growing by leaps and bounds. I was completing projects for Y.E.C. without any problems. I became proficient in the window business, and Steve had an idea—he was going to make me the poster child for Y.E.C. The storyline was, "South Bronx youth and high school dropout comes to Y.E.C., learns a trade, gets his GED, and is now a crew leader supervisor. Look how great this program works, and who better to lead it than someone who's been where the kids enrolled in it have been."

The idea sold like hotcakes. Steve was able to secure grants from different organizations, and Y.E.C. started to grow financially. Whenever Steve would go to a meeting with potential donors, he brought me along—all spit and polished—and would lay it on thick. The donors were mostly, if not all, white.

T came by the job a few times, acting like a fool, and Steve told me I needed to "handle it." We had a good thing going, and he didn't want to see me get arrested for something dumb. If that happened, he would have to fire me. I knew it was just a matter of time.

T didn't understand about growing as a person. All she knew was that job equals money. She didn't care what kind of job her men had, even if it was at Burger King, as long as she got some money out of the deal.

I wasn't just a ghetto bastard high school dropout anymore. I was in a position to grow and meet new and different kinds of people besides street people. I decided to move back in with T and my son in an attempt to pacify her. I figured if I was living with her, the fights would be at home, and not at my job or in front of Nana's door. The plan worked. I was spending more time with my son, and I was still hanging out with Jason. I was, once again, playing the perfect spouse and father. When I was with Jason, it was the same old Russell, but this time, I was a little more cautious with the women I dealt with.

Jason had found himself hooked on a new girl. She had two kids and a job. Nothing fancy, but she supported herself. The girl's name was Susie. Jason really liked her. He wanted to double date with me. Jason told Susie I had a wife, trying to impress her with the people he hung around, and told her that we were going to go on a double date. Susie was divorced from an abusive husband, but she respected the sanctity of marriage. Jason knew I wasn't taking T anywhere, so I asked Julie's best friend, Helen's daughter, to go with me. Helen's daughter was named Judy.

Judy was half-white and half-Spanish. She was a big girl, but not fat, and white-looking, with brunette hair. She was very tall. I knew Judy, but she was always with her boyfriend, this guy named Angelo. I knew Angelo, too, and he even hung out with Jason and me sometimes. Judy was a good-looking woman, and was also sexy. She had a hustle selling Social Security numbers to illegal Mexicans. I don't know where she got the numbers and I didn't ask, but she was a very street-savvy woman.

Angelo was out of town. He went to Los Angeles for some reason or another, so Julie suggested that I ask Judy to come with me. I asked Judy, and she said no problem. She and I were always cool with each other.

I met Judy at Julie's, and the three of us picked up Susie in a cab and went to a dance that someone Susie knew was throwing. I heard Jason and Susie arguing, and she went to the bathroom. Jason said she was mad because Susie had asked if Judy was my wife, and he told her no. Jason said that my wife was sick and couldn't come. Susie asked Jason who Judy was, and he told her Judy was just my friend. Susie said, "Oh. Is that how it works? His wife can't come, so he brings another woman?" Jason had no answer for that.

Needless to say, that night didn't go well, because Susie was acting somewhat stink toward Judy, and Judy wasn't the type to take crap from another woman, especially since she was tall and big and could put a beatdown on the average female. Susie was on the petite side.

I told Jason that Judy and I were going to leave. We caught a cab back to Julie's. It was about 2:00 a.m., and Julie was about to go to sleep. She gave us the keys to one of the vacant apartments. (Julie would sometimes show apartments to people for the landlord.) Then we went to the corner store, which also sold illegal liquor, and bought a large bottle of Bacardi, ice, and cups.

Judy and I went to the vacant apartment, and the first thing she asked me was if I was alright.

I said, "Yeah. Why?"

Judy gave me a long, passionate kiss and said, "That's why."

I rolled a blunt while she fixed our drinks, and they were strong. We both smoked and talked a little. I wasn't expecting this at all. My plans were to drop her off, and then head over to the old lady's house. I was thinking, *What if Angelo finds out?* But then, the Bacardi started to kick in and I said to myself, *Fuck Angelo. If he's dumb enough to leave this fine woman alone while he goes three thousand miles away, then who am I to turn her away?*

Judy and I had sex all night long. It was hot, nasty, passionate sex. It wasn't as good as Melanie's, but it ran a close second. Judy told me she had wanted to fuck me for the longest time, but the opportunity never came up. When we were done, I sent her home in a cab and I slept the Bacardi off on Julie's couch. Julie didn't even know I was there until she woke up and saw me.

She looked at me and said, "I'm not going to even ask, I already know."

I asked her what she meant, trying to spare Judy's reputation.

"Don't try to play dumb with me. I know that girl been wanting to fuck you for the longest time. Do you want something to eat? I know she wore you out."

Julie fixed me some eggs and grits, and I went home to a pissed-off T. She asked me where I was all night. I told her I was drunk, so I stayed at Julie's.

After that, Judy and I started a clandestine affair. The only people that knew were Jason and Julie. Judy didn't want Helen to know anything, because she was still with Angelo. Judy and I would leave Julie's house with Jason, and then go our own way to throw off

257

suspicion. Soon, Jason was getting a little jealous and thought he was entitled to some of Judy's secret sex.

Sometimes, when we were leaving him, he would say, "Hey! What's up with me?"

Judy never beat around the bush, and she wasn't the type of woman that was going to let you run a train on her unless she wanted it. She would tell Jason straight out, "Look, muthafucker, you ain't getting any of this pussy." Jason didn't like that. What Judy and I had was good, strictly fun sex with no strings attached. We liked each other, and neither of us was catching feelings.

Now, Jason was what you would call a cockblocker. Since he saw me getting free sex from a good-looking woman, he thought he was entitled as well, so he would make a brouhaha. It wasn't the sex part, because Jason could always go to the old lady or get some crackhead. It was the fact that the sex was free and with a good-looking woman.

Judy and I would laugh about it. Then she said she had a cousin from Long Island that liked black guys, and we could hang out. I told Jason about it, and he was more than willing. Judy called her cousin, and we picked her up at the Long Island Railroad Station on Fordham Road. That night, the plan for hanging out consisted of sniffing cocaine, drinking Bacardi, and wild, uncommitted sex.

Judy's cousin was a cute, short, white girl, but she had a trashy look, too—she was perfect for Jason. That night, we sniffed cocaine, smoked marijuana, drank, and had sex in two beds right next to each other. When we were done, Jason and I walked with Judy and her cousin down Fordham Road. What a sight! Two black guys with two white girls in the Little Italy section of the Bronx, in the wee hours of the morning. I didn't think we were going to make it home that night.

After that night, Jason left Judy and me alone to do our thing without implying he should get some. Also, I never saw Judy's cousin again. Jason may have hooked up with her without me knowing. So now, I was seeing Judy and still playing the committed spouse and father. I was a committed father, but I started to understand that this thing with T was never going to last.

Denise was a sometimes on, sometimes off thing, depending how things were going with her new man. It was the same type of relationship I was having with Judy; the only difference was that I had feelings for Denise. I knew in my heart that, sooner or later, T and I were going to end. I was so unhappy, but I didn't want to lose my son. At this point in my life, I only had two things that I would die for: Nana and my son.

I didn't even care about the job that much. It was nice to be the boss, but I was so unhappy in my personal life. I decided to give it one last shot. Maybe it was me. Maybe if I really committed to T and stopped acting like I was committed, she would change. Maybe I would start to love her—I at least owed it to my son to try. After all, I did make him a promise when he was born: to do all I could do for him. I promised to give him the world. Now, all I had to do was love his mother and make us a family. Didn't I owe him that? Didn't I promise him that? In life, no matter how hard you try, or how genuine you are, sometimes you can't always keep the promises you make. But with all my heart and might, I was going to try. Even at the expense of my own happiness, I was going to try.

I started to spend more time with T and my son. I would hang out with her at her mother's house, and sometimes at her sister's, to become a part of her family. T's sister and I had a falling out again, and I stopped talking to her, so T and I didn't go there anymore. I went straight home from work every day. Jason and I didn't hang out so much, and anything T wanted, I gave her. I bought her leather coats. I bought her kids things. I would spend most of my time in the house with her. I even started to say things like "honey" and "baby," and show her more affection.

I was doing everything right. I wasn't seeing Judy, or Denise, or making trips to the old lady's house. I would just go to work, come home, smoke a blunt, and watch TV. T was still being a bitch, but I let things go. I didn't want to fight anymore. I did this for a few months, but like always, a person like T would take your kindness for weakness. The following string of events would be the final straw.

Incident #1

I was still young, so I didn't really understand things like tax refunds. When I would get my W2s, I would just leave them lying around the house. T would take the forms and have one of her ghetto tax preparers do my taxes, and then T would sign my name and file my taxes. She did this for two years before I found out. When I did, she still filed them. The only difference was this time, the checks would come to me.

Sometimes I would leave the state refund lying around the house, and that would disappear. When I would ask T if she had seen the check, she would say no, that maybe she threw it away by accident when she was cleaning up the house. But she never cleaned the house—she was a slob.

When I would see Julie, I would tell her about the tax issues and she would say to me, "That's a no-good bitch if she would steal from you, especially with the things you do for her and her kids." I would listen to Julie, but since I wasn't counting on the money anyway, I wouldn't make a big deal about it. But next year, I would do my own taxes.

Incident #2

One day, around October, T showed me a credit card that she had gotten in the mail. She told me the card had a $300 limit on it, and now we could rent cars. So, we started to rent cars, and she would let me drive most of the time. Sometimes, I would take her with me to hang out with Belinda and Kim. Since we now had some wheels, we could go bar hopping. T and I would fight often around Kim and Belinda, but one occasion stands out. I was driving, with Kim and Belinda in the back seat. In the middle of the highway, T got mad and pulled the steering wheel. I noticed that she had the same look on her face as when she pulled the trigger of my gun.

I said, "You fucking bitch. I could have wrecked the car. Somebody could have been killed."

T said, "Fuck you, muthafucker."

I told her, "Never mind about me, but there are two other people in the car that could have been hurt." I turned around and apologized to Kim and Belinda. I pointed to T and said, "Take a good look at this bitch, because you ain't ever going to see her ass out with me again."

T turned to Kim and Belinda and said, "Yeah, right. Fuck him. You'll see me again, girls. This muthafucker is talking shit. He ain't going nowhere."

I drove to Belinda's house. Kim and Belinda exited the vehicle. I drove a block away, got out of the car, and told T, "Fuck you. I don't want to drive your fucking car."

I took the train home. When I arrived, T was there and wanted to argue, but I didn't have it in me. But again, I was thinking of my son. What could I do? I was stuck.

I saw Belinda the next day at work, and she said, "Russell, can I talk to you for a minute?"

I said, "Sure," and we went into her office. I sat down at Belinda's desk.

She said, "Russell, please forgive me if I'm overstepping my bounds, but I care about you and I been where you're at in a relationship. My ex-husband and I used to fight like that, and I've pulled the steering wheel a few times myself, but she's no good for you. She doesn't respect you, and if you don't get out of the relationship, things are going to end very badly. You've got a lot going for you, and she's got nothing to lose."

I thanked her for her advice, and again apologized for the incident. I knew she was right, but my hands were tied. I needed to be there for my son.

Incident #3—The Final Straw

Around the beginning of November, T came to me and said, "Hey, you want to rent a car for Thanksgiving so we can drive around and see family and stuff?"

I said, "Yeah."

T said that she needed $250 to put on the card, because it was at the limit and she needed the money to rent a car. I gave her the $250. T rented the car on Thanksgiving, and we went out to Queens to see my father with the baby, then to Nana's, and then to her mother's. The night went by without any major incidents.

A few days later, T showed me an envelope and said that she applied for a credit card for me—one just like hers. When I opened the card, it was just like hers, but had a $1,500 limit.

T looked at the card and said, "That's fucked up. My card has a $300 limit and you get $1,500."

I didn't think anything of it. Of course, T wanted to use the card to buy all kinds of stuff she didn't need.

I barely used the card, mostly just on T and the kids. I was home one day, and there was opened mail on the table. It was the credit card bill. I saw the $1,500 limit on the card. I looked further and saw all the purchases from restaurants, bars, and women's clothing stores, but the purchases were from June and July. I got my card in November.

As I examined the bill more closely, I saw that it wasn't mine—it was T's. She had gotten the card in May, and she also had a $1,500 limit. My mind raced. Why would she lie about her limit? Why would she have me give her $250 on Thanksgiving, saying that the card was over its $300 limit?

When I got my card, I let her spend on it, very freely, without any questions. She didn't even tell me she had the card until four months after she had gotten it, and never spent anything on me. I know it may have seemed obvious before, from all the other things she had done. But this was such a slap in the face, especially since I was making a genuine effort to be a good, committed man to her. I finally realized that I could never trust her.

I sat on the couch, lit a cigarette, and waited for T to come home. I wasn't mad, I was fed up. I was disappointed. I just continued to ask myself why. Instead of working with me, she was doing everything against me. I thought back to her mother and her upbringing. That might have explained T's behavior, but I couldn't understand her deviousness and her deceitfulness, especially to someone who was treating her well.

T came home, greeted me with a "Hi, honey," and walked toward the bathroom. She was putting some things away and making small conversation.

I just looked at her while she was talking. I was thinking, *How can she be so calm and cool with all the secrets she's been hiding?*

Finally, I said, "You know, you're really fucked up!"

T turned and looked at me with a dumbfounded look. "What now?"

I didn't speak angrily. I spoke like a man that was done with the situation. I spoke like a man that was at his wit's end.

I calmly spelled it out for her like a teacher to a first grader. "I saw the credit card bill. I saw your limit, and you're fucked up. You had that card four months before you even showed it to me. You were out spending, and when you needed a payment, you showed me the card so I could make it. Then, when I got my card, you continued your deceit by playing it off like you were upset that I had a $1,500 limit and you had a $300 limit. How could you treat me like that, after all you've already done to me? You went out of your way to break up Denise and me, knowing we loved each other. You've disrespected my grandmother and disrespected her home on several occasions. You've humiliated me in front of my friends and coworkers. You've called the police on me several times. You stole my income tax checks. You've even stepped out on me with other men, and you still haven't come clean about who that guy was that Jason saw you with. On top of all of that, now you're stealing from me just to do it. Just because you can. You even tried to shoot me with my own gun. I'm done. I can't do this anymore. I can't be with a woman I can't trust. I'm out of here."

When I was done talking, she just stood there with her mouth open. She didn't say anything. She couldn't say anything. Everything I said was true, and she had no justification whatsoever. I packed what little belongings I had and went to Nana's house. I knew if I wanted to get away from T and her drama for good, I had to leave New York.

I thought about how this was going to affect my son. He wasn't even a year old, and here I was, leaving him. I was, creating another ghetto bastard like me.

At work, I told Steve that I had broken up with T. I asked if I could spend as much time in the field as possible, so as not to bring any drama to the office. Steve said, "Fine."

I was hanging out at Julie's straight after work, so as to break my regular routine that T was well aware of. I came home to Nana's when I was ready to go to bed. T called Julie's a couple of times looking for me, but no one ever let her know I was there. She called Nana's, but she wasn't giving any information. T even showed up at the job, but I wasn't there for her to start her drama.

chapter **TWENTY-THREE**

I was keeping a good distance from T. I did miss my son, but I knew I had to create a distance between him and me as well. I had to give the appearance that I didn't care about my son. I had to act like all the other men T had kids by, but it couldn't have been further from the truth. I tried to figure all the angles around how I could be with my son without him being used against me. But for now, I was going to have to just stay away.

I was back to the old Russell again, this time without any boundaries whatsoever. Jason and I were at the Tunnel and the Goat on a weekly basis. I even got to know a couple of girls from the Goat on a personal level. They were cool with me because I never tried to pay them for sex in the club. Jason and I would usually get there about 7:00 p.m. and start drinking and smoking blunts. I had such a routine that all I had to do—even if the girls were talking with another guy—was walk up behind them and whisper in their ear, "Do you want to smoke a blunt?" Without turning around, they would know who I was, excuse themselves from the man they were talking to, and come smoke and hang out with me.

The Goat also had pay-per–view TV, so when there was a major boxing match coming on, Jason and I would watch it there for free. When boxing was on, all the other activities would cease, and the women would hang on the arms of the men, cheering on the fight. I would have two or three beautiful women holding on to me, bringing me drinks, laughing, and joking. Other men would look at me and wonder what was up, since I wasn't giving the women any money.

What the other men in the club didn't understand was that I had my experience with a prostitute already. If a prostitute knows she can manipulate you because you want to have sex with her, then all you're good for is getting money. The women knew I didn't want to have sex with them—well, I did want to have sex with them, but I wasn't going to do it there—so all we had was a friendship. For the first time in my life since I started to have sex with women, I was a single man. There was no one to answer to, and no one to go home to. I could be with any woman I wanted, when I wanted, and without hiding it or worrying about getting caught. I was loving it.

After about a month, T caught up to me at Nana's, thinking that things had blown over and the relationship would go back to normal. I reiterated to her everything that she had done to me, and, like all ghetto rats, her response was, "What about the baby?" Now she wanted to know all my plans for my son, and how much she was going to get, and how often was I going to pick him up. She wanted to know everything then and there, from his first day at preschool to his college graduation.

I told her what most men leaving a woman with a child behind say: "I don't know."

T tried to minimize what she had done by saying that other couples had gone through worse, that she was sorry and wouldn't do it again.

I told her in no uncertain terms, "I don't want to be with you anymore. I don't trust you. I can't be with a woman that I don't trust. Now I know why Denise left me. It wasn't that she didn't love me—she couldn't trust me. You went out your way to make sure of that. Then you had me, but you couldn't keep me, because you can't be trusted. I don't care what the price is that I have to pay. I'll never be with you again."

T was mortified that I brought up Denise and said, "You never loved me. You always loved her, and you know it."

266

"You're right. I always loved her, and still love her. And you're right again. I never really loved you, but I tried. I gave you everything you wanted that I could afford. I treated your kids like they were mine. I loved your daughter like she was my own, but all that wasn't good enough for you. You still had to be a lying, stealing, cheating, devious, self-centered bitch, and no matter what you say, you're always going to be like that. That's never going to change, because that's you. That's T, from the day I met you to today. It's how you are."

T left Nana's crying. I didn't care. I didn't have one morsel of empathy for her.

As time went by, T still didn't believe things were over between us. She thought I was still this eighteen-year-old boy she could manipulate. She didn't understand that I was older, and I had suffered emotionally from the loss of my first love, the embarrassment she had caused me on many occasions, and the humiliation in the courtroom. My emotions were those of a hardened man.

I thought, *At last! My plan has come full circle.* With a lot of detours, of course. It cost me the first woman I ever loved and a lot of pain and humiliation, but finally, T was feeling the hurt that I wanted her to feel. Finally, I was getting the retribution I wanted for all the things she had done to me.

T even tried to entice me with sex on several occasions, but that was to no benefit. I did sleep with her a couple of times, but the sex was different, and she knew it. I was treating her like a whore—have sex with her and leave. Sometimes, to add insult to injury, I would throw $20 on the table before I left. T would be pissed off, but she still took the money. The truth was, sex with T was never really that great. Most of the time—if not all of the time—it was angry sex, and boring at that. The only exceptions were the few time she would surprise me with public sex, like in a cab while the driver was watching her give me oral gratification, or some office building stairwell. I could live without it.

I wasn't eighteen anymore. By now, I had been with numerous women, beautiful women, and women that were professionals at sex. Now, a woman couldn't pussy-whip me. Now, women were there for my pleasure and enjoyment. Whatever I wanted sexually, I could buy, so the tools that T used to manipulate me before were useless. They were a dime a dozen.

As time went on, T would often show up at Nana's house, unsolicited, with gifts, pleading her case and apologizing for everything that she had done to me. It was kind of like the way I was apologizing to Denise when she was leaving me. T would tell me she wanted me to be the way I was before, but it was too late. I was just leading her by a string for my own benefit. Once in a while giving her sex, making her think that there was maybe a chance, although there wasn't (kind of like what Denise had done with me).

I knew it was just a matter of time before the pleading became anger and drama.

chapter TWENTY-FOUR

I was talking with Grammy on the phone. She had an aunt that lived across the street from her in the housing projects, the Castle Hill houses. Grammy said that her aunt wasn't well, and had to go to a nursing home for a while, but didn't know if it was going to be permanent or not. Grammy asked me if I would be interested in staying at her house. She had heard from Nana that T and I weren't together anymore, so she was offering me my own place. I jumped at the opportunity.

This was perfect. Now, I wouldn't have to be concerned about T acting a fool in front of Nana's house. There was no Denise she could blackmail me with. The only thing she had was my son, and I was slowly distancing myself emotionally from him, even though I didn't want to. It was my first place, a one-bedroom apartment and truly a bachelor's pad in every sense of the word. Jason and I were hanging hardcore now that we had somewhere to take women besides a hotel. Jason introduced me to a drug called mescaline for the first time while hanging at the apartment.

There was this girl Jason was seeing—nothing serious—and she brought a friend over. Jason said he had something for me to try. I asked him what it was, and he said it was acid. I refused. I had heard bad things about acid. Jason told me he took it a couple of times, and the girls we were with gave their approval, also. Jason pulled these small purple pills out of his pocket. They almost looked like mouse droppings, they were so small. I asked him what to do with it, and he said to just put it under my tongue and let it dissolve.

I asked a whole lot of questions before I would engage. What does it do? How does it feel? How long does it last? What are the side effects? What could go wrong?

The three of them were laughing at me. They all took it and said, "Just take it, it's not going to kill you. You're just going to laugh a lot."

I asked, "What's a lot?"

Their answer was about twelve hours.

I put the purple pill under my tongue and waited for some type of reaction...and waited, and waited, and waited. But nothing was happening. I said, "Man, someone must have sold you some bull-shit, because I don't feel nothing." The four of us were drinking, and still, I didn't feel anything. Then, about two hours later, I found myself laughing at anything and everything. The four of us were laughing, having sex, and drinking for hours. When the women left, it was well into the afternoon of the next day.

When I finally came down, I couldn't explain the high. I just knew it was fun. I took it a couple more times with Jason, just to see if the first time was a fluke. The last time was the funniest. Jason had taken me to a party—a Spanish party. We had taken the hits of mescaline about an hour before we arrived. Jason and I were the only black guys there. The music was playing as we were standing against the wall, watching the Spanish girls dance. We were laughing, and the people at the party were looking at us because we were having such a good time.

We had been there for about four hours when Jason turned to me and said, "Hey, you know how I know we're fucked up?"

I said, "How?"

"Because we've been here about four hours, and they haven't played anything but Spanish music, and you and I haven't even no-ticed."

He was right. I didn't even realize there was music playing. I had fun on mescaline, but didn't make a habit out of it. The high lasted too long.

270

Every week, Jason and I had different women in my apartment, partying—so many that I can't even remember their names. I was having a ball with my newfound freedom. Denise even came up a couple of times, and we were intimate. This would have been a perfect time for us to get back together, but she still hadn't forgiven me for the past, so she would just use me for sex and move on. I even let T come up and had sex with her. It gave me great pleasure to put her out when I was done with her, recalling the many times she had the cops put me out of her house.

The job was going well, but I wanted to get out of New York. Denise wasn't going to get back with me, and I wanted to get as far away from T as possible.

I called my uncle in Milwaukee. By this time, he had parlayed his drug business into a legal liquor store. I told him I wanted to make a new start of my life, and asked if it would be all right if I came to live up there. Now, I no longer called him Uncle Reesy; I called him Mo. Mo said it was cool, and he would line up a couple of jobs for me. He asked what timeframe I was looking at. It was April, so I asked him if July would be okay. He said it would be.

There were still a couple of projects that Y.E.C. needed to finish, and I didn't want to leave them out in the cold or burn my bridges with them.

I let Steve know when I was planning to leave. He wasn't happy, but told me he could see that I was a young man that was a go-getter, and he could understand why I had to move on. He thanked me for staying until the end of the contract.

This was going to be a good thing—a new start in a new place with some contacts. I was anxious to get started. The only reason to stay in New York would have been for Denise, but it would have been to no avail. The women I was seeing were nothing special, and the further I got away from T, the better. I just saw her sometimes to pacify her until I made some moves, and this was the move.

I told Julie and Jason about my plans, and told Jason that if I could get something started, maybe he could come down and start anew. Jason wanted to move out of the ghetto too, but didn't have any place to go.

The plans were made and in motion, but like the saying goes, "The best-laid plans of mice and men often go astray."

There were only two months until I was to leave for Milwaukee. Jason and I were hanging out one night in a park on the Grand Concourse and Kingsbridge Road. We called it Poe Park because it was named after the writer, Edgar Allen Poe. This night wasn't unlike any other. Jason and I were just sitting on the benches, like many other people in the neighborhood, smoking a blunt, waiting to see where the night would take us.

.While we were smoking, Jason said to me, "Look. There goes Tito's sister, Virginia."

Virginia was walking with another girl, and I asked Jason who she was. Jason said it was Tito's and Virginia's cousin, Vivian. Virginia didn't like Jason, but he was cool with Vivian, and he mentioned that both girls liked to sniff cocaine. The plan was set: we would invite the girls to sniff some cocaine at my place, he would fuck Vivian, and I would fuck Virginia.

Jason called the girls over and introduced me to Vivian. I already knew Virginia because of Tito. She didn't like me too much, either, but Jason and I knew Virginia's love of cocaine would override her dislike for us. We all made small talk, and then Jason said the magic words: "Hey, you girls want to sniff some blow?"

That was it. The plan was in motion. The four of us left the park, caught a cab back to Julie's block, bought some cocaine, and then caught another cab back to my place. Both girls were attractive, but in different ways. Virginia was short, with short, jet-black hair and a petite body. Not much of a chest, though. Vivian was a little taller, with medium-brown, slightly curled hair—not like a black person's curl, but not bone-straight white hair like Virginia's. She was also petite, but heavy-chested.

When the four of us arrived at my place, we started to drink Bacardi rum and smoke a blunt, and then we broke out the cocaine.

At first, neither of the girls was with Jason or me in particular. We were just hanging as a group, and then, during the course of the night, Virginia was sitting next to Jason, and Vivian was sitting next to me.

One thing about Jason and me: when we were on the prowl, we didn't hound the women about having sex. To us, sex was easy to obtain. The women we were with always picked up on that vibe. They never felt any pressure to have sex with us, but it seemed like every weekend, we were having sex with different women, and they always came in pairs.

When you're high on cocaine, alcohol, and marijuana, time seems endless. On the drugs, I was a good listener, especially when I was trying to have sex with a woman. I knew women loved a man that would listen, and that was my method of seduction. I sat next to Vivian as she sniffed the cocaine Jason and I bought, drank the alcohol I had, and smoked the blunt I rolled. And she was a talker. I got to hear her whole life story, and it was a sordid tale of drugs, suicide, jail, and the ghetto. This was her story.

Vivian was the same age as me—twenty-one. She had three sisters and two brothers, and was raised by her grandmother. Vivian was the youngest of all of the children. Most ranged from thirty to forty years old. Vivian didn't know who her father was. The reason there was such an age gap between Vivian and her brothers and sisters was that they were really her aunts and uncles. When Vivian was seven years old, her mother committed suicide and tried to kill Vivian, too. The story was that Vivian's mother was going out with this big-time heroin dealer. She was trying to leave him, but he didn't want her to leave. Vivian said her mother was a very beautiful woman who was also a heroin addict. She had brought her mother out of an overdose many times by dragging her to the bathtub and putting her in a tub of cold water.

When her mother was trying to leave the heroin dealer, he would follow her. Wherever she stayed, he would show up the next day. The man was also very abusive toward her mother, who was in a state of despair and hopelessness.

Vivian told me that they were in Puerto Rico, and her mother had finally given up on life. They were in a park, and her mother pulled out a gun and shot herself in the chest. When Vivian came running toward her, she pointed the gun at her and fired. The bullet grazed Vivian above the forehead, but she still ran toward her mother. Vivian's mother died in her arms. After that, Vivian went to live with her grandmother.

She told me that her aunts and uncles would call her, "You little black bitch," even though she was Puerto Rican—she was a little tanner than they were. She also told me of a couple of instances when the uncles tried to molest her while her grandmother wasn't around. Vivian said she always felt like a stepchild, and was treated like one by her aunts and uncles, but never by her grandmother. That was why she called them her brothers and sisters, not her aunts and uncles.

As she got older, Vivian rebelled and ran away from home. She started to sell drugs and was busted several times. At the age of eighteen, she went to jail for a year on Riker's Island. There, she had to fight a lot to survive. She told me of her first encounter when she arrived in prison. A woman walked up to her, acting very friendly and asking if she wanted a cigarette. Vivian took the cigarette, and the woman gave her a light. The woman proceeded to school her on the ways of the jail and told her that when someone borrows a cigarette, they pay back a pack, so now Vivian owed her one pack of cigarettes. Vivian had taken about five drags.

Vivian didn't have any money on the books, nor was anybody going to send her anything, but the woman was ready to work things out. "To work things out" meant being with the woman sexually. Vivian said she was with the woman and was her girlfriend for a while, but she only did it to survive in jail. When she got out, she said she was strictly dickly.

274

She met this guy named Flacko, a cocaine dealer and an ex-heroin addict. He was about twenty years older than her, but took care of her really well and supplied her with all the cocaine she wanted. That's who she was with now, but he had gotten busted and just got out of jail six months ago. He was broke because the cops and lawyers took all his money. He was on probation, and they lived with his brother, around the corner from Julie's. Yes, she knew Julie, too. Everybody in the neighborhood knew Julie.

That night, I listened to her story and felt that she and I had some things in common. I wasn't looking for a girlfriend. I was just looking for someone to have sex with. Vivian and I sat on one couch, while Jason and Virginia sat on the other. Soon, Vivian and I retired to the bedroom, leaving Jason and Virginia to sleep on the pullout couch. In the morning, we gave them cab fare for the ride home.

When the women were gone, Jason asked if Vivian told me who her boyfriend was. I said, "Yeah. Some guy named Flacko."

Jason said, "Yeah. He used to be big-time, but he ain't shit now. He just tries to live off his old reputation."

I didn't care. I wasn't trying to take his woman. I already had sex with her; I didn't need to know his whole life story.

I had had a good time with Vivian, and the sex was pretty good—not great, but since I had already had sex with her, it was easier than picking up new women. So I told Jason if he saw her to tell her that I wanted to hook up again. Jason did, and told her to call me. We made plans, but she had to find a way to get away from Flacko.

The next weekend, I met her at Julie's, and we took a cab back to my place. I asked how she was able to get away, and she said she started a fight with Flacko about him not wanting to take his medicine. I didn't know what the medicine was for, and I didn't care. Once we settled in, we repeated the first time we were together, only now, we had more time and solitude.

We talked as much as we had sex. Vivian didn't have a job and wasn't looking for one. We did have some things in common, though, one of which was a troubled childhood. We both smoked cigarettes, sniffed cocaine, and smoked marijuana. She was cool to hang out with, but not girlfriend material. I wasn't looking for a girlfriend, anyhow—I was leaving for Milwaukee soon.

As she and I were talking, I found there was something else we had in common—we were unhappy in our current relationships. I told her about T and all that dirty business, and that we weren't together, but did have sex from time to time. I never mentioned Denise.

Vivian told me how she and Flacko were broke. She stayed because he had guilted her into it. He did this when he was in jail, saying to her, "Oh, you were just with me for my money. I treated you good, and now that I'm going in jail, you're going to leave me." She told him she would stand by him, but she was tired of the relationship.

I told her that she was young, and if she wasn't happy in a relationship, she should move on. She had a lot of life to live. He was twenty years older than she was, and she didn't want to be forty and him sixty and find herself taking care of an old man. Her whole life would pass her by. I was just talking common sense to her, and she said, "You know, you're right."

I told her to be honest with the guy and tell him that she wasn't happy. Vivian said she was going to do it the next day, because she knew there was going to be a fight when she got back home after staying the night with me. She was going to leave him and take her things to her mother's. (She called her grandmother her mother.)

I said if she wanted to, she could swing by after that, and we could hang out some more. I was going to be at work, so I gave her the key to the bottom lock and told her to wait for me inside the apartment. I didn't care that she would be in the apartment by herself. I didn't really have anything in there to take, or that I was concerned about her seeing.

276

When I came home, she was there. I asked her what happened, and she said she left Flacko and dropped her things off at her mother's.

"Cool." Then, I looked in the corner of my bedroom and saw a small suitcase. I pointed to the suitcase and said, "What the fuck is that?"

Vivian looked at me and gave me a small smile and said, "Well I didn't want to be running back and forth to my mother's, so I brought a few changes of clothes here." I made it clear that she was not living there, but one day became two, and two days became three, and so on. I would come home, and she would have the house clean and dinner cooking. We would have sex twice a day during the week, and three times a day on the weekends. I figured I was leaving anyway, so if she stuck around until I left, then it was to my benefit. What wasn't to my benefit was that she didn't have a job, and she had every habit that I had. I was smoking two blunts and half a pack of cigarettes a day, and now it was times two, plus food.

I made it a point for her not to answer the phone, and for about three weeks, everything was going well. She and I would hang out at Julie's, sometimes with Jason. And then, word got to her ex-boy-friend. He would make idle threats about going to get a gun or stuff like that, but when people would come and tell me, I would say to tell Flacko, "I'm right here, come and get some."

No one ever came. I felt a little empathy for the guy, but what was done was done.

People from the block would even tell me that he would be drunk and screaming in the street, "That bitch gave me AIDS!"

All his actions seemed desperate. When I would hear of them, it reminded me of when Denise left me and I was calling her job at New York University. I knew a hurting man would say anything to get a woman back.

My birthday came, and Jason, Kim, Vivian and I celebrated by having a cocaine party at Frida's. While there, I had an idea. Frida knew I was leaving in about a month, so I asked her if she would consider letting Vivian stay with her. I told Frida that she was going to be living with her mother when I left, but she wanted a little more independence. Frida said it was okay, but I needed to do her a favor first. Dennis needed a job. She knew I had a lot of influence with Steve. I told Frida I could do it, and then she said that Vivian could live there, and that we would work out the plans and money later. I thought that was a good deal. At least, this was a step for Vivian to move toward her own independence, without relying on a man. I told Vivian she was going to have to get a job, and she was all for it.

I even introduced Vivian to Grammy and Pete. After meeting her, Grammy said to me, "You can't be around other women with her. She is very jealous and possessive."

I told Grammy that we weren't serious, but Grammy was right about her. It was a characteristic I didn't like about Vivian, but I was leaving soon, so it didn't matter to me.

During the week, I went to see my son. T wanted to come to the apartment, but I told her no. I had gotten home a little later than usual, and Vivian asked me what had taken me so long. I told her that I went to see my son.

Vivian started asking me a lot of questions, and then she finally got to the real one: "Did you tell your son's mother about us?"

I said, "What about us? There's no need for me to mention us."

She became very hostile, and told me I needed to handle this shit. I was somewhat confused as to what she was talking about, because we were supposed to be just hanging out. I never said she was my woman. She was just the maid, the cook, and my sex outlet until I left for Milwaukee. I liked her, but I wasn't all head-over-heels.

In the heat of the argument, the phone rang. In an act of defiance—as I had told her not to answer my phone, in case Denise called—Vivian picked up and in a tone that said this was her house, said, "Hello. Who is it?" And then she said, "Hold on." She handed the phone to me and said, "Now handle this shit, muthafucker."

I took the phone without even knowing who it was. I hoped it wasn't Denise. I hadn't seen or talked to her in about a month, and I was still in love with her, so I didn't want to mess up the little time she did allow me to spend with her.

I said, "Hello."

It was T. She had an attitude in her voice and said, "So that's how it is, Russell?"

All I could say was, "That's the way it is."

"Okay, muthafucker, you're fucked up." She hung up the phone.

I looked at Vivian and said, "You see what you started?"

Vivian was unapologetic about her actions. She knew what she was doing—she was making a claim on me and letting all the bitches know she was in the picture. I knew a shitstorm was about to begin, and I wasn't wrong.

The next day, I went to work, told Steve what happened, and that I would be going straight to the job sites until things calmed down. I also told Steve about Dennis. Steve said that if I was recommending him, I should bring Dennis in to fill out the paperwork, and he'd have the job. Dennis went in and started as my assistant the same day.

Steve beeped me on my pager, so I called the office. T came by with my son, looking for me. Steve said she called the house and spoke to Vivian, in front of everybody. All he could make out of the conversation was that T was asking Vivian who she was, Vivian asked T who she was, and T said, "I'm his wife." Steve didn't know what Vivian said, but T hung up the phone after whatever response Vivian gave her.

When I got home, I asked Vivian what happened, and she pretty much reiterated what Steve had said. I asked Vivian what she said to T. T didn't know that I had told Vivian about the whole marriage scam. So, Vivian told her she knew all about it, and if she was stupid enough to leave a nigger like me in an apartment by himself, then she was a dumb bitch. That was when T hung up the phone on her.

I knew that wouldn't be the end of it, but at least it was out in the open. T didn't dare come to the apartment. She knew by the way Vivian was talking that she was likely to cut T's face or something—she was one of those fighting women.

Maybe this wasn't a bad thing; it was definitely a way to get rid of T.

About a week later, Julie called me and said, "Russell, T called me. Malik is in the hospital emergency room. She said, 'Julie, you tell him to get his ass over here right away.'"

Julie told me that Malik was at Columbia Presbyterian Hospital in Manhattan. I asked what was wrong with him, and Julie said, "I don't know. T didn't say."

My mind was racing about what was wrong with my son. Did T do something to him? Did he hurt himself? How serious was it?

I got up to get dressed, and Vivian started to get dressed to come with me. I told her, "No, you can't come." She tried to argue, so I had to curse her out. "Look bitch, you ain't coming. You ain't getting into no fight at the hospital while my son is sick. I don't even know what's wrong with him, so stay the fuck here."

Vivian was pissed off and started to talk shit back. "Oh, there's probably nothing wrong with him. She just wants you to come running when she calls." I told her that might be the case, but until I found out, she wasn't coming with me. I stormed out of the house and caught a cab to the hospital.

I walked into the emergency room and asked the attending nurse where I could find Malik Russell. I said I was his father. The nurse escorted me to a section of the emergency room where Malik was lying in a bed with IVs in his arms and an oxygen tube in his nose. He didn't look good. T was sitting by his bedside and saw me as I approached the bed.

T started right away. "About time your ass got here."

I just ignored the comment and asked what was wrong with Malik.

T said they ran some test and were waiting for results. He was at her mother's house, and he became unresponsive and was lying there motionless, so they called for an ambulance. Then she added, "You would have known that if you wasn't with your Puerto Rican bitch."

I ignored her comment once again. All I could concentrate on was the question of why my son was lying in this hospital bed. I felt helpless to do anything for him.

I thought, *How could I have let this happen? I promised him that I would protect him.* I thought that I'd been neglecting him lately. No one could have been harder on me than me, but T was trying. Every other word out of her mouth was condemnation for my actions, for leaving her, for not being there for my son.

In the middle of T's tirade, the doctor came and told us what was wrong. Malik had a bowel obstruction, and he was going to need emergency surgery immediately. The doctor had papers for T and me to sign, and said the nurses would be back to take him and prep him for the operation. My son wasn't even a year and a half old, and these doctors were going to cut into him. I was beside myself with grief and fear. I knew any surgical procedure was dangerous, but it was especially dangerous with young children when they had to go under anesthesia.

While all this was going on, T decided this was going to be her show. She started to rip into me about what was going on between us. She went on what seemed like and endless tirade of insults and a barrage of "How could you do this to me and your son?" condemnations.

I can remember her words like they were yesterday—not because they were so effective in their purpose, but because I kept thinking, *Does this woman have no shame? Here we are, with our son getting ready to be operated on, and all you can think about is you, you, you, you. What was done to you. Not the things you did to deserve it, but what you were feeling. Have you no decency at all?*

"You're a fucking bastard. You make me sick. You left me for a Puerto Rican. You're disgusting. I swear to God, if it's the last thing I do, I'm going to get you, muthafucker!"

I interrupted her and said, "Can't this wait? Your son is lying in a hospital bed, deathly sick to the point that they have to do emergency surgery on him, and you're at his bedside, cursing me out."

T's response was, "He'll be fine, but you're a fucking bitch."

It seemed as if she was trying to provoke a reaction out of me, but I had no energy for her.

Just as she was done with her tirade, her sister, Lisa, walked into the emergency room. Now, I had two of my archenemies staring daggers at me. I just got up, walked away from the bed, and waited in the waiting room.

Malik's operation was fine. After that night, I saw him once more, and then I didn't see him for another six years. His mother took him to Tacoma, Washington. I tried many times in the court system to get visitation rights, but because I didn't live in that state, it made the process very cumbersome. What wasn't cumbersome was T getting child support from me, even though she was in a state 3,000 miles away.

When I returned home from the hospital, Vivian was very apologetic about her earlier comments—the ones regarding nothing being wrong with my son. I was so emotionally drained, I just let it go.

Now, a couple of days of Vivian staying with me had turned into a month, and it was almost time for me to move to Milwaukee. I went by Frida's one day after work to secure the plans we had discussed about Vivian staying there, and Frida dealt me a wicked blow. She did a 180-degree turn on me—she didn't want Vivian to stay with her.

I argued that we had a deal, and I had done my part. Dennis had been working for about six weeks now, and Frida was surely benefiting from his employment. I also looked out for him when he screwed up, since he wasn't qualified for the job in the first place. I pointed all these things out to Frida to remind her of the great lengths I went to in order to help her out. I asked her why was she doing this, and she said she didn't trust Vivian. She said Vivian looked like she smoked crack.

I was offended by her remarks, but I wasn't angry with Frida. I was hurt not by her words, but by her actions. I thought she and I had something special after Mitchell had died. I looked to her as one of the few people I could trust, but here she was using me and betraying me like an enemy.

I asked her to reconsider, but she said, "No. That's it. I don't want to talk about it anymore."

I didn't argue the point any further. I left the apartment feeling that I had lost someone close to me. I knew I wasn't going to be able to forgive her for this. She had used me to get Dennis a job. She knew I was leaving, so it wasn't like I could take the job back. I recollected the tone and look on her face—smugness, like she had gotten one over on me.

When I got home, I told Vivian what had happened. She called her sister, Gloria, and asked if she could come and stay with her in a couple of weeks.

Damn, I was played. Vivian never went to her mother's to drop anything off. She had come right to my house when she left her boyfriend, intending to stay with me. That was a lot to handle in one day. I discovered two acts of betrayal against me by two people that were in my inner circle.

I didn't mention to Vivian that I recognized her actions; I was leaving, so what did it matter now?

A couple of days later, Grammy called and asked me to come over. She said that if I wanted to be on the safe side when I left, Vivian could stay at the apartment—just in case things didn't work out in Milwaukee and I wanted to come back. At least I would have a place to live. I didn't even think about things not working out in Milwaukee. It was a good idea, but there was a catch—Grammy said I had to give her two months' rent for the apartment before I left. The rent was only $130, so it wasn't a big deal. However, I had planned to go to Milwaukee with $1,500, but with Vivian living with me—with no job, buying food, cigarettes, marijuana and, on occasion, cocaine for two people—the two months' rent was hitting my pocket hard. I agreed anyway.

The only thing that always rang in my mind was if I could trust Vivian. I hadn't known her that long, only about six weeks now, and I saw how coldly she left her boyfriend of two years because he wasn't rolling in the dough anymore. If I really thought about it, she was using me, too.

The next incident proved that I couldn't trust her. If I was smart, I would have dropped her ass then. But at twenty-one years old, I wasn't that smart, and I was very prideful. As the expression goes, "Pride comes before the fall."

It was about a week before I was going to leave for Milwaukee. Jason, Virginia, Vivian, and I were hanging on Julie's block. Jason and Virginia had started to see each other on a regular basis by now, and the four of us would hang out a lot. Jason and I left the girls in front of Tito's building while we went to go buy some marijuana. By this time, we were no longer buying nickel and dime bags—we were buying ounces and half ounces. We told the girls we would be back in about an hour, but the transaction only took about twenty minutes.

Jason and I returned to the block much earlier than expected, a group of people was in front of Tito's building. I saw Tito, Virginia, Vivian, and this guy that was standing very close to Vivian. They had not seen Jason and me coming down the block, because we had come back in a different direction than we had left. Vivian and this guy were being very flirtatious, and she was even holding his hand in a playful manner. I had seen the guy before; his name was Max. He was nobody in particular, just a guy.

Max saw Jason and me coming from up the block, and I saw his eyes get big. He said something to Vivian, she dropped his hand really quickly, and he walked off. Jason saw the incident, too.

We walked up to Vivian and Virginia. I said, "Who the fuck was that, bitch?"

Vivian responded very quickly, "Oh, that was my cousin."

I looked at Virginia and asked her, "Who the fuck was that?"

She also said it was their cousin, Max.

I didn't believe either of them. I looked at Tito, who knew better than to lie to me, and asked him.

Tito said, "Man, I ain't in this," and walked away.

I knew then that both those bitches were lying. The four of us took a cab to Virginia's house, and the cab ride was silent, the atmosphere thick.

I was festering the whole ride, thinking, *This bitch must think I'm a fool. She thinks she's going to play me.* My mind started racing, going over all that had transpired during the last six weeks.

I thought about how Frida and I were now at odds with each other because of Vivian. I thought about the situation with T. Even though I was leaving her, I had my own way of doing it. Now, I had to accelerate the process. I thought about how I planned to have $1,500 to go to Milwaukee with, but now I'd be lucky if I had $300 when I left. I thought about how, for the past six weeks, I had been taking care of her, buying her drugs, buying her cigarettes, buying her food, and this was how she repaid me. My blood was boiling.

When we got up to Virginia's apartment, I sat in a chair by myself. Jason, Vivian, and Virginia sat on her bed and rolled a blunt with the marijuana Jason and I had just bought. Virginia had a bottle of Bacardi rum in the bedroom, and I started to take straight shots of it. The more shots I took, the more I started to think about how Vivian was playing me.

I started to make little cynical remarks to her as the night went on, like, "You know that's not your fucking cousin, you lying bitch." I would even make remarks to Virginia. "Why the fuck you lying for her? Fuck both you bitches." I continued to taunt them all night. I told Vivian, "Just come clean. You know you lying. He ain't your cousin."

By the second hour, I was very drunk and furious that the two women were continuing to lie to me. Jason was telling me to cool down and lay off the Bacardi, but his words fell silent in my ears. Finally, I had enough. I jumped out the chair, grabbed Vivian by her neck with both my hands, and picked her up off the floor, choking her.

"So he's your cousin, bitch?"

Vivian tried to remove my hands, but I had a solid grip on her neck. Jason and Virginia had to pull me off her. I dropped Vivian to the floor. Jason held me back while Virginia helped Vivian up.

I continued my assault. I reached past Jason, grabbed Vivian by her hair, and tried to pull her toward me. Again, Jason and Virginia intervened between us. Now, Vivian was swinging at me, trying to strike me in the face. This was now a knockdown, drag 'em out fight between Vivian and me. Jason and Virginia were in the middle, trying to break us up.

Virginia said, "You guys got to leave. You're tearing up my house."

I agreed and said to Vivian, "Yeah, bitch. Let's take this shit home."

As we walked out of Virginia's apartment, I grabbed Vivian by her hair again and slapped her in her face. She fell down a landing.

Virginia and Jason were still in the apartment and heard the commotion. They came out to intervene once again. Vivian and I fought from the fifth floor to the first floor. I was slapping her, and she was fighting back. Jason and Virginia were trying to stop us. It was a wild scene. People were stopping and looking in the building as the commotion continued.

Finally, when we were both out of breath, we stopped, left Virginia's building, and caught a cab. In the cab, Vivian said, "You want me to go, Russell, then I'll go when we get to the apartment. I'm packing my things and leaving."

I was still drunk, and my mind was racing, still on the question of who was that guy was. Vivian still hadn't come clean.

When we got to the apartment, she started to pack her stuff. I had bought her a couple of outfits, and when she packed them, I ripped them from her suitcase and said, "You're not taking shit I bought you, bitch. Go get Max to buy you shit."

Vivian responded by trying to swing on me, and another physical fight broke out. This time, Vivian took a different approach: she was destroying things in my house. She ran into the kitchen, pulled out the glasses from the cabinet, and started to throw them on the floor. I grabbed her by her hair and pulled her out of the kitchen to stop her. When I let her go, she ran to my TV set and pushed it over. It fell to the floor. Sparks came out and the screen glass broke. Then, she ran into the bedroom and started to break my cologne bottles.

I grabbed and dragged her by her shirt collar out of my room and said, "Just take your shit and get the fuck out, bitch."

After Vivian left, I took a visual survey of the house. It looked like a hurricane had run through. I didn't even have the strength to clean it up that night; I just laid down and slept the Bacardi off.

chapter **TWENTY-FIVE**

I got up the next day, hungover. Jason stopped by to see if everything was cool and said, "Man, I never seen you act that way with a female. Even when T was bugging out, you didn't go off like that." Jason also told me that Vivian was around the block, telling people that I beat her up.

I just said, "The bitch was trying to play me."

When Jason left, I cleaned up the house.

That night, by some strange coincidence, Denise called me. All that time Vivian was there, Denise never called. She wanted to come by. She visited later that night, and we talked. She said that her friend Rosemary was moving in with her boyfriend, and was going to let Denise have her apartment. I didn't know why she was telling me this; she knew I was leaving for Milwaukee in a couple of days. I thought she was trying to tell me that we couldn't see each other on the down-low anymore. Probably because her boyfriend was moving in with her, or he would be spending a lot of time with her and it would be hard for her to get away.

When Denise left that night, I had a sorrowful feeling in my heart. Up to this point, she had lived with her parents. But now, she was going to have her own place, and she and her boyfriend would have more time to be intimate. Who knows where that would lead—maybe marriage. When Denise left that night, I didn't see her for three years.

The next day, I was in a slump. I was thinking about Denise, and how things could have been if I hadn't screwed up, and how things could be if she would just forgive me. I still loved her, and even the slightest thought of her being married to someone else was agonizing. I thought about my son—how he was taken from me, and how I would not be able to see him grow up. I felt so alone in the world. I thought about how Frida and I were on the outs. I was thinking that it was going to be a good move to start a new life in Milwaukee. There was nothing here for me anymore; Denise was growing closer to someone else. My son was 3,000 miles away, and I didn't even have a phone number. I couldn't wait to go and leave all this misery behind me. I was only twenty-two; I could start over, and this would be all a bad dream.

As I was wallowing in self-pity, the phone rang. It was Jason. He said that Virginia was in the emergency room at Lincoln hospital. I asked what happened; he had a sense of anger in his voice. Jason said that Virginia was jumped by some girls around her block, and that they beat her and stripped her naked in the street, and she ran home naked. He said he had been sleeping and heard her banging on the door. When he opened it, she was standing there, bloody and naked.

Jason was calling me from the hospital, and I told him I would get dressed and meet him there. When I arrived, Jason, Virginia, and a couple of her family members were coming out of the emergency room. Virginia was beaten badly. Her face was swollen, her left eye was closed from the beating, and the other eye was black. The left eye had a golf ball-size contusion on it, and her top and bottom lips were busted with the crust of blood on them. When I saw her, I knew that retribution was definite.

Jason was full of rage and talking out of his head. He was saying, "Muthafuckers going pay for this shit. Fuck this, I'm going to kill someone for this shit. Do this shit to my girl, fuck that."

I told Jason to calm down and worry about that later.

Virginia and her family members got in a cab and went to her mother's house.

Jason and I went to my apartment, sat down, and discussed re-venge. Before we got to the details, I asked Jason more about the incident: the who, what, when, where, and why. All I knew was that Virginia was jumped by some girls, and before I went out to engage in warfare, I needed to know what we were fighting for.

Now, all the sordid details came out. Jason said that Virginia used to mess with some married guy. She used to sniff cocaine with him. Virginia was out early in the morning and walked by the guy's building, and the wife saw her. The wife lived on the first floor, so when Virginia walked by, the woman hit her in the head with a flower pot. Then she and two other women came out to beat Vir-ginia up. They ripped her clothes off and laughed at her as she ran home naked. Jason said that the people lived right around the corner from Virginia.

When Jason finished, I tried to be the voice of reason. I asked him what Virginia was doing out so early that morning. I asked if there was a chance that Virginia was still seeing the guy, and if not, how long had it been since they were together? I asked Jason to consider the aftermath of our retribution. Was Virginia going to be safe, since the people lived right around the corner? And who were we going after, the guy or the women?

Jason was full of rage and didn't want to hear any of what I was saying. "Fuck all that bullshit. If that was Denise, you wouldn't be asking all those muthafucking questions. Do you got my back or what?"

I was surprised he mentioned Denise, but he was right. I now understood what he was going through.

All we needed to do was get our small army together, get some more weapons, and make a plan. I told Jason it would be wise to strike right away, because they wouldn't be expecting us to return the same day. We took a cab to Julie's and gathered the troops.

When we got to Julie's, she had already heard what happened. Her stepson, George, was there, and Tito, Virginia's brother, had met us there as well. Jason called this guy named Rob that he worked with and we hung out with a couple of times. Rob owed Jason and me because one time, some guys were going to jump Rob after work. He was an undercover security guard, and some of the people he busted were threatening to come back and hurt him. I loaned him my .25 auto so he would feel safe if anybody showed up. So now there were five of us, and we needed to take stock of our weaponry. I had the .25 automatic, and Julie gave us her .32 automatic. Jason had a .22 rifle that he had bought some time back, but it was too large to carry in the street, so he hid it in Julie's closet. I took the rifle and sawed off the butt, so it would be smaller and have a pistol grip.

The five of us went to a vacant apartment to map out the block and plan our attack. I made the entire plan. I was leaving in two days for Milwaukee, so I wasn't letting hotheaded Jason plan anything. I decided we would approach the block from both directions. George and I would come from the far end with the rifle. Rob would come up from the other end by himself with the .32 automatic and stand by the building. Jason and Tito would be together with the .25 automatic, and draw the attention of the people we were after, since they knew who Jason and Tito were.

The plan was set. We all took separate cabs to our destination. George and I got in one, Jason and Tito in another, and Rob in a cab by himself.

Rob got to the building first, got out of the cab, and calmly leaned on a car and smoked a cigarette. Five minutes later, George and I arrived up the block and got out within view of the building. I could see Rob from where I was. I put the rifle in a nearby garbage pile until it was needed. About five minutes later, Tito and Jason came walking through the block in the middle of the street.

The plan had worked so far—Tito and Jason caught the attention of the woman that hit Virginia with the flowerpot. She was unafraid, and walked right up to them in the middle of the street and said, "Hey, you looking for me?"

Jason looked at the woman and his eyes turned red with rage. Now there was a target. Now there was someone to unleash his fury on. Now there was a face to put on the crime.

Jason didn't even answer the woman. He just reached into his pocket, and all hell broke loose.

Jason pulled out the .25 automatic and slapped the woman in the mouth with it, knocking out her two front teeth. Blood came pouring from her mouth. As the woman held her mouth in pain, Jason came down on top of her head with another strike from the gun, and she fell to the ground. Jason and Tito started to kick her body and stomp her head into the ground. George and I saw the activity, so I grabbed the rifle and ran down the street.

A small crowd was forming around Jason and Tito as they beat the woman. I fired two shots in the air, and the crowd quickly dispersed.

Jason and Tito continued the savagely beat on the woman. Her husband came running out of the building with a baseball bat raised, attempting to strike Jason over the head.

Rob came up behind him, put the .32 automatic to his head, and said, "Put that shit down, muthafucker."

The man dropped the bat, and Rob struck him in the head with the gun. The man fell to the ground. Rob put his foot on the man's neck as the man helplessly watched Jason and Tito stomp and kick the woman until they were out of breath.

I yelled to both of them, "Come on! Let's get the fuck out of here."

By this time, people were all around, but not as close, since everyone saw the guns. People were looking out of their windows with faces of horror at the vicious beatdown. The five of us ran around the corner to Virginia's building with guns in hand.

When we got in front of it, people were outside watching the incident too, since the buildings were so close by. Jason decided this was his time to make a statement on the block, since he was staying there sometimes, and he wanted people there to know what he was capable of.

Jason took the .32 automatic, since it was a bigger gun, and walked back and forth in front of Virginia's building. Then he fired a shot in the air and said, "Fuck that shit! Muthafuckers want to fuck with me, this is what the fuck is going to happen."

Tito, George, Rob, and I all hid behind a car, fearing that the police would come soon due to the gunfire. Jason wasn't hiding anything; he made sure people saw and heard the gun.

Finally, I yelled to Jason, "Yo, nigger, you gonna get us busted! Stand the fuck down, and let's get the fuck off the street before the cops come!"

Jason heeded what I said and we all entered the building separately, in intervals, all the while people on the block watching our every movement.

The five of us ran up to Virginia's apartment on the fifth floor, hid the guns, and watched from the fire escape as police cars circled the block with their lights on. The cops didn't get out of their cars, and soon disappeared from sight. The five of us started to laugh and go over what happened and what we saw from our vantage points. The adrenaline was coming down, but there was still danger. I brought up that the people we just attacked knew where Virginia lived, and we should be ready in case they decided to strike back in the wee hours of the morning. I tried to think how I would retaliate if the same situation happened to me.

Rob had to leave; he was married, and had a kid at home. Truth be told, he had no business out there with us. The four of us that remained were in it until the end. I figured the attack could only come from one of two directions, or both directions if they had enough people. I wasn't willing to make any assumptions, so I planned for the worst-case scenario.

George and Tito stayed in Virginia's apartment, while Jason and I stayed in Tito's, since it was right across the hall from Virginia's. Tito would stay by the window with the fire escape, holding the .25

automatic. George would stay by the entrance door to the apartment with a large knife.

Jason and I were across the hall. He was at the entrance door, looking out the peephole at Virginia's door. I was at the fire escape window. This way, all angles to the apartments were covered.

The four of us waited and waited, but no one came. We were ready for anything. We stayed up all night, and I can remember watching the sun come up. When we decided the coast was clear, George and I left and caught a cab. Jason and Tito stayed behind with the guns in the apartment.

When I got home that morning, I took a long shower. I was thinking how thankful I was that no one was killed. It was two days until I was on a plane to Milwaukee.

Jason called that afternoon and told me that two guys came to Virginia's mother's house. Virginia opened the door, and it was the woman's husband—the guy she used to mess with, the cause of all the trouble. Jason told me that the guy begged Virginia for the situation to be over. He said he didn't want any more trouble, that his wife was in the hospital with broken ribs and needed dental reconstruction on the front of her mouth. The man said the police asked them if they knew who did it, but they didn't tell them about Virginia. The man was sincerely scared for his wife, and begged Virginia to call off the dogs.

Virginia didn't admit to anything, since there was a witness present. She thought the other man may have had a gun—they would have been dumb to come into enemy territory without one. Virginia just told the guy she would see what she could do, and the two men left. Jason said that Virginia's mother was a little disturbed, but she understood the situation.

The next day, I went to Y.E.C. to pick up my final check. Steve told me he was sorry to see me go, but if things didn't work out in Milwaukee, I always had a place at Y.E.C.

Before I left, Dennis approached me and said, "Hey man. Sorry about that thing that Frida did. Hope you don't have any hard feelings towards me. It all worked out anyway, right?"

I didn't tell anyone that Vivian was gone. I did mention she was going to be able to stay at my place. I told Dennis that I didn't hold anything against him. What was done was done. I thought, *What could I do about it anyway?*

That afternoon, Jason called and told me that he was coming up so we could hang out before I left. I called Denise to say goodbye, but she wasn't home. I was all packed and ready—ready to leave all the bullshit behind. I was thinking about the last time I was in Milwaukee—I was thirteen and taking cocaine orders for my uncle. The last night I was there, I was up all night sniffing cocaine. I wondered what it would be like know.

All I wanted to do when I got there was hit the ground running. My uncle said he had some construction jobs lined up, and I just wanted to start to work. I wasn't looking for any handouts. I was no stranger to hard work, and I was ready. I didn't have the $1,500 I wanted to go down with; I had $400. But if I started work right away, it shouldn't be a problem.

There was a knock at the door, and I looked through the peephole. It was Jason. I opened up, and there was Vivian, standing right next to him.

I wasn't angry like the night Vivian left. I let them both in, and Vivian and I went to the bedroom and talked. We didn't talk about who Max was; the conversation consisted mostly of whether she could still stay at the apartment. I figured I had already paid two months' rent for it, and I didn't tell anybody about what happened between Vivian and me, so I let her stay there. I was playing it safe, just in case things didn't work out. I never liked putting all my eggs in one basket.

TWENTY-SIX

I left for Milwaukee the next day, anxious to start my new life. The plane ride took about two hours. My uncle Maurice picked me up at the airport. I was happy to see him and ready to get started. I asked him various questions about the jobs he had lined up for me. He told me to take my time and cool out for about a week, then I could get down to business.

My uncle took me by his new liquor store to show it off. The place was huge. His girlfriend Michelle's nephew, Wayne, was running things for him. Wayne was about my age, and he had a couple of his friends working there. A few of Maurice's old dealer friends worked there, too.

Everyone at the store called my uncle Mo, like they did in his drug-dealing days. Mo showed me around and explained the operation. He told me that the business grossed half a million a year. I wasn't really interested; I just wanted to get started on my own thing.

The people that worked at the store were a tight group. They did everything together, kind of the way mafia people do. That night, we all went out to a fair. I was watching everyone interact, feeling like an outsider. They busted each other's balls all the time, but it seemed kind of silly to me.

During the fair, I passed by a long-distance phone call promotion table, where they would let you make a long-distance call for free to promote their product. I took the opportunity to call Vivian. It was about 2:00 a.m. in Milwaukee, so that meant it was 3:00 a.m. in New York. I called, but there was no answer. It did run through my mind—where could her ass be at three? But I couldn't focus on that down here. I had to keep my mind on the prize.

During the first week, my uncle had me work at the store with him a couple of times. On Friday, when everyone got paid, I thought I would be getting something. However, when I inquired, he started to act a little funny. He said, "Why should I pay you any-thing? You're staying in my house for free."

This was a bad sign.

Later on that night, Michelle told me that my mother had called him and said, "If I knew you wanted to take care of a grown person, I would have come down there a long time ago." I wasn't surprised that she would do that. God forbid anybody did anything to help me. My mother was a jealous person, even of her only son, and any good fortune anybody would bestow upon him.

During that first week, Vivian called every day. I told her I called her that first night at 3:00 a.m., and she wasn't there. She gave me some bullshit story that she was hanging out with Virginia.

After the first week, I was ready to get started, but there was nothing coming my way. I asked my uncle about the construction jobs he had told me about, and he said that they fell through. I kept working at his liquor store for free.

My uncle was on this health food kick where he didn't eat any-thing dead, so there was barely any food in the house that I could eat. My money was running low from buying fast food for myself. Besides that, Vivian had called and asked me to send her $50 be-cause she was broke. I didn't let the fact that my uncle didn't come through for me with a job stop me from trying to get work. I started to go to job placement companies, but this presented another prob-lem: I didn't have a car. When I would ask my uncle or his girlfriend to take me someplace, I was met with resistance. One time, when I asked my uncle to take me, he had a nasty tone in his voice and told me that I needed to learn how to get around. In other words, I needed to learn how to take a bus.

I also started to feel animosity from the workers at the store. They were treating me as if I was there to spy on them for my uncle, and this couldn't have been further from the truth. The crews of fellows were always at the house, and when Vivian would call, they would make smart comments about me being pussy-whipped.

I did notice something strange while I was there. This guy named Dallas kept calling the house, but neither Mo nor Michelle would take the calls. I remembered Dallas; he was Michelle's mother's boyfriend, and they were both in the drug game. The last time I saw Dallas, he was wearing diamonds so large that when you looked at him, they would blind you. I knew that he and Mo were in some kind of illegal business together. I was able to figure out what took place.

A while ago, I heard rumors of the FBI coming to Mo's house. Mo gave a bullshit story about them wanting him to testify against someone in the drug game, but when he got on the stand, he pulled an "I don't recall." I wasn't dumb. If the FBI comes to your house and tells you to testify, that really means either you testify or you go to jail. Mo said that Dallas was broke and selling used cars, which meant Mo snitched on him. That's why they weren't taking his calls. Dallas was probably trying to set them up, as well.

This situation was not working out for me. I had been there for three weeks and hadn't made a dime. Michelle's brother-in-law, Ron, had a cleaning service and needed people to do cleanup jobs in a warehouse. He gave me some work for two days, which was nothing steady.

This was not working out like I had pictured it. I just wanted to work and earn some money. But the only steady work I was doing was in my uncle's store, and that was for free. I was sold a bag of false goods. I was led to believe that a job was waiting for me, and it wasn't. So from the outside, I looked like a freeloader.

I decided that this wasn't what I signed up for. I called Steve in New York at Y.E.C. and told him about my situation. I asked if his offer was still good, and he said, "Most certainly." I called Grammy and told her that I would be returning to New York. I also told my uncle. I tried to smooth it over, saying that Milwaukee just wasn't for me, but the true reason was that he had lied to me. I wasn't going to be an indentured servant to him. I wanted to make my own money and have my own place, but it would be almost impossible to do that here without a car or knowledge of the area.

I had been here for exactly one month. My uncle bought me a plane ticket home. He took me to the airport, gave me $100, and sent me back to New York.

When I got to New York, my first stop was at Y.E.C. to confirm things with Steve. He had me hit the ground running—he already had a meeting set up with some potential customers, and wanted me to accompany him. I wasn't even dressed for a meeting. I had on shorts and a t-shirt, but Steve said it was fine. He needed me to pull this off, so he insisted I go with him.

We went to the meeting and landed the contract. Next, he wanted me to see the two buildings that needed to be completed for the state contract. There were about 500 windows that needed to be installed, and in addition, we now had this new repair contract.

Steve asked me if I could find some more people to work so that Y.E.C. could get the jobs done. At the moment, there was only Dennis and Bumpy—the other crew leader—to work steadily. That was no problem. I was able to recruit Jason and Eric, who I worked with when I first started at Y.E.C.

I jumped right into my old position as crew leader supervisor. Steve had let Dennis do my job on a probationary basis, to see if he could do it. But Dennis didn't know what he was doing. He was ordering the wrong size windows, and was a no show/no call a couple of times. Steve said he was between a rock and a hard place. He needed Dennis, since he had knowledge of the projects.

All of this was laid on me the first day back. I hadn't even gotten home yet, but there was really only one definite thing on my mind. First things first, Dennis had to go. I hadn't forgotten how Frida crossed me. Even though it all worked out, she and Dennis weren't going to reap the rewards of my generosity. I realized something about myself—I was a spiteful and vindictive person.

When I got home, Vivian was there, happy to greet her meal ticket. After the formal hellos, I told her that if she and I were going to be living together, there were going to be some rules in place. Rule #1: bitch, you got to get a job. I told Vivian that playing Suzie Homemaker was fine when I was in Milwaukee, but now that I was back, she had to contribute to the household. There was no argument from her.

I had her go to a temp agency, and she got a job in Queens doing piss tests for a probation office. I guess they didn't do background checks on temps, because she wouldn't have been able to get that job with her criminal record.

Jason and Virginia were no longer together. Jason told me that Virginia came around with some hickeys on her neck and tried to convince him that he had done it. He said he didn't have time to be playing games with dumb bitches like that.

A few weeks after I got back to New York, Jason called and told me his cousin, Maurice, got out of jail. I thought, *I haven't seen Maurice in about four or five years.* I remembered the last time was the day before he had to surrender himself to do his time. All this time, Jason and I never mentioned him, or even thought to visit him in jail. I wondered what he looks like now, or what his plans were. I told Jason to bring him by the house so I could see him.

Jason brought Maurice (who now went by Mo) up to the apartment later that day. When I saw Mo, he looked the same, but a little more mature. Of course, this was five years later; what else was he going to look like? Mo was still tall and skinny, but had a little more muscle to him—not bulk, but more tone and definition. Vivian was home when Mo and Jason arrived, and as the three of us sat down, reminiscing about old times, I noticed something about Vivian. She kept interjecting herself into our conversation. I wasn't concerned about her engaging, but it was truly three men talking, and she was making herself a part of the conversation—even to the point of talking about her mother killing herself, being raised by her grandmother, and calling her aunts her sisters. Jason, Mo, and I all looked at each other while she was talking, like we all knew she was out of place. I didn't want to pull her coat in front of the guys, so I waited.

After Mo and Jason left, I said to Vivian, "You need to know when to shut the fuck up. You don't know Mo from Adam, and here you are telling all your fucking business. When I'm with my friends like that, and you're the only female, go in the room or something. Mo ain't your friend, he's mine, and he don't give a shit about what you're saying anyway."

Of course, this erupted into a fight.

Vivian's response was, "I can say whatever the fuck I want to whoever the fuck I want. What am I supposed to do, sit in the room like a good little girl?"

I tried to explain that there was a time and place to hang out with people, and there was a time and place to shut the fuck up. Vivian was hardheaded, so I put an end to bringing her around or having my friends around her.

The argument wasn't just those words. There was a lot of physical abuse on my part, and a lot of throwing and breaking stuff— my stuff—on her part. That's how fights always were with Vivian and me. I wasn't usually the one to initiate the first assault. That was her thing in a fight—break my stuff. She knew I would replace it. I realized early on that this wasn't the type of relationship I wanted to be in. I thought about all the times Denise and I were together and I never raised my hand to her. Now, T was a different story, but even that wasn't abusive the way this one seemed. It almost seemed like Vivian wanted to be beaten—as in, if I didn't beat her, I didn't care about her. This was new territory.

The job was going well, and Dennis was in my crosshairs. I had to come up with a way to get rid of him, but not make it look like retaliation for the Frida incident. My plan was to hold his feet to the fire, to make him accountable for all his work. Up until this point, I had carried him and covered for him before I left for Milwaukee, but he still didn't know what he was doing.

Eric was in charge of the repair contract, and I assigned Dennis to him. I pulled Eric aside and told him, "Make Dennis earn his money. Don't do his work for him, and ride his ass. Know what I mean?" Then I gave Eric a wink.

Eric said, "Got you, Russ."

While I was planning Dennis's demise, Jason and I would still hang out with him after work, smoke a blunt and drink a forty of malt liquor. I made Dennis feel like we were all buddies even as I planned his downfall. Eric was doing a good job riding Dennis's back, because about a week after my plan was initiated, Dennis called the office and demanded a meeting with Steve, Linda, and me. I asked Steve if I could take the lead in the meeting, since I was the one who brought Dennis into the organization. Steve said that was a good idea because Dennis seemed kind of hostile over the phone. Maybe he would be calmer since he and I had a prior relationship outside of Y.E.C. Steve didn't know about the arrangement I had with Frida, or why I got Dennis the job in the first place. This situation looked like regular company business. The four of us sat down, and I asked Dennis what the problem was. He said that he couldn't work with Eric anymore, and asked to be placed somewhere else. Dennis thought that since he knew me, I would accommodate his request without a problem. He thought we were cool like that. He was wrong.

I asked him what was wrong with Eric, like I didn't have any idea what was going on. Dennis said Eric was riding him hard, and that he expected him to do a certain amount of repairs a day. Also, he didn't like the way Eric was talking to him. I knew that Steve and Linda were watching to see how professional I could be. Up until this point, they still thought I was just a young, thuggish punk from the ghetto. At that point, I let Dennis know how vindictive and cunning I was, and I let Steve and Linda know that I wasn't just the dumb thug.

I said, "Dennis, you have to understand that we are under contract with that building complex to repair a certain amount of windows per day. Therefore, you are required to repair a certain amount of windows per day. Everyone must pull his own weight, and Eric is the supervisor there, so it's his job to make sure that everything is run in an orderly and timely manner. As far as you being offended by the way Eric talks to you, I think you need to be a little more thick-skinned. I mean, you just can't demand that you be assigned to another job site just because you don't like the boss. What kind of example would we be setting for the youth that we're training? Remember, it's all about the youth."

Dennis, Steve, and Linda sat there with their eyes big and their mouths open. Dennis couldn't believe what was coming out of my mouth. Up until now, he always saw me when I was getting high and in my ghetto mode, never my professional mode. Linda and Steve had never heard me speak without some kind of profanity coming out of my mouth.

Dennis knew at that moment that the fix was in. He knew I was behind everything because I just got totally professional on him.

He stood up and said, "Well, shit going to have to change, or else I'm outta here." Dennis started to show his ghetto ignorance by cursing at the three of us during this meeting.

I stayed calm and asked Dennis what he meant by that.

Dennis stood up over me and said, "It means if shit don't change, I quit."

I glanced over at Steve and Linda, then I looked up at Dennis and said, "Well then, I accept your resignation."

Dennis just stood there in disbelief. After a moment, he tried to backtrack, saying, "Now, wait a minute. I want to talk about this."

I told him there was nothing to discuss. He quit, and we accepted, and we would send him his last check in the mail.

Dennis stormed out the office and slammed the door. Steve looked at me and said, "Russ, that was a great job. You were very professional—cool, calm, and collected. I thought for sure when he stood up over you, there was going to be an altercation, but you held your cool. Good job."

I thanked Steve and said, "There wasn't going to be any altercation, Steve. This was just business. Nothing personal, just business."

After work, Jason, Eric, and I celebrated with a blunt and a forty. The deed was done, but Dennis wasn't. I thought that, even though Dennis lost his job, he knew he didn't deserve it. Besides, Frida did double-cross me. It was just payback for that. It was like a bank repossessing a car if you didn't pay on the loan. I just repossessed the job.

Dennis didn't see it that way. He felt he was done wrong, and everyone was going to pay. He then did the most vicious, vindictive, and, what we call in the ghetto, bitch move that you could possibly pull. Dennis called the director upstairs in the rehab program and told her that Jason, Eric, Willie, and I all got high on drugs on a regular basis.

The director called Steve upstairs for a meeting. Dennis was trying to destroy the program; he was trying to make sure nobody had a job, even Willie. Willie didn't even do anything to Dennis. After Steve met with the director of the program, he called me into his office and told me what Dennis had done.

I was furious. This was Ghetto 101: never snitch about other people's habits of getting high—only your own.

I asked Steve what happened at the meeting, and he said that the director wanted to have us all drug tested on the spot. My heart started to beat just a little faster as he continued to speak. Steve had refused the director's demand, stating that none of us were ex-addicts, and we had no prior history of drug use. This was just a blatant attempt by a disgruntled employee to defame our characters. After a lot of back and forth with the director, Steve prevailed.

Steve knew that Dennis was probably telling the truth, but he wasn't from the drug rehab scene, so he didn't care what we did on our free time as long as we came to work and did our jobs. After the meeting and after work, Jason, Eric, and I decided to pay Dennis a visit at Frida's. Steve saw the fury in my eyes and asked me to please not do anything stupid. He needed me and the other guys for work. I told Steve that I wouldn't. I just wanted to clarify some things, and we would all be at work the next day.

The three of us showed up at Frida's door that night. I knocked, and Dennis answered. He opened the door about a quarter inch and said, "What's up?" I told him we wanted to talk to him. Dennis wouldn't let us in. He said he would meet us downstairs. The three of us waited for him in front of the building until he came outside. I did all the talking as Jason and Eric stood by.

I asked Dennis about what he did, and he flat out denied it. He said he didn't know what I was talking about.

I told him, "I just got out of a meeting with Steve, and he told me everything you told the Director. You even included Willie."

Dennis denied everything, and then tried to justify his actions by saying, "Even if I did, what you did to me was fucked up anyway."

That was his confession with a justification behind it. I then began to verbally assault him. I was yelling at the top of my lungs. "Oh yeah, well you're a piece of shit, muthafucker! I got you the job and I took it away! That's what the fuck you get when you and your bitch cross me, muthafucker! You didn't know what the fuck you were doing anyway, you fucking crackhead. I carried you all the way, and you're lucky we didn't lose our jobs, you piece of shit, or I would have come here and cut your balls off and sent them to your mother! I would kick your ass up and down the street right now, but I see what kind of pussy you really are, and you would probably call the cops, you fucking punk."

Dennis tried to be defiant by raising his voice a little. "Oh yeah?"

"Yeah, muthafucker!" I stepped right up in his face, as if to say, "Don't press your luck."

Dennis backed down.

I went inside the building and rang all the doorbells. As people were looking out their windows, I started yelling to everyone looking down at us, "Dennis is a crackhead! Dennis smokes crack! He lives in apartment 4B!"

Jason and Eric joined me in our announcement; this went on for about five minutes. Frida was looking out the window, furious. I didn't care. I thought, *Fuck her, too!*

When we were done, the three of us walked up the block, still yelling, "Dennis is a crackhead!" When we were out of range, we all started to laugh.

Frida made two phone calls the next day—one to Nana to tell her what I had done, and the other was to the office. Frida was trying to talk to the director upstairs, but the receptionist wouldn't put her through. When Frida told Nana what I did, Nana did exactly what I thought she would do—she defended me. She told Frida that if I did something like that, her boyfriend had to have done something to me first. She said, "Malik wouldn't just do something like that out of the blue. I raised him better than that."

Frida lied, of course, but Nana didn't believe her. Nana called me later and asked me what happened and I told her. She said, "That's what I thought."

I never saw or spoke to Frida again after that. I felt bad for the loss. She was someone I felt very close to at one time, but in the end, she was willing to use me and throw me under the bus. I couldn't help but think about all the women that have hurt me: Nana (Emma's mother), Emma, my mother, Denise, Melanie, T, and now Frida. I think I was starting to develop a serious distrust for women.

chapter **TWENTY-SEVEN**

V
ivian and I were continuing our relationship. We'd have sex every day without protection, yet she never ended up pregnant. I asked her again why she never had kids. Vivian told me that she previously needed to have an operation to turn her womb around. That's why, up to this point in her life, she never had kids. I thought, *Good, because I don't want to have kids by this woman anyway.*

Vivian was okay, but there were a few things I needed to work on with her. The first was her wardrobe. Vivian dressed tacky. The first time I realized this was when we were going to Nana's Thanksgiving dinner. Up until this point, all she really wore were jeans and some type of top, no dress clothes. I told her about Nana's dinners and that everyone in my family was going to be there, so she should try to make a good impression. Vivian went into her suitcase in the corner and pulled out a tacky short dress and tried it on. She thought it was cute, but when I saw it on, I asked her what else she had. She pulled out several other tacky outfits. I told her that none of them were acceptable. I took Vivian shopping and picked out a dress and a pantsuit.

Vivian liked how she looked in the clothes, but I could tell she wasn't used to wearing classy stuff. She thought slutty was classy. I took her to Nana's Thanksgiving dinner, and as long as she kept her conversations to a minimum, she was fine. Vivian was a good-looking woman, but not very cultured. Her dialogue was limited to drugs and things of the ghetto. If you wanted to speak about current events, she would try to involve herself in the conversation, but would sound stupid.

At that first Thanksgiving dinner, Vivian made a good impression; she didn't talk much. To me, she was a step up from T, because she had a job and no kids.

I eventually realized that I was looking for another Denise. Vivian was no Denise, but then again, nobody could fill Denise's shoes for me. I was looking for a model, and Vivian was a start. She was very attractive, she didn't have any kids, and she had a job, for now. She also cooked and cleaned the house. I figured I could work with it. Those were the good points. The bad points were that she wasn't very smart, she had a very bad temper, she was insanely jealous, she smoked cigarettes (but so did I), and she liked cocaine.

I knew all these things, but I wasn't contemplating a long-term relationship with her; we were just hanging out. I realized by no means was I perfect, so I was going to try and see how things worked out with her. We had no kids, so it wouldn't be hard to get rid of her. I would just take it day by day and see how it went.

Jason and Mo ended up living together. Mo's grandmother died, so his father let him and Jason stay in the apartment. It was a studio in the Lennox Terrace Apartments complex on Adam Clayton Powell, Jr. Blvd. in Harlem. Mo needed a job, so, of course, I got him one at Y.E.C. Mo wasn't qualified, and he had a criminal record. It didn't matter, though, because Y.E.C. never did a background check on him. Steve just hired him on my word.

Mo and Jason's place was a swinging bachelor pad. Two things that were always there were prostitutes and cocaine. They were both single men. I was with Vivian now, so I couldn't hang out with them much at night. Besides, I would see them at work. However, the few times I did hang out with them at their apartment, it was always the same sequence of events.

The night would start off with Mo and Jason wanting to get some cocaine. They would have me walking around with them in the Fort Washington area, looking for the best price. Mo and Jason were very particular. They wanted the best quality for the best price and the most quantity. Sometimes, we walked around for an hour. I always had my own marijuana on me, so we didn't have to look for that.

There was a liquor store right on the corner, and we would buy a half-gallon of Bacardi. Then, the party would begin. The three of us would start by sniffing some cocaine, smoking some marijuana, and drinking the Bacardi. As the night went on, Mo would say that he was going for a walk and leave. Within the hour, he would come back with some street woman ready to sell her soul for some money or drugs. Mo was a professional at picking up desperate women of the night. He was a smooth-talker, and by the time he went to pick up one of these women, his standards were lower from all the cocaine and alcohol he had consumed. (He wasn't much of a marijuana smoker.)

Jason and Mo would call the women strays. Once the woman or women—sometimes Mo brought back more than one—were in the apartment, what followed was a night full of uninhibited sex. The scenes were right out of a porno movie. Sometimes, even Mo's brothers (two older brothers that were fraternal twins) would come over and indulge in the orgy of sorts.

Since I had a woman, I would never partake in the activities. I would often come back home around five or six in the morning, and I never wanted to take the chance of Vivian smelling my genitals, or find the smell of another woman on me. I would just smoke my blunt, drink my Bacardi, and enjoy the show. I did this with them four or five times.

Every day at work, they would tell me about the freak fest they had the night before. I saw that both of them were looking a little rough at times, and I also noticed that Jason was sniffing cocaine a lot more than he had before. Mo seemed like he was just making up for lost time from when he was in prison.

As time went on, I got to meet Vivian's family. These people were the epitome of ghetto. Every ghetto stereotype there was, her family had it. Where do I start?

Vivian's grandmother was about sixty-five and looked like she had lived a hard life. She had eight kids by six different men—six girls and two boys. She had been on welfare her entire life. The woman lived in the first-floor tenement on Crotona Avenue in the Bronx.

The oldest of her children was Vivian's mother. The next oldest was a woman they called Gigi; she had two kids and was very religious. Her husband was a dope fiend. Vivian said Gigi was a party girl until her sister had killed herself, then she gave her life to God.

The third was Papito. He was a grown man, but had been in and out of mental institutions his entire life. He had the maturity level of a ten-year-old. Vivian said he had tried to molest her when she was ten. He still lived with Vivian's grandmother.

The fourth was a woman named Margie. Margie was a recovering dope fiend who had three children—the oldest was fatherless, the second by a dope fiend, and the youngest was born as a result of her prostituting for heroin.

As for the fifth child, Lily, she had five kids by two men—four girls and one boy. Lily had been married to the father of the four girls. She had the boy with some guy she hooked up with that worked as an usher at a movie theater. Vivian said that Lily's husband tried to rape her when she was twelve years old, and it was always a point of contention between Vivian and Lily.

The sixth child was this woman named Gloria. She had two kids by two different men. This was the sister that Vivian was going to live with before we knew she could stay at the apartment. Vivian was closest to Gloria out of everyone.

The seventh child was a woman named Carmen. She was Tito and Virginia's mother. She had three other kids beside them.

The last and youngest of the eight kids was a guy they called Junior. Junior was about thirty years old and still lived at home. He had an under-the-table job working at some Chinese man's store, and slept on the couch in his mother's living room. Vivian told me that she and Junior would go to bars where Vivian would pick up men with the premise that she was going to have sex with them. Junior would follow them, and when Vivian and the mark got to the destination, Junior would rob him. Vivian would scope the men with the most money.

Everyone, from Vivian's grandmother to all of her seven living kids, was on welfare and lived at home or in some sort of public housing. I really didn't get along with any of them; I tolerated them. Once, I went to a Christmas party at Gloria's with Jason. They all knew him from when he was dating Virginia. The place looked like a day care center. The women all dressed in cheap, slutty dresses like the ones Vivian used to have, and all of the women's boyfriends were bums. Out of all the men with Vivian's aunts at the party, none of the kids were theirs.

That night, Jason hooked up with Margie and came back to the apartment with Vivian and me. Vivian was upset that they had sex in our living room, but I said to her, "You didn't care when you and Virginia were in the same situation, did you?"

Jason and Margie just hooked up for that night. Even though Margie was on methadone and a recovering junkie, she was rather cute and sexy. Funny thing was that out of all the family members, Margie and I got along the best. She was cool with me because she was real. I didn't judge her because she was a junkie or a former prostitute. Everyone else talked behind her back. The more I knew about Vivian's family, the less I ever wanted to become a part of it.

Vivian was holding down her job, and Y.E.C. was growing by leaps and bounds. I had my two boys working with me and watching my back, and the state started to train me in weatherization. Energy Conservation was the wave now, and there were all kinds of new technologies being developed. Not to mention that the state was sending me to all kinds of other trainings. I was learning about boilers, how buildings lose heat, the different types of oils that large buildings burn. And there was this new invention called the Minneapolis blower door that worked in unison with a laptop computer for one- and two-family homes. In a nutshell, I would take a measurement of a house, input the information into the computer, and give a ratio of a hole in the home, which would then indicate how much fuel the homeowner was wasting. I would then develop a plan of action including, but not limited to, window installation, possible boiler replacement, and weather-stripping to assist in closing the hole and saving the homeowner money while also conserving energy.

I was learning more, and becoming more of an asset to Y.E.C. Not only was I the crew leader supervisor, I was now their lead man in the weatherization department because I was the only one going to trainings. Because Y.E.C. was trained in the weatherization technology, we ended up scoring a contract with Con Edison, the main supplier of electricity in New York. I was the go-to guy. I made all the decisions regarding the Con Ed contract. Animosity started to develop from Linda, both because I was in charge of something that was out of her control, and because I started to become more important to the company.

Linda had a problem with Jason and me ever since that thing with Dennis. She was a recovering heroin addict, and recovering addicts hate when they see people that get high and still function without losing control like they did. I would smoke a blunt in the morning before I came to work, after work, and before I went to bed. I still came to work every day, worked hard, and did my job. There were no complaints from anybody about my performance, and Linda hated that. Jason and Mo were doing the same, but their daily rituals also included cocaine and alcohol. Truth be told, I really didn't like alcohol or cocaine so much, but I would indulge because it was around. My preference, above all, was always marijuana. Like I said before, I noticed that Jason and Mo looked pretty rough sometimes, but as long as they came to work and did their job, I didn't care.

As always, just as my professional life was growing, the relationship with Vivian became strained. She was insanely jealous, so I couldn't even go over to Julie's the way I used to because Judy might be there. Even though nothing was happening, Vivian was jealous that Judy and I had been together. That was something I told her before I went to Milwaukee, and now she was holding it against me. Judy and I were good friends, and now I had to treat her like I didn't know her. Judy was upset about that.

Vivian and I would get into fights over stupid things, and it was always the same nonsense—she would swing on me and break things. One night, I can't even remember what the fight was about, but I can remember what happened like it was yesterday.

Vivian and I were arguing, and it was a heated one. She picked up a ceramic ashtray and tried to hit me in the head with it. I was able to get the ashtray away from her, and I started to hit her on the legs with the ashtray and say, "You see how this shit feels? And you're trying to hit me in the face and head with it, bitch."

I was furious, and during one of the swings with the ashtray, the ceramic cracked. I noticed it in mid-swing, but was unable to stop myself. I heard the flesh tear from her leg.

Vivian screamed in pain, and the blood started gushing and running down her leg. She said, "You muthafucker! I can't believe you did this shit to me!"

I told her to calm down and then went to get a cloth to hold against her leg to help stop the bleeding. I was scared that she would call the police. I knew if it was T, she would have.

After she calmed down and removed the cloth from her wound, we both looked at it and saw a deep, four-inch-long gash, down to the bone. We could see the fat under her skin. She needed to go to the hospital. I called a cab and told her if they asked what happened, to say that she cut her leg on the edge of a glass table when she was trying to get her cat.

We went to the Jacobi Hospital emergency room, and they took her right away. Vivian stuck to the story. They took her to get an x-ray, just in case there were any glass fragments in her leg. When she was in the x-ray room, the nurse asked her if she was pregnant, and Vivian said that she couldn't have kids. The nurse had Vivian place a lead protective blanket around her anyway. She said it was hospital policy, just in case. There weren't any fragments, and Vivian ended up getting six stitches.

During the cab ride home, she was telling me that she was going to get me back for her injury. I told Vivian I was getting tired of this battling, and if it kept up, I didn't know if I wanted to continue the relationship. She didn't have a response to that.

Life went on as usual. A few weeks after the fight, Vivian came to me and said, "I didn't get my period this month."

I said, "So, you can't have kids anyway, right? So you ain't pregnant. What you telling me for?"

Vivian said that she never missed her period, and she wanted to take a home pregnancy test just to make sure. Vivian brought an EPT test, and it came out negative. I thought, *Well, that was close.*

Three more weeks went by, and still no period, so she brought another test. This time, one that was more expensive…and the results were positive.

chapter TWENTY-EIGHT

I pretended to be happy, but truth be told, I felt like I was being played. All this time in this woman's life, she didn't get pregnant, and I was supposed to think that I had some kind of super sperm or something? Vivian went to the doctor's to confirm her findings. Once it was confirmed, the first thing she did was quit her job. The doctor told her that she was eight weeks pregnant. I thought, *Why does she need to quit her job?* Vivian wasn't too cool with working in the first place, so this was the perfect opportunity for her to quit.

I couldn't help but have a selfish thought when it was confirmed that she was pregnant—this was really going to seal the deal regarding Denise and me getting back together. I hadn't heard from Denise in about six months. This was the longest I'd ever gone without talking to her, though I thought about her often. Usually, she would call Nana's or my job, but no calls came. I didn't know her home phone number, since she moved into her own place.

I thought, *Here I go having a child with a woman I really don't want to be with again.* I took full responsibility for this one, because I should have been using protection. I just accepted it and took things as they came. I hadn't really trusted Vivian ever since that Max thing, so who's to say that the baby was mine? But I didn't take that road. I just took a wait-and-see approach.

Vivian tried to play me right from the start, "You know I'm not going on welfare."

I had to curse her out. "Bitch! Are you fucking stupid? You been on welfare your whole life, and now you got a problem being on

welfare? Besides, you quit your fucking job. I don't know what you
think is going to happen here, but you ain't going to be sitting on
your ass, sucking my pockets dry."

There wasn't even an argument after that. I told Nana, Grammy,
and Pete, and they all had the same reaction: "I thought she couldn't
have kids."

To this, I had no answer.

I buckled down and got ready for another baby. I painted the
apartment and bought new furniture. I figured I would at least try.
I didn't have any other prospects, anyway. I thought maybe this
baby would calm Vivian down a little. I told her that she had to stop
smoking marijuana while she was pregnant. She agreed, but every
time I smoked a blunt, she was right there smoking with me. I would
say, "How you think your child would feel knowing that you got
high every day you were pregnant with them?"

Vivian's answer would be, "I'll tell them that you gave it to me."

I didn't understand what she was saying, because if I refused to
let her smoke with me, a fight would ensue. I couldn't let the fights
escalate like they did before she was pregnant, so I just let her have
her way.

The job was going well, and it was time to finish up another
contract with the state. Jason and Mo were partying hard. I wasn't
hanging out with them much, but I could see that they were looking
rougher and rougher as time went by. From time to time, Jason or
Mo would call off, but it was a good time in between, so I didn't
take too much notice. Then, one day, it all came crashing down.

The state inspectors were coming to look at the finished buildings, and Steve needed everyone at the job to show them around.
Jason and Mo were a no-call/no-show that morning. The job
started at 8:30 a.m. By 9:00, Steve was getting a little nervous and
asked me to call Jason and Mo, but they didn't have a telephone.
Steve then asked me to run by their house. I had Linda drive me.
There was no answer at the door.

At 10:00 a.m., Jason called and told Steve that he wasn't going to be able to make it. Steve told Jason it was urgent that he come in because of the state inspectors. Jason said that his cousin was hit by a car. I could hear Steve on the phone pleading with Jason to come in, but they didn't.

We were able to get all the inspections done, but it was by the skin of our teeth. Steve was furious, and when the day was over, he asked me if I knew what was going on. I told him I didn't know, and I didn't know what cousin Jason was talking about. When I went home that night, I expected a call from Jason to at least let me know what was going on, since I was his best friend and his supervisor.

But Jason didn't call, and the next day, he and Mo didn't show up for work again, and didn't call at all. I was pissed off, because now Steve was like, "Hey! I hired these guys on your word. You're supposed to handle stuff like this." Steve asked me several times that day if I knew what was going on. He even wanted me to speculate what might be wrong, but I had no idea whatsoever.

I called Julie and asked if she had heard from Jason or Mo. She hadn't heard from them, and she was a little worried after I told her what had happened.

It wasn't like Jason not to keep me in the loop. This was my homeboy for seven years, through thick and thin. This was my best friend. He was there when my son was born. This was the guy who taught me about the streets. This was the guy who showed me how to roll a blunt. This was the guy I sold drugs with. This was the guy who introduced me to buying women, and we even had shared a few. I just knew something had to be wrong, because he would have called me by now.

Three days passed by, so I went to their apartment once more, but still there was no answer at the door. I decided to give up. On the fourth day, when I was returning to the office from a job site, Steve called me in and said, "Russ, I need to talk to you. Jason called me this morning."

What Steve told me then infuriated me to the point that I wanted to kick Jason's ass. I was twenty-two, and had known Jason since I was fifteen. I couldn't ever recall a time that I wanted to hurt him. It turned out that Jason and Mo were on a cocaine binge.

My jaw dropped. This thing with Dennis just happened. I was able to deflect that attention away from me doing drugs, and now my best friend was calling Steve, saying that he was on a cocaine binge for two days? Everyone knew we hung tight, so it would be easy to make the connection. I wondered why he would call and say that, and why he didn't call me beforehand.

Steve asked me if I knew that Jason had a problem with cocaine. I told him that since Jason moved in with Mo, and I was with Vivian, I didn't really see him outside of the job too much.

That day, Steve had a staff meeting. He made the announcement that Jason and Mo were no longer working there, and indicated that it was surrounding drugs. As the meeting was taking place, I could see Linda's eyes piercing through me. She had an inner grin, like I was next to go. I thought my job was in jeopardy. All it took was the director upstairs to get word of this and she would demand that I be drug tested. It would have been over. Here I was with a baby on the way; the last thing I needed was to lose my well-paying job. I was beside myself.

I called Julie and told her what happened, and she was surprised. I went home that night, waiting for a call from Jason. There was no call. I was furious, so I didn't go by his apartment out of fear of what I might do.

A few days passed, and again Steve called me into his office. He told me that Mo came by to pick up his check and apologize for what happened. Mo said he didn't know why Jason would call and tell Steve what he did, but what was done was done. I was even more pissed, because no one called or came by to see me.

Steve told me not to worry about what was going on, then he sat me down in his office and schooled me. "Russ, you may be from the ghetto, but you're not going to stay in the ghetto," he started.

"You will outgrow the people you hang around because you're ambitious, and have some kind of integrity. You're a leader, and this might be a hard pill to swallow right now, but maybe things worked out for the best. Better you find out in a situation like this how loyal your friends are, than in a situation where you're facing jail time."

Steve was right, but it didn't take away the embarrassment I felt when I would come into work. All that drama died down, but now, I felt down. I just stopped talking to Jason; I didn't even try to contact him anymore. I had no friends—I couldn't even call Denise a friend. She wasn't trying to contact me, so I just decided I was going to put everything I had into my family.

Vivian had a sonogram and found out that we were having a girl. I thought this would be a second chance with a child. Again, I made all these promises of what I was going to do for my child. This baby was going to be daddy's little girl.

I heard through the grapevine that Jason and Mo had lost the apartment, and Jason had to move back in with Julie. Mo had gone back to jail on a gun charge, and this time, he was going to be gone for a while, because he was still on probation when it happened.

I became a devoted family man. All I did was go to work and come home. I was also making all kinds of plans with Vivian. I thought that I had no one and nothing else, so I would put all I had into this relationship. I had to give it a fighting chance. After all, there was no way Denise was ever going to take me back now. Who knew—she might have been engaged or married by now. I figured the worst case scenario, since she hadn't contacted me.

Vivian was getting bigger, and we were getting along well. Things seemed to be working out. I thought I had life all under control. I came to a place in my life that I accepted the loss of Jason's friendship, and the inevitability that Denise and I would not get back together. Now, I had a baby girl to think about, and I was okay with what life had dealt me. This wasn't too bad. I was heartbroken about some things, but I thought that time would heal all my wounds. I was in a good place.

And then the hammer came down.

It was June of 1991, days before my twenty-third birthday. It was like any other day when Vivian and I went over to Grammy and Pete's, just to visit. Grammy and Pete were health food nuts, so they were always making some kind of fresh juice or something like that. Grammy gave Vivian a glass of carrot juice, and Vivian drank it. This wasn't the first time that Grammy had offered Vivian a glass of carrot juice, but this time, she drank it, and I thought it strange for some reason. Vivian and I stayed about an hour, and we left to go home.

As we were walking across the street to the projects, Vivian said, "Russell, there's something I need to tell you."

"What is it?"

"I don't know how to tell you."

I started to become concerned. Vivian was never one to be shy about saying anything. I saw her eyes watering up, and then I really became serious.

I started to raise my voice. "What is it?" I thought it may have been something with the baby. "What? What? Tell me what it is!"

Vivian looked me in my eyes, and with a cracked voiced, she said, "Russell, I'm HIV-positive."

Vivian's words echoed in my ears—positive, positive, positive.... I didn't know what to say, and I wasn't sure if she was saying she gave it to me or that I gave it to her. My mind went back to when her ex-boyfriend, Flacko, said that she had given him AIDS— I just brushed it off as a desperate man saying anything to get his woman back.

Vivian and I walked back to our project apartment in dead silence. When I opened the door, I just sat on the couch in the living room while my mind ran a mile a minute. I couldn't accuse her of infecting me because of all the women I had slept with without protection. I thought about every woman I had slept with, without protection, that may have been sleeping with someone else at the same time. Out of all the women that I slept with, I couldn't recall one that was only with me—Lori, Denise, T, Tracy, Melanie, Judy. I knew this for a fact. So how could I be sure it was Vivian that infected me? I knew I had been with a lot more women than just them, too, but with the other women, I used protection.

Vivian came into the living room. I wasn't mad, but I was still in shock. I told her that I had been with a lot of different women, and I guess this was the consequence for my actions. I told her not to tell anybody, and that we would just deal with it.

Here I was, twenty-three years old, and I was just told that I had a death sentence. It was 1991. At that time, people with AIDS were dropping like flies. Those that were infected would develop sores and lesions on their face and body. They would lose weight fast, and walk around looking like skeletons. The stigma of having the virus was almost worse than having the virus itself. People were scared to death of it, and didn't want people with it around them.

I feared for my unborn child. There were commercials on TV all the time about babies being born with HIV and dying soon after.

The next day, I went to work, and all I could think about was that I was going to die. And from what I had seen, it was going to be a horrible death. I thought, *Who would care if I just became another ghetto statistic?* I needed to talk to someone, so I asked Steve if I could speak to him in his office, in private.

Steve said, "What is it, Russ?"

I couldn't even bring the words to come out of my mouth. My eyes started to water and I put my face in my hands to hide the shame. I started to weep uncontrollably. Steve was surprised at the scene before him—this tough ghetto bastard crying like a young child.

"Russ, what is it? It can't be that bad. Tell me what it is."

Finally, I found the strength to form the words to come out my mouth. Between sobs, I said, "Last night, Vivian told me that she was HIV positive."

Steve looked at me with such empathy. "Ahhh, Russ, I'm sorry." He asked if I had gotten tested.

"No, I just found out last night."

He said, "Well, before you go assuming the worst, go and get yourself tested."

I told him about my fear of people finding out that I was infected. Steve told me to go to a clinic that had anonymous testing. He then told me to take the rest of the day off to get that done. "Russ, you don't need to be walking around with that uncertainty on your mind."

I wiped my tears, got myself under control, and walked out the office like nothing was wrong.

I went to a clinic by Montefiore Hospital and took the HIV test. The counselor at the clinic told me it would take about two weeks for the results to come in and gave me a number. Since the test was anonymous, I would return in two weeks and they would match the number with the results. This was good. *At least no one will know about this,* I thought on my way out the door, and then I was spotted by this guy named Cisco. He was a janitor at the rehab center, and it was well known that he had AIDS. Cisco was there receiving treatment, and he asked what I was doing there. I played it off and told him I was just getting tested to be safe.

"No big deal," I told him.

Cisco said, "Hey, let me know how things work out."

"Sure," I said, and walked away.

Those two weeks were the longest of my life. I went back to the clinic and sat down at the desk with the counselor, a black man in his mid-forties, and gave him the ticket with my test number on it. The man went to another room and came back with a folder, sat down, opened it, and read it to himself. Then, he closed the folder, looked at me, and said, "Well, it's positive."

I just stared at the man.

He said, "Don't give up hope. They're coming up with all kinds of new treatments in the medical field." He then told me about a doctor in Harlem that was running trials of a new drug for AIDS called Kamron—it was promising, but years away from FDA approval.

I asked for the doctor's name and number, and then left the office. Her name was Dr. Barbara Justice.

I went to work, and told Steve what the results were and what the counselor had told me. Steve asked me what I planned to do.

"What can I do? I'm going to keep on living until it's time to die. Right now, my biggest concern is providing for my family and taking it one day at a time."

Many people in the early days of AIDS would fall apart with the news of their infection and just run wild. They'd say, "I'm going to die anyway, so it's party time." I just went on with life as usual. My biggest fear was being exposed. I was also scared that the baby would be born sick, and then everyone would know my secret.

TWENTY-NINE

That September, my daughter was born. There was no big hoopla; just Vivian and me at the hospital. No one came to visit with us. It was like no one cared. I was somewhat glad that no one came, though, just in case the doctor or one of the nurses mentioned Vivian's status. I asked the doctor how the baby was regarding the HIV, and he told me that all babies born to an HIV-infected woman are positive for the first fifteen months because they still have their mother's immune system. Once they develop their own, then we can tell if the baby will still remain HIV-positive.

My baby girl was beautiful. I named her Ashley, after the character on the sitcom *The Fresh Prince of Bel-Air*. I went home that night and called Grammy, Pete, and Nana to let them know about Ashley. I went to the hospital the next day, and the doctor said that the baby needed to get a special shot. I asked what kind, and the doctor said it was related to a sexually transmitted disease. I asked the doctor to clarify. He looked at Vivian. She said, "It's okay, you can tell him."

The doctor said that Vivian had been treated for a venereal disease before, and that it was still in her system. Therefore, as a precaution, they would treat the baby so that she would not develop symptoms. I was upset with what the doctor was saying, but held my cool until he left. I was silent while sitting there with Vivian.

Vivian asked me if I was upset about her having had VD and not telling me about it. I said, "It is what it is." She said it happened about two years ago, and she was treated for it before we met, so she didn't feel she had to mention it.

I wasn't mad; I was disappointed. When I met her, I thought, *This is a pretty woman with no kids. I can work with her.* I thought as long as she wasn't like T, she had potential. I thought I could make her into Denise—get her working and teach her class. But Vivian wasn't Denise; she was a wolf in sheep's clothing.

When it was time to take the baby home, we took a cab. Grammy and Pete didn't even ask if we wanted a ride home, and they lived right across the street from us. This reminded me of when my son was born—nobody cared. I was just a ghetto bastard having another ghetto bastard.

I didn't care. I didn't need anybody. I was going to work hard and provide for my new family. I felt there was nothing else I could do. I was damaged goods now, so who else would want me?

I went to work the next day to find people standing in a circle in the office, talking about the developing news on the TV. I walked into the crowd and asked what was going on, and someone said Ervin "Magic" Johnson, the basketball player, had just announced that he was retiring because he was just diagnosed with HIV.

This was a shock. People started to say ignorant things about him dying, and how he was going to get scabs and lesions on his face. I started to defend him somewhat, saying that there were new medications for people, and maybe he wouldn't end up like that. In a sense, I was defending myself.

Steve said, "Russ, can I talk to you in my office for a second?" I followed Steve into his office, and once he closed the door, he said, "Russ, you don't need to defend Magic Johnson, he can defend himself. You should be careful about talking about HIV, because someone may think to themselves, 'Why does he know so much?' And then, they may suspect that you have it, and then your secret will be out."

Steve was right. I never mentioned it at the job again.

Later, I ran into the janitor, Cisco, in the hallway, and he asked me how everything went. I told him everything was all good. Cisco was in the later stages of AIDS, and he looked it. When I said everything was all good, he seemed a little disappointed, like if I said I were positive he and I would become friends or something. Cisco died about six months later. I thought about my own mortality, but I also remembered that Cisco was an ex-IV drug user, too, so he may have had numerous diseases that contributed to his rapid death.

That Thanksgiving, Vivian, the baby, and I went to Nana's for her annual dinner. Everyone was there, including Uncle Mo, my mother, and several other family members. Of course, everyone was giving their fake "Oh! How cute she is!" comments. Ashley was about two months old now, and my mother had seen her one time before that for about five minutes, when she was visiting at Grammy and Pete's. Neither my mother nor anyone else sent so much as a card for my daughter. That Thanksgiving, my cousin Sunni was having her baby. Sunni was Aunt Shirley's daughter, Nana's granddaughter, and my mother's first cousin. She was a year younger than I was.

Aunt Shirley called the house and told Nana that Sunni had the baby and had almost died during the delivery. Nana made the announcement to everyone at the house, and then it cleared out with people going to see Sunni and her new baby girl. I knew then, in my heart, that neither my children nor I meant shit to my family.

• • • • •

Work was going well. Linda ended up getting fired; I knew that was going to happen sooner or later. The job was becoming too difficult for her. It was becoming really high-tech, and she thought she could talk her way out of everything, but not this time.

Roland, the guidance counselor, started to have an affair with the secretary, and both of them were married, so they left their respective husband and wife and ran away together. I was on the bus one time and saw them walking down the street with a baby carriage. They didn't look too happy. I guess the novelty of the affair was gone.

When Linda left, Steve made me the second signer on the company checks. Now, I was signing everyone's paychecks. Linda was replaced by a lady named Mildred, who was married to a judge. The secretary was replaced by a woman named Quinn, and the guidance counselor was replaced by a Spanish guy named Juan. Juan was an ex-cocaine addict, but he didn't come from the program upstairs.

The company was growing by leaps and bounds. We even started a repair outlet branch. The state increased our funding every year, and we now had a million-dollar contract with them. As the contract increased, so did job positions in the office. Quinn was moved up to a better position, and we hired a new secretary name Jezebel. The program did so well with the state contract that we were invited to a weatherization conference in Upstate New York, at a prestigious resort called the Saratoga.

Steve let me take Vivian along. Everyone there knew who I was and just drooled over what a good-looking family I had. They knew my story; Steve had marketed me just right. He had made me a success story: troubled youth from the South Bronx, a high school dropout who, against all odds, beat the system. I enrolled in the Y.E.C. job training program, learned a skill, put it to use, learned all aspects of the trade, and was now signing people's paychecks.

That weekend, Y.E.C. won three awards from the state. Every time the presenters called the company name, Steve, Mildred, and I would go up and accept it. I was being applauded by a room of at least 300 people—300 industry professionals—and they were paying homage to me. I started to believe my own hype.

What would these very people say if they knew I was HIV-positive? What would they say if they knew I smoked blunts every day? Would they still applaud my success? No matter how successful I became, the back of my mind always harbored the fear of being exposed. But as time went on and the company grew, I started to believe there was nothing that could bring me down. I started to think I was invincible. I would soon realize that the higher up the ladder I went, the further I could fall.

I was being the perfect father and make-believe husband. All I did was go to work and come home. I started to speak to Jason again, slowly, but things between him and me would never be the same, because I no longer trusted him.

Vivian started up with her old habit of sniffing cocaine, only this time, it was becoming a big problem. Every time I came home, she was high. I could tell because when she sniffed, she had a telltale giveaway: her eyes would become wide and buggy. Sometimes, when I got home, she wouldn't be there. I would go to her friend's apartment—in our building—to find five or six people sitting around with that wide-eyed, buggy look. The worst part was that she was sitting there with my daughter. No matter how upset I got, no matter how much I yelled and screamed at her, she still sniffed cocaine. I guess she figured, what was I going to do about it? Leave her?

Vivian knew that I was signing people's paychecks and how much I was growing. The problem was, I was not only growing on the job, I was starting to outgrow Vivian. She didn't want to get a job. I suggested numerous times she put Ashley in daycare and get one, but for someone who in the beginning was so against being on welfare, she sure was enjoying the ride.

Then there came the time Vivian thought that since I was the boss at my job, she could call up and talk to the secretary, Jezebel, any old kind of way. At one point, Jezebel complained to Steve about the verbal abuse, and Steve asked me to talk to Vivian about it. I told her not to call the job anymore.

The cocaine use continued, so I thought that maybe if we moved to a different environment—out of the projects—she would stop her foolishness. I moved us to a two-bedroom condominium in Park Chester. The rent was $860 a month. Vivian was getting a

$175/month rent stipend from Welfare, so that left me with $685 to pay, because the utilities were included.

The move didn't work either; she just made friends with the people in the building that sniffed cocaine and hung out with them.

I felt trapped. I felt there was nothing I could do, so I just accepted my circumstances and continued to provide. I didn't want to lose my daughter. I knew in my heart that this relationship was not going to survive the way things were going, but what was I going to do? I was damaged goods now.

started to become somewhat depressed by my circumstances. I was sitting at my desk at the office one day, thinking about Denise. It had been about two years since I spoke with her or seen her. My mind was running wild with thoughts about how she was doing, and a whole lot of what ifs.

What if I had been honest with her? What if I never cheated on her? What if I never got T pregnant? What if she and I were married? What if she had children by now? What if she was married to that guy she was in love with? The "what ifs" went on forever. I thought, *There is no chance in the world for the two of us to be together anyway, considering my current medical condition.* She was on my mind so much that I decided to try and call her. I still had an old job number of hers and thought, *What the heck. Let me give it a try.* I didn't even know if she still worked there or not.

I pumped myself up and finally had the courage to make the call. I dialed the number. The phone rang once, then twice, and then a woman answered. She voiced the company name and said, "How may I help you?" I knew the second she started speaking that it was her. Her voice was like a cup of ice water to a man dying of thirst in the desert. There could have been no sweeter sound to my ears.

I said, "Hi."

She recognized my voice immediately, just as I had recognized hers. She said, "Well, this is a surprise."

I told her that I was thinking about her a lot, and I just wanted to hear her voice.

She said she was thinking about me, too. We both started to make small talk, and then I started to ask her questions that I was curious about. I asked her if she was married, and she said no. She asked me if I was still married, and I said no. I asked her if she had any children, and she said no. She asked me if I had any more children. I paused for a second and said, "Yes." She paused for a moment and let out a deep breath of disappointment. She asked me what the gender of the child was, and I said it was a girl. She asked what her name and birthday was. I told her that Ashley was born September eighteenth. That was three days before Denise's birthday.

I asked how her love life was going, and she said that she was living with someone, but the relationship was kind of shaky at the moment. I asked if it would be alright if I met her for lunch sometime, and she said it would be nice. I knew there wasn't a snowball's chance in hell that I could be with her, but I just wanted to see her again.

It was nice to talk to Denise, but it was also a double-edged sword. I was happy to hear her voice and happy to know that she was thinking about me, also, but it was painful to know she was living with someone, and painful to know that she and I could never be together due to my medical condition.

Ashley was fifteen months old now, and she was tested for HIV again; she was negative. The new fear I had was if Vivian and I died, who would take care of Ashley? Nana was too old now to be taking care of a young child, and I would have rather seen her die before staying with Vivian's family.

The relationship between Vivian and me was becoming even more strained. Whenever I asked her not to do something, she would do it anyway and look at me like, "What you going to do about it?" I didn't want to get into physical fights anymore, now that we had the baby. I remembered what it felt like when Lamar was beating my mother.

Besides being a cocaine addict and disrespectful to me on a constant basis, Vivian was an extremely jealous woman. If she and I would go over to a friend's house and she perceived that I was paying too much attention to any female—even just in general conversation—there would be a long, drawn-out fight about me wanting to fuck the woman, even if the husband or boyfriend was there. Vivian was also self-centered; if the attention wasn't focused on her or about getting high, she didn't want to hear what anyone else had to say. I started to not go places with her anymore.

Grammy's cousins were having a family reunion in Virginia, and she wanted the whole family to go. She and Pete even rented a car for me so that I could drive down there. Grammy wanted to give the impression that she had a big, happy family, and against all my better judgment, I let Vivian come with. I told Vivian that if I brought her, we needed to lay down some ground rules beforehand. I asked her to please not smoke around Grammy's family in Virginia, because they were very religious people. I told her to wait until we were at the hotel, or at least step outside, away from people, if she had to smoke. Vivian agreed. I also asked her not to show her ass in front of people, because I didn't know them that well, and I didn't want to embarrass Grammy. Vivian assured me she would be on her best behavior.

It was a three-day trip. The first day went fine, but soon after, it was as if Vivian and I never had that conversation. The second day, we had a backyard picnic at one of the cousin's houses, and everyone was playing games like volleyball and cards. We all had matching t-shirts, and it was a beautiful day. I was talking to some people when I looked up and I saw Vivian standing by the backdoor of the house, holding Ashley in her arms as she smoked a cigarette.

I walked over to Vivian, slowly as not to cause a scene, and said, "Didn't I ask you not to smoke around these people, and you're smoking while you're holding the baby."

Vivian said, "What's the big fucking deal? The only person tripping is you, muthafucker."

332

I didn't want to fight in front of people, so I just took Ashley from her arms and walked away. The rest of the trip, she just lit up her cigarettes at will. Every time she did, I just looked at her with the expression of being annoyed. She didn't care in the least. After she saw that I wouldn't engage her in any verbal confrontations in front of family members, she just became the same old Vivian from New York.

On the third day, Grammy and her cousins were sitting at a dining room table, reminiscing about their childhood days. The rest of the family was sitting throughout the house, also conversing. Vivian got bored and started to roll her eyes and suck her teeth loudly, constantly, and everyone noticed. I would give her a stern and disapproving look every time, but she just continued. Finally, my Uncle Maurice looked at me, and in a loud voice said, "Hey, I guess it's time for us to go."

Vivian said, "Thank God."

I was so upset I couldn't hold my tongue any longer. "He was talking to me, not to you, Vivian, so we don't need your smart-ass comments."

Vivian, in order to get the last word, replied in an even louder voice, "Well, I'm talking to you."

I gave her a dirty look and walked out the door.

After that, I swore to myself that I would never take her ass with me anywhere again. My uncle pulled me aside before I left to go back to New York and said, "I would like if you would come down to Milwaukee for your mother's birthday. And bring Vivian and Ashley, too."

My uncle wanted the whole family there, and even offered to pay for the plane tickets. I wanted to go and take Ashley, but I knew I couldn't take Ashley without taking Vivian. About two months later, my uncle sent three tickets for Milwaukee.

Everyone stayed at my uncle's house. My mother pulled me aside when no one was looking and said, "You know, my brother paid $600 for your tickets. I hope you're going to pay him back. This is my birthday, not yours." Then, she walked away. My mother was the most self-centered person I knew, though Vivian was a close second. My mother figured my uncle could have spent that $600 on her; she didn't care about having her son and granddaughter there on her birthday.

I approached my uncle about the money and told him what my mother said. He said "Don't worry about that. I invited you to come."

I was only there for two days, and Vivian was true to form for the whole trip. First, we were all sitting around looking at old pictures of the family and came across an old picture of me and Denise. When Vivian saw the picture, she jumped up from the table, stormed off to the bedroom, and slammed the door so hard that she broke the lock. Everyone was looking at me, and I was so embarrassed. I got up and went into the bedroom. I didn't go in to fight with her; I went in to get away from the rest of the family.

The first thing Vivian said was, "What the fuck is that picture doing in that box?"

I didn't even argue with her, because it was so stupid to me. I just said, "What do you think? When I got with you I called everyone in my family and told them to throw away all the pictures they have of me and any ex-girlfriends?"

Vivian had an attitude for the rest of the trip, so I couldn't wait to go home. Between her and my mother, I was miserable.

Before the weekend was over, my uncle said, "Hey, I'm going to make a run to the store. You want to come?"

I went along for the ride. When we got in the car, he drove for a minute and then stopped. He said that he didn't really need to go to the store; he just wanted to pull my coat to something. He said, "I'm not trying to get in your business, because I know I've had my fair share of crazy bitches, but nephew, I'm telling you that you really need to control your woman. I know she's pretty and all, but the way she was acting leaves a lot to be considered."

I thanked him for the advice and told him I was handling it.

334

Again, I swore I would never take her anyplace with me again.

Again, I went against my better judgment. This time, would prove to be the final straw. Another weatherization conference was coming around, and everyone expected to see me and my family again. I had to live up to the persona that I had established the last time.

The conference was at another resort in upstate New York. Ashley was about two now, and everyone commented on how pretty she was and on how much she had grown. Mildred and her husband had a room right next to ours. The conference only lasted two days, and on the last night, the people from the various weatherization agencies all met downstairs at the hotel bar to unwind, mix, and make contacts. I told Vivian I was going downstairs with my coworkers, and she said she wanted to go. I told her that she couldn't, because she had to stay with Ashley.

I went downstairs and sat with a few people from the state and local agencies. I had a couple of drinks, and we spoke about current events and new weatherization technologies. I was there about an hour when, out of the corner of my eye, I saw Vivian walk into the bar and start looking around. Everyone at the table noticed her, as well. The first thing that came to my mind was, *Where is Ashley?* I excused myself from the table, walked over to Vivian, and asked her what was up. She said, "Oh, nothing. I just wanted to get out for a little while." I asked her where the baby was, and she said, "She's in the room, sleeping."

"You left a two-year-old alone in the room by herself? What the fuck? Are you crazy? What if she wakes up?" I rushed out of the bar, up to the room with Vivian. Ashley was asleep in the middle of the bed. I didn't even bother to go back downstairs to the bar, I was so embarrassed. I took off my work clothes, but Vivian remained dressed.

She said, "I'm going downstairs to the machine to get a couple of sodas, since we don't have anything to drink up here."

I said, "Fine, whatever."

It was about 10:00 p.m. I waited, and waited, and waited, and the next thing I knew, it was 1:00 a.m. I didn't go looking for Vivian, because I didn't want to leave Ashley alone, but my blood was boiling. At two, Vivian knocked on the door.

I opened the door and said, "Where the fuck have you been?"

Vivian said, "I was hanging out at the bar, having a few drinks."

I lost it. I started to yell at the top of my lungs, "Bitch, what the fuck you mean you was hanging at the bar? You said you were going to get us some sodas."

With arrogance in her tone, she said, "Well, I changed my mind, so fuck it. What's the big deal?"

Again, I was yelling at the top of my lungs and said, "What gives you the right to be hanging at the bar with the people I work with? This is business. This is how I make contacts and get to know people. You come down to fuck that up for me, and then you go hang with them?"

Before I knew it, I had swung my open hand and slapped her across the face, knocking her onto the bed.

As Vivian fell, she reached for a large ceramic ashtray on the nightstand and threw it at me. I moved and it hit the window, but since the shades were closed, the window did not break. The both of us were hitting, yelling, and cursing at each other. The noise could be heard in the hallway, and in the room next door. The phone in the room rang, and I picked it up.

The person on the other line said, "Russell?"

I said, "Yeah."

It was Mildred, my supervisor. She said, "Look, you need to knock it off before the people in the hotel call the police, and you get arrested and lose your job."

"Okay." I hung up the phone.

Vivian just sat there, unfazed by the whole incident. "Who was that?" I told her, and she said, "That bitch needs to mind her own business, and when I see her tomorrow, I'm going to tell her."

I almost slapped her again. I said, "Look, bitch, you ain't telling nobody shit. I work with these people."

The rest of the night was calm, but I swore—and this time I meant it with every essence of my being—that I would never, ever, take that bitch with me anywhere ever again. In fact, I had to seriously contemplate if I was going to stay in a relationship with her.

The next morning, I had to get up early because Steve had made an appointment with a reporter for a popular weatherization magazine. It had national distribution, but if you weren't in the weatherization field, you would never know it existed. The magazine mainly had information about the new technologies and in between, a couple of feel-good, human interest stories.

The reporter wanted to do a story on Y.E.C. because of the great success the company was having. I met the reporter around 9:00 a.m. Mildred was supposed to be there, but she didn't show up, so the reporter interviewed me alone. He asked a lot about the company, but also about me and how I started out in the company, where I was from, my background, and so on. The interview went on for about an hour, and we finished up about ten a.m.

I went to get some breakfast and headed back up to my room. I was waiting for the elevator. When the doors opened, Mildred stepped out. We exchanged good mornings, and then she asked me if everything was okay from the night before. I told her that everything was fine. She apologized for calling.

Then Mildred asked me where I was going. I told her I was going back to my room to pack. She asked if I was going to the interview with the reporter, and I told her I had already met with the reporter at nine. She seemed very surprised. She thought the meeting was at eleven. I told her, "No, it was at 9:00 a.m. I tried to wait for you, but the reporter said he had other appointments, and he wanted to get started." Mildred didn't seem upset; she just seemed a little confused about the time.

Mildred and her husband gave Vivian, Ashley, and me a ride back to the Bronx. It was a two-hour trip, and Mildred talked quite a bit about how the company could make more money through little loopholes in the state contract, and kept elaborating about how Steve wouldn't allow it. There was a hint of disloyalty toward him in her voice.

I listened very carefully. When Mildred was hired at Y.E.C., I didn't really get her backstory. I knew her husband was a judge, and I knew people from the state were familiar with her, because they were the ones who recommended her to Steve in the first place. The only other thing that seemed odd was that when Steve first told me about her, he said she had been out of work for ten years. But I thought since her husband was a judge, she didn't have to work. Mildred was a middle-aged woman, about forty-five, and somewhat attractive for a woman her age. She was big-boned, not overweight, and had a medium dark complexion.

The next day, I went to the office, and Steve said he wanted to speak to me privately. Once in his office, Steve asked me how the interview went, and about the trip altogether. I told him the interview went well, and the trip was fine. Steve said the reporter had called him the same day and told him that he was going to do an exposé on me for the article he was writing. Steve and I were overjoyed. The reporter was so impressed with how I handled myself that I gave him a totally different opinion of young, at-risk black men from the South Bronx.

Then Steve closed his door and said, "Now, on a serious note, I heard about what happened in the hotel room. Russ, I'm not trying to get in your business, but can I be honest with you?"

"Sure, Steve."

"Russ, you've outgrown Vivian. How long have you been with her now?"

"About two and a half years."

"Russ, I can remember when I first met you. I've seen how much you've matured, and what a hard worker you are and what a great work ethic you have. I'm telling you that Vivian will bring you down. You've outgrown her. Right now, you're the best thing that has happened to her. She knows it's just a matter of time before you leave her behind. You could have lost your job this weekend if the police were called and you were arrested. Did you think about that?

"Look at all the things that are getting ready to happen for the company. You're going to be the poster child for the program, and what a great success you and the program are. The possibilities are limitless, and all it would take is something stupid—like a fight with your girlfriend—to make it all come crashing down."

I knew that what Steve was saying was true, and I appreciated him telling me. But when he continued, I thought, *There's more?*

Steve asked, "How do you feel about Mildred?"

I said I thought she was cool, I had no problems with her, and she was fine to work with.

"Russ, you've got a lot to learn about women. How do you think I knew about what happened in the hotel room? Here's an even better question: why do you think she told me?"

Steve began to educate me on my newest nemesis. "Yesterday, Mildred came by the office after she dropped you off at your house, and she was livid. She said that you did the interview without her. I told her that it was a good thing, because the reporter wanted to do an exposé on you and that would give more publicity to Y.E.C. I told her you are the face of Y.E.C., because I can sell the program to many charity organizations because of your backstory. After I told her that, she told me about the incident in the hotel room. She was trying to convince me that you were a woman beater. Now, Russ, I want you to be careful with Mildred. I never trusted her.

"I'm going to tell you something else—she also wanted me to take you off the checks as the other signatory, and replace you with her a couple of months ago. She didn't think it was right that she was your supervisor and you were signing her paycheck. Now, let me tell you a little about her background. Mildred used to work as the director for a weatherization program in Brooklyn. The company was suspected of various incidents of fraud. Mildred resigned

her position before there was an official investigation. The only reason I hired her was because, at the time, we needed someone to fill
the spot to finish the contract. But I knew I had to keep an eye on
her, and I have been. You need to be careful, because she's going to
try and get you to do something crooked because you sign the
checks. Now, Russ, I know you're smart, but you're young. This is
an older woman, and let me tell you something about women—
they're smarter than you think they are, but not as smart as they
think they are."

I was dumbfounded by Steve's words. For the most part, I
trusted Mildred. I asked Steve why he didn't tell me all of this information before, and he said, "Russ, I know how you are, and I didn't
want her to become an enemy of yours before she even started. I
wanted to give her a fair shot."

After hearing everything Steve told me about Mildred, I told
Steve everything Mildred was saying in the car ride from the conference. Steve wasn't surprised; he said she had come to him with a
couple of shady things in the budget, and he had shot them down.

This was new territory for me. In the streets, you knew who
your enemies were, and it was plain as day that you better watch
your back. If anyone caught you slipping, they were going to take
you down. This woman smiled in my face and got me to trust her.
If this information hadn't come from Steve, I would have thought
that he was lying. I even confided in her sometimes about my personal problems and sought advice, and all along, she was planning
my demise.

Steve told me not to treat her any differently, because she would
catch on. He said, "Russ, have you ever seen *The Godfather?*"

I said, "Yes."

"Remember what the main strategy was that Michal Corleone
used in the movie?"

"He killed everybody."

"No, Russ, it was keep your friends close, and your enemies
closer."

340

This was all new to me. Before, when I had an enemy, he knew he was my enemy. Now, I had to smile in my enemy's face and befriend her. And now, my enemy was a woman, and that was a whole different battle. In the past, my enemies were all men. I know a few women that would consider me an enemy, but to me, an enemy in the street was someone you tried to hurt physically, or even kill. I never wanted to hurt a woman like that, or kill one.

From that point on, Mildred was my best friend; I wanted to give her a false sense of security. I was humble, and made her feel even more like the supervisor. I let her feel like she had me wrapped around her little finger. Her wish was my command. Every important decision that needed to be made, I brought to her—unlike before, when I would make a decision and then tell her what I did.

For a period of time, she had gotten into a car accident and didn't have a vehicle. I would get up an hour early, drive to Queens to pick her up, and take her to work until her vehicle was repaired. Now, even though she was out to get me, she felt that she controlled me, so she didn't have an urgency to bring me down. All I needed to do was be patient and wait for her to slip up. I remember thinking, *This may take a while.*

Meanwhile, at home, Vivian started to hang around with this girl named Carmen. Vivian said that she had known her for years, and the girl just left her husband for this guy named Jay who just got out of jail. I came home one day, and Carmen and Jay were sitting in my living room. Vivian introduced me to the two of them. I sat down and smoked a joint with the guy to feel him out.

He seemed younger than the woman, and the woman seemed older than Vivian and me. He may have been around my age, twenty-two to twenty-four, and the woman looked like she was in her thirties. He was medium-height, with a stocky build—like he just got out of jail—and had a darker complexion, but he was Spanish. She was about the same height as he was, with short, blondish-dyed hair, a little on the heavy side, and about Vivian's' complexion.

341

When the two of them left, I asked Vivian what they were doing in the apartment. Vivian said they were doing business together—they were breaking into mailboxes and stealing Social Security checks. She told me Carmen had a hookup at the supermarket that would cash the checks for them.

I said, "What the fuck! Are you stupid, bitch? If you get caught, you could go to jail for that, and it's a federal crime."

"I'm just getting my hustle on, trying to make some money. What the fuck is your problem? You didn't have a problem breaking the law when you were selling crack on the street, or when you go and buy your weed every day. You do know you can go to jail for that, too, don't you?"

I didn't have anything to say to that, and walked away. Two things came to mind about what she said. The first thing was that Steve was right—I was outgrowing Vivian. If this had been three or four years ago, I wouldn't have had a problem with what she was doing. In fact, I may have even looked for a way that I could be down with the hustle. But now, I was a company man on the rise, with a lot to lose.

The second thing to come to mind was, as far as I was concerned, smoking marijuana was a victimless crime. On the other hand, breaking into mailboxes and stealing old people's and disabled people's Social Security checks was not victimless. I knew it was just a matter of time before this bit her in the ass. And worst of all, she was taking my two-year-old daughter with her.

I just let her do whatever she was going to do. It made no sense to argue or fight with her. I couldn't even get her to treat me with respect, much less do what I asked. I knew that when the shit hit the fan, I was going to have to be the one to clean it up. When I was sitting and smoking a joint with Jay, I got the sense that he and Carmen were some shady people, and Vivian was pretty shady herself. There's an old saying: "There is no honor amongst thieves."

A few weeks had gone by since Vivian started her new career as a thief, and she never told me if she had any money or not. If she did, she kept it all to herself and just bought more cocaine, I suppose, because I wasn't giving her any money to buy drugs.

One day at work, out in the field, I got a page on my beeper. This was 1993, so there were no cell phones. I called the office, and it was Quinn. Vivian had called and asked Quinn to contact me and tell me that this guy, Jay, had slapped her in the face, in the street, in front of Ashley.

I called the house. Vivian answered. According to her, she got into a dispute over money with Carmen and Jay, and he called her a greedy bitch and slapped her in the face. Ashley saw him do it and was crying. I knew everything was fine at the moment, but I was pissed off that she called my job with this.

When I got home, Vivian laid it on thick about how Jay was cursing her out, how scared Ashley was, and how he said to her, "Go get your man now, bitch." I had a feeling that Vivian had embellished a lot in order to get me raging, and it worked. By the time she finished telling me about what happened, I was ready to put my foot in someone's ass—not really for Vivian, but because he scared my daughter.

I asked Vivian more about the guy, since he knew where I lived and I didn't know anything about him. Vivian said he and Carmen lived with his mother in a house near the Bronx River Projects, and he also went to a probation officer somewhere near Westchester Avenue. I asked her if she had a phone number for them, and she did.

I called Julie and asked her to contact George, her stepson, to come and watch my back. George was like a brother to me. If Jason or I were ever in trouble, George was always ready to come to our aid. He was about 6'2" and 250 pounds, and was an ex-con.

I also called this guy I worked with named Phil, who I also hung out with. Once, he drove me to Maryland to buy a riot gun—a small shotgun you usually see in the movies—since he had a driver's license for that state. He was a little crazy and had spent some time in a nuthouse, so he was always ready for some action. Phil was loyal to me because I always treated him well on the job. He was about 5'10" with a very stocky build. Together, the three of us looked very intimidating and made a dangerous group.

I had the two men meet me at my house. I explained what happened, and they were ready for whatever I wanted to do. I had two guns, a .32 automatic that I bought from Julie and the riot gun.

My plan was to get Jay to come to my house. I called, and his mother answered. She said Jay wasn't there. I told her I was Vivian's boyfriend and asked if she knew Vivian. She told me she did. I repeated what Vivian had told me. I told her that I knew where she lived, and that I was going to kick her son's ass—and if I couldn't find him, then kicking her old ass would suffice.

My plan was, if the guy had any heart, he would come looking to kick my ass since I threatened his mother. The three of us waited in the apartment until about 11:00 p.m. No one showed up. Jay was a punk. I called the mother again, told her that her son was a pussy, and hung up on her.

The next day, Vivian, Ashley, and I, along with George and Phil, took a walk to the house. I was packing my .32 automatic. I banged on the door, but no one would answer. The way we looked, I wouldn't have opened the door, either. I looked across the street and saw a kid I knew, Chris, who had worked at Y.E.C. a couple of years back. I asked him if he knew the people that lived in the house. Chris said he didn't, but the day before, he saw the dude and his girlfriend moving out in a hurry.

The four of us left. The next day, George and I went by the probation office and waited outside to see if Jay would show up there, but he didn't. I was done looking for this punk. I called his mother again and said, "I got people looking at your house, and if I hear that that muthafucker moved back in, I am going to burn the fucking house down with your old ass in it!"

Vivian was smiling while this was going on, as if I were defending her honor. I said to her, "I don't know what the fuck you smiling for, bitch. I didn't do any of this for you. I did it because he scared

Ashley. This is all your fault, with your breaking into mailboxes and shit. If something would have happened to my daughter, it would have been your ass that got fucked up."

I was surprised that the woman never called the cops, because afterward, I thought about what I had done. If she had, I could have been arrested for terroristic threats. I figured she didn't because her son was on probation, and the mailbox scam would have come out. What Steve had said sunk in even more. Vivian was going to bring me down.

At the job, I had thrown George some subcontract work for Y.E.C. He was an unemployed mason, so I had him do a few brick-work jobs—with Mildred's permission, of course. Steve was going on vacation, so Mildred was in charge now for two weeks—when the cat's away, the mice will play. It had gotten to the point that Mildred was using George for more and more little jobs. Because Steve was away, Mildred thought it was time to make her move. Just like Steve said, women are smart. Mildred was a very, very smart woman. But, like Steve also said, she wasn't as smart as she thought.

I had gained Mildred's trust. She called me into her office one day and said, "You know, there's a way for you, George, and me to make some money." This was it—this was what Steve was talking about. Y.E.C had a contract with Con Edison, the electric company for the New York area, to replace regular light bulbs with the new energy-efficient light bulbs. Con Edison supplied the light bulbs, and the state allowed a certain amount in the contract for subcon-tractors to install them. Since the company was a job training pro-gram, we didn't hire a subcontractor to install the bulbs, which was just screwing them in. We had the trainees do it. Then, the money was just redistributed for other costs.

Mildred's plan was simple. Just like in her previous job, there was a little loophole in the state contract that she was going to try and scam. Mildred told me that the state allowed up to $6 a bulb to be paid to a subcontractor. So, the plan was to get George to install them for $2 a bulb, and submit a bill for $6 per bulb. Then, she and I would split the leftover $4. Mildred would pay George in a check, and he would give us back the difference in cash. Mildred figured that George was my friend, so we could trust him with giving us back the money. She also figured that George would be happy making a few easy dollars. We were talking several thousand bulbs through the course of a year. We could make a lot.

Mildred asked me if I was interested, and I agreed. Then, she asked if I thought George would cooperate, and I said sure he would. This was it. This was the moment I had been waiting for. But I had to play it just right, or else the opportunity would slip through my fingers. I couldn't just tell Steve what Mildred asked me to do, because all she would have to do is deny it. It would be my word against hers, and she would know I was out to get her.

I called George and told him of Mildred's offer, not letting him know what my true intentions were. George came by the office, and Mildred explained. Her intention was to get it started before Steve came back from vacation. That way, all he would see were the sub-contractor bills allowed by the state that came trickling in and wouldn't become suspicious.

Now I had her right where I wanted her. I even had a witness. The only thing left was to drop the bomb. I went by Julie's to see George, tell him what my plans were, and apologize for using him. George didn't have any hard feelings. He was just glad he was able to make the few dollars that I had thrown his way already.

The next day, Mildred was expecting George to show up, ready to begin her scam. But he was a no-show. Mildred beeped me out in the field, and asked if I knew where George was. I played dumb and told her I would try to contact him and get back to her.

I waited all day to go back to the office, ignoring her beeps the entire time. I returned at 3:00 p.m. Mildred was livid, and scolded me for not answering my beeper. I waited until she finished her tirade, calmly sat down in her office, and dropped the hammer on her.

346

I said, "Fuck you, Mildred."

She said, "What did you say? How dare you?"

"You think you're so fucking smart, don't you? You thought you could corrupt me into doing your dirty work, didn't you? Well, guess what? I've been playing you all the time, ever since the conference. I know what you did. You thought you were playing me, and guess what? You got played. George isn't going to do your dirty work, and when Steve gets back, I'm going to tell him everything."

Mildred blurted out, "Well, I'll just deny it."

I told her, "I knew you would say that. That's why I had George come in and play along, so I'd have a witness to stick a fork in it. You're done, bitch."

I got up and walked out of her office.

Steve was due back in two days, but he was home, so I called him there and met him for dinner to fill him in. Steve smiled the whole time while I was telling him about the situation.

He told me to write up everything I just said and to put it on his desk. He was still going to come back to the office in two days, but he was going to act like he didn't know anything about it. Then, he was going to act like he just read the memo and call Mildred into the office. I agreed.

Steve said, "Russ, I sure wouldn't want to piss you off, because when you play, you play for keeps."

I told Steve, "I do unto others before they do unto me." But he didn't have to worry about that, because I was loyal to him.

For the next two days, Mildred kept trying to meet with me alone, but I refused. She might have tried to make false rape allegations against me or something. I know it was far out there, but you never know what a desperate person will do.

When Steve returned, he said good morning to Mildred and the rest of the staff, and then went into his office. He came out about five minutes later, highly upset, walked over to Mildred's office and said, "Mildred, did you see this?"

Mildred said, "No."

Steve handed her the paper and asked her to come into his office. He called me in as well. Steve asked Mildred what she had to say for herself.

Mildred said, "I deny it."

I reminded Mildred that I had a witness who was willing to come in and confirm what I had written.

Steve said, "Mildred, I'm sorry, but due to the circumstances, I'm going to have to let you go. And considering the seriousness of the situation, I'm' going to have to ask that you to leave right now."

Mildred said, "Fine." She cleaned out her desk and left.

Steve told me he knew I was telling the truth because if she had a leg to stand on, she would have been talking about suing, since her husband was a judge.

After that incident, Steve and I became closer than ever. I looked up to him like a father figure, and now, he knew he could trust me. It was going on five years that Steve and I were working together. He had big plans for me. The one thing I really respected was that he never treated me differently when I told him about my medical condition. In fact, he always asked me what I was doing to follow up on any kind of treatment.

I told Steve that I would finally call the number that the counselor at the clinic gave me for Dr. Barbara Justice, and the next week I did. Dr. Justice's office was located on 145th and Convent Avenue in Harlem. Coincidentally, it was right across the street from where Denise lived with her boyfriend. I made an appointment and was fearful that I would see Denise, but it was in the daytime, and she was usually at work.

The doctor's office was located inside of a brownstone on the first floor. When I stepped into the office, it was very low-key. There were a couple of very sick-looking people sitting around, and they had the same thing I had. I thought, *Is this what the future holds for me?* They were all very skinny, their skin was discolored, and they looked very gruesome.

348

I signed in with the receptionist and waited my turn. When I was called into the doctor's office, I sat down across from a very dark-skinned woman with her head wrapped in some type of Afrocentric scarf. She looked at the application and asked me what the problem was. I could barely muster up the words.

I said, "I went to an anonymous clinic and was told that I was HIV-positive. The counselor there gave me your number and said that you were involved in some new breakthrough and untraditional treatments."

The doctor told me that I would need to go to her lab to get tested, so she could see what my numbers were. Later, I found out that one of the reasons she wanted me to go to her lab was because many large drug companies did not want her using the new drug she was promoting. At that time, the companies were promoting AZT. She wanted to make sure that I wasn't a spy trying to set her up.

I went to her lab and had blood drawn. I returned to her for the results two weeks later. When I got there, she confirmed what the clinic told me. She told me that the new drug she was giving her patients was called Kemron. It was produced in Africa, and was showing promise in people with HIV, improving their T cell count and their quality of life. While she was talking, hope started to build up inside me. *Maybe I'm not going to die. Maybe I won't get sick.*

But then, the hammer came down.

She said that since the drug was not FDA approved, my insurance would cover my lab work, but not the treatment itself. I would need a treatment once a month at a cost of $1,000 each time. The doctor continued to speak, but after she said $1,000 a month, I knew I couldn't afford it, so everything else was meaningless.

I decided just to live my life and take it one day at a time. I started to take some vitamins and read up on my sickness as much as possible. But the most important thing I was thinking about was keeping my condition a secret. I heard the way people talked about others they knew that had HIV, and it was horrendous. They talked about people with HIV and AIDS like they were modern-day lepers.

I knew if anyone else found out, it was over for me. As of now, the only other people that knew of my condition were Vivian and Steve.

Ever since the situation with Mildred, Y.E.C. needed to hire a new director. I remembered that when I was at the conference, I had met this guy named James. I didn't really know him that well. The only thing I knew was that he and I held the same position, but at different companies, and he knew the paperwork involved with weatherization contracts. In fact, he was one of the people I was sitting with in the bar at the conference when Vivian walked in that night. I suggested him to Steve, and Steve told me to set up an interview for James.

I called James, and he was interested in the position. He came in, and Steve and I interviewed him and offered him the job. James accepted, and I walked him to his car. James knew I had recommended him for the job, and before he got in, he gave me a firm handshake and said, "Hey, Russ, thanks for looking out for me, man. I won't forget it."

I told him, "No problem."

I thought he and I would work well together. I was wrong. James soon became my biggest and most dangerous adversary to date.

chapter THIRTY-ONE

D enise and I talked a few more times and started writing to each other. Both of us had to send the letters to our jobs because we were involved in other relationships. In every letter I wrote, I professed my love for her and how sorry I was about the past. I told her that if I could turn back time, I would. I let her know that I was older, and now realized what a great woman she was and how much she loved me. I wasn't telling her to come back to me. I knew that was impossible, for a number of reasons. I just wanted to let her know how much I loved her.

Surprisingly, her letters mirrored mine. She, too, told me how much she loved me. But the wounds of my betrayal, even after five years, had still not completely healed. It was hard for her to trust me, even though she loved me a great deal.

Denise and I finally decided to meet for lunch and spend an afternoon together. I took off work that day, and when Vivian went to some appointment, I left the house, dressed decently. Denise and I decided to meet in front of Radio City Music Hall, and then go to the Metropolitan Art Museum. I was supposed to meet her at 12:30, but I had gotten there early. My heart was beating fast. The anticipation was overwhelming. I hadn't seen her in almost three years, and I wondered what she would look like. I wondered if I would still see her for the beautiful woman she was, inside and out. Or had time and volatile relationships diminished my view of women in general?

It was a beautiful spring day. It was around the beginning of May, and the temperature was about seventy degrees. The sun was shining brightly, and there wasn't a cloud in the sky. This was a perfect day. As I stood in front of Radio City, I saw strolling toward me this slim woman. As she came close, I saw it was Denise. She was as beautiful as ever. She looked like she had put on about ten pounds, and it looked great on her.

She was smiling as she approached. Her smile outshined the sun in my eyes. When she came closer, we gave each other a kiss on the lips. I was overjoyed to see her. Denise and I began to walk toward Central Park, and we both gave each other compliments about how good we looked. When we got to the park, we sat on a bench and made small talk about our jobs and current events, but neither of us mentioned the people we were living with.

As we were talking, I leaned over and tried to give her a sensual kiss on her lips, but she didn't reciprocate. With a smile on her face, she said, "I'm not going to do that with you."

I didn't complain or ask her why. I just figured she was being true to her boyfriend, and was probably in love with him. Meeting with me was bad enough, and she didn't want to betray him any further. I respected that.

From the park, we went to the museum. We talked, and talked, and talked. It was like we were never apart. She was so intelligent, and conversing with her came so easy. There was no conversation about drugs, or welfare checks, or drama; it was just pleasant.

It was about 4:00 p.m. when she said she had to head home soon. I didn't want the day to end. I didn't want to go back to my relationship at home. I wanted to continue this fantasy of us being together. I wanted to believe that she and I had a chance, but I was only fooling myself. I was damaged goods. Even if she wasn't with anybody, who would want me, with what I had?

I walked Denise to her train station, and we kissed on the lips and embraced. Then she walked down into the subway station. I was glad we spent the time we did together, but leaving was reminiscent of the time when she left me in the park with my son. I knew it was going to be a long time before I would see her again.

I rode the train home in a state of depression. I felt trapped by my circumstances. I didn't want to be with Vivian anymore. I saw, just by being with Denise for those few hours, that I couldn't even talk to Vivian. She was satisfied with her life, and didn't have any ambition at all—she was happy being on welfare and riding the Russell gravy train.

I didn't have the courage to leave. One reason was that I didn't want another child growing up without a father. I made all the same promises to Ashley that I had made to Malik, and here I was contemplating not fulfilling them. The other reason was I thought Vivian would reveal my secret. She didn't tell anyone that I knew of, but she also didn't have any shame about her. I was miserable and had no way out. Vivian was increasing her cocaine use and becoming more daring in her actions and disrespect toward me.

It was the first of the month, and the rent was due. I relied on Vivian's portion. I always tried to make sure that the rent was paid by the second day of the month at the latest. It was a Friday, and I had just gotten paid and was waiting for Vivian at the apartment. But it was getting late, and she was nowhere to be found. Around 11:00 p.m., Vivian walked through the door. I could see that her eyes were wide-eyed and buggy. I demanded her portion of the rent money and she said, "Fuck you, muthafucker. Wait!" I was furious with her for having such a smartass attitude with me.

Once again, I demanded her portion of the rent, and she said, "You'll get it when I give it to you, muthafucker!"

I slapped her in her face, and she fell to the couch. Ashley was standing right there, watching me. I was so angry. Vivian didn't try to hit me back. Instead, she said, "Now you ain't getting shit. How you like that shit, muthafucker?"

Then, I snatched her bag and started to rummage through it, looking for the money. She just kept antagonizing me about not finding it and how she wasn't going to give it to me. I was pissed that she was using the rent money as a tool to screw with my mind, and I struck her again. My daughter just sat there and watched. She was about two at the time.

After that, Vivian got up, went into the bedroom, and started to pack a suitcase. I really didn't care. All I cared about was how I was going to pay the rent the next day. I thought this was a blessing in disguise. If she was leaving me, then there was no fear of her revealing my secret to anyone as revenge. I didn't say anything as she was packing. I watched from the window as she walked out of the building with Ashley and caught a cab.

As I sat there alone, I felt bad about striking her in front of my daughter. I thought, *I'm no Lamar. I'm not like him.* However, I couldn't help but think about the physical altercations I had gotten into with Vivian and T. I started to think that I was more like Lamar than I wanted to admit. I also thought about Denise. I never, ever laid a hand on her. I never even thought about it. I never cursed her out the way I'd cursed at Vivian and T, or called her a bitch like I had them—and these were the mothers of my children.

The next day at work, I told Phil what happened, and he loaned me $200 to pay my rent. I didn't even call or look for Vivian. I was glad to be rid of her. I was making plans already to compensate for the rent. Two or three days passed by, and then the phone rang. It was Julie. Vivian knew that Julie was like a mother to me, and that I listened to her. Julie asked me what had happened. I told her, and let her know how embarrassed I was to have to ask a subordinate at my job for the loan.

Julie spoke to me in a soft tone. "Mijo," she said. That's an endearing term used by older Spanish women which means "my son." She went on, "Mijo, listen. I know you're upset, but Vivian says she is very sorry for what she did and she wants to come home."

I told Julie I didn't want her home, and she could stay wherever she was. I was fine with her being gone.

"Mijo?" Julie asked, "What about your daughter? Do you want her mother wandering from house to house with her? You're a better man than that. I know that about you."

Julie's words made sense, and I said, "Fine, but she had better give me the rent money."

Julie said, "Mijo, she said that she spent all the money. That is why she asked me to call you."

"Julie, this is bullshit."

Julie agreed, but again reiterated about Ashley.

Again, I said, "Fine." I let Vivian come back.

After that incident, I started to make plans to leave Vivian. I was no longer committed. I wanted to move out of the condominium and into an apartment in a lower-income neighborhood so that when I left, Vivian would be able to afford the rent and I would know that Ashley had a place to stay. This was going to take some time because I had to save the money. But from now on, I was going to be back to my old self again.

I started to hang out with Phil and a couple of other guys from the job after work. I started to hang out at strip clubs like the Goat again. It was like I never missed a beat. I also ran into an old friend who I hadn't seen in a couple of years.

I was driving down Brook Avenue in the Bronx after dropping off a crew at a repair site when I saw Jazz walking down the street with a baby carriage. Jazz had put on a little weight, but she was still very attractive. I called out to her, and she waved for me to come over. I stopped the truck, walked over, picked her up, and gave her a big hug. I was twenty-five now, and she was thirty-three. She told me she still lived in the same building as before, but on a different floor. I asked her about the baby in the carriage, and she said it was her daughter. I asked her about her son, Alex, and she said he was at school. She lived with this guy named Julio, who worked for the telephone company, but he was an asshole.

When she said Julio, I remembered it was the same guy that came up to Jazz and me in the park when I was out with her and

Alex. I remembered so well because it was the first time I had met Denise. Jazz told me that she heard about me and Frida, and I told her, "Fuck Frida!" Jazz told me to stop by sometime during the day, and I told her I would come by tomorrow after I dropped my crews off. She complimented me on how grown I was and told me not to forget to drop by; she was looking forward to it.

I got in the truck and drove away. My mind went back in time. I remembered how in love I was with Jazz when I first met her, when Mitchell got killed. I remembered how much I wanted to have sex with her then. I knew her before I knew Denise. She was the first woman I was ever in love with. It just wasn't the right time—I was fourteen and she was twenty-two. I thought now was the perfect chance to make up for lost time. I also remembered how Jason was having sex with her for a while. I couldn't wait until the next day. I wanted to see exactly what she had in mind because, at this point, I was down with whatever she wanted to do.

The next day, I went by. Julio was at work, and Alex was in preschool. Jazz opened the door in just a shirt and invited me into the apartment. I asked her where the baby was, and she said she was asleep. I tried to make small talk and asked her what her daughter's name was. She had named her after herself—Giselle. I asked her why she wanted me to drop by, and she told me not to play dumb. Did I want to fuck her or not? I was a little shocked at her straightforwardness, but then again, I remembered that when I was fourteen, Frida and her friends would call her a nymphomaniac.

I answered, "Yes." I had protection with me, anticipating that this was going to happen. The sex was worth waiting for all these years. It was as good as Jason had told me—Jazz was very uninhibited.

From that day forward, Jazz became my side chick. I would go by her house three or four times a week during the day. Sometimes Julio would be there, and Jazz would just wave me away. She didn't want anything from me but sex, and I didn't want anything but sex from her as well.

From time to time, I would give her a few dollars, but she never demanded anything. I treated Jazz the way I should have treated T. I realized that I had showed T too much respect, instead of treating her like the ghetto rat that she was.

Jazz was the same kind of ghetto rat. She had three kids by three different men and was on welfare. She didn't work, but she also didn't play head games with me. She didn't want me to be her man. We had a good understanding, and it was working out well.

Now, all I had to do was get rid of the ghetto rat I had at home. I went about my daily routine. I paid the bills and took care of both my daughter and Vivian. As long as she could get high and ride the Russell gravy train, everything was fine with her. I was just biding my time. Jazz made the time just a little more tolerable, but I needed to get rid of Vivian.

At the job, we completed another contract and our funding increased. By this time, James started to show discontentment toward me. He felt that he was the boss, and everything had to go through him. James's envy was showing its ugly face as his position started to go to his head. He was no smarter than I was; he was just able to do the paperwork better. But in the other weatherization companies, his position held a lot of power. Just like Mildred, he felt that I held too much power, especially since I signed his paycheck.

Every chance he got, James complained to Steve about something I had done. Steve finally got sick of it and told him that he was the director, so he should be able to express his concerns to me directly. James tried to do that, which made me really see his cowardly colors. He didn't know that Steve told me every time he complained about me.

So one day, James called me down to a basement work and storage area. He called this a "man-to-man talk." James gave his speech, and it went something like this: "Look here, Russell, I'm the director of this program, and I run things. From now on, first thing in the morning, I want a briefing about the day's activities. Also, I want a weekly schedule of the projects that you are working on. Is that clear? Things are going to be different from now on, and I just want you to know that I'm not going to tolerate any insubordination. Is that clear?"

After James was done, I asked him if I could speak, and he said, "Go ahead." I could see the weakness in his eyes. If he were a real man, he would have had his "I'm the boss" speech long before he was snitching to Steve about everything I did.

I closed the door and said, "Look here, muthafucker. You ain't running nothing but your mouth. You know something? You're a piece of shit. I got you this job, muthafucker, and now you coming in here acting like you King Shit. Well, guess what? I been here going on six years, and we finished every single contract without any problems. So I say, if it ain't broke, don't fix it. You know something else? You're an ungrateful mutherfucker. I know you been complaining to Steve about me all the time, instead of coming to me. That's some pussy ass shit. From now on, muthafucker, if it ain't job-related, don't say shit to me. And one more thing—fuck you!"

I turned and walked away. From then on, I had to watch my back, because any chance he got, he was going to try and burn me. At least I knew he was out to get me. It wasn't like with Mildred.

Besides James, the job was going great. Steve's plan was working, and I was growing every day. Our funding increased to over a million dollars, and some people came from California to look at the job training aspect of our program. Of course, I was the centerpiece. Steve was showing me off, as well as the awards the program had received during my tenure as the crew leader supervisor.

Steve laid it on thick about me being raised by my great-grandmother and being a high school dropout. He continued by praising the job skills I learned from Y.E.C. and how I put them to work, which led me to become a productive member of society. It didn't hurt that I had never been arrested and sent to jail. After the men went to visit various job sites with me and got feedback from different customers, by the end of the day, they wanted Steve to send me out to California to start up a program there. They would pay all expenses.

I was at the top of my game. That year, the state was giving out an award for people that worked with kids called Decade of the Child. Steve and Juan nominated me, so I had to go to the courthouse for the ceremony and was presented with the award by the Bronx District Attorney himself.

During my rise, you could see the envy and hatred in James's eyes. Steve often found himself playing referee between the two of us. I started to believe I couldn't be touched. I was getting away with so much. I smoked weed every day, and I disrespected my immediate supervisor all the time. I started to believe the image that Steve was selling to other people. I started to think I was Y.E.C. I started to believe that Y.E.C. couldn't run without me.

Besides James, I really didn't have any other enemies on the job. Most of the guys were people I had hired as favors for friends. I had it so that they were loyal to me. Everyone hated James. He knew that I hired most of the people, so he would take his contempt for me out on them at every opportunity.

THIRTY-TWO

There was one person that I didn't have any part in hiring, and that was the secretary, Jezebel. Steve always hired the secretaries on his own. He liked eye candy, and Jezebel was eye candy to the max. She was a very beautiful woman—Dominican, about 5'4", and a medium-light complexion. She had jet-black hair that ran down her back, and she was built very well—not too busty, but she had a very curvy figure.

Sometimes, James would take Jezebel out with him to collect documentation from buildings we were going to service, and he would use Jezebel to translate for the non-English-speaking tenants. James would often make passes at her, but she would reject his advances. James was married, so he wasn't making a pass to get together with her—he was looking for a booty call. He would even ask her to have oral sex with him in the car on the way to job sites.

After a while, Jezebel finally complained to Steve. So, Steve reprimanded James and informed him that Jezebel would no longer go out to any job sites with him. That led to great enmity between him and Jezebel. I now had a new ally in the fight against James. Jezebel and I weren't enemies, but we weren't friends, either. This stemmed from when Vivian would call and disrespect her on the phone, and from an incident when Denise had written me a letter and sent it to the job. Jezebel had opened and read it. When I asked her about it, she said she was supposed to look though all the mail that came across her desk. I had to tell her not to open any mail addressed to me.

But now, she and I had a common enemy.

After a while, Jezebel and I became cool because we would take every opportunity to grind James up. Sometimes, Quinn, Jezebel, and I would have lunch together and laugh about how hard we were making things for James. Jezebel even arranged for me to buy a used car from her father, a 1985 Buick Skyhawk. This was my first car, and Steve loaned me the $800 to buy it. These interactions made Jezebel and me a little bit closer.

The program became so successful that we ended up moving to a bigger location, and I got my own office. James had to share one with the bookkeeper. The office was located on West Tremont Avenue, and it had twice the amount of space that the old one did. There, we didn't have to answer to anyone.

Soon, the opportunity for me to move to a lower-income neighborhood came. A building we were working on became a co-op, and Phil had moved in. It was located on Monterey Avenue, right off Tremont, and the neighborhood really sucked. It was the kind Vivian deserved to live in. The rent was only $400, and the first chance I got, I made arrangements to move.

Vivian had no idea what I was up to. I just told her that we were moving so that I could save money. We downgraded from a two-bedroom to a one-bedroom. The day of the move, I got a couple of guys from Y.E.C. and Chris, who lived across the street from Jay and Carmen, to help.

At the end of the day, when I was dropping Chris off at his house, I saw Jay and Carmen across the street. They stood in front of his mother's house, talking. My blood started to boil, but he was with a couple of guys. Even though I was with Chris, I didn't want to get him involved in my fight.

Jay and Carmen didn't see me pull up, so I watched them while my mind contemplated what I could do to them. Chris was drinking a bottle of juice. I told him to finish it and give me the bottle.

Chris looked at me and said, "You're going to piss in it, aren't you?"

I didn't answer. Chris finished drinking the juice and handed me the bottle. I filled it up. I told Chris to get out, and he walked into his house.

I rolled down the window, put the car in drive, sped up quickly in front of Jay, and threw the bottle of piss in his face from the window of the car. Jay and other people standing close by were in shock. Jay was momentarily blinded by the urine, and I yelled out the window to him, "Hey, muthafucker! Remember me? I'm Vivian's man. You know what I just threw in your face? It was my piss, muthafucker! The next time I see you, you ain't gonna see it coming, either."

Then, I sped off.

I drove to my new place. I had moved right next to Phil. I didn't even tell Vivian what I had done. Like I said before, I didn't do it for Vivian; I did it for Ashley. A couple of weeks later, when I got home one day, Vivian said that she was on Tremont Avenue and this guy she didn't know walked up to her and said, "Hey bitch. You know who I am? I'm Jay's cousin. I was with him when your man pulled up in a car and threw piss in his face. Your man is lucky, because we went by the place you used to live and you guys moved out. Your man better watch his back."

Vivian said that she was with Ashley, and she thought the guy was going to strike her, but she put up a front and started to talk shit to the guy. She said, "Muthafucker, you don't know my man. He ain't got to watch his back. You need to watch your back, and you're the one who was lucky that when you came by the other house, we had moved out. Because, believe me, you ain't got the balls to step to my man. Matter of fact, if you think you're a bad muthafucker, meet him on this corner at seven o'clock tonight. We'll see what kind of man you really are, muthafucker."

The guy said, "That's a bet. I'll be here tonight at seven, and we'll see, bitch," Then, he walked away.

When Vivian was finished, I confirmed to her that I did throw piss in Jay's face. I asked her how the guy found her, and if he knew where we lived. She didn't think so, and said Jay and his cousin probably saw her walking down the street and took the opportunity to step to her. She made sure no one followed her home.

I knew I had to end this once and for all. I didn't know where Jay or his cousin lived, so I just hoped they would be stupid enough to actually meet me on that corner. Since Vivian told them to meet me there at 7:00 p.m., I decided to get there at 5:00. I took a sledge-hammer with me and put it in the trunk of my car. I put my .32 automatic in the passenger seat for easy access and covered it with a sweatshirt.

I parked about two blocks away, where I could still see the corner. My plan was to wait until they arrived, follow them to their house—since I didn't know where they lived—and then take action against them.

By seven o'clock, no one had arrived. I waited until eight and thought they weren't going to show up, so I started to drive down Tremont to go home. As I was driving, I passed by the spot that I was supposed to meet the guy. I looked in my rearview mirror and saw Jay and this guy looking and pointing. They didn't even realize I was right in front of them. I pulled up a little ahead of them, made a U-turn, and positioned my car about two cars behind them. I followed them for about five blocks, but lost them to a traffic light.

I parked on Tremont and 3rd Avenue in the hopes that they would circle around again. I waited for maybe twenty minutes. Just as I was about to leave, I looked, and there in front of me was Jay and Carmen, in a car with a baby that looked about one year old. They were stopped at a red light on 3rd Avenue.

I followed closely. This time, I wasn't going to lose them. They stopped at a store that Jay went into, leaving Carmen and the baby in the car. My first instinct was to walk up to the car and pistol whip Carmen. Jay would come out and see her all bloodied up. I really didn't want to do that in front of the baby, and I still needed to know where they lived. Jay came out, got back in the car, and drove off. I followed them. They pulled up to the housing projects near

Story Avenue. I drove past as they were parking. They never noticed me.

I parked approximately 100 feet away and watched as they got out of their car. I was going to run up on them and put a bullet in both of Jay's kneecaps, but when he got out of the car, he was holding their baby. I'd heard of too many situations where a baby accidently gets killed because of gunfire, and I didn't need that on my head. Besides, if Jay got shot in the kneecaps, as long as he didn't die, the police wouldn't really look into it too much. They would just see it as an ex-con who pissed someone off. On the other hand, if a baby got hit or killed by a stray bullet, it would be a major investigative event.

I watched as Jay and Carmen walked up and spoke to a couple of people for a minute or two before entering the building. Once they were inside, I started my car, backed it up, and pulled in right next to their car. I put my gun in my waist, then popped open my trunk and pulled out the sledgehammer. In a heated rage, I started to attack their car. I busted out every window. I busted out the headlights and the rear lights. I caved in the roof, the doors, and the hood. I destroyed the car beyond repair. People were looking at me like I was crazy.

One of the people that Jay was talking to before he went into the building walked up when I was done and said, "Hey, yo, that's my boy's car."

I dropped the sledgehammer, pulled the gun out from my waist, and pointed it at the guy. "You gonna do something about it, muthafucker?"

The guy stood there, silent and scared to death, and didn't say a word.

I said, "That's your boy, right? Well, you tell that muthafucker the only reason he ain't dead is because he had that baby in his arms. You tell him the next time he or anybody goes near Vivian, not even the baby is going to save him. You got that, muthafucker?"

The man just nodded.

"You tell them I know where they live now. You got that?"

He nodded again. I could see the fear in his eyes. I picked up the sledgehammer, threw it in my car, and sped off.

The next day, I drove back to the same area to see the damage in broad daylight. I had taken Vivian with me so she could see, also. Jay had the windows covered with garbage bags, and I could see that the car was a total loss. I told Vivian, "The next time, if there's a next time, someone steps to you, remind them muthafuckers about this."

I never heard about Jay and Carmen again after that.

The move into the new apartment allowed me to save a few dollars, and I was able to pay Steve back right away for my car. Vivian was still getting the $175 stipend from Welfare, but she decided it was her money and she was just going to indulge her drug habit even more. Whenever I asked her for the money when rent time came around, she would just disrespect me by saying, "Fuck that. This is my money. You don't need it."

I sat her down one day and told her that I wasn't happy in the relationship, and that if things kept going the way they were, I was going to leave. Vivian responded just as I knew she would—disrespectfully.

"What, muthafucker? Who do you think you are? You ain't nobody. Go ahead and leave. I made it in this world without you before I met you, and I'll make it when you're gone. So go ahead, leave! What the fuck you waiting for? Leave!"

At that moment, I had no place to go, but at least I put her on notice. After that conversation, Vivian would taunt me at times when I came home. As I walked in the door, she would say things like, "You still here, muthafucker? I thought you were leaving." Since I didn't leave right away, Vivian thought I was bluffing. She also knew how much I loved Ashley. But no matter how much I did, I wasn't going to stay in this toxic relationship.

Soon, Vivian's actions became bolder than ever. One Friday night, she just walked out the door without a word, leaving Ashley with me. I didn't care, but I did have to go to work the next day. Vivian never came home that night and didn't call, so in the morning, I had to make last-minute arrangements for Ashley so that I could go to work.

The next day passed, and Vivian still hadn't shown up. I called Julie and asked if she had seen Vivian. Julie said she hadn't. As I was talking to Julie, Vivian walked in, looking like she had been partying for the whole two days she was gone.

Vivian looked at me, waiting for some type of angry reaction, but I took a deep breath and walked away.

Vivian tried to provoke a response. "You ain't got nothing to say, muthafucker? I know you want to hit me."

I told her, "I don't want to hit you. I just don't want to be with you." I walked away, rolled a blunt, and sat and watched TV.

I knew that in Vivian's mind, if I argued with her or hit her, it would mean that I cared. I didn't care anymore. The sooner I got out of there, the better.

After her disappearing act, I would hang out after work with Phil or Willie. My goal after work was to eat, get high, and when I got tired, go home and just go to sleep. I would have hung out at Jazz's house, but her boyfriend got home at 5:00 p.m. So instead, it was usually strip clubs or Willie's house. Sometimes, Willie's wife would even cook for me. Willie was a dark-skinned Puerto Rican guy who was the job developer at Y.E.C, since Juan had found a new job. Willie hung out with me a lot after work because he cheated on his wife a lot. Sometimes, he would use me as an excuse to get out of the house.

The job was going well. James had finally pissed Jezebel off to the point that she was now threatening to file a sexual harassment lawsuit against him. James, in an attempt to avoid any kind of litigation, up and resigned. I felt that a weight had been lifted from me, but Steve was a little upset about the situation and had a meeting with me about it. He felt that I may have contributed to James leaving because I was always giving him a hard time.

Steve said, "Russ, I know you had a problem with James, but you have to learn that you can't always be in battle mode. If you would have worked with him, you could have had him wrapped around your finger. It seems that you're always up against someone. Let me tell you, Russ, you can't always fight on all four fronts. You need to fight one battle at a time. That way, you can give each your full attention."

Steve also gave me a warning. "Russ, watch that Jezebel. She's dangerous. People think you're the one who brought James down, but you and I know it was her. She is a spiteful and vindictive woman, and you don't want to get on her bad side."

Steve said that until we found a replacement for James, I would be taking over his duties. This was a way of punishing me for giving James such a hard time.

That afternoon, after work, Quinn, Jezebel, and I went out to celebrate James's demise. We had a good time, and Quinn left the bar first. Jezebel and I stayed and hung out together for a couple more hours. I didn't want to go home, and although she had a four-year-old son, she said her parents were watching him that night and she didn't have to be anyplace soon.

The two of us seemed to talk for hours. I found out a lot more about her. She was in the Army. She was separated from her husband, who was half-black and half-white. She had graduated high school. She was a native of Brooklyn, and had a plan to open a business with a GI Bill loan from the Army. The longer I talked to her, the more I realized that she was a very intelligent woman, and not just a secretary.

As the night went on, we moved locations. We went to the South Street Seaport and stood by the water and talked. Then, we went to another bar and hung out some more. At the end of the night, we headed back to the Bronx for a nightcap and to pick up her car. I walked her out of the bar. When we got to her car, she gave me a passionate kiss and I returned it. We stood there for about five minutes, making out. It had been so long since I kissed a woman like that. I hadn't kissed Vivian like that in at least a year, and I didn't kiss T like that at all. There wasn't any kissing at all with the other women that I was involved with.

When we unlocked lips, she said, "Go home now, before I don't let you." She got into her car and drove off.

When I got home, it was about 2:00 a.m., and I went right to sleep. The next morning, as I rolled a joint before work, I realized that I hadn't smoked the whole day before. I was so entranced in conversation with Jezebel, I didn't even think about smoking. I didn't even smoke a cigarette. Jezebel definitely had my attention. I was absolutely attracted to her, but I didn't want to make any assumptions about her being attracted to me. After all, we were drinking, and sometimes alcohol made things seem more than they actually were. All we really did was kiss—no big deal.

The next day when I went to work, both of us were acting awkward toward each other. Finally, I asked her if she wanted to go for a drink after work, and she said yes. While we were out, I found out that I wasn't making any assumptions at all. She told me how she had been attracted to me for a long time, but never said anything because I was her boss. She told me that on many occasions, she wanted to just come up and kiss me on the lips, but she feared embarrassment. I told her that I always noticed she was a beautiful woman, but I never got to talk to her that much. After last night, I realized that she was as intelligent as she was beautiful.

She also told me that once, when Vivian came by the office, she said to herself that I deserved a better woman than that. I told her Vivian and I were on the rocks, and about the plan I had of moving to a lower-income neighborhood and leaving her. She told me she had just broke up with a guy who was a drug mule, and she and her husband had been separated for two years. He lived in Texas.

The two of us repeated the night before, hanging out all around town. At the end of the night, when I walked her to her car, the make-out session lasted about fifteen minutes. She got a rise out of me, and when she noticed, she said, "Not tonight. Maybe next time." Then, she got in her car and drove away. I went home and went to sleep.

The next morning, when I got up, I started to roll a joint. I realized that I hadn't smoked again the night before. I went to work. Jezebel and I stayed away from each other, so as not to let on that something was happening. I didn't really know what was happening; I was just going with the flow.

Later on that day, she called me on the intercom from her desk. She asked if I wanted to come over to her place that night, and I said yes. She gave me the directions and told me to come around 7:00 p.m. I went home, changed, and just walked out of the door without saying two words to Vivian. I drove to Brooklyn and arrived at Jezebel's place at 7:00 p.m. on the dot. She had her parents watching her son; they lived just down the block. She lived in the Williamsburg section of Brooklyn, right off the Williamsburg Bridge off Delancy Street.

She had a small, one-bedroom apartment in a three-unit house. That night, she had dinner waiting for me when I got there. She was an excellent cook. I didn't even know what she was serving; I just knew it tasted good. It had been so long since I had a home-cooked meal. Vivian stopped cooking for me right after the baby was born.

When dinner was over, Jezebel asked me if I wanted to take a shower with her, and, of course, I agreed. I watched her undress, still mesmerized by her beauty. When she took her clothes off, she was just as beautiful as with her clothes on. In the past, when I would sleep with some women, when they took off their clothes, there was a lot left to be desired. The women would have had a C-section scar, or stretchmarks galore, or cottage cheese thighs.

This woman didn't have a mark on her body. She looked like she stepped out of a magazine naked. When we made love, she was aggressive. She wanted to be on top and took over. When we were done, I was hooked. My nose was wide open.

I spent the night there and got up about six a.m. to go home, change my clothes, and go to work. I didn't say a word to Vivian. She looked at me strangely, but she knew after she pulled that disappearing act for two days that she couldn't say shit to me.

This routine went on the next night, and the next night, and the next night. Finally, Jezebel said to me, "Why don't you just move in? You're here every night, sleeping over. Vivian has to know by now that it's over between the two of you."

I agreed. That morning, I didn't go home. I went straight to work and took half a day off. When I got home, Vivian was sitting on the couch, watching TV. I just pulled out a bag and started to pack my things. Vivian jumped off the couch and said, "What are you doing? Is this it?"

I said, "Yeah! This is it, bitch. I'm outta here."

What came out of Vivian's mouth next was classic of ghetto rat mentality. "What about the baby?"

I said, "What about the baby?"

This woman wanted me to give her every detail about how I was going to take care of Ashley, right then and there. I told her that I was going to take care of Ashley, but the days of riding the Russell gravy train were over. I told her that since she wanted to act like a welfare bitch, she could live like one.

I walked out the door with my bags.

I drove my things to Jezebel's, and I had a new residence. I was so happy. I had a new woman now. In the morning, we would drive to work in the same car, but I would drop her off about a block away so our relationship could stay secret from the rest of the staff, especially Steve. I knew he didn't like her.

I was in love. And, wouldn't you know it, just at that time, Denise called the job. I hadn't heard from her since that day we went to the museum together. Jezebel answered all the phone calls, so when Denise called, she knew who she was and how I felt about her. Therefore, she watched the light on the phone to see how long the conversation went on. It just so happened that Denise was calling to tell me that she and her boyfriend were breaking up, and that he would be moving out soon. She thought that maybe she and I could see how things would go between us—slowly.

I thought, *Isn't this a kick in the head? This was what I've been waiting to hear for the past five years, and she says it now.*

As much as I wanted to say, "Sure," I had to tell her of the situation. I told her that I was seeing someone new right now, and that I worked with her. I asked Denise to please not call the job from now on; I would call her.

Denise seemed a little taken aback by what I said, but she said, "Fine," and hung up.

Jezebel was upset about the phone call. I had to explain why I had to take it, and that I had told Denise about us. I thought, *If this was a week earlier, I never would have gotten involved with Jezebel.* When Denise and I met the last time, I had thought that she was in love with her boyfriend.

I was heartbroken about the situation, but I was in love with Jezebel. We had sex every single day. The novelty of the new relationship was intoxicating. I wanted to do all the things with her that I had wanted to do with Denise, and the relationship was moving fast. And, yes, I used protection, but, no, I couldn't bring myself to tell her.

The first thing we did was open up a joint checking account. I wanted to show her that I trusted her, and that I meant business. I wasn't just trying to use her as a booty call. Besides Melanie, this was the most beautiful woman I had ever been with, and I was proud when I walked down the street with her. Men would look at me with envy.

I even took her to meet Julie, but a strange thing happened. Jezebel had a bit of a superior disposition toward Julie and her house. We didn't stay long, and later, I called Julie to ask her what she thought.

"Mijo," Julie said, "I love you like you were my own son, but I want you to listen to the words I'm going to say to you very carefully. Yes, the woman is very beautiful, but remember that beauty is only skin-deep; ugly is to the bone. I am glad you are happy."

Then, we ended the conversation.

I was a little surprised at what Julie had said. Now, there were two people I trusted that gave me a less-than-favorable opinion of Jezebel—first Steve, and now Julie. But then again, love is blind.

This was a whirlwind romance. I wanted everyone to see my new woman. I guess I was always a little embarrassed by Vivian, so I wanted to let the people in my family see my new, beautiful, intelligent woman. I took Jezebel to Washington D.C. for the weekend so that my mother could meet her. I wasn't looking for her approval; I just wanted her to see how good I had it.

Jezebel and I stayed at a hotel and hung out with my mother and one of her boyfriends for a night. We went to some nightclub, and she and I danced the night away. I could see men gazing at her with desire in their eyes—even the guy my mother was with. We were only supposed to stay overnight, because I had a job to do on Sunday for Walter Cook, but Jezebel talked me into staying another day.

She said, "Hey, why do we have to go back tomorrow? You're the boss aren't you? Why don't you just have Phil do it?"

I thought, *She's right!* So, I called Phil and ask him to do the project for me, and he said he would.

When I got back to New York, I found out that Phil was unable to do the job. His excuse was that he was unable to get into the equipment room. When I got to the office, Cook was already on the phone with Steve, ripping me a new asshole. Steve asked me what had happened, so I told him I went away with my new girlfriend, and we were unable to get back.

Steve said, "Oh, you have a new girlfriend? Well, it seems like she's already causing you to screw up. Try to keep yourself together, Russ. Now, go see Cook and make arrangements to finish that job."

It had been about three weeks since I had left Vivian. She called me at work. She asked if I could watch Ashley for the weekend, because she had some things to do. I was glad to watch Ashley, since I hadn't seen her in about three weeks, so I agreed.

I picked her up on a Friday and took her to Jezebel's. Ashley and I slept in one bed, and Jezebel and her son slept in his bed together. We took both of the kids to the park and to McDonald's, as well as to a couple of indoor playrooms. Ashley would look at me funny whenever I would show Jezebel any kind of affection, but I felt she had to get comfortable with it sooner or later.

I dropped Ashley off that Sunday, and on Monday morning, Vivian called the job with a raging tirade. "You brought my daughter around your new bitch, muthafucker! I hate your fucking ass! I swear I'm going to get you for this shit, muthafucker!"

I just hung up the phone on her.

The next day, Phil came to work and told me that Vivian was tearing the apartment up. I didn't care; I didn't live there anymore. I had taken everything that I needed from the apartment when I left. I guess the reality of me leaving had finally hit Vivian.

I went by the apartment after work to check on Ashley. I opened the door, since I still had the key, and when I looked inside, the place was a wreck. It looked like a tornado had hit. Phil told me that he saw Vivian and Ashley leave a couple of hours before I came. That was fine, as long as I knew Ashley was okay.

A week went by, and I didn't hear anything. Phil was keeping an eye on Ashley for me, since he lived right next door, so I wasn't worried.

I was about a month into the relationship with Jezebel when I realized something: I hadn't smoked marijuana or cigarettes the whole time. This was amazing—I didn't even miss it! I had no desire at all to smoke. Besides, Jezebel was adamantly against me smoking anything. I thought this was good thing. Julie and Steve might think she was bad for me, but this was something good. For the past six years, I had smoked marijuana and cigarettes every single day and barely missed one. I did notice that I was drinking a little more than usual, but I was drinking with Jezebel. It wasn't a lot, just wine and an occasional cocktail when we went out together.

Up to this point, Steve knew I had a new girlfriend, but he didn't know it was Jezebel. I was on top of the world. I had a new, beautiful, intelligent, independent woman. I was making about $40,000 a year. I was second-in-command at a company with a $1.5- million contract with the state and growing, and another half-million in repair contracts. There were also plans set for me to go to California to start a spinoff program of Y.E.C. We were about to go national, and I was leading the charge. I felt unstoppable. I was in control. I was the boss, and I was the man, so I thought.

I was in for a rude awakening.

chapter **THIRTY-THREE**

I t all started so unassumingly. It was a normal day. I woke up just like any other morning for the past month. Jezebel and I took separate cars to work, because Steve and I had to go to small claims court. Some woman was upset that her house was still cold after she bought new windows. We tried to explain that, besides new window installation, she would also have to invest in weatherization supplies because it was a brownstone building. The woman didn't want to hear that, so here she was, trying to get the windows for free.

We were in night court around 6:00 p.m. While Steve and I were in the courtroom, my pager kept going off. When I looked at the number, it was Jezebel's; she had paged me about four times. I excused myself and called her on a pay phone. She told me that while she was driving home, her car started to act funny, so she pulled into a garage. The mechanic told her there was some kind of construction sand in her gas tank, and it was going to cost $400 to fix. Jezebel was calling me to find out if she should have it fixed there. I told her that we didn't have a choice, to just get it done, and we would figure what was going on later.

It was Friday, and when I got home, we discussed the oddity of the sand being in her gas tank. We thought it might be James, seeking revenge for the trouble she had caused him, but there wasn't any proof.

The next afternoon, the apartment bell rang. It was Jezebel's ex-boyfriend. She went downstairs to talk to him. I stayed upstairs and looked out the window with my gun in hand, just in case there was trouble. Her ex-boyfriend was a small Spanish guy—not a physical threat to me at all, but if he had a gun, I was ready.

He and Jezebel had a brief conversation, and then he got in a car and drove away. When Jezebel returned upstairs, I asked her what that was about. She said, "Same old, same old. He wants to get back together and he wanted to come upstairs, but I told him no. He said, 'Why, because you got that nigger upstairs?' Then he got in his car and drove away."

I asked, "How do you think he knew I was upstairs?"

"Because he saw the car. I was with him when my father sold it to you, so he knows it's yours."

I didn't think much about it. As long as he didn't come upstairs looking for an altercation, I was cool. I could understand him wanting to get back with her. She was a hell of a catch.

That Monday, when we went into work, Jezebel told Steve about the sand in her gas tank. She also told him of her suspicions, but that she had no proof. Steve understood and offered to pay for the repairs. He would allow Jezebel to park in our lot that was secured with a gate and chain from now on. Problem solved.

The next day was a Tuesday, two days before Thanksgiving in 1994. I can remember it like it was yesterday. After work, Jezebel and I were going out to dinner. I drove by Grammy and Pete's to officially introduce Jezebel to them as my new woman. They had met her one time before when they came by the job, but not on a personal level.

The plan was to go to dinner downtown after the visit. I drove to their house and parked my car across the street in front of their building. Jezebel and I held hands and walked inside. We visited for about a half-hour, said our goodbyes, and got on the elevator to the lobby. As we stepped off the elevator, I could see a whole lot of flashing lights and heard the loud sirens of fire engines almost in front of the building. As we got closer to the entrance, I looked out the glass of the door. In slow motion, I started, "Hey that looks like…" then yelled, "my car!"

My car was a roaring fire, all ablaze. Jezebel started to cry, and I immediately rushed her back upstairs and told Grammy and Pete what was happening. Pete got dressed and came downstairs with me, while Jezebel waited upstairs with Grammy. When Pete and I got back downstairs, the fire was almost out. A firefighter standing nearby asked me if it was my car. I told him it was and asked if it was some kind of electrical fire.

The firefighter said no and pointed to the driver's side window. "Someone threw a Molotov cocktail through the window."

All I could think was, *Vivian did this.* Pete and I went back upstairs and told Grammy and Jezebel what the firefighter said. Jezebel and I called a cab and went to dinner anyway.

That night, we talked at great length about our recourse. We thought about calling the cops on Vivian, but we had no proof, just suspicions. We even thought it could have been James. He did hate both of us with a passion. If he knew we were together, I'm sure it would have only fueled his rage even more.

The next the day, before Thanksgiving dinner, I went to work and told Steve what had happened. We called Walter Cook, since he was an ex-cop. I gave him my suspicions, and he responded with his expert opinion: "Muthafucker, that ain't James doing that bullshit. That sounds like bitch shit to me. Bitches like to fuck with niggers' cars and shit."

After talking with Cook, I was convinced that it was Vivian, but I still wasn't 100% sure. I thought, *How would she know where I was going to be?* She would have needed help. But no one in her family would dare cross me, knowing what I pulled off that time Virginia got jumped.

Jezebel was more than convinced and wanted to retaliate. She said she could get some cousins to break into Vivian's apartment when she wasn't home. They would plant a bunch of drugs in the apartment. We could call the police with an anonymous tip and have her apartment raided. Then Vivian would go to jail, and I would get Ashley.

I was stunned by her cold, cunning, and calculating mind. I told her that I was pissed at Vivian, but I wasn't trying to hurt her, ruin her life, or traumatize my daughter just to get even with her. It was just a fucking car. Jezebel got upset, because she thought that I was defending Vivian. I told her she was going to the extreme with the situation, and to just be cool. I reminded her that we were not gangsters.

I called Vivian and accused her of setting my car on fire. Of course, she denied it. She sounded angry about the breakup, but I still wasn't convinced that she did the deed.

Then it was Thanksgiving. I went to Nana's annual dinner, and the talk was how my car got set on fire. My mother had a ball telling the rest of the family of my misfortunes, like she was getting some kind of high out of it. I would think that someone with as many domestic disturbances as her would understand the embarrassment that came with it and have some sort of empathy for me. But not her. She was jealous of my rise in my professional career, and she was happy to let people know that I wasn't shit.

After dinner, Jezebel picked me up at Nana's house, and then she, my uncle, my mother, and I went to the movies downtown, near my uncle's hotel. After the movie, Jezebel and I went home. We had sex, and then went to sleep.

At 3:00 a.m., there was banging on the door. I grabbed my gun and ran to it. I held the barrel firmly against the door and said in a deep voice, "Who is it?" It was the lady that lived downstairs, under us. She said, "Excuse me for banging like that, but your car is on fire."

We looked out the window and saw the car ablaze. The fire department arrived a short time later and put the blaze out. Jezebel was furious. She started saying, "That bitch is dead. She's a dead fucking bitch!"

I told Jezebel to calm down and that we should get some rest. We would figure this shit out in the morning.

That morning, we were awakened by the phone. It was a female, but not Vivian, and she was taunting Jezebel, saying, "Hey, bitch! This is the fire department."

Then, another woman got on the phone and they were both singing, "Burn baby burn, disco inferno!"

Jezebel hung up the phone and told me what was said. I asked her if it was Vivian, and she said no, but didn't sound convinced.

I said, "How can we be sure it was her? How would she know this phone number? I never called her from this house. Something is strange about this, but I can't figure it out right now."

Jezebel didn't want to hear any reasoning. She just knew it was Vivian. So, she picked up the phone and called her. "Hello, Vivian, this is Jezebel. You done fucked with the wrong bitch. I'm going to have your fucking heart cut out. I'm going to have your fucking nipples cut off, bitch! You better watch your back, bitch!"

Jezebel then hung up the phone and called the police. I asked her what she was doing, and she said she was going to call and say that Vivian called and threatened her.

I said, "But she didn't call. You said it wasn't her on the phone."

"I don't care. Fuck that bitch! Are you going to back me up or not?"

The cops arrived about ten minutes later. Jezebel filed a false police report and said that Vivian had called and threatened to set her car on fire. When the police asked Jezebel if there were any witnesses to the phone call, Jezebel pointed to me. I reluctantly confirmed that Vivian did make the call.

After the police left, I told Jezebel that we were in danger. I said, "Look, someone's been following us. They have your phone number, and no matter what you say, we're not sure it's Vivian. It could be anybody. It could be James, it could be your ex-boyfriend, it could be Vivian. We don't know. All we do know is that this is serious. They know everything about us, and we know nothing about them. Until we find out, we're sitting ducks. We don't have cars now, and they have the upper hand on us."

Jezebel asked, "Well, what are we going to do?"

I told her that we needed to get out of the apartment right away, and then we had to skip town.

I called my uncle at the hotel and told him what happened. He was upset for me. I asked if Jezebel and I could come to Milwaukee until things cooled off in New York and I had time to figure out who was behind all of this.

My uncle said some very comforting words. "Well, nephew, I love you and I don't want to see anything bad happen to you. So if you need some place to stay, it won't be a problem."

I thanked him and told him I would call him later with the details. I just needed to close some things out before I left.

Jezebel and I packed some small bags and took a cab to Y.E.C.'s office in the Bronx. I had the keys to the office, so I opened the door and took a set to one of the work vans. At first, we drove around with no destination in mind. I was in a state of shock. Everything was happening so fast. I was paranoid that we were being followed, so I drove to out-of-the-way places. Finally, I stopped at the Whitestone Motel right off the Whitestone Bridge.

Once we got settled in, I called Grammy and Pete. My uncle had already filled them in on what had happened. My mother was staying with them for the Thanksgiving weekend. She said that she was leaving for Washington, D.C. on Tuesday morning. If we wanted to leave with her and then go to Milwaukee from there, it was fine, but she was leaving very early—5:00 a.m. I told my mother that I would think about it. I knew any help I got from her was going to come at some kind of cost, either monetarily or emotionally.

It was Saturday, and we were on the run. I felt safe in the motel, but I needed to plan my next move. Monday, I had to go to the office, face Steve, and tell him everything, especially about Jezebel and me. This wasn't something I was looking forward to. I thought maybe I could go away for a little while and come back, and things would be just like they had been. I thought I could still fix everything. I didn't want to admit to myself that I had lost control of my life, and everything had changed in the course of a week.

It was all over, but I just couldn't see it.

That night, Jezebel said, "I need you to take me someplace."

I asked her, "Where?"

"To Brooklyn, to this Santeria spiritual lady."

"For what?"

She told me the lady was a fortuneteller. I had forgotten that Jezebel practiced Santeria. I remembered when we first slept together. She had candles of St. Michael burning in the bathroom. Also, when I had first left Vivian, I found a cucumber in the bathroom by the candle, with a hole on each end and a piece of paper in each whole. When I asked her what the cucumber was about, she picked it up and pulled out the paper from each end. One piece had Vivian's name on it, and the other had James's. I asked her what was it about, and she said she had cast spells on them—a spell on James to lose his job, and on Vivian so I would leave her.

I drove Jezebel to Brooklyn that night. We stopped at this two-unit house. Jezebel led me to the front door and knocked. A dark-skinned woman opened it. Jezebel conversed with her in Spanish. The lady led us to a basement door, and Jezebel led me down the stairs as if she had been there before.

When we got to the bottom of the stairs, there was a closed door to my right. Jezebel knocked, and a woman said to enter in Spanish. There was a somewhat heavyset Spanish woman sitting on a bed in a very small bedroom, with a small table in front of her and several candles burning around the room. The woman didn't speak any English, so Jezebel had to tell me everything that she said. I sat on a chair in front of the lady, on the other side of the small table.

The lady pulled out a deck of cards and placed a couple on the table. She then turned to Jezebel and started to speak Spanish to her. Jezebel asked me what I wanted to know. I told her to ask the lady who was out to hurt me. Jezebel translated what I said, and the woman spoke to Jezebel for about two minutes in Spanish. Then, Jezebel told me it was a woman with Indian-colored skin. Vivian didn't have Indian-colored skin.

I asked the woman, "Should I kill whoever is doing this to me?"

The woman said, "No."

I then asked the woman what the future held for me. After I said this, Jezebel translating, the woman started to speak very fast for about fifteen minutes. While she was speaking, I looked at Jezebel and her eyes became wide, looking at the woman very intensely. While the woman was still speaking, I asked Jezebel what she was saying. Jezebel waved me off so as not to miss anything. She became very serious once the lady was done.

The whole time the woman was talking, she would not make eye contact with me. When she was done speaking, I asked Jezebel what she had said.

Jezebel hesitated for a moment, then said, "Oh, she said everything was going to work out fine, and don't worry."

I knew she was lying because of her tone and the way her face had looked while the lady was talking. She also said that I was going to go and work for a family business; I thought this might have meant my uncle's liquor store.

I gave the woman $20 and got up from the chair. The lady said one more thing in Spanish to Jezebel and pointed to me. I asked Jezebel what she said.

"Burn white candles for peace."

I thought, *Well, this was a waste of time.*

We drove back to the motel and stayed another night. The next day, we went back to Brooklyn to pick up Jezebel's son from her parents. Her parents had seen her burned car and were concerned. She told them that it was an electrical fire.

I had an uneasy feeling about what the Santeria lady had said, so I kept asking Jezebel about it, which made Jezebel become defensive. I told her I wanted to go back to the lady, but this time I wanted someone else to translate for me. Jezebel was adamantly against taking me back, so I knew she was hiding something. But what?

The next morning, Jezebel and I went to the Y.E.C. office, bright and early. Jezebel stayed at her desk with her son, and I took the long walk to Steve's office. Steve greeted me with a big smile and a "Hi, Russ." I closed his door and sat down in the chair in front of him. Steve asked me what was wrong. I was so ashamed about my actions that I couldn't even look at him. I held my head down, looking at the floor, and let it all out.

"Steve, I've been in a relationship with Jezebel for about two months now. On Thanksgiving night, someone set her car on fire, also, and then called and taunted her over the phone about it. I need to leave town until I can figure all of this out. I'm sorry I kept this from you. Right now, I'm on the run."

I picked my head up, looked at Steve, and could see the disappointment in his eyes. It looked like his eyes were watering, and he was shaking his head.

Finally, Steve said, "Russ, do you know what you've done? You've blown it. First, you're sleeping with a subordinate. And does she know that you're HIV-positive?"

I shook my head.

Steve continued, "You better not tell her, because she will destroy you. Russ, I'm telling you, that woman is no good for you. I know she's very attractive, but like I told you before, she is cunning, spiteful, and vindictive. Look at all you had going for you. You were making a great salary, and that was going to go up. You were on your way to California to start a new program, and in a few years, you could have been sitting where I am, as the president of this company. But here you are, willing to throw it all away over a piece of ass."

I said, "Steve, she's not just a piece of ass. I love her."

"Love her? Russ, you don't even know her. Just a couple of months ago, you were telling me about that girl, Denise. Now, all of a sudden, you love this bitch?" Steve just kept shaking his head.

"Well, I guess you're going to need a few dollars, so I'll get you a check. And then, give me a call, and I'll get the bookkeeper to tally up all that we owe you. I should have it ready for you in a week."

I followed Steve into the bookkeeper's office, and he told her to cut a check for me for $2,000. Then he signed it, and I signed it. It was my last check to sign for Y.E.C. Steve walked me to the front door. Jezebel was standing there, but Steve didn't even speak to her. He had a look of loathing on his face.

Steve opened the door and said, "Good luck, Russ."

That was it. Everything that I had worked toward for the past seven years went up in smoke in the course of one week. But I didn't care, as long as I had Jezebel. All I wanted was to be with her at all costs. I figured we could start over in Milwaukee. I was still young, so fuck Y.E.C.

The next stop was Nana's. I knew I was going to need some more money. I knew that Nana had heard a whole lot of things by now, and I just wanted to let her hear it straight from the horse's mouth. Jezebel and I took a cab to Nana's, and Jezebel waited in the taxi.

I sat Nana down and told her that I was in trouble. People were after me, and I didn't know who it was. She told me that my mother had already informed her. I said I was going to need money, and asked if she could lend me $2,000. She said she would give me $1,000, but that she had to go to the bank to get it. I said, "Okay," and got up to leave. She asked me when I was coming back for the money, and I told her to just hold it for me; I would be back for it. I gave Nana a kiss on her cheek and left.

Jezebel and I went back to the motel and mapped out our game plan. We decided to take my mother up on her offer and go to Washington, D.C. with her, lay low for a week, and then come back to New York, clean out the apartment, and catch a plane from New York to Milwaukee. I didn't care about anything else, as long as I was with Jezebel.

Early that Tuesday morning, Jezebel, her son, and I arrived at Grammy and Pete's. My mother was surprised to see the child with us, but didn't say too much about it. Jezebel and I told her that we were just going down to D.C. for a week to get off the radar, and then we were coming back to New York to catch a plane to Milwaukee. My mother was fine with that, and we all got in her car and drove down.

The ride with my mother was smooth. I kept thinking, *Something isn't right. She has something up her sleeve.* My mother was nice as pie to Jezebel and me during the ride. When we got to D.C., we stayed in the living room. Even though there was an extra bedroom, we didn't want to get too comfortable, since we planned on leaving in a week. My mother lived in a two-bedroom condominium with a front entrance that led right to the outside, so there was a bit of privacy, but was still part of a complex.

Jezebel and I would rest during the day, recovering from the emotional train wreck that we had just gone through. When my mother got home each day, she would make drinks, she and Jezebel would chitchat, and sometimes they would go into the back bedroom together. My mother would even show her old pictures of Vivian and me. I didn't know why, because afterward, Jezebel would be a little upset and make smart comments to me like, "You looked happy."

About three days into our stay, Jezebel said, "You know, instead of going to Milwaukee, we should just stay here. It's closer to New York, and Milwaukee's a thousand miles away. That way, I would be closer to my family when I wanted to see them."

I asked Jezebel how she came up with that idea all of a sudden. I had told her about the tense relationship I had with my mother, so why would she think I wanted to live with her?

Jezebel said that she and my mother had been talking, and my mother felt bad about how she didn't raise me, and wanted to take this time for us to get closer. Jezebel said, "She really wants us to stay, baby. And we can stay in the other bedroom. Please, please?"

I knew this was a bad idea. I knew my mother just wanted us to stay there to help her pay her mortgage. During the car ride, she had mentioned a friend's niece had been staying with her and paying half the bills. The niece had just moved out, and the bills were heavy on my mother's pocket. I realized that's why she had been nice as pie. And now Jezebel was falling for it.

I wanted to please Jezebel, so I agreed to stay. I called my uncle and told him that we were staying in Washington. My mother wanted to guarantee we were coming back, so she even rented a car for us to go to New York to clean out the apartment and bring whatever things we needed back. I called Steve and let him know I was coming to pick up a check, and he said he had one for $8,000 for me, which included my sick time and vacation days. But he would rather I not come by the office.

I asked him if he was pissed at me, and he said it wasn't that. Vivian had come by the job with the police, looking for Jezebel and me. They were going to arrest us for making terroristic threats over the phone. I told Steve I understood and asked him to give the check to Phil for me.

Steve also said he would allow Jezebel and me to file for unemployment insurance. He was still looking out for me, even though I had disappointed him.

I told Phil to meet me at Julie's house. I had called Julie earlier to have George pick up a pistol. I wanted him and Phil to follow me in Phil's car, just in case whoever was after me was waiting. I met Phil and George at Julie's, and they followed us to Brooklyn. Then, Jezebel and I cleaned out the apartment. She sold Phil and George her furniture.

They followed us to the George Washington Bridge, and then we were on our way back to Washington, D.C. to live with my mother.

The full impact of what I had lost hadn't hit me yet. I still thought I was in control of my life. I still thought I was something special. I almost believed what Jezebel had said about my mother wanting to have a closer relationship with me. At least, I wanted to believe it. I was just happy to be with Jezebel. I was in love. I was walking on clouds, and all I thought about was being with her, and how beautiful she was, and how we had sex every day and how much I enjoyed it. I was willing to walk through fire for this woman, and I just knew she felt the same way about me.

I thought, *Just look how she up and left everything behind just so she could be with me.* That's really all I wanted—a woman that had my back, a woman that was in my corner. The kind of woman Denise was to me, until I messed up. She fell in love with someone else, and then she didn't have my back. She wasn't in my corner; she was in his.

I felt I had a second chance with this woman, and I was going to do right by her. She and I were going to grow old together, and I would show Steve and everybody that what I was giving up for Jezebel was worth it.

When we got back to Washington, the first thing I did was get the money matters out of the way with my mother. Even though she never said anything about money, I knew it was coming up. It was just a matter of time—I knew her well. (Jezebel didn't know her at all.) I had $10,000 in the bank. I asked my mother what her monthly expenses were, and she gave me some roundabout number. I told her I would give her $700 for now.

My mother, trying to sound caring and motherly, said, "Oh, Malik, I can't take that kind of money from you guys. I know you're going through a bad time, and you guys need to get back on your feet."

For a moment, I thought, *Wow, my mother is really trying. She really does want to have a closer relationship with her only child. She really does want to make up for her past mistakes.*

Just for a moment, though, because in the next breath, she said, "I'll take $500."

I gave her the cash right there. Later that night, Jezebel was pissed off. She was asking me why we needed to give my mother

$500. She was complaining that the room was small, and I was her only child. I told Jezebel, "That's how she is. But you wanted to live here, so now we live here. I know my mother. She doesn't care about me; all she cares about is herself. That's why she offered to let us say here—because she wanted someone to help her with her bills."

Jezebel felt deceived. But the deed was done, and right now, this was where we were, so I told her we should try and make the best of it.

The honeymoon didn't last long. My mother started to show her true colors. After she saw we were moved in and had no place to go, she became the woman I always knew. She was sarcastic and condescending toward us. When she talked on the phone, we could hear her telling her friends how we fucked up and that people were after us, and now we were living with her and had no jobs. She didn't tell them that we gave her $500; she made us sound like lowlife freeloaders.

The first week was annoying, but we survived it. My mother kept asking me to fix things for her, like I was a live-in handyman or something. In the morning, when Jezebel and I got up, there would be a list of things my mother wanted us to do taped to the refrigerator. Jezebel would say things like, "She acts like we're living here for free and paying off our debt in trade." I agreed. Then, we would refuse to do anything on the list.

One day, Jezebel and I were going food shopping. We were going to take a cab to the store. My mother asked us to go by the liquor store on our way back and pick her up a bottle of rum. She asked Jezebel if she knew how to drive a stick-shift, and Jezebel said yes, so my mother offered her a twenty-year-old Renault 18i, since we were going to the liquor store for her.

Jezebel, her son Mikey, and I went to the supermarket. On the way back home, we stopped at the liquor store. Jezebel put her hazard lights on, and I exited to go into the liquor store while she and Mikey waited in the car.

I purchased the bottle of rum, exited the store, and walked toward where the car was idling. As I got closer, I could see the flashing lights blinking off and on, but it was as if my vision was off. Then, I saw the car was up on the sidewalk, and the rear was damaged. I saw another car. An older man got out and started to curse, saying, "Oh shit, oh shit." The man had rear-ended Jezebel and Mikey while the car was idling. He had hit them so hard that it pushed our car up on the sidewalk.

I ran up. There wasn't any blood or anything, but Jezebel was injured and Mikey was crying uncontrollably in the backseat. Someone had called an ambulance, because it arrived moments after I ran up. The EMTs were on the scene, putting a neck brace on Jezebel and one on Mike. Then they took them out of the vehicle. I rode to George Washington Hospital in the ambulance. We were in the emergency room for about six hours. Neither Jezebel nor Mikey were seriously hurt, but she was told by the doctor to wear a neck brace for a few days due to the shock from the impact of the crash.

During our time at the hospital, I didn't even think to call my mother for two reasons: I didn't have her number on hand, and if I had called from the hospital, there was going to be a lot of drama. At the immediate moment, my main concern was that Jezebel and Mikey were not seriously hurt.

When they were discharged, they were both in neck braces. We took a cab back to my mother's. I knocked on the door, and my mother answered with an attitude, saying, "Where the fuck were you people?"

"She was in an accident. The car struck her from behind."

My mother didn't even ask about the neck braces. She just went into a tirade about her owning a house, and how the people were going to sue her because she owned a house. (My mother considered the condominium a house.)

I said to her, "But they hit her from behind. The car was parked. She didn't do anything wrong."

My mother continued her tirade. "I don't give a fuck. Once they find out I out I own a home, they're going to be out for money. I can't believe this shit. And why didn't you call me? The fucking phone book! You could have looked me up."

I told her that, in the moment, I was concerned about Jezebel and her son being hurt. Jezebel was just crying during the scene, emotionally wounded by my mother's obvious disregard for her recent trauma. I helped Jezebel to the bedroom as my mother continued her rant.

It was about 3:00 a.m. Jezebel cried for an hour, not believing this Jekyll and Hyde woman was for real. I was embarrassed by my mother's actions.

That morning, at about 7:00 a.m., we were awakened by yet another tirade. My mother was banging on the bedroom door, saying, "Where's my fucking car?"

I told her that the police had the car towed, and she asked me where. I said I didn't know.

"You better get my fucking car. I want my fucking car back today, muthafucker," was all she said.

I was getting angry and said in a deep voice, "Fine, I'll get your fucking car."

After my mother saw that I was becoming angry at her attack, she continued her verbal assault while she was walking out the door. Jezebel was disgusted by my mother's actions, and just kept crying.

I got up, got dressed, and then called information to find the local police station, since the accident happened right up the block. I took a cab to the station, asked for the police report, and asked where the car was towed. The police gave me all the information I needed, including the name and insurance of the driver that hit Jezebel. I took a cab to where the car was, paid the towing fee, and paid to have it towed to my mother's house. The groceries that we had bought were still in the car.

When I got home, Jezebel was still crying. "I can't take much more of this."

I comforted her, but didn't have any words.

Later that day, my mother returned home. But this time, she was in a whole different mood. Now, my mother wanted to talk about the accident. She was asking Jezebel and me all kinds of questions, and asked us if we got the other driver's insurance information. I told her that we had.

My mother said, "Oh, well, I called an old friend of mine who is a lawyer." ("Old friend" meant a married man she used to screw.) "And he said you guys have a good case because you were struck from behind."

There it was. This was why she was in a different mood. She started to see dollar signs. The night before, she didn't give a rat's ass about what happened. Now, when she thought Jezebel might get a few dollars, she wanted to be so caring and concerned.

My mother gave us the lawyer's number, and Jezebel and I made an appointment for the next day. It was a very nice place, right in the middle of downtown Washington, D.C., overlooking the Capitol Building. The lawyer told Jezebel that she had a good case and gave her the number of a doctor to go see. He told her to go three times a week, and not to worry about any bills; the doctor was a friend of his, and it would be worked out in the settlement. The lawyer had Jezebel sign a paper stating he would receive a third of the settlement.

When we got home, my mother was all hugs and kisses, now thinking she was going to get some money, or maybe a new car. Every day for the next week, my mother continually asked about Jezebel's doctor's appointments. However, she continued to leave notes around the house about things she wanted me to do.

My uncle called me and asked about the accident. I told him what had happened. He mentioned that the same night, before Jezebel and I returned home, my mother had called him and Grammy. She thought Jezebel and I took her car and went to New York with it, since we were gone so long.

I was furious hearing this, and I told Jezebel. We could have been dead someplace, but instead of being concerned for us, she called New York and Milwaukee to trash talk us.

The animosity between us and my mother grew, until one day, my mother said, "Hey, I think we need to have a sit-down."

This meant we were doing things to aggravate her, like not following her daily written instructions. My mother told us the next night would be a good time. Jezebel and I had talked and decided it would be better if we tried to get our own place.

The next day, when my mother called us into the living room, she started her little speech with an air of sarcasm. "Look, I know we need to get used to each other's habits, but since you guys are going to be here for a while, I think we need to put some rules in place so that we can have harmony in the house."

I waited until she was finished, then said, "You know, Jezebel and I were talking, and we think it would be better if we got our own place. We may need a reference from you, okay? That way, your house can go back to normal, since I know we are making things somewhat uncomfortable for you by being here."

Immediately, my mother became defensive and argumentative. "Why? Why you want to get your own place? I thought you were going to be here for a while."

I tried to sugarcoat it as best as I could. "I just think it would be best if we had our own place, that's all." My mother kept insisting for an explanation, so finally, I just said, "We don't like it here."

Again, my mother asked, "Why not?"

"We don't like the way you treat us. The way you leave notes around the house for us to do things for you, even though we paid you $500. You act like we're your gofers. And the way you went on that tirade the night of the accident, and didn't even inquire about the wellbeing of Jezebel or her son, even though they both had neck braces on. And the fact that you called New York and Milwaukee, trash talking us while we sat up in an emergency room. We could have been dead, for all you knew. I just think it would be best to get our own place."

I could see the rage in my mother's eyes. "Well, fine, then. Let me know what you need from me." She stormed off into her bedroom and slammed the door.

After that episode, the tension in the house became overbearing. For the next couple of days, my mother would walk right past Jezebel and me without speaking. And if she did speak, it was with a hardcore attitude. From the way she was acting, I knew we couldn't depend on her to give us a favorable reference to any landlord.

Jezebel and I knew we just couldn't keep living like this, so we decided to move into a motel. We didn't say anything to my mother; we just waited for her to go to work one day, packed our things, and called a cab. When the cab arrived, he saw that we were moving our things out and made a comment like, "You guys look like you're flying the coup." We just gave a friendly acknowledgement and continued to pack our things into the cab. I remember this so vividly, because what happened next was so trivial at first, but later on had such a philosophical impact.

The cab driver made a comment about God. I don't remember what he said, but I just gave an acknowledgement that God was good, yeah, yeah, yeah. The cab driver turned around and gave me a wide smile. He was a reddish black man with a large, reddish afro, and a very round face. He wore glasses and had freckles. He handed me a very small red book of Bible verses. It was a little bigger than a matchbook. I took the book, put it into my coat pocket, and forgot about it.

The cab driver drove us to the Days Inn. Once we unpacked our things, we took a nap as if a weight had been lifted. We woke

up about 7:00 p.m. I knew that my mother would have already realized we were gone by then, and also probably made her calls to New
York and Milwaukee.

Jezebel and I discussed a new game plan. We decided to go with
our original idea and head to Milwaukee. I called my uncle, told him
of the current situation, and said we would be coming to Milwaukee
in about a week. Jezebel wanted to go back to New York first to
visit her family before we left, since Milwaukee was so far away.

Jezebel demanded I call my mother and demand our $500 back.
She said, "We were only there for two weeks, and just from the
mental abuse alone, she should be paying us."

I agreed. I called the house. "Hello, Rosemary. This is Malik. As
you know by now, we no longer reside at your premises, and we
would like a refund of the $500 we gave you. We are staying at the
Days Inn motel. Please make arrangements for us to get our money,
or would you like me to come to your job looking for it?"

I hung up the phone.

I waited a couple of days, and Rosemary had her assistant from
her job drop off an envelope at the motel's front desk. When I
opened the envelope, it had $250 in it. The envelope also had a pa-
per stating, "2 weeks' rent at $125 a week. Refund due: $250."

Jezebel looked at the letter and said, "That is a petty bitch."

I told Jezebel not to sweat the small stuff; we had bigger fish to
fry. While we were at the hotel, we ate out every day. Jezebel decided
to buy some new clothes. I also noticed something about myself: I
had slowly developed a drinking habit. I had drank alcohol every
single day since my misfortunes started happening, usually Bacardi
151.

Jezebel reserved the tickets to be picked up at the airport. They
cost $860 for the three of us. My money was dwindling. I needed to
get by Nana's also to pick up that $1,000 when we stopped in New
York. I called Grammy and Pete to let them know. We ended up
staying at the motel for seven days, and the final bill came out to

around $700. It seems like money goes a lot faster when there's no money coming in.

Jezebel and I took the bus from Washington to New York, since it was only a three-hour ride. Jezebel had an older sister who loaned us her car so we could drive around and handle our last-minute details.

First, we went by Grammy and Pete's to say goodbye. Grammy gave me a soft-worded rebuke about calling my mother by her name. I respected Grammy, so I didn't argue the point, but I knew I would never speak to Rosemary again—not after the way she acted the night of the accident. If I did, I would continue to address her as Rosemary. She didn't deserve any acknowledgement of being a mother.

The next stop was Nana's, where she gave me $800. I told her to hold on to the rest for me, in case of an emergency.

I asked Jezebel to take me by the Santeria lady's house once again before we left, and once again, she was adamantly opposed. She even became indignant about it, saying, "Fuck that bitch. What's the big concern about going to that lady? I told you everything that she said, so we're not going."

I left the subject alone after that, but my gut was telling me that she was hiding something. That Santeria lady told her something Jezebel didn't want me to know.

That night, Jezebel's sister and her husband drove the three of us to the airport. We boarded a plane for a two-hour flight to Milwaukee. During the flight, Jezebel fell asleep. I couldn't sleep. My mind was racing about the past month. I kept pondering who had done this to me, who was able to destroy my life in the course of a week. Was it Vivian? Or James? Or Jezebel's ex-boyfriend? Or maybe Jay and Carmen spotted me and did the same thing I did to them, except they kept their identities concealed.

As I thought about all the possible suspects, Steve's words rang in my ears: "Russ, you can't always fight on all four fronts. You need to fight one battle at a time. That way, you can give each your full attention."

Well, all of that is behind me now—Vivian, Denise, Jazz, T, Y.E.C. I'm going to start a new life with the woman I love. We have survived this adversity in our relationship, and it has only made us stronger. I'm going to go to Milwaukee and bust my ass like I did at Y.E.C. And now I have a woman who's willing to bust her ass, too. There's nothing but blue skies ahead.

I had about $4,000 left, and I felt like I could do anything as long as I had the love of a good woman by my side. There was nothing left that anyone could do to hurt me anymore. I took the worst hits that life could deal me, and look at me—I was still standing. I still had a woman who loved me. I had money in my pocket. What else could life possibly do to me that it hadn't done in the past twenty-six years?

I would soon find out.

GHETTO BASTARD

BOOK II

I would soon be shaken to the core of my sanity. My spirit would soon be broken to the point that, for a split second, I would think about killing myself. I would be left broken, destitute, betrayed, and abandoned. I would soon realize that I had no control of my life. I would soon be at the mercy of strangers who, at a moment's notice, would cross me and leave me for dead, with no one to miss me.

I thought I had taken the worst hits that life could deal, but then I realized that they were just love taps. Life was about to give me the knockout blow.